AF619165

UBUNTU AND WOMEN

BUILDING COMMUNITY IN URBAN AREAS

Musa W. Dube
Senzokuhle D. Setume
Tirelo Modie-Moroka
Rosinah M. Gabaitse
Malebogo Kgalemang
Pulane E. Motswapong
Mmapula D. Kebaneilwe
Tshenolo J. Madigele

Ubuntu and Women: Building community in urban areas

Published by African Sun Media under the SUN MeDIA imprint
Place of publication: Stellenbosch, South Africa

First edition 2023

ISBN 978-1-991201-98-0
ISBN 978-1-991201-99-7 (e-book)
https://doi.org/10.52779/9781991201997

Set in Adobe Garamond Pro 11/14

Cover design, typesetting and production by African Sun Media

SUN MeDIA is an imprint of African Sun Media. Academic and general works are published under this imprint in print and electronic formats.

Our publications can be ordered from:
orders@africansunmedia.co.za
Takealot: bit.ly/2monsfl
Google Books: bit.ly/2k1Uilm
africansunmedia.store.it.si *(e-books)*
Amazon Kindle: amzn.to/2ktL.pkL
JSTOR: https://bit.ly/3udc057

Visit africansunmedia.co.za for more information.

This volume is dedicated to

Dr Peggy Mulambya-Kabonde,

a founding member of the

Circle of Concerned African Women Theologians.

CONTENTS

PART TWO: *Botho/Ubuntu*, Naomi/Laban Showers and In-Laws

PART FOUR: *Botho/Ubuntu*, Love and Bedroom Talk

ACKNOWLEDGEMENTS

Many people and institutions played an important role for this book to come into being. We wish to thank and acknowledge some of them here as follows:

1. John Templeton Foundation for funding the research and Nagel Institute for assessing and awarding the grant.
2. University of Botswana – the Department of Theology and Religious Studies, Faculty of Humanities and the Administration, for research support, provision of an office space for the study, and management of funds.
3. UB colleagues who provided methods analysis and other technical assistance. We are thinking here of Professor Keoagile Thaga (may his soul rest in peace) and Professor Gabriel Faimau, without whom we may have never managed to submit the proposal before its deadline. Many colleagues also read and reviewed our papers at the presentation of our findings and raised the quality of our work.
4. Project managers and research assistants, Amanda Matebekwane, Tebogo Sentsima, Sidney K. Berman and others were the oil that kept the project running.
5. Members of the study who were there at the beginning but had to leave due to other commitments include Sana K. Mmolai, Gomang Seratwa Ntloedibe-Kuswani and Doreen Sesiro. Those who stayed, the authors of this book, are also highly appreciated for making it happen.
6. Candler School of Theology, who provided space, time and facilities for the principal investigator to finalise this book.
7. Lastly, the hosts of the numerous social gatherings that conducted bridal showers, Naomi/Laban showers and baby showers for opening their private spaces and creating time for us to collect data and to interview them.

This project was conceived and carried out by the University of Botswana Circle of Concerned African Women Theologians. We, therefore, wish to thank the founders of the Circle of Concerned African Women Theologians for providing the forum and vision for women to network and work together. We all grew as we learnt how to give *botho-ubuntu* to one another, and how to deconstruct and resist patriarchy that teaches women to fear working with one another and to compete against each other. To all we say, "*Le ka moso betsho*".

Musa W. Dube
Principal Investigator of the study
10 February 2023

PREFACE

Contemporary *Ubuntu* – its place in urban spaces and on the global stage

Tinyiko Maluleke[1]

Late in the 1990s, while Southern Africa was still basking in the euphoria of Namibian and South African independence of 1990 and 1994 respectively, I wrote two short pieces on *Ubuntu*.[2] My concern then, as it has continued to be for a long time, was the prevalent mis(appropriation) of *Ubuntu* for perversely counter-intuitive purposes. I realised then that whatever else the last instalment of African democracies meant, it was unlikely to trigger a cultural re-awakening or a return to authentic *Ubuntu*. A few years into the South African democratic era made it clear to me that, if anything, the centuries-old colonial caricature of African culture and *Ubuntu* was intensifying.

The radical Mandela, who undertook what he called "the long walk to freedom",[3] which included 27 years in jail, was rebranded as a dancing, nice, baby-kissing old man whose *Ubuntu* consisted of loving his enemies more than he loved his allies. Similarly, Desmond Tutu, once demonised and persecuted by the apartheid regime for his fearless opposition to injustice, was repackaged as a man who loved peace, but so much so that he would take any form of peace ahead of equal rights and justice. I feared that something perverse was going on. *Ubuntu* was being hollowed out and portrayed as an indiscriminate and limitless form of cultural niceness.

I am, however, excited and most pleased to say that, in contrast to the foregoing, this magnificent volume, titled *Ubuntu and women: community building in the urban space*, is a breath of fresh air. This book will restore the faith of even the most critical reader in the continued viability of the notion of *Ubuntu*, as well as its pivotal place, not merely in the African past, but in both the African present and the global future.

1 Tinyiko Maluleke, a professor of theology, is currently Vice Chancellor and Principal of the Tshwane University of Technology, Pretoria, South Africa.

2 Maluleke, T. 1998. "Contesting ubuntu". *The Natal Witness Echo*, 29 October; Maluleke, T. 1999. "The Misuse of Ubuntu". *Challenge Magazine*, 53(April/May):12-13.

3 Mandela, N. 1994. *Long Walk to Freedom*. London: Little Brown Company.

My two short pieces of the late 1990s observe that one of the mistakes committed in the effort to rehabilitate the treasured notions of *Ubuntu*, has been the temptation to essentialise the African experience and practice of *Ubuntu* as static, immutable and indifferent to context and impervious to all external stimuli. But thankfully, much like the book *Unfolding Narratives of Ubuntu in Southern Africa*,[4] this volume on *Ubuntu* and women does not only locate *Ubuntu* in contemporary Africa but also moves away from the usual association of *Ubuntu* with the past and the rural.[5] Instead, contributors to this volume track and trace *Ubuntu* in contemporary urban African spaces. For example, several chapters in this volume tease out the conceptions and practices of *Ubuntu* through such contemporary and very urban rituals as premarital counselling, bridal showers, baby showers, and urban courtship patterns. Nor do the chapters in this volume shy away from the thorny issues pertaining to the associations and contaminations between *Ubuntu* and its malcontents, namely patriarchy and the related. Yet, none of the contributors tackle these issues from a purely abstract and philosophical manner. All contributors situate themselves in their very specific contexts of Botswana.

If *Ubuntu* were not such a pivotal aspect of African culture, and if the world was not so patently in need of *Ubuntu*, I would have been the first to advocate that we consider abandoning the notion altogether, seeing how corrupted, trivialised and misconstrued it has become. Given the many wrong-headed conceptions of *Ubuntu* that are in circulation, it has been tempting to simply let go of the contaminated notion and go searching for alternative concepts. In my mind, such a predilection towards abandonment of *Ubuntu* has also been occasioned by several of the recent works on *Ubuntu*, which have not inspired much confidence, but have vacillated between the wryly philosophical[6] and the extremely utilitarian.[7] Many such works have inadvertently tended to bury *Ubuntu* rather than resuscitate it.

Nonetheless, the book *Ubuntu and Women: Community Building in the Urban Space* will definitely help resuscitate the concept of *Ubuntu*. Its foregrounding of women as conceptualisers and practitioners of *Ubuntu* provides a rare and unique perspective on the subject. Previously, works on *Ubuntu*, being inadvertently patriarchal, have

4 Müller, J., Eliastam, J. & Trahar, S. (eds). 2019. *Unfolding narratives of ubuntu in Southern Africa*. New York: Routledge.

5 Ogude, J. (ed). 2019. *Ubuntu and the reconstitution of community*. Bloomington, IN: Indiana University Press.

6 Praeg, L. & Magadla, S. (eds). 2014. *Ubuntu: curating the archive*. Pietermaritzburg, South Africa: UKZN Press; Praeg, L. 2014. *A report on ubuntu*. Pietermaritzburg, South Africa: UKZN Press; Ogude, J. (ed). 2018. *Ubuntu and personhood*. New Jersey, NJ: Africa World Press.

7 Msila, V. 2015. *Ubuntu: shaping the current workplace with (African) wisdom*. Randburg, South Africa: Knowres Publishing; Msila, V. & Gumbo, M. (eds). 2016. *Africanising the curriculum: indigenous perspectives and theories*. Stellenbosch, South Africa: African Sun Media; Ogude, J. & Dyer, U. (eds). 2019. *Ubuntu and the everyday*. New Jersey: Africa World Press.

tended to ignore women's place within the *Ubuntu* space. Indeed, the common denominator of the works I critiqued above is that the *Ubuntu* discourse presented in them is dominated by males, surprisingly white males, a few white females, and very few black females. Now, the demographics alone of the contributors to *Ubuntu and women: community building in the urban space* make the present volume a very special book. It is truly a breath of fresh air, a book that takes us several steps forward in the discourse about the continuing relevance of *Ubuntu* in troubled Africa and the unequal world of the 21st century.

1 INTRODUCTION

Botho/Ubuntu "must permeate every aspect of our lives"

In 1997, the government of Botswana established a task force to draw up *Vision 2016: The Long-Term Vision for Botswana.* This national policy document was considered a dream and a roadmap for the type of society the country aimed to become upon turning 50. The task force added *Botho/Ubuntu* to the four existing principles of the nation, namely democracy, development, self-reliance and unity (1997:5). *Vision 2016* was not only the first attempt to transform a cultural concept into national policy, but it also gave us some of the most beautiful definitions of *Botho/Ubuntu*. According to *Vision 2016*:

> *Botho* defines a process for earning respect by first giving it, and to gain empowerment by empowering others. It encourages people to applaud rather than resent those who succeed. It disapproves of anti-social, disgraceful, inhuman and criminal behaviour, and *encourages social justice for all. Botho* as a concept must stretch to its utmost limits the largeness of the spirit of all Batswana. It must permeate every aspect of our lives, like the air we breathe; so that no Motswana will rest easy knowing that another is in need [emphasis added].
> (Vision 2016, 1997:2)

In 2016, Botswana celebrated 50 years of independence and *Vision 2016* saw its final year, when a new *Vision 2036* was drawn up. The new vision document upheld *Botho/Ubuntu* as the fifth principle of Botswana (Vision 2036, 2016:22), although with comparatively less emphasis. By adopting *Botho/Ubuntu* as a national policy, *Vision 2016* implies:

> Just as individuals must embrace *Botho/Ubuntu*, our communities and society at large should have a social and moral obligation to build *Botho/Ubuntu-centred* families, groups, departments, sectors and institutions [that] strive to serve justice with and for all. [The] *Vision 2016* ... definition highlights that *Botho/Ubuntu* makes us strive to be a nation that has zero tolerance for all

> social issues that diminish the human dignity of any of our citizens, such as poverty, violence of any form, corruption, ethnic bias, gender oppression, unemployment, homophobia, ageism or racial-based discrimination.
>
> (Dube, 2021a:vii)

Although we did not seek to measure the impact of *Vision 2016*, we decided in 2016 to investigate how *Botho/Ubuntu* is expressed in the urban settings of Gaborone, the capital city of Botswana. Our research project was named *Botho and Community Building in the Urban Space.* Our study sought to investigate how *Botho* (commonly known as *Ubuntu*) is expressed in urban areas, using multiple case studies of bridal, baby, Naomi and Laban showers in Gaborone, Botswana. Bridal and baby showers are social gatherings commonly known for supporting a new bride and anew mother, respectively. The Naomi and Laban showers are new events created in Botswana for parents and in-laws to prepare them for receiving numbers in their homes and communities following a new marriage. The John Templeton Foundation sponsored the research project in 2016 and completed data collection in 2018. The project initially involved ten scholars from the Faculties of Humanities, Social Sciences and Education at the University of Botswana.[1] The objectives of the project were as follows:

- Explore the theological and spiritual base of *Botho/Ubuntu* values/ethics.
- Examine how *Botho/Ubuntu* ethic was understood and manifested in traditional Botswana communities.
- Analyse how the *Botho/Ubuntu* ethic is expressed in contemporary urban settings of Botswana.
- Investigate how *Botho/Ubuntu* activities in the urban space construct and reconstruct gender.
- Highlight how *Botho/Ubuntu* spirituality can inform the building and maintenance of justice-loving communities.

This book, therefore, presents our data-based findings and contributions to the discourse of *Botho/Ubuntu*, gender and community building. In addition to *Vision 2016*, many other scholars in Botswana and the region of Southern Africa have also researched and written about *Botho/Ubuntu*; to them we are highly indebted. Dumi Mmualefe has researched *Botho/Ubuntu* (2004, 2013); Joseph Gaie (2010, 2013); Musa W. Dube (2009); Sana Mmolai (2013), and Dube et al. (2016), among others. Recently, Zimbabwean writers have been making significant contributions to *Ubuntu* and gender, characterised by the work of Manyonganise (2015), Chitando (2015),

1 The initial research team included: Musa W. Dube, Senzokuhle D. Setume, Malebogo Kgalemang, Rose M. Gabaitse, Seratwa Ntloedibe-Kuswani, Tirelo Modie-Moroka, Elisabeth Motswapong, Tshenolo Madigele, Mmapula Kebaneilwe, Sana Mmolai and Amanda K. Matebekwane.

Chirongoma (2022) and Chisale (2020), among others. South African thinkers have also made significant contributions (Desmond Tutu, 2011; Maluleke, 1999; Motlhabi, 2009; LenkaBula, 2008, etc). It is important to sketch the contributions of these writers as the foundation upon which we present our research findings.

Botho/Ubuntu and Botswanan thinkers

In 2004, Dumi Mmualefe wrote his master's dissertation, 'Towards authentic Tswana Christianity: revisiting Botho', where he argued:

> *Botho* has been mistaken especially in the Western thought as emphasizing the community to the detriment of personal freedoms and individuality ... Instead of the individual being neglected, the emphasis of one's individuality is always related to the person's identity as a member of an extended family and to the total social and historical context. 'The individual, whose identity is constantly being created through a series of becoming', does so not apart from, but with. One's becoming therefore becomes part of the community becoming. (2004:7)

In a follow-up chapter, titled 'Botho and HIV and AIDS: a theological reflection' (2013), Mmualefe develops his ideas on *Botho/Ubuntu and community building.* Though the African concept of *Botho/Ubuntu* has been explored from different angles in academia, Mmualefe (2007) makes his theological reflection of *Botho/ Ubuntu* within the context of HIV and AIDS. Mmualefe contextualises *botho* as 'relational'. When defining a person, *motho*, he explains that *motho* "is a relating thing ... one who is conscious of himself" (2007:3) or herself. He further explains that in *botho* there is always 'us', never '*them*' (ibid.). By avoiding othering, society becomes a better place/space for caring for those in need, such as those infected and affected by HIV and AIDS and those grappling with life challenges in the urban spaces. Mmualefe explains the importance of *botho* as acceptance versus rejection; thus, "when one is welcome and embraced, one feels part of it" (2007:13-14). They feel that they are a person, *motho.*

Concerning *Botho/Ubuntu* and gender, Mmualefe highlights the "danger and challenges of gendering God" (2007:14). He argues that to understand why women and the girl-child are more susceptible to HIV and AIDS than men, there is a "need to deal with gendering God" (2007:17). Mmualefe (2007) further asserts that when God is depicted as male, by implication, men are supposedly godlier than women, leading to the abuse of women and girls by men. Mmualefe stands firmly against intergenerational sex, where older men take advantage of young girls. This has led to moral decadence as young girls no longer respect older men due to the inappropriate behaviour of men. Mmualefe, though acknowledging that Setswana is equally gendered, explores the possibility of applying gender-neutral terms about God. He laments the failure of the Christian community to live up to the expectations of *botho*. He says that by focusing on individual and personal salvation, the Christian community has lost the essence of botho because the church fails to serve the community: it does not build the community anymore but is inward-looking. The church community has lost its "saltiness" and "light".

In their chapter, 'The African ethic of *Ubuntu/Botho*: implications for research on morality', Thaddeus Metz and Joseph Gaie (2010) define *Botho/Ubuntu* as afro-communitarianism. They explain that this is a strain of sub-Saharan moral thought that emphasises the importance of community in a person's life. The spirit of *Botho/Ubuntu* is expressed in the phrase, "a person is a person through other persons" or simply, "I am because we are". The phrase carries with it ideas about what it means to be human, implying that an individual could either be less human or fully human, where the latter is the ultimate desire for all persons. The achievement of full personhood or genuine humanness is essentially relational. People cannot realise their true selves in opposition to others, or even in isolation. This means that individuals get deeper and deeper into the community with others to achieve their full personal humanity. The authors do not make any specific links between *Botho/Ubuntu* and gender. They, however, elaborate on the intersection of *Botho/Ubuntu* and community building. *Botho/Ubuntu* is a vital ingredient in community building as it emphasises an individual's moral duty and obligation to exhibit solidarity with others. One must belong with others in a harmonious community where each member must necessarily ensure that they play their part to achieve the good of all (Metz & Gaie, 2010:276, citing Gbadegesin, 1991:65). According to Metz and Gaie (2010:276), community building depends on an individual's humanness, as expressed in their solidarity and identity with others by their friendliness and love towards others, as though in familial relationships. The extended family is a fundamental expression of the *Botho/Ubuntu* African idea of community (Metz & Gaie, 2010:276, citing Shutte 2001). Accordingly, one is obligated to promote, exhibit, and extend one's familial relationships to all human beings, which essentially sees all as potential family members worthy of being loved. Consequently, the *Botho/Ubuntu* ethic esteems community highly, encourages and enables true sharing of life in community as integral to human existence. Each member of the community participates voluntarily and in a friendly, caring, and loving manner towards improving the quality of life for all group members.

In their chapter, 'Condomisation as a method to fight HIV and AIDS: implications for Botho', Joseph B.R. Gaie and Sana Mmolai (2006) describe *Botho* as a series of attempts by an individual to try to assist others when they need assistance; or if one is unable to assist directly, then they should be able to point others to where they can receive help. Gaie and Mmolai link Botho and gender through their discussion of marriage, age differences, sexual rights, faithfulness and HIV and AIDS prevention. The age difference is a social factor that creates new power dynamics, for elders are to be respected and obeyed by the younger generations. Because of the age difference, Gaie and Mmolai argue, women hesitate to ask their partners to use condoms, for in so doing, they will be disrespectful to their elders and fail to practise Botho. The authors also discuss Botho and the community in the HIV and AIDS context. They argue that men, women and young people must all participate in reducing the spread of HIV by using effective methods of prevention. Gaie and Mmolai insist that both men and women are expected to be faithful to their partners, and they use the word *people* to demonstrate how HIV prevention should ideally be a community affair. The two scholars call both men and women to take responsibility for practising faithfulness, since this would reduce the spread of HIV and protect the whole community. In so doing, they place the community at the centre of the manifestation of Botho, HIV prevention, as a collective and communal effort. For other chapters dealing with *Botho/Ubuntu* and HIV and AIDS in Botswana, see Dube (2009:178-188; 2016:531-542).

Botho/Ubuntu and Zimbabwean thinkers

While many authors' expositions of *Botho/Ubuntu* concepts of the community are beautiful and might shelve critical analysis, we know better – that no culture or theory is perfect. Most cultural concepts are double-edged swords. In the past fifty years, when the world has become more attuned to human rights, we have come face to face with the fact that most of our beautiful thoughts and concepts need further interrogation. In short, we need to apply the 'hermeneutic of suspicion'. Thus, many African scholars have argued that as Africans, we need a critical concept of "I am because I am", given that the African context is riddled with civil wars, poverty, corruption, dictators, etc. – it seems to show a stark contradiction to the proclamation of 'community' that is often underlined. If it is proclaimed without critically engaging it in our context, the concept of "I am because we are", easily slides into 'blind romance' about Africa, African life and thinking. In recent times, the Zimbabwean thinkers have not only begun to engage *Ubuntu* in large numbers but also critically. Here we look at Molly Manyonganise's (2015), Ezra Chitando's (2015), Sophie Chirongoma's (2022), and Sine Chisale's (2018, 2022) take on *Ubuntu*, gender and community building.

In her chapter, 'Oppressive and liberative: A Zimbabwean woman's reflections on *ubuntu*', Manyonganise (2015) uses a womanist lens to critique the deployment of *Ubuntu/Unhu* in the Zimbabwean Shona culture, and its negative impact on women's experiences (in general) and the Zezuru ethnic group (in particular). The womanist framework propounded by Alice Walker suggests that understanding human relationships brings insights into moral life based on ethics supporting justice for women, survival and productive quality of life through a holistic approach to the community's struggles. Womanism is transformative in orientation; hence, it uses the power of individual and communal resistance to oppression. The womanist paradigm becomes relevant in shaping the future of *Ubuntu* in African communities because of its close affinities with African ethics. In this chapter, Combs, through accepted definitions of the concept of *Hunhu*, connotes being human; *munhu* (a person) refers to a person who is expected to have *hunhu* (the trait of being human). Despite *Ubuntu* being a reclamation of the dignity of the black person from the effects of colonialism, associated with love, compassion, and humility within the Shona culture; its ambivalence in practice has resulted in women and girls being 'denied their humanity', and declared non-existent at birth and throughout the lifecycle Manyonganise asserts. She acknowledges that the field of African philosophy has been male-dominated and has treated women philosophers and ethicists as subordinate figures, hence the convenient disregard for the implications of *Ubuntu* on gender. Manyonganise (2015) contends that glorifying the concept without due analysis of its gender implications is practised by the beneficiaries of the patriarchal dividend.

Manyonganise outlines several cultural practices to make her point on *Ubuntu*: several practices within the Zezuru ethnic group uphold male normativity, such as the stereotypical representation of women through proverbs and sayings; the socialisation of women into a code of secrecy; the belief in and respect of ancestral spirits who are of patrilineal descent; the practice of polygamy; the high regard for male over female children; the linking of male children to carrying the family lineage and homestead forward; exclusion and silencing of married women in decision-making processes; the expectation of women to implement the decisions taken by men in the traditional courts, and the exclusionary identities around marriage, all of which reinforce exclusionary boundaries in both families of birth or the families to which they are married. Other practices include hetero-normativity and exclusionary tendencies in the political environment, land ownership, paying *lobola* to the woman's family upon marriage, and condoning violence against women in public and private spheres.

Manyonganise (2015) contends that *Ubuntu*, in its current form, has been used to marginalise and silence women. The *Ubuntu* practice has depended on silenced women to increase moral and cultural landscapes that inevitably exclude women. Manyonganise's (2015) chapter interrogates the definitions and utility of a 'concept' often taken for granted, such as *Ubuntu*, and repositions it with gender expectations and prescriptions within the socio-cultural context. The second-order explanations, the conceptual assumptions, often differ from their contextual assumptions, which are the conditions that restrict when, where, and for whom *Ubuntu* is assumed to hold or where it applies. Not specifying the contextual boundary conditions of *Ubuntu* as applying equally to both men and women and in all socio-cultural contexts has reduced its power of explanation and prediction. Therefore, Manyonganise's (2015) chapter contends that male and female African philosophers should actively define women's place and relevance in the *Ubuntu* or *Hunhu* philosophy, considering the central human beings of inherent dignity and beings within the transformative ethos of gender equality and equity.

In his chapter, 'Do not tell the person carrying you that s/he stinks: Reflections in *Ubuntu* and masculinities in the context of sexual and gender-based violence and HIV', Chitando (2015) reviews the concept and practice of *Ubuntu* and its ever-glorified path against the backdrop of the emerging interest in masculinities in Africa. Chitando (2015) questions the relevance or applicability of the constructions of masculinities in contexts of sexual and gender-based violence and HIV, and the need to recover indigenous values in contemporary democratic spaces. Chitando (2015) observes that men have been socialised to dominate and control women's bodies and to enjoy gender-prescribed privileges that include being pampered, leading, getting their demands met, 'doing' violence, and receiving preferential treatment. These masculine gestures not only support simplistic notions of what men supposedly are but also highlight how reigning definitions of masculinity undergird notions of bloated conceptions of male power, control and dominance over women, which justify the worst kinds of violence against women and girls.

Therefore, the journey to redefine *Ubuntu* is a progressive one, which revisits the patriarchy that is embraced in *Ubuntu*. The struggle toward redefining *Ubuntu* in practice should invoke upending hegemonic meanings and institutions that deny women the space to see whole human beings on an equal footing with men. Practising a de-patriarchalised *Ubuntu*, Chitando insists, includes a redefinition that considers women's rights violations manifested through the horrendous acts of domestic violence and HIV infection. There is a need in the African community to re-characterise gender roles that do not stigmatise women, with men having to learn to accept that women are human beings with rights, equal to them. Men must try through *Ubuntu* to advocate for women's rights. For *Ubuntu* to work, there is a need for society and men to challenge sexual and gender-based violence and promote gender justice. Through a progressive *Ubuntu*, men should adopt a non-violent masculinity that appreciates women from an early age. Though these prescriptions are central to the influence of the *Ubuntu* ethic, various parts of Africa have recoiled from adopting this progressive way of thinking for fear of being labelled Western-influenced. Chitando (2015) contends that if *Ubuntu* is de-patriarchalised, it can be deployed to detoxify aggressive masculinities, assist men in challenging sexual and gender-based violence, and embrace more harmonious, life-giving, and transformative/liberating masculinities. Such a brand would further support and nurture gender equity, oppose and not engage in violence against women, and appreciate the critical role played by women in sustaining families, communities, and nations.

Sinenhlanhla Sithulisiwe Chisale's chapter, '*Ubuntu* as Care: Deconstructing *Ubuntu*' (2018:1-8), adds to Manyonganise's and Chitando's critical view. She argues that *Ubuntu* is a caring ethic in the context of Africa, which is characterised by harmony, homogeneity and interdependence. Those are the characteristics that should consistently run across all aspects of life. It is, however, unfortunate that caregiving has become a gendered notion. It has seemingly become an exclusive role of women in Africa, a norm that has been perpetually reinforced by masculine authority and patriarchal values. According to Chisale, care is not gendered, as it is characterised by un-gendered values such as dignity, responsibility, caring, compassion, fairness, regard, respect, hospitality and responsiveness. Those who practise *Ubuntu* are to possess the mentioned qualities and more. Moreover, being human is better expressed through interdependence and homogeneous relationships. In that regard, men and women must embrace working together while extending pastoral care services to those in need (Chisale, 2018).

In her chapter, 'Politics of the Body, Fear and *Ubuntu*', Chisale explores *Ubuntu* concerning disability and feminist theology. Chisale (2020) argues that *Ubuntu* generally addresses two core questions: 'What is it to be human?' and 'What is necessary for human beings to grow and find fulfilment?' First, to be human is to be caring, empathetic, respectful of other people's dignity, welcoming and compassionate. They are further expected to exhibit associated values (2020). From this understanding of what it is to be human, we notice that more emphasis is on good interpersonal relations and the possession of good values. That is basically what the original meaning of *Ubuntu* entails. Chisale points out that *Ubuntu* comes from the Nguni maxim, *Umuntu ngumuntu ngabantu*. It translates as "A person is a person through other persons". In core understanding, *Ubuntu* is about interpersonal relations, interconnectedness, and interrelatedness of the web of life (Chisale, 2020). Chisale maintains that African women's theology of disability that *Ubuntu* informs can curb discrimination against women with disabilities (Chisale, 2020, 2022). The ableist approach, however, is widespread in academic circles where functionality, good looks and physical health are promoted. It is, however, unfortunate that feminist discourses generally exclude "other women's" lived experiences in their deliberations. African women's theology of disability is challenged to be inclusive of the body. African women's theology of disability should be an alternative community that vigorously, without compromise, challenges socially constructed politics of gender separation and difference among disabled and abled women. A communal-oriented approach accompanied by commitment, advocacy and praxis development should be adopted in academic cycles. Women and men should be united regardless of their differences, and theology should be used to fight against any form of oppression from the perspective of *Ubuntu. Ubuntu* protects all against any form of discrimination and encourages all to collaborate in maintaining and sustaining the humanness of the other (Chisale, 2022).

In their chapter, 'Reigniting the principle of *Ubuntu/Unhu* in the aftermath of cyclone Idai in Chimanimani, Zimbabwe, in the light of sustainable development goals', Sophia Chirongoma, Sibiziwe Shumba and Susan Dube have taken strides to define *Ubuntu/Unhu.* The authors define *Ubuntu/Unhu* as the promotion and enhancement of the well-being of others. In the process, the person becomes open and available to others where there is pure affirmation. This affirmation gives an individual reassurance that they are not an island but rather belong to a greater whole. This further explains why their will to survive ceases, especially when others are humiliated or diminished, or are subjected to inhumane tendencies. This move situates an individual in a safe space due to being inclusive. Hence, they conclude that the principle of *Ubuntu* becomes enshrined in understanding what it means to be human and what is needed for humans to mature and flourish. The discovery of harmony and peace is much needed, especially during times of upheaval and uncertainty, as was the case with the people of Chimanimani when cyclone Idai hit.

Furthermore, Chirongoma et al. (2019) make a fascinating link between *Ubuntu/Unhu*, and their conclusion can be highlighted as '*Ubuntu* is gendered'. In their chapter, they reiterate that in a disaster of such magnitude, the hardest hit and most affected are women, children and the elderly. This translates into women being on the receiving end, because they are the caregivers to the children, the elderly, and even males – all of whom depend on them. Notwithstanding, the majority of people who perished were women and children. Similarly, we notice the mothers who lost their children did not have emotional space to deal with grief because cyclone Idai eroded the traditional burial and mourning rituals. While men drown their sorrows in alcohol and drugs, women wake up sober and have to keep a stiff upper lip and take each day as it comes, oblivious to the devastation and hurt they are experiencing. Not only that, women, in this case, do not even have the space or time to heal because they have to think of where the next meal for their surviving relatives will come from. As such, they do not have closure, and the pain lingers on to the point of desperation. Worse still, abuse and violence against women and children escalated because many families camped in temporary shelters in schools, churches, and public spaces. Women and children became victims because of their vulnerability.

building and *Ubuntu* as critical tools during the devastation left by cyclone Idai. As much as African communities are communal, the devastation's aftermath eroded several rites associated with *Ubuntu* and community building. For instance, failure by the community to come and pay their last respects and celebrate the lives of their dearly departed relatives meant the therapeutic role they usually provide could not be enacted. Hence the family and the community did not have a sense of closure. That meant failing to play their role in the community's emotional building, a critical component in the healing process of the scars left by Idai due to either missing people or where deceased people were found, the roads were inaccessible, making it impossible to reach the relatives destination and offer support. For material support, there was urgency to assist children by offering child-friendly spaces in the affected areas and the main concern is that these children are assured of a safe home, while making sure that their education is guaranteed. In conclusion, despite the devastation of the Idai aftermath, Chirongoma et al. maintain reigniting the principle of *Ubuntu* is the best antidote to the shattered and grieving people of Chimanimani.

Botho/Ubuntu and South African thinkers

Many South African thinkers have deliberated on *Ubuntu* (Tutu, 2011; Maluleke, 1999; Munyaka & Motlhabi, 2009). Nonetheless, this chapter will focus on Puleng LenkaBula's chapter, 'Beyond Anthropocentricity – *Botho/Ubuntu* and the Quest for Economic and Ecological Justice in Africa' (2008:375-394). LenkaBula provides a compelling elaboration of *Botho/Ubuntu.* LenkaBula transcends the conventional meaning of *botho* linked with human connections in the humanities and social sciences. First, she acknowledges that *botho* has been reduced to anthropocentric understandings that prioritise human values and requirements. She contends that these human approaches and interpretations of the '*botho* framework' are inadequate (2008:377). This framework explains humanity's relationship to itself while ignoring the relationship to ecological life.

She admits that anthropocentric interpretations of *botho* have been boiled down to favouring human values and desires. She claims that when examined and interpreted with the aid of human logic, "frameworks linked with *botho* are inadequate" (2008: 377). According to LenkaBula (2008), *botho* does not engage in or promote simple compliance or dictatorial relationships that prohibit the autonomy and flourishing of the person. *Botho*'s objective is inspiring, as it encourages people to "encounter the difference of their humanity to inform and deepen our own … *ubuntu* respects the particularities of the beliefs and practices of others" (2008:377).

After recognising and critically discussing the limitations of an anthropocentric definition of *botho*, LenkaBula (2008) contends that *botho* has the potential to be defined by "ecological well-being and human relatedness with ecology" (ibid.:380). Her emphasis on *botho's* ecological paradigm runs counter to normative understandings and constructions of *botho* as a concept that "conveys the values of respect, humane relationships, and compassion, as well as caring for other human beings" (ibid.:380).

In her intersectional approach to the spirit of *botho*, LenkaBula (2008) asserts that *botho* calls for "an understanding of the ontology of people as embedded in that of others (human beings), in creation and God" (ibid.:386). The ontology of *botho* defines their essence. The religious rituals of ethnic groups demonstrate the connection to the Earth. Ethnic cultures' religious rites prove their relationship to the land. LenkaBula (2008:386) uses the Basotho ethnic group to illustrate "the interconnection of all of creation". Other ethnic groups, such as the Bakwena (crocodile people) and the Batloung (elephant people), describe their "identity, their being, and their self-conception regarding ecology and communities in which they live" (2008:386) and refer to their connection to animals as a form of connection to the Earth and God.

LenkaBula's (2008) discussion does not focus on *botho* and gender, because her focus and definition of *botho* emphasise its interconnectedness to ecology. On the other hand, her focus is dominated by an emphasis on botho's communal logic. Community is essential to *botho* because "a person's humanity is affirmed by acknowledging the humanity of others" (2008:385). She defines community as "human and biotic communities, as well as webs of life" (2008:386). Her definition returns us to her reading, which goes beyond the anthropocentric understanding of *botho*. She contends that "a more organic, holistic, and inclusive understanding of community lining human relations to relations with nature is relevant in Christian theology and ethics…" (2008:386).

Gaborone showers and the spirit of *Botho/Ubuntu*

The above perspectives and concerns were central to the research project on '*Botho/Ubuntu* and community building in the urban space'. The study sought to investigate how *Botho/Ubuntu* is expressed in cities and towns of Botswana by focusing on the women-driven events of Naomi/Laban, bridal and baby showers in Gaborone. It took cognisance that the community spirit can be lost in urban areas, and poverty can easily encroach. Therefore, the question was: "How does *Botho/Ubuntu* mitigate isolation and poverty in urban settings?" While the study began in 2016, fieldwork ended in 2018, and several chapters were published in various journals.[2]

2 Some of the group authored chapters include: '*Botho*, Community building and Gender Constructions in Botswana', *Journal of the Interdenominational Theological Center*, 42(2016):1-22; "Exploring the Concept of *Africa*, 2/3(2017):173-191; '"A Little Baby is on the Way": *Botho/Ubuntu* and Community

However, the researchers deemed it necessary to share some of their findings and recommendations with various stakeholders through this book, a collection of pre-published articles in book form. We hope it will contribute to the ongoing academic debates on *Ubuntu*, illustrated by the above reviews.

However, the researchers deemed it necessary to share some of their findings and recommendations with various stakeholders, by collecting these chapters into a book publication on '*Botho/Ubuntu*, Gender and Community Building in the Urban Space'. As attested above, *Botho/Ubuntu* has been and still is, intensely researched and discussed regionally and internationally. This volume enters these debates with fieldwork-based data. In other words, we carried out fieldwork with non-academic women in their normal life settings in an urban area to investigate how they express and maintain *Botho/Ubuntu* and how they challenge or maintain patriarchal and other oppressive social categories. The volume will, perhaps, be the first of its kind produced by women in conversation with other women concerning *Botho/Ubuntu*. We hope that the publication of our findings will contribute towards an evidence-based deeper understanding of *Botho/Ubuntu* philosophy and how *Botho/Ubuntu* can continue to empower African communities and their members, are manifested and interpreted in specific contexts, such as urban spaces of Botswana addresses (or an address), social injustices such as gender, class, race, ethnicity, sexuality, and other differences that intersect with Christianity. The biblical text and other traditions can inform African governments to become *Botho/Ubuntu*-centred economies and political systems that seek to empower all its members.

The reader will glimpse some of our findings and recommendations from various chapters in this anthology. To serve the interest of different readers (those who might be interested in other showers), the book has endeavoured to maintain each chapter's independence while attempting to create a structural, thematic, and ideological coherence. The main disadvantage is that when read continually, a reader may find some repetitions in the descriptions of aims, fieldwork methods and some findings.

This book is structured as follows:

- Introduction
- Introductory Chapter 2

building in Gaborone Baby Showers', *Gender Studies*, 16/1(2017):50-70; 'Reproducing or Creating a New Male: Bridal Showers in the Urban Space of Botswana', *Journal of Gender and Religion in Africa*, 24/1(2018):79-95; 'Pathways to Social Capital and the *Botho/Ubuntu* Ethic in the Urban Space of Gaborone'. *Botswana. Global Social Welfare: Research, Policy and Practice.* (2019):1-13; 'Emergent Rites of Passage in Botswana: The Case Study of Naomi/Laban Showers', *Pula Botswana Journal of African Studies*, 33/1(2019):61-79; 'Pre-marital Pastoral Counselling/*Go Laya* on Issues of Gender and Human Sexuality: Naomi/Laban Showers in Gaborone, Botswana', *The International Journal of African Catholicism*, 10(1), Winter 2020). See also *Journal of the Interdenominational Theology Center*, 50 (2021) and 51(2022).

- Part 1: *Botho/Ubuntu*, Bridal Showers and Marriage
- Part 2: *Botho/Ubuntu*, Laban/Naomi Showers and In-laws
- Part 3: *Botho/Ubuntu*, Baby Showers and Mothering
- Part 4: *Botho/Ubuntu*, Love, and Bedroom Talk

Although one would have thought the parental shower (Naomi/Laban) should come first, it is featured after the bridal shower, for it is only organised after a couple intending to marry has officially announced their intentions and made advanced preparations for the wedding day. The second chapter, 'Mother Economies – *Botho/Ubuntu* and Community Building in the Urban Space: A Focus on Naomi/Laban, Bridal and Baby Showers' gives a broad sketch of theories, methods, origins, main aims of each shower, and the findings, while arguing that women are, more often than not, guardians of *Botho/Ubuntu* philosophy. This analysis and presentation of findings begin by exploring Mercy Oduyoye's proposal for mother-centred economies (2004:57-66) and the concept of *Botho/Ubuntu*. The chapter proposes the intersection of the model of mother-centred economies with the principle of *Botho/Ubuntu*. It argues that the ethics of mother economies hold the best hope for the survival and expression of *Botho/Ubuntu*. In other words, mother economies seek to build *Botho/Ubuntu*-oriented communities, social structures and relations, which, when applied at national and international levels, will assist us in building a justice-oriented world. Therefore, Gaborone's women-centred showers are seen as a practice, creating and maintaining mother-centred economies, exuding the *Botho/Ubuntu* ethic. Lastly, the chapter draws its conclusions from all showers, calling for a *Botho/Ubuntu*-based 'Earth Community' founded on the pillars of serving justice with and to all members.

Part 1 on '*Botho/Ubuntu*, Bridal Showers and Marriage' focuses on bridal showers, featuring four chapters. The third chapter, 'Exploring the Concept "*Botho/Ubuntu*" through Bridal Showers in the Urban Space, Gaborone, Botswana', explores *Botho/Ubuntu* using the lens of the agency. Agency aids in understanding how women in the urban space navigate and create their own space that would allow them to empower, help and support each other. In the rural areas of Botswana, *Botho/Ubuntu* was the basis of all social relations as reflected in economic and cultural practices such as *mafisa*[3] and *molaletsa*.[4] While in the village, the space for exercising *Botho/Ubuntu* is a given. It has to be created in the urban space. Researchers attended

3 '*Mafisa*' refers to a Setswana socioeconomic structure that allowed the lending of cattle by the rich to the poor. The poor would take care of the cattle on behalf of the rich; in the meantime, the poor would use the cattle for milk and draught power (Rankopo, Osei-Hwedie & Modie-Moroka, 2007).

4 '*Molaletsa*' is a mutual self-help system to enable people to provide the much-needed labour to each other in a reciprocal way. Through this system the communities were productive and self-reliant (Rankopo, Osei-Hwedie & Modie-Moroka, 2007).

14 bridal showers with a total of 230 attendants, where they conducted 40 in-depth interviews and administered 110 questionnaires. The study shows that women in the urban space express *Botho/Ubuntu* through 'creating a new family' presence at bridal showers, and giving advice and presents to the bride. While the study found that in the urban bridal showers, patriarchal gender roles/ideologies are still reproduced, it also found that they are also deconstructed. Chapter 4, on 'Unsettling Patriarchy: *Go Laya* in Gaborone Bridal Showers', utilises theories of gender and agency to read and analyse the content of counselling (*go laya*) provided during the shower events. The chapter seeks to assess the process and content of *going laya* in Gaborone bridal showers to understand how it confronts, reconstructs or cohabits with patriarchal structures and note its agency. The chapter finds that there are multiple ways utilised to unsettle patriarchy, which include the procedure of holding counselling (*go laya*), dress code, inclusive participation and the content of the advice given. Chapter 5, on 'Reproducing or Creating a New Male? Bridal Showers in the Urban Space in Botswana', recognises that each society has specifically constructed images of acceptable maleness and femaleness. The chapter utilises theories of masculinities and gender to explore how Gaborone bridal showers construct and reconstruct gender. It explores how women gathering in an exclusively female space of the bridal shower construct the image of a Motswana man, the husband-to-be, as they counsel each other on the challenges and tricks of maintaining a successful marriage. While remaining within the constraints of patriarchal hegemonic masculinities, there are many indications that the Gaborone bridal showers also endeavour to construct *Botho/Ubuntu*-informed masculinities.

Chapter 6, 'Pathways to Social Capital and the *Botho/Ubuntu* Ethic in the Urban Space in Gaborone, Botswana', underlines that since independence, Botswana has experienced urbanisation and industrialisation, which has prompted rural-urban immigration, leading to weakened family and community spirit. Be that as it may, the chapter notes that very few studies have investigated how rural and indigenous values are maintained and practised in urban spaces. Using the concept of *Botho/Ubuntu* and the theories of social capital, the chapter examines themes such as social norms of mutuality, social networks, reciprocity, and collective efficacy. The data analysis from the bridal showers leads to the conclusion that participation in showers brings social empowerment, satisfaction and improved social relations. The findings agree that while bridal showers still embrace many forms of patriarchy, they have also shifted the game's rules by disregarding age and marital status as required criteria for counselling the bride-to-be. The Gaborone bridal shower space welcomes every adult woman to participate without making marital status and age a requirement. In so doing, they challenge patriarchy that forces women to define their humanity concerning patriarchal marriage. The kind of *Botho/Ubuntu* community space

Gaborone bridal showers seek to embrace and promote is constantly in friction with established patriarchal norms in their struggle to birth inclusive and liberating communities. Their endeavours to empower a new bride to start a home are also in constant confrontation with poverty. They seek to ensure that new couples are psychologically empowered to build thriving families and materially empowered to start a home through gifting.

Part 2, on '*Botho/Ubuntu*, Laban/Naomi Showers and In-laws', features three chapters. Naomi/Laban showers are designed for parents and the communities that will receive new daughters- and sons-in-law. They started to address the apparent gap – namely the assumption that parents automatically know how to receive, welcome and live with their in-laws without training. Such an assumption, the trainers argue, is false. Ignorant parents and other in-laws often mess up their children's marriages and sometimes even cause divorce. In particular, the gendered relationship of the mother-in-law and her daughter-in-law is noted for its conflict-laden history that is based on two women competing for the same man, primarily since economic power used to, and to some extent still does, lie in the hands of sons and fathers. The Laban shower recognises that fathers-in-law are also known to exploit their sons-in-law, as attested by the biblical story of Jacob and his father-in-law, Laban. Therefore, the Naomi/Laban showers seek to empower parents and all in-laws with skills of welcoming the new daughters- and sons-in-law into their families, homes and communities – and how the daughters- and sons-in-law should also accept, support and welcome their new parents. The shower primarily uses the biblical book of Ruth and the story of Laban in Genesis 24-31, although there are references to several other biblical passages.

Three chapters analyse data from the Naomi/Laban shower. Chapter 7, on 'Emergent "Rites of Passage" in Botswana: A Case Study of Naomi/Laban Showers', utilises the ritual theories holding that rites of passage are "ceremonies that mark important transitional periods in a person's life, such as birth, puberty, marriage, having children, and death. *The ceremonies* usually involve rituals and teachings designed to strip individuals of their original roles and prepare them for new ones". Rites of passage mark a process by which an individual is separated from their old self or status to transition into a new self and status and be incorporated into a new position and stage in life. The Naomi/Laban is an emergent rite of passage, first because it is new and invented in Botswana; second, it helps both the parents and the new couple cross-cultural/legal boundaries into new roles through the marriage contract. The chapter explores how the Naomi/Laban ritual is, in fact, a manifestation of *Botho/Ubuntu*.

Chapter 8, on 'Naomi/Laban Showers and the Creation of a Womanist-*Botho/Ubuntu* Ethic of Communal Living Spaces', takes cognisance of the fact that mother-in-law and daughter-in-law relationships are often conceived within a patriarchal economy, breed competition and conflict in these relationships. It utilises social theory, intersectionality, and womanist/womanhood theories to analyse the data collected and how it intersect with the philosophy of *Botho/Ubuntu.* The chapter thus theorises the Naomi/Laban shower as a reconstructive space that seeks to create communal living spaces that are informed by the ethic of *Botho/Ubuntu.* It is concluded that Naomi/Laban showers create a womanist *Botho/Ubuntu* ethic of communal living, in which the mother-in-law and daughter-in-law exist in a harmonious relationship.

Chapter 9, 'Premarital Pastoral Counselling/*Go Laya* on Issues of Gender and Human Sexuality: Naomi/Laban Showers in Gaborone, Botswana', begins by exploring Botswana's family and marriage situation. It highlights how the country is confronted by low marriage rates exacerbated by high divorce rates, resulting in a fragile family institution in Botswana. The chapter highlights that the Naomi/Laban shower takes cognisance of this context and actively seeks to offer premarital counselling to new couples and their in-laws to address and prevent conflicts that often lead to marital breakdowns. The chapter assesses nine themes addressed by the Naomi/Laban shower, highlighting how they build *Botho/Ubuntu*-oriented relationships in families, homes and communities by offering premarital counselling that addresses gender-based conflicts. Naomi/Laban counsels older and younger women to be reconciled with one another and to work as a team rather than compete against one another.

Part 3 on '*Botho/Ubuntu*, Baby Showers and Mothering', features one chapter (10), titled '"A Little Baby is on the Way": *Botho/Ubuntu* and Community Building in Gaborone Baby Showers'. This chapter uses theories of gender and the "good mother" to analyse how the Gaborone Baby shower manifests *Botho/Ubuntu* and how in the process it swings between deconstructing patriarchal gender roles and re-imaging male-female relations within the space of raising children. It was in the baby showers, where there was more demand for male participation than others. The chapter underlines that the arrival of a baby has always played a significant role in many societies across the globe. Hence, there is a need to shower the mother-to-be and her future baby with gifts and advice to welcome the baby and the additional member into the family. The objectives of the chapter seek to establish what baby showers entail, how these initiatives started and how they are conducted. But most importantly, the chapter highlights that baby showers are a community building initiative in the urban space that *Botho/Ubuntu* drives. As the data indicate, gathering for the baby showers is not only to celebrate the baby but also an opportunity for the community to celebrate being a community.

Part 4 on '*Botho/Ubuntu*, Love and Bedroom Talk' consists of two chapters. Chapter 11, 'How I Met My Husband: Bridal Narratives at Bridal Showers in Gaborone', explores the stories shared on how the prospective brides met their suitors. The chapter investigates how such stories may exhibit *Botho/Ubuntu*, embody gendered relations, or create a space for reconstructing gender relations while building community. The art of storytelling is in itself a cultural space of building community, normally around the fireplace. Given that in Setswana and many Bantu cultures, an open discussion concerning sexuality is not the norm, Chapter 12, on 'Sex in the Shower: Bridal Showers and Sexuality', seeks to analyse how sex-talk in Gaborone bridal showers empowers women to deconstruct patriarchal, heteronormative perceptions. Further, the chapter demonstrates how sex conversations embody life-giving values and ideals of *Botho/Ubuntu* within marriage.

Some recommendations

One significant confirmation was that Batswana women in Gaborone are led by *Botho/Ubuntu* to make efforts to make more humane the arrival of a new bride into her new home, the arrival of a new mother and a new baby, and the arrival of new parents-in-law and their daughters/sons-in-law. Women voluntarily organise events, contribute money, give material goods and give moral guidance to ensure that the new home, new couple, new baby, and new-in-laws are well grounded and are materially equipped to begin their new roles in their homes and community. As the theories of agency propounded by Avishai and Mahmood, drawn from religious women, underline "agency as resistance that might also appear as 'the negotiation with oppressive social structures and partial compliance', thereby indicating that 'docility did not necessarily compromise agency'" (Avishai, 2016:267). The analysis of the data from all showers also highlights that these women movements often work within and with patriarchal frameworks; they often work in contexts where poverty and ethnocentrism is a threat, yet they endeavour to create a space of justice by small and various strategies and acts that displace patriarchy, poverty, ethnocentricism, racism and ageism by calling into being *Botho/Ubuntu*-oriented communities. Building *Botho/Ubuntu*-oriented communities and relationships are, therefore, a process, a movement, a journey, and a commitment to building relationships that uphold the dignity of all members. In other words, the Gaborone showers help us to understand "*Botho* as a ***process*** for earning respect by first giving it, a process of gaining empowerment by empowering others … and the spirit of encouraging social justice for all through our programs and the skills that empower all our citizens to serve *ka Botho*" (Vision 2016, 1997:2). Where the ethic of *Botho/Ubuntu* exists, we should find ourselves restless against any form of injustice among us and within us.

In light of *Vision 2016*'s definition of *Botho/Ubuntu*, of the findings of our fellow researchers discussed above, and our fieldwork-based findings, we would like to add that *Botho/Ubuntu* is not just for one segment of the community such as young people, women, or servants. It is for the young, the adults, men and women, bosses and workers, leaders and followers, and for people of all ethnic groups and races, who realise their *Botho/Ubuntu* is not only concerning other humans but the entirety of the creative community on Mother Earth. Just as individuals must embrace *Botho/Ubuntu*, so our communities and society at large should have a social and moral obligation to build *Botho/Ubuntu*-centred families, groups, departments, sectors and institutions, which strive to serve justice with and for all (Dube, 2021a:viii).

References

Battle, M. 2000. 'A theology of community: the *ubuntu* theology of Desmond Tutu'. *Interpretation: A Journal of Bible and Theology*, 54(2):176-186. https://doi.org/10.1177/002096430005400206

Chirongoma, S., Shumba, S. & Dube, S. 2019. 'Reigniting the principle of *ubuntu/unhu* in the aftermath of cyclone Idai in Chimanimani, Zimbabwe in light of the sustainable development goals'. *The Fountain: Journal of Interdisciplinary Studies*, 3(1):15-29.

Chisale, S.S. 2018. '*Ubuntu* as care: deconstructing the gendered *ubunTu*'. *Verbum et Ecclesia*, 39(1):1-18. https://doi.org/10.4102/ve.v39i1.1790

Chisale, S.S. 2020. 'Politics of the body, fear and *ubuntu*: proposing an African women's theology of disability'. *HTS Teologiese Studies/Theological Studies*, 76(3):1-10. https://doi.org/10.4102/hts.v76i3.5871

Chisale, S.S. 2022. 'Covid-19 and *ubuntu* disruptions: curbing the violence against women and girls with disabilities through African women's theology of disability'. *Journal of International Women's Studies*, 24(4):3.

Chitando, E. 2015. 'Do not tell a person carrying you s/he stinks: reflections on *ubuntu* and masculinities in the context of sexual and gender-based violence and HIV'. In: E. Mouton, G. Kapuma, L. Hansen & T. Togom (eds). *Living with dignity: African perspectives on gender equality*. Stellenbosch, South Africa: African Sun Media. 269-284.

Denbow, J. & Phenyo, C. 2006. *Culture and customs of Botswana*. Westport, CT: Greenwood Publishing Group.

Dube, M.W. 2009. 'I am because we are: giving primacy to African indigenous values in HIV&AIDS prevention'. In: M.F. Murove (ed). *African ethics: an anthology of comparative and applied ethics*. Pietermaritzburg, South Africa: UKZN Press. 178-188.

Dube, M.W. 2016. 'Let there be light: birthing ecumenical theology in the HIV and AIDS apocalypse'. *The Ecumenical Review*, 67(4):531-542. https://doi.org/10.1111/erev.12186

Dube, M.W. 2021a. 'Introduction: towards *ubuntu/botho*-centred individuals, communities and nations. *Journal of the Interdenominational Theological Center*, 50(Spring):iii-xix.

Dube, M.W. 2021b. 'Postcolonial *Botho/Ubuntu:* transformative readings of Ruth in the Botswana urban space'. In: J.L. Claassens, C.M. Maier & Funlola O. Olojede (eds). *Transgression and transformation: feminist, postcolonial and queer Biblical interpretations as creative interventions.* London: T&T Clark. 161-182. https://doi.org/10.5040/9780567696274.ch-011

Dube, M.W., Setume, S.D., Modie-Moroka, T., Gabaitse, R.M., Kgalemang, M., Motswapong, P.E. Kebaneilwe, M.D. & Madigele, T.J. 2021. 'Mother economies: *Botho/Ubuntu* and community building in the urban space, a focus on Naomi/Laban, bridal and baby shower'. In: L.C. Siwila & F.A. Kobo (eds). *Religion, patriarchy and empire: festschrift in honor of Mercy Amba Oduyoye*. Pietermaritzburg, South Africa: Cluster Publications. 61-112.

Gaie, J.B.R. & Mmolai, S. 2006. 'Condomization as a method to fight HIV and AIDS: implications for botho'. *BOLESWA Journal of Theology, Religion and Philosophy*, 1:2.

Gaie, J.B.R. & Mmolai, S.K. 2007. *The concept of Botho and HIV/AIDS in Botswana.* Eldoret, Kenya: Zapf Chancery. https://doi.org/10.2307/j.ctvgc61hd

Le Grange, L. 2015. '*Ubuntu/Botho* as ecophilosophy and ecosophy', *Journal of Human Ecology*, 49(3):301-308. https://doi.org/10.1080/09709274.2015.11906849

LenkaBula, P. 2008. 'Beyond anthropocentricity: *Botho/Ubuntu* and the quest for economic and ecological justice in Africa'. *Religion and Theology*, 15(3-4):375-394. https://doi.org/10.1163/157430108X376591

Maluleke, T.S. 1999. 'The misuse of *ubuntu*'. *Challenge*, 53:12-13.

Metz T. & Gaie, J.B.R. 2010. 'The African ethic of *ubuntu/botho*: implications for research on morality'. *Journal of Moral Education*, 39(3):273-290. https://doi.org/10.1080/03057240.2010.497609

Mmualefe, D.O. 2004. 'Towards authentic Tswana Christianity: revisiting *botho*'. Unpublished Master's thesis, Eden Theological Seminary, Missouri.

Mmualefe, D. 2013. '*Botho* and HIV and AIDS: a theological reflection'. In: J.B.R. Gaie & S.K. Mmolai (eds). *The concept of Botho and HIV/AIDS in Botswana.* Eldoret, Kenya: Zapf Chancery. 1-29. https://doi.org/10.2307/j.ctvgc61hd.4

Munyaka, M. & Mokgethi, M. 2009. '*Ubuntu* and its socio-moral significance'. In: F. Murove (ed). *African ethics: an anthology of comparative and applied ethics.* Pietermaritzburg, South Africa: UKZN Press. 63-84.

Tutu, D. 2011. *God has a dream.* Random House.

Vision 2016. 1997. *Vision 2016: long-term vision for Botswana.* Gaborone: Botswana Government.

Vision 2036. 2016. *Vision 2036: achieving prosperity for all.* Gaborone: Botswana Government.

2

MOTHER ECONOMIES – *BOTHO/UBUNTU* AND COMMUNITY BUILDING IN THE URBAN SPACE

A focus on Naomi/Laban, bridal and baby showers in Gaborone

'*Botho*' defines a process for earning respect by first giving it, and for gaining empowerment by empowering others … '*Botho*' as a concept must stretch to its utmost limits the largeness of the spirit of all. It must permeate every aspect of our lives, like the air we breathe, so that no [one] will rest easy, knowing that another is in need (*Vision 2016*).

> *Botho* is what constitutes God's image in us, and that which is divine knows not what is male and female. (Mmualefe, 2007:26)

Introduction

This chapter[1,2,3] and the rest in this book are based on the findings of the research project *Botho/Ubuntu and Community Building in the Urban Space*. The project sought to investigate how *Botho/Ubuntu* and community building are manifested in the urban space by focusing on Naomi/Laban, bridal and baby showers of Gaborone, in Botswana. Naomi/Laban showers are celebrations organised by women for parents who will either receive a daughter- or son-in-law; a bridal shower is organised for a woman who is engaged to be married, and baby showers are organised for a woman who is about to become a mother. These showers have become a common female-centred movement in Botswana's major cities 'presumably' expressing the *Botho/Ubuntu* ethic and spirituality in urban areas. The *Botho/Ubuntu* ethic is a communal

1 This study was graciously funded by John Templeton Foundation through Nagel Institute of Calvin College.

2 The article, 'Mother economies: *Botho/Ubuntu* and community building in the urban space: a focus on Naomi/Laban, bridal and baby showers' by Dube, M.W., Modie-Moroka, T., Setume, S.D., Ntloedibe, S., Kgalemang, M., Gabaitse, R.M. & Sesiro, D., was first published in 2021 in L. Siwila & F.A. Kobo, *Religion, patriarchy and empire: festschrift in honour of Mercy Amba Oduyoye* by Cluster Publications, Pietermaritzburg, South Africa. It is republished in this volume by permission.

3 Gaborone is the capital city of Botswana in Southern Africa.

spirit that holds that one's humanity is only expressed through the capacity to uphold the dignity of another person, expressed through welcoming, respecting, caring and empowering the Other (Vision 2016, 1997:2). As used here, the 'Other' refers to that which is outside (but interconnected) to oneself physically, ethnically, racially, sexually, culturally and in relation to class, Earth, gender and health, among others. Botswana cities are a product of rural-urban migration, where the community spirit can easily give way to isolation, individualism, and pockets of dehumanising poverty. This research project set out to investigate how *Botho/Ubuntu* is expressed in the Botswana urban space using the examples of the above-listed showers.

The analysis and presentation of findings begins by exploring Mercy Oduyoye's proposal for mother-centred economies (2004:57-66) and the concept of *Botho/Ubuntu*. The chapter proposes the intersection of the model of mother-centred economies with the principle of *Botho/Ubuntu*. It argues that the ethics of mother economies hold the best hope for the survival and expression of *Botho/Ubuntu*. In other words, mother economies seek to build *Botho/Ubuntu*-oriented communities, social structures and relations that, when applied at national and international levels, will assist us to build a justice-oriented world. The women-centred showers of Gaborone are, therefore, seen as a practice, a creation and maintenance of mother-centred economies exuding the *Botho/Ubuntu* ethic. Simultaneously, the spirituality and ethic of *Botho/Ubuntu* are highlighted, which is a spirituality of recognising and welcoming the 'Other' through upholding their dignity. The second part of this chapter presents the problem statement, hypothesis, objectives, and fieldwork methodology of the study. The third and major part of the chapter analyses the findings of the study. These are presented first by describing the participants, origin, and purpose of each shower. This is followed by presenting some key findings under three subheadings, namely: (a) *Botho/Ubuntu* as a Driver of Showers in Gaborone; (b) Community Building in Gaborone Showers, and (c) Gender Cultural Base and Cultural Reconstruction in Gaborone Showers. Lastly, the chapter draws a conclusion from all sections, calling for a *Botho/Ubuntu*-based Earth community that is founded on the pillars of serving justice to all members.

Mother economies: "I am not a mother, but I have children"

In her article, 'Poverty and Motherhood', Mercy Amba Oduyoye highlights that African women raise children under adverse social, economic and political contexts, and in doing so highlight that not only is "mothering a religious duty", but also "what a good socio-political and economic system should be about, if the human beings entrusted to the state are to be fully human, nurtured to care for, and to take care of themselves, one another and their environments" (2004:57). African mothers model what good governance should be: caring and serving justice, not just to humanity but to the whole Earth community. Oduyoye argues that

> The quality of a sense of duty and fulfilment and achievement that must go with the determination to see another person become human, cannot be associated with poverty of understanding about the value of humanity. It (motherhood) may be exercised in the midst of abject lack of material needs and that makes it more of a marvel that women continue to mother. Scarcely ever does one find a deliberate choice of childlessness among African women and furthest from our understanding of life is to make that choice for economic reasons. (2004:58)

According to Oduyoye, "Mothering, biological or otherwise, calls for a life of letting go, a readiness to share resources and to receive with appreciation what others offer for the good of the community" (ibid.:58). Oduyoye thus says an association of poverty and motherhood is a strange and unacceptable combination, since motherhood is the epitome of understanding what it means to be human through the capacity to know how to nurture the life of the 'Other'. Motherhood, therefore, entails both biological and social mothers, that is, it is "a principle of human relations and the organization of human community" (ibid.:58). Drawing examples from the mother-centred Akan, and from her own biological mother, Oduyoye asserts that "I have accompanied my mother through her motherhood. Motherhood has not made my mother poor. *My mother is rich.* She has a community of people whose joys and sorrows are hers. I am rich because I have this community and hold a special place in it. I am not a mother, but I have children" (ibid.:57). In the latter, she acknowledges that while she does not have biological children, she embraces the ethic of African mothers, who are driven by the "determination to see another person become human." Oduyoye offers the model of mother economies as a critic of capitalism and neo-liberal economies (Dube, 2006:178-192) whose focus is the accumulation of goods through exploitation of the majority and our Mother Earth, thus creating the anomaly of associating motherhood with poverty.

In a similar but different take on the issue, Brigalia Bam argues that

> ...the first challenge to mention here is that (African) women bear the brunt of all crises that African nations are faced with – HIVAIDS, POVERTY, WAR, VIOLENCE Genocide – HIT WOMEN hardest. In this sense, African women are the bearers of the cross alongside the crucified Lord. The first challenge facing churchwomen in Africa is all the challenges facing the continent put together. This is a mammoth challenge [emphasis original]. (2005:4)

In suggesting that African women are crucified alongside the crucified Lord, Bam implies that they do not only carry the cross of suffering, but they also fly the banner of the resurrection power, thereby bearing the light of salvation from death-dealing oppressive structures that deny life and its quality. It is this light of salvation that Oduyoye underlines, to which we need to turn our attention. A Setswana saying goes, "*mmangwana o tshwara thipa ka fa bogaleng*", which literally translates as "a mother grabs a knife by its cutting edge". The saying means that mothers will do and must do all they can to protect life – to protect their children. The protection of life is not optional; rather, it is imperative, and mothers do all that is in their power to accomplish it. As Oduyoye underlines, motherhood is beyond biological mothering – rather, it refers to the principle of holding all life in sanctity and working for maintaining the same. Motherhood, she underlines, is the process of being "co-creators with God and imitators of God's management." She thus proposes that the ethic of mothering should apply to all other aspects of life – economically and politically informing the ethics of our social relations and structures. It is the proposal of this chapter that African women's commitment to mothering is, therefore, the embodiment of *Botho/Ubuntu*, as well as the radiation of godliness in a world where evil and exploitative structures devalue the dignity of communities, individuals, and the whole creation community at large. African mother-economies' resurrection power lies in challenging death-dealing capitalist and neo-liberal exploitative structures through their life-redeeming practices that seek to build *Botho/Ubuntu*-oriented communities and social structures. An exploration of *Botho/Ubuntu* philosophy and its intersection with the concept of mother economies is therefore in order.

Botho/Ubuntu philosophy: "A person is only human with and through others"[4]

The word *Botho/Ubuntu* is derived from Ba**ntu**/Ba**tho**[5] (people), which refers to an African linguistic group spreading from southern, east, central and some western parts of Africa. *Isi**ntu**/Se**tho*** refers to the cultural ways of the Ba**ntu**/Ba**tho**. *Botho/Ubuntu*, on the other hand, is the philosophy of being human, or what constitutes one's humanity (Dube, 2009:178-188; Mmualefe, 2004). *Botho/Ubuntu* is measured by one's capacity to uphold the dignity of the 'Other'. It encompasses human, economic, environmental and divine relations that underline the sanctity of the creation community as a whole, by acknowledging that *Botho/Ubuntu* – or humanness – is and can only be measured by the capacity to care and respect the 'Other'. In Bantu thinking, one who lacks this capacity, without any form of physical challenge, is described as "*gase motho*", that is, inhuman (Munyaka & Motlhabi, 2009:70-71). The saying, *Umu**ntu** ngu mu**ntu** nga banye/mo**tho** ke mo**tho** ka ba bangwe* (a human being is only human with/through others) highlights that community building is a central part of exercising *Botho/Ubuntu*. The saying best

4 This is the translation of the Bantu saying, "umuntu ngu muntu nga banye" in Nguni languages, which in Setswana language is "motho ke motho ka batho".

5 Bantu (people) is Nguni, whereas Batho (people) is Sotho-Tswana. I have highlighted the stem of the term for easy recognition.

captures *Botho/Ubuntu* as a process of realising one's identity and of being fully human as an experience that occurs within the type of relations and communities that we build, namely through each member of the community taking the mantle of building empowering and affirmative relationships.

Botho/Ubuntu as a core relational principle encompasses being in communion with the environment and the Divine (Lenka Bula, 2008:375-379). This is because respecting the Earth is prominent in the Bantu philosophy (Ramose, 2009:308-314). It was (and is) attested by regular Earth cleansing rituals that preceded farming season and followed the harvest. They included the practice of communal self-interrogation whenever environmental disasters such as drought occurred (Dube, 2014:157-172). The Bantu communities were keenly aware that they could pollute the Earth and thereby change its seasonal balance. Although the Bantu people were not living in the industrial and capitalist societies, cleansing the Earth from human pollution was a regular annual practice in preparation for the coming of rains (Molato, 2020:53-64). There was thus a spirituality of awareness of living in a close relationship with the Earth and the full understanding that the Earth could raise a voice in protest whenever human beings polluted the environment (Dube, 2014:317-340; Habel, 2000; Matholeni, Boateng & Manyonganise, 2020). Similarly, Ancestors are regarded as the living dead who reinforce healthy relational *Botho/Ubuntu* ethics (Dube, 1999:315-328; Le Grange, 2015:301-308; Gaie and Mertz, 2010:273-290). Mercy Oduyoye's proposed ethics on mother-centred economies has implications for Earth care as well as maintaining economic and political structures of justice, for she underlines that these African "mothers are co-creators with God and imitators of God's management of creation" (2004:62).

Mluleki Munyaka and Mokgethi Motlhabi elaborate on *Botho/Ubuntu* characteristics, pointing out that

> Ubuntu is inclusive ... its manifested in living in community, it is best realized in deeds of kindness, compassion, caring and sharing, solidarity and sacrifice. Such acts produce positive results for both individuals and community. They make it possible for an individual to count on and expect the meaningful support of fellow human beings. People are expected to share the resources with which they are blessed. Furthermore, Ubuntu is a call to participation. It demands service to humanity in a practical way. Through positive acts within community, one is connected, linked and bound to others. The best way to contribute to society is through practical communal action to alleviate human suffering. Ubuntu is the source or basis of feelings of compassion responsible for making life more humane for others, in particular the disadvantaged, the sick, bereaved and poor, as well as strangers. There is commitment to advance their interest and concerted effort is made to do so. These acts help bring sense not only to one's own life, but also to the lives of others. (2009:74-75)

Oduyoye's definition of motherhood intersects with the *Botho/Ubuntu* ethic as she maintains that "Mothering, biological or otherwise, calls for a life of letting go, a readiness to share resources and to receive with appreciation what others offer for the good of the community" (2004:58). According to Oduyoye, the ethics of mothering may hold the best hope for the survival of *Botho/Ubuntu*, as it offers "a principle of human relations and the organization of human community" (ibid.:58). In the face of exploitative and anti-communal capitalist and neo-liberal economies, which expose women (as well as children, communities as a whole, and nations) to poverty and compel us to think that mothering is a source of poverty, Oduyoye maintains that "What we need to turn our attention to, therefore, is the poverty of the human spirit that ignores the humanity of women as persons made in God's image and mothers as co-creators with God and imitators of God's management of creation" (ibid.:62). The portrait of God as a creator and the process of creating life presented in Genesis 1:1-30 characterises God as the mother-economist. Not only does God create all members of the Earth community in interconnectedness, but also blesses all members with divine dignity, and spreads resources equitably to all. Genesis 1 thus presents God as the 'mother creator' who births, loves, cares for and does all to sustain the whole creation community. God's management of creation is best seen in the creation of a balanced, blessed and beautiful Earth community. Here the dignity of all members of creation is guaranteed by the sacredness of their origin and they are pronounced as such. In other words, all members are created by God, declared good by the same, and hence deserve full dignity as members of Earth community and against any form of exploitation and discrimination (Dube, 2015:1-17). It goes without saying that when human beings seek to build *Botho/Ubuntu* and mother-centred economies, they are seeking to be in touch with God's image within them and their communities.

In her paper, '"I am because we are": giving primacy to African indigenous values in the HIV and AIDS prevention', Musa W. Dube (2009) has underlined the primacy of *Botho/Ubuntu* in maintaining the sanctity of life in the creation community. She holds that

> The community is where the divine is experienced and the individual is groomed. The community is where values are embedded, passed on and practised. All life is sacred by virtue of being part of life, and the business of living is about being continuously involved in respecting the other, each other and one another ... Such a community is founded on the values of *Setho/Isintu/Cjithu* which, when embodied by people becomes *Botho/Ubuntu/Buthu*. As the Botswana *Vision 2016* tells us, '*Botho/Ubuntu* defines a process for earning respect by first giving it, and to gain empowerment by empowering others ... and *encourages social justice for all ... Botho* as a concept must permeate every aspect of our lives, like the air we breathe ... so that no one will rest easy knowing that another is in need.
> (2009:20 & 13)

Underlining the spirituality of *Botho/Ubuntu* concept in community, in individuals, in godliness and in the practice of faith in general, Dumi Mmualefe maintains that "without *Botho*, we cannot worship God, for *Botho* is an expression of God's image in us" (2007:26). As Dube argues, "The community is where the divine is experienced and the individual is groomed", for a *Botho/Ubuntu*-founded community reflects the image of God by honouring/respecting/empowering all its members. It follows that a community that lives by the *Botho/Ubuntu* ethic will reflect the image of God in its economic and political structures and environmental care by practising mother-centred ethics. Such an economy is guided by care for the 'Other' and does not entertain isolation and poverty, for poverty is the ultimate dehumanisation and violation of God's image in creation.

Botho/Ubuntu, community building, women-centred showers

With the above theoretical description of *Botho/Ubuntu* and mother economies, we return to the research project on '*Botho/Ubuntu* and community building in the urban space', which sought to investigate how the ethics of *Botho/Ubuntu* and community building are manifested in the Botswana urban space by focusing on Naomi/Laban, bridal and baby showers. At this present stage, the chapter will present the problem statement, hypothesis and objectives, and describes the fieldwork methods before focusing on presenting the findings and analysis of the study. Then the chapter will focus on aspects that will assist us to measure how *Botho/Ubuntu* and community building are expressed in urban settings and within the women-centred movements of Naomi/Laban, bridal and baby showers. Cities of Botswana are borne of migration from rural areas under circumstances that are antagonistic to the community spirit but are prone to isolation, individualism and pockets of dehumanising poverty. The aspects covered in this chapter seek to establish from the data the women centredness of these movements, the origin and purpose of the showers, and the construction and deconstruction of gender roles. In conclusion, these three aspects will be analysed for the works of the *Botho/Ubuntu* ethic and their community-building practices in the urban space. It is in such spaces that mother economies are expected to manifest as cradles of *Botho/Ubuntu* ethic.

Problem statement

In rural Botswana communities, relationships within the family, village and community are guided by the *Botho/Ubuntu* spirituality and ethic that underline our humanity as perpetually dependent on recognising, respecting, affirming and welcoming the 'Other'. They also inform communities' practices of affirming the human dignity of each member by building the economic base of the needy and vulnerable through practices, such as *mafisa, letsema, molaletsa* and *motshelo*.[6] *Botho/Ubuntu*, therefore, prevents the encroachment of dehumanising poverty amongst its members, for it would negate both the communal and individual dignity of its members.

Botswana has a growing urban population in towns, cities and urban villages where encroachment of poverty becomes a real threat. Unfortunately, it is undocumented how the *Botho/Ubuntu* spirituality and ethic are practised in such urban settings, where communities do not necessarily share ethnical, geographical or established histories of close coexistence. The lack of such analytical documentation is a major theological and national loss. This leads to policymakers', developmental planners' and community leaders' failure to rely on evidence-based research to cull contextual productive energies for building self-reliant and self-respecting communities. Therefore, this research sought to come up with evidence-based conclusions on how *Botho/Ubuntu* is still expressed in urban cities, which it did by studying women-centred showers.

Hypothesis

The study on *Botho/Ubuntu* and community building in the urban space sought to test the following hypothesis: 'Naomi, Laban, bridal and baby showers are forms of community-building activities in urban spaces informed by the *Botho/Ubuntu* ethic, which has the effect of forging African spirituality; mitigating the encroachment of dehumanising poverty and empowering women'.

Objectives of the study

This study sought to:

1. explore the theological and spiritual base of the *Botho/Ubuntu* ethic/values;
2. examine how the *Botho/Ubuntu* ethic was understood and manifested in traditional Botswana communities;

6 Mafisa is an indigenous Setswana cattle loan, which is given to an economically challenged family. The family would take care of someone's cattle while using them for ploughing, milk, and draught power. In addition, every year the concerned family would be given one cow by the owner. The loan enables economically challenged families to move out of poverty and establish themselves as self-reliant within approximately five years. 'Letsema' and 'molaletsa' are corporate labour movements where members of the village provide one another with free labour for any big project, such as harvesting, building a house, roofing or digging a well, etc. Motshelo is a micro-lending practice that women use to pool funds and give themselves interest-free loans and groceries for seasonal celebrations. When they have pooled significant funds, they loan the money to non-members with some percentage of interest, thereby becoming micro-lenders.

3. analyse how the *Botho/Ubuntu* ethic is expressed in contemporary urban settings of Botswana;
4. investigate how *Botho/Ubuntu* activities in the urban space construct and reconstruct gender; and
5. highlight how *Botho/Ubuntu* spirituality can inform the building and maintenance of justice-loving communities.

Methodology of the study: desktop and fieldwork research

The study first carried out desktop research to review relevant literature (Dube et al., 2016:1-23). The desktop research sought to address the first two objectives stated above. The literature review also sought to investigate the concept of *Botho/Ubuntu* and how a new daughter-in-law, son-in-law, married person and baby were traditionally received in the community. This investigation served to lay the foundation for assessing continuity, discontinuity and hybridity in the urban-based Naomi/Laban, bridal and baby showers, against which fieldwork data will be interpreted. The research also sought to investigate how *Botho/Ubuntu* cohabits with patriarchy (Maluleke, 1998, 1999; Manyonganise, 2015:1-7; Chitando, 2015:269-284), how *Botho/Ubuntu* challenge each other and how *Botho/Ubuntu* can become a prophetic framework against gender oppression and all other forms of discrimination that reduce the human dignity of some members in African communities and sanction the oppression of the Earth (cf. Mmualefe, 2013:26; Dube, 2009:178-188). The proclamation of *Botho/Ubuntu* should, therefore, have zero tolerance for gender, race, age, ethnicity, religion, disability, health, or sexual-based discrimination, or any other form of oppression in relationships.

Whereas earlier on it was pointed out that one who does not live by the ethic of *Botho/Ubuntu, gase motho*, that is, they are inhuman. Mmualefe extends this concept, holding that theologically, one who does not have *Botho/Ubuntu, ga ana boModimo* lacks godliness and fails to acknowledge the humanity and godliness of others. One who fails to welcome and empower the 'other' fails the divine test, for the Creator God, who welcomed us into the Earth community and blessed every member with sufficient resources, is the *Botho/Ubuntu* God. In other words, where *Botho/Ubuntu* is proclaimed as the embodiment of humanness and godliness, any form of discrimination would be contradictory and unacceptable. Nonetheless, gender, ethnic, religious and sexual discriminations, among others, are rife among Bantu speakers, where *Botho/Ubuntu* is proclaimed. Nonetheless, unlike Manyonganise, whose critique almost equates *Botho/Ubuntu* with patriarchy, in this chapter, the philosophy of *Botho/Ubuntu* is best viewed as a prophetic ethic that constantly reminds and challenges African individuals and communities to remember what it means to be human and to carry the obligation to create structures that are informed by the same ethic socially, economically, politically and environmentally. African mother economies are best sites for bulleting *Botho/Ubuntu* as a constant call to justice and justice-oriented social structures, institutions and relationships for the whole Earth community.

For fieldwork, the approach of the study was an embedded case study with more than one case, which adopted a mixed methods design. The significance of the mixed design was to use multiple data collection techniques (qualitative and quantitative) as they play supportive roles for each other (Mertens, 2010; Creswell, 2009). Qualitative data were collected through participatory observations (Bryman, 2001) and in-depth interviews from five key informants from each shower, such as organisers and the recipient of the shower. The researchers attended the showers and recorded the events and the teachings that go with it. Narrative descriptions of the setting and all activities were written. Interviews allowed researchers to collect data about "ideas, experiences, beliefs, views, opinions and behaviors of the participants" (Wagner, Kawulich & Gardener, 2012:133) at the Naomi/Laban, bridal and baby showers in relation to *Botho/Ubuntu* and community building in an urban setting. In addition, quantitative data were collected through a self-administered questionnaire to all participants of the showers who concerted. So, although it used a mixed-methods approach, it was dominated by the qualitative approach.

Fieldwork research addressed the third objective of the study stated above. Researchers used various avenues to identify showers, to contact organisers and to ask for permission to attend. This included approaching churches, magistrate courts, gift shops and health clinics, advertising in the radio, public noticeboards, and social noticeboards. Altogether, 31 showers were attended, involving 451 participants. The last two objectives of the study are addressed below through the analysis of the findings and the application of gender, feminist, and *Botho/Ubuntu* theories. Both qualitative and quantitative data are analysed to address objectives three to five, and some findings are presented below within the framework of mother economies as the practice of *Botho/Ubuntu*, which is best modelled by the ethic of African mothers.

The project used a mixed method to collect data, but the study was primarily qualitative. First, we reviewed literature concerning the area of study, particularly to establish how traditional Setswana handled the arrival of the daughter-in-law, son-in-law and a new baby. The project sought to establish both continuity, discontinuity, and hybridity. Our instruments for collecting data included an interview guide, self-administered questionnaire, recorded data in video and audio, as well as an observation instrument.

Female-centred showers: "Why will you go with me?"[7]

From our participatory observations, all showers were largely, if not exclusively, female-centred events and movements. The analysis of biographical data by gender, age and educational status gives an idea of the showers' participants. In the Naomi/Laban shower, 89% are women while 10.6% are men; in the bridal shower, 100% are women and 0% are men, and in the baby shower, 98% are women and 1.2% are men. The female centredness of the Botswanan showers legitimises the claim made here, that they are women-centred movements that maintain and cultivate mother-centred economies. As said above, Oduyoye proposes that African women's commitment to mothering under adverse economic, political and social contexts attests to an ethic of commitment to seeing another human being come into life successfully. In doing so, they offer us an ethical model of being in community and building *Botho/Ubuntu*-oriented economic structures whose primary aim is to welcome, care, respect and empower the 'other' into full dignity. The analysis of Botswanan women-centred shower movements will explore how they build mother economies and challenge us to commit ourselves to *Botho/Ubuntu* founded communities and structures, as well as to embody *Botho/Ubuntu* spirituality.

To start with the Naomi/Laban shower, it is supposed to be attended by parents of the couple, the soon-to-marry couple, their friends, and relatives, yet it remains clear that it is also a female-centred movement (Kebaneilwe et al., 2019:62-79). From the participatory observations made, we noted that all the facilitators of Naomi/Laban showers are exclusively female. Save for two events of the ten, where males were in the range of seven in attendance; in most cases the males who might be there would be the bridegroom-to-be and his future father-in-law. In several cases, both the future bridegroom and fathers-in-law were absent, leaving the mothers-in-law with the future bride. Although males were invited, we were frequently informed that they did not come, since they assumed that showers were exclusively female.

The female centredness of Naomi/Laban perhaps has historically female roots. It was founded by four church women. Their initial aim was to encourage their friend, whose son was getting married. Concerned that their friend had too much control over her son, they thought she would be unable to let go of her son, welcome his wife and successfully foster a healthy relationship with her new daughter-in-law. In their search for a good role model for a healthy mother- and daughter-in-law relationship, they landed in the biblical book of Ruth, from where the name of Naomi is derived.

7 This question was posed by Naomi to her widowed daughters-in-laws Ruth and Orpah, when she was underlining to them that due to her ageing body, she can no longer bear children who could grow up and remarry them (Ruth 1:11). Nonetheless, Ruth chose to remain with her, thereby indicating that there is more to their relationship than patriarchal marriage ties.

In the biblical book of Ruth, Naomi had two daughters-in-law, Ruth and Orpah (Masenya, 1998:81-90; Nadar, 2001:159-178; Dube, 2001a:67-80; Kanyoro, 2001: 101-113). When we first meet the three women in Ruth 1:1, they are all widowed and living in Moab. Naomi decides to return from her foreign country of residence, Moab, to Bethlehem of Judah, her indigenous country. Her daughters-in-law walk or attempt to return with her. Naomi stops, kisses them, weeps and says to them: "Turn back, my daughters. Why will you go with me? Do I still have sons in my womb that they may become your husbands? Turn back, my daughters, go your way, for I am too old to have a husband. Even if I thought there was hope for me, even if I should have a husband tonight and bear sons, would you then wait until they were grown?" (Ruth 1:11-13). Orpah kissed Naomi good-bye and returned to her mother's house as advised by Naomi. The story, however, does not detail her future (Dube, 1999b:145-150).

Ruth, however, stayed on, clinging to her mother-in-law. She utters the classical words that have been adopted as marriage vows: "Do not press me to leave you or to turn back from following you! Where you go, I will go; where you lodge, I will lodge; your people shall be my people and your God my God. Where you die, I will die – there I will be buried" (Ruth, 1:15-17). Naomi returns, therefore, to Bethlehem with Ruth, where she is welcomed by a group of women. They resettle, and Ruth begins to work to support her aged mother-in-law. She goes to harvest in fields and gleaning what was left behind by harvesters for their upkeep. Naomi organises for Ruth to be married to a close relative, Boaz. They marry, and Ruth gives birth to a baby boy, and the women of Jerusalem rejoicing with Naomi do not only say, "a son has been born to Naomi" (ibid.:4:17). They also say, "your daughter-in-law who loves you, who is more to you than seven sons, has born a child" for you (Ruth, 4:13-16). And the text says, "Then Naomi took the child and laid him in her bosom and became a nurse" (Ruth, 4:16).

The formation of the Naomi shower quickly led to the need to address the father-in-law. This shower was named after Jacob's father-in-law, Laban (Genesis, 29-32). Unfortunately, Laban was the opposite of Naomi, demonstrating how parents-in-law can fail to welcome their sons and daughters-in-law and see them as sources of labour to be exploited for their own ends. Laban received Jacob in his home, who wished to marry his daughter, Rachel. He asked Jacob to work for seven years for his dowry, which Jacob did. On the day of the wedding, however, Laban tricked Jacob and gave him Leah, the elder sister of Rachel, because Laban declared that the younger cannot be married before the older sister. Jacob, who was still interested in marrying the woman he loved, had to work another seven years, bringing it to fourteen years. Laban also gave Jacob some sheep, but whenever he realised that Jacob's sheep were multiplying he would take them and give him a new set of sheep

(Genesis 29). In the end, Laban did not even want to release Jacob to start his own family. Jacob, together with his two wives, concubines and property, had to secretly escape during the night (Genesis 30-32).

Naomi/Laban showers are held simultaneously, bringing together the parents, friends and relatives of the engaged couple. Although male facilitators were invited to participate, they have not demonstrated a marked interest, leaving the Naomi/Laban shower as a female-driven and dominated movement. Although both men and women (parents) are expected to attend, it is dominated by female participants. Often fathers are absent, or only one father is available (the latter could reflect that marriage rate in Botswana is very low, featuring 6203 marriages a year, from 2.2 million people (Burton, 2019:7, 34)). Comparatively, the age range of the Naomi/Laban shower is predominately higher, that is, 76% of the participants are 40 years old and above, indicating that it is indeed a parents-oriented shower. According to the Naomi/Laban shower facilitators, the shower was formed because they believed that marriage was founded by God and no one should break it up. However, no one prepares parents-in-law to receive daughters- and sons-in-law. Consequently, they end up breaking up the marriages of their children. This is how the facilitators introduce the Naomi/Laban shower session:

> We are here, to explore how to receive daughters-in-laws in our families and to build affirming relationships. We are holding this shower so that we can honor God the creator of marriage, so that we can avoid the curse of Miriam. We realize that while there are numerous bridal showers held for the soon to be brides, to prepare them for the marriage institution, no one, on the other hand, prepares the parents of the couples who are about to marry. There is an assumption, rather, that these parents know how to receive a daughter-in-law or a son-in-law. Evidence on the ground, however, indicates otherwise, since mothers-in-law are known to oppress their daughters-in-law leading to marriage break-ups. Reading the book of Ruth gives us a good example on building a healthy relationship with our daughters-in law.

Although gifts were featured in some of the Naomi/Laban showers, they were not central. Gifts were sometimes given to the mother-in-law to assist her to prepare for the forthcoming wedding. The gifts could be in a form of money contributed by each participant or by the associates of the recipients, or women from one's church or cell group. Sometimes plates for serving during the forthcoming wedding or anything recommended by the organisers of the events in consultation with the recipient were given. In the majority of the Naomi/Laban shower, there were no presents. The shower's emphasis was primarily the presence of people and the gift of building firm and healthy relationships with new and old families and their larger communities through guidance and advice. The statistical survey confirms that about 80% participants disassociated the shower with material presents as Table 2.1 below indicates.

Table 2.1 The main purpose of the Naomi shower is to give presents to the mother-in-law

Responses	Frequency	%
Strongly disagree	16	24.2
Disagree	19	28.8
Agree	18	27.3
Strongly agree	7	10.6
Do not know	6	9.1
Total	**66**	**100.0**

Bridal shower: participants, origins and purpose

Turning to the bridal shower, we attended 14 bridal showers in Gaborone consisting of 230 attendants (Setume et al., 2017:173-191; Gabaitse et al., 2018:79-95). From our observations, participants consisting of organisers, friends, workmates, church mates, hosts, family and other associates, were primarily young women. Consequently, our interview guides participants were all women. Statistical data confirm that Gaborone bridal showers are both female- and youth-centred movements. For example, while participating in the Naomi/Laban shower, 89% of participants are largely adult women and 10.6% are men; in the bridal shower, 100% are women and 0% are men. The age range of bridal shower participants is predominantly youth-oriented, for 90.4% are between 20–40 years, while only 9.6% participants were 41 years and above. Educationally, bridal shower participants ranged from high school Form 3 to PhD, with the highest number of participants possessing a degree and postgraduate training (41.4%). The marital status of the bridal shower participants indicates that the majority of participants are single (76.8%) while only 20.7% are married and 2.4% widowed. The youth-oriented and single participants of the bridal showers dominated by friends and non-blood related people, such as workmates, church mates, neighbours (89%) of the bride-to-be, with blood relatives constituting only 11%, and mostly sisters, is statistically significant. It indicates that the Gaborone bridal shower movement is not driven by blood relations, but most likely by *Botho/Ubuntu*, as other forms of data will confirm. Figure 2.1 highlights the phenomenon. Further, it confirms Mmualefe's assertion, that there is a direct link between godliness and *Botho/Ubuntu* (namely that without *Botho/Ubuntu*, we cannot please God). Figure 2.1 shows that church mates are as likely to give *Botho/Ubuntu* as friends. The most disappointing findings indicated by the figure, is that workmates are the most unlikely to give *Botho/Ubuntu* to one another. This finding has deep implications for our workplace and possibly for customer service as well. It would seem the workplace is more dominated by the belief that "*disela mmapa ga di ratane*", that is, colleagues tend to compete with rather than support one another.

This certainly calls for training on mainstreaming *Botho/Ubuntu* in the workspace of Botswana.

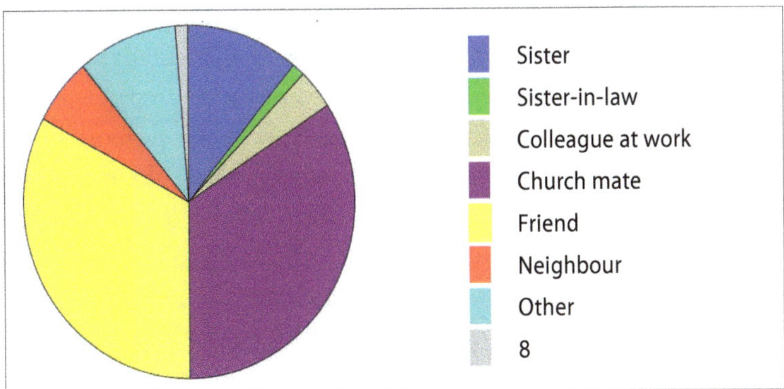

Figure 2.1 Relation to the shower recipient

Concerning the origin and role of the bridal shower, the participants gave various answers during interview guides. Some participants associated its origin with media (TV and Internet); others associated its origin with Western cultural influence and others linked it to cultural practices of offering guidance and counselling to the bride, *go laya*, which was done during the wedding (Ellece, 2011b). Others, however, linked, the origin of the bridal showers with purpose, namely that it seeks to celebrate with the bride-to-be, to support her through giving her moral support, advice/guidance/counselling on how to maintain a successful marriage and to give her gifts in preparation for her wedding day and new home. As data from interview guide participants attest, a bridal shower:

> Brings women together to learn from each other, to advise the bride-to-be from the life experiences of married people, to give gifts and financial help, to celebrate with her ... to unite as sisters, married and single, to enlighten her process towards marriage ... to make the bride feel supported with women encouraging her; without them there is no way, there is no joy!

The above articulations indicate that both *Botho/Ubuntu* and community building are central to the Gaborone female-centred bridal shower movement, since women of different marital statuses and age are brought together to accompany the bride-to-be as she prepares to cross to her new status as a married woman. As stated, the bridal shower seeks more than just to focus on the bride-to-be, for it also seeks "to unite sisters, married or single." Not only does the shower "bring women together", but it is also underlined that the bride-to-be's journey would be impossible and poorer without the community that gathers around her, that is, "without them there is no way, there is no joy!" The *Botho/Ubuntu* empowerment strategy comes in the form of the gathering – through their presence, the community itself is the gift to the bride-to-be. This empowerment comes in the form of presence, advice, support, encouragement, enlightenment, sharing, learning and material gifts (Modie-Moroka et al., 2019:1-13).

How central are material presents to the bridal shower? Consistent with the Naomi/Laban shower, they are appreciated, but they are not above presence (community). As Table 2.2 indicates, only 40.2% thought that the main purpose of the bridal shower was to give presents, while 59.8% disagreed. Thus, the majority believed that presents are not central to the event. Much emphasis is laid upon giving moral support, giving advice, guidance, and social networking that is community building. This, however, does not mean that presents are not important to bridal showers. Indeed, the group of friends who constitute the organising committee always contribute agreed amounts of monies, which are also contributed by her close circle of friends. The money gathered is used to buy presents for her new home, buy food for the shower event, as well as in some cases giving the bride-to-be hard cash. Rather, by insisting that "presence is more important than presents", there is recognition that community comes first, for indeed the material gifting is dependent on a solid foundation of a supportive community. It is within the community that *Botho/Ubuntu* is expressed, and it is *Botho/Ubuntu* that maintains the community. The Botswanan women's shower movement is an important part of this community-building process, for they seek to empower young and new couples to realise their plans to be family, professional persons and productive members of the community by accompanying them into the institution of marriage.

Table 2.2 The main purpose of the bridal shower is to give presents to the future wife

Responses	Frequency	%	Valid %	Cumulative %
Strongly disagree	16	24.2	28.0	28.0
Disagree	19	28.8	31.7	59.8
Agree	18	27.3	34.1	93.9
Strongly agree	5	6.0	6.1	100.0
Subtotal	**82**	**98.7**	**100.0**	
(Missing from system)	1	1.2		
Total	**83**	**100.0**		

Baby shower: participants, origins and purpose

Turning to the role and origin of the baby shower, the participants give various answers in the interview guides (Motswapong, 2017:50-70). Some participants said the baby shower origin was prompted by contextual needs, such as single parent-hood, which is high in Botswana, and the urban setting, where women are separated from their extended families. According to the *Vital Statistics Report 2017*, 73.3% of children were born to single mothers and only 26.4% were born to married mothers in Botswana (Mnguni, 2019:26). For others, the occasion of a pregnant mother and her baby calls for celebrating both the mother and the baby through gathering to support the mother. The support takes the form of gathering to share experiences, to give moral support, to advise/counsel/guide as well as to give material goods to the expectant mother. Some participants associated the origin of a baby shower with the influence of media and Western culture. Others, however, link its origins to Setswana cultural practices of *mantsho a ngwana* (the outdooring ceremony for a baby), which was done three months after the birth of the child. From the gathered interviews, the role and purpose of baby showers were expressed by some participants as follows:

> To get advice from other mothers, friends and family on the importance of motherhood. Also, to help prepare the mother-to-be about what to expect. It is also a form of *motshelo* as well ... to bring friends, relatives, and colleagues together as a way of celebrating the coming of the baby and also to extend a helping hand to the friends by giving them presents and advice ... To bring friends and family together as well as to celebrate the arrival of a baby ... To give the mother-to-be advice and gifts as well ... to welcome the new baby into the family ... to support the new baby by bringing gifts.

As Tables 2.3 and 2.4 indicate, participants of the baby shower underlined that baby showers are important (96.4%), and that presence (community) and presents (material gifts) for the forthcoming baby are a must. Unlike in the other two showers, Naomi/Laban and the bridal, baby shower participants underlined that it was less acceptable (64.3%) to come to a baby shower without a present for the expected baby.

Table 2.3 Baby showers are important

Responses	Frequency	%
Strongly disagree	2	3.6
Agree	26	46.4
Strongly agree	28	50.0
Total	**56**	**100.0**

Table 2.4 It is okay to attend without bringing presents

Responses	Frequency	%
Strongly disagree	16	28.6
Disagree	20	35.7
Agree	18	32.1
Strongly agree	2	3.6
Total	**56**	**100.0**

Be that as it may, the purpose of a baby shower is beyond the mother and her forthcoming baby. It is about building community and being in community. That is, the mother-to-be and her future baby are celebrated as part of the community celebrating being a community. It is an assertion that "it takes a village to raise a child." The expected coming of a child is thus beyond the immediate parents and family, but rather calls for the village and city to reclaim its community spirit. It calls upon the caring, empowering community of *Botho/Ubuntu* to live up to its standards. The mother-ethic thus challenges the oppressive and exploitative economic and political structures of our world to rethink their purpose, thereby inviting them to embrace the mother-centred economy, which is grounded on being co-creators with God and managers of God's resources. Consequently, data from the interview guide found much emphasis laid on the purpose of baby showers in the following fashion:

> The purpose of a baby shower is to connect with new people and socialize as well as to network ... to liaise and meet as well as make new friends to support each other especially women ... to bring people together, to mould or build community as well as for them to know each other ... I think it is mainly to forge relations and support each other as women.

The findings of this shower indicate that in Botswana, a baby shower focuses on three entities: the expectant mother, the forthcoming baby and community. The occasion of celebrating the forthcoming baby is also the occasion to remember and to strengthen the codes of being community. The event of gathering to empower an expectant mother and her forthcoming baby is indeed as the Figure 2.2 below on *Botho/Ubuntu* comes out as explicitly affirmative.

Botho/Ubuntu as a driver of showers in Gaborone

Since our hypothesis held that 'the Naomi/Laban, bridal and baby showers are forms of community-building activities in urban spaces informed by the *Botho/Ubuntu* ethic, forging African spirituality, mitigating the encroachment of dehumanising poverty and empowering women', the first concern we sought to establish was the presence of *Botho/Ubuntu* as a driver of showers. The main research question here was: "How does the *Botho/Ubuntu* ethic drive the Naomi/Laban, bridal and baby shower events in the urban space?" The answers to this question were sought through the interview guides, observations, recordings (audio and video) and quantitative survey.

If we consider that the *Botho/Ubuntu* ethic is the belief that one's humanity is only defined through one's capacity to respect, welcome, care for and empower the 'other', it seems the purpose and the organisation of all three showers exude this philosophy, as the above statistical survey affirms. Data from the interview guides on the whole support the data from the survey on the centrality of *Botho/Ubuntu* in the showers: As one Naomi/Laban participant said: "*Botho* drives one to have a loving heart, willingness to support one another, a spirit of oneness and being there for one another. Therefore, showering one another is in itself a practice of *Botho*." One participant from the bridal shower said: "*Botho* is sharing and caring. We demonstrate *Botho* here by donating money. We accept help from each other." According to a participant from the baby shower: "*Botho* means a lot of things: love, respect and support. Baby showers promote these principles extensively."

The statistical survey was affirmative as indicated by Figures 2.2 and 2.3.

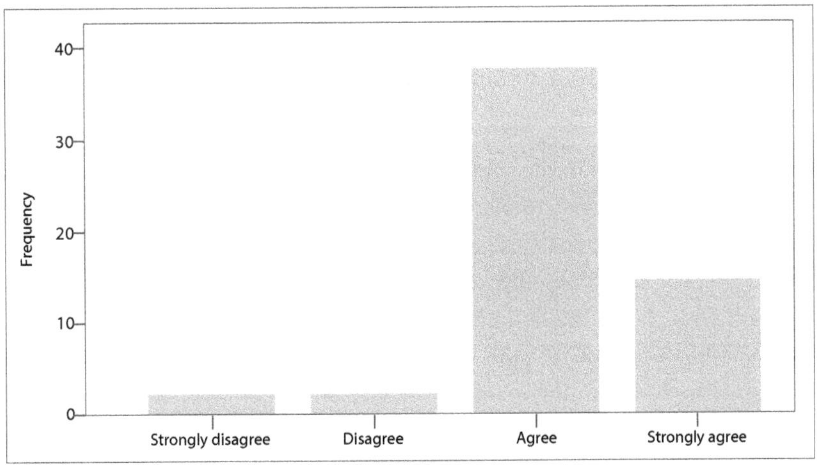

Figure 2.2 Baby showers demonstrate *Botho/Ubuntu*

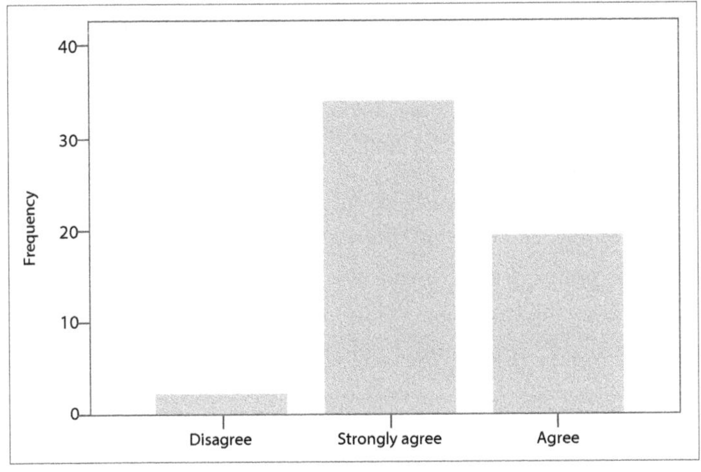

Figure 2.3 Naomi/Laban showers demonstrate *Botho*

Both Figures 2.2 and 2.3 present a strong attestation to *Botho/Ubuntu*. Almost 98% of participants viewed baby showers as demonstrating *Botho/Ubuntu*, while 88% of the Naomi/Laban participants attested to the same. Both percentages are significantly high.

Community building in Gaborone showers

The above analysis of the data has already shown that participants view showers as a form of networking, meeting new people and supporting each other (Modie-Moroka et al., 2019:1-13). The content and purpose of showers seek to strengthen relationships and prepare people to be well integrated in their social relationships and communal roles, be it marriage, motherhood, professional career or in their larger communities, which is promoted by all three showers, which is undoubtedly communal.

Yet, community building in the urban showers involves more than the teachings and training. It is also practised through the processes of organising and preparing for the shower, which may be three to six months before the actual event. This often begins with the closest friends calling the first meeting to set up an organising committee in consultation with the recipient, although sometimes it is a surprise. The organising committee often consists of representative people from various departments of the recipient, such as family, neighbours, church mates, workmates, club mates, depending on her social connections. Once the organisers are constituted, they meet several times to plan the event. Here, people who never met begin to regularly meet and work together until the event is achieved, thereby building new relationships. The overall evidence that showers are driven by non-blood relations (see Figure 2.1 above) is a significant indicator of the *Botho/Ubuntu* ethic and African spirituality at work in these movements. Further, it is clear that Botswanan urban areas have found ways of building community that are not based on ethnic, class or blood relations; rather, it is grounded on the ethic of *Botho/Ubuntu*.

Turning to the Naomi/Laban shower, community is built through uniting the families of the new couple and uniting the mother-in-law and daughter-in-law. Two rituals are usually performed following the intensive teaching on this unity. This teaching appropriates the language of 'blood relations' to underline the importance of building unbreakable relationships. Hence the new mother-in-law (mother to the bridegroom) is informed that she is highly pregnant and shall give birth to a new daughter on the day of the wedding. The speaker indeed does all to reconstruct the language of mother-in-law and daughter-in-law to 'mother and daughter', underlining that "there is no such thing as daughter-in-law – she is your daughter!" A demonstration of how a loving 'mother' carries the child of her new 'daughter' follows, highlighting that she ties the baby behind, so that if she trips and falls, she will not fall on the baby. Similarly, the new bridegroom has been born into a new family where he is a son (not son-in-law). Following this teaching on birth into new families, two rituals are performed to demonstrate their new positions and roles. Both rituals underline that *Botho/Ubuntu* must be given by all sides, to all involved members and in all our relationships.

Figure 2.4 Naomi/Laban shower participants performing a demonstration of the bonding of the two families

In the first ritual (demonstrated in the above picture), the bride-to-be has been born into a new family as a new 'daughter', while the groom-to-be has been born into her new family as a new 'son'. The new couple envelope their parents within. Further, the bridegroom-to-be is now facing his new parents, hence he is better equipped and responsible for hearing and seeing their needs. Similarly, the 'bride-to-be' is facing her new parents and is now fully responsible to see to their needs and hear their concerns. Both have been born into new families. The facilitator (standing at the rear in Figure 2.4 above and wearing eye glasses) explains the meaning of the ritual to both parents and their children. Notably, the father to the bridegroom is missing, possibly due to the extremely low rate of marriages in Botswana (Burton, 2019:7, 34).

The second ritual focuses on the 'new mothers', who are now ordained for their new role, which must be characterised by their capacity to let go, and let their married children run their own show while they support them to be their best in building their home, building their professional careers, parenting and playing their roles effectively in the wider community. There are no dichotomies between the private and public space according to gender. Both the man and woman are expected to be their best in all spheres of life and are to be mentored accordingly by their new families.

The following garbing words open a window into the purpose and intention of the ritual:

> Do you see this shawl? What is its color? I believe your heart is pure, white with joy. As I put this shawl on you, I remind you the words that you heard. Children are blessings from God. God blessed you today. You are both giving each other children. Receive these children and put them under your wings. Your job is to carry the burdens of these children and take them to God as you pray on your knees. The shawl represents the glory of the Lord. It indicates that God's presence is surrounding and protecting your children and their marriage.

On the day of the shower, larger numbers of guests arrive, and there is great occasion for socialising, networking and meeting new people. Here, community is built through several activities, such as dressing in the same colour (normally stated in invitation cards), cooking together (in preparation for the event), teaching and learning together, playing theme-oriented games, eating and finally, in some showers, partying thereafter.

Statistically, the survey indicates that participants agree that showers build community (71% and 78.6% in Tables 2.5, 2.6 and 2.7 below) and that they expect to continue meeting with at least half of the people they meet at these events, as indicated by Tables 2.6 to 2.8 and Figure 2.5. That is, 63.6% said they would visit the mother-in-law after the Naomi/Laban shower; 58.9% of baby shower participants said they will have long relations with recipients of the shower, while 78.6% said they will visit the baby after the shower, as indicated by Figure 2.5.

Table 2.5 Naomi/Laban showers allow community building in the urban space

Responses	Frequency	%
Strongly disagree	1	1.5
Disagree	1	1.5
Agree	22	33.3
Strongly agree	25	37.9
Do not know	17	25.8
Total	66	100.0

Table 2.6 After shower, I will visit my mother-in-law (Naomi/Laban)

Responses	Frequency	%
Strongly disagree	4	7.1
Disagree	8	14.3
Agree	36	64.3
Strongly agree	8	14.3
Total	56	100.0

Table 2.7 I will build strong relations with people from the bridal shower

Responses	Frequency	%
Strongly disagree	2	3.0
Disagree	14	21.2
Agree	23	34.9
Strongly agree	19	28.8
Do not know	8	12.1
Total	**66**	**100.0**

Table 2.8 I will build a long-term relationship with baby shower people

Responses	Frequency	%
Strongly disagree	3	5.4
Disagree	20	35.7
Agree	22	39.3
Strongly agree	11	19.6
Total	**56**	**100.0**

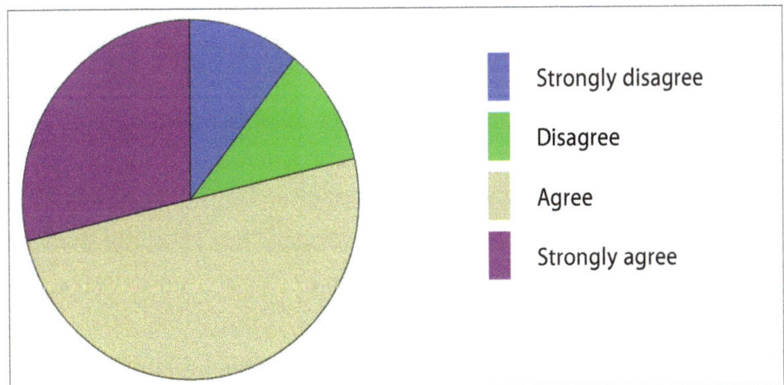

Figure 2.5 After the shower, I will visit the new baby

A significant indicator of *Botho/Ubuntu* as a driver and community-builder in the shower movements of Botswana was the emphasis on inclusivity. When participants of the baby showers were asked if showers are for rich people, the answer, as Table 2.9 below attests, was 100% a 'no'. This finding is very significant since it suggests that the participants believe that every member of the community deserves to receive *Botho/Ubuntu* regardless of their class. Similarly, when participants were asked if showers are exclusively urban events, the response (as attested in Table 2.10) was 87.5% weighed towards 'no', thereby suggesting, among other factors, that the spirit of *Botho/Ubuntu* pervades the whole country or is expected to cater for everyone.

Table 2.9 Baby showers are for the rich people only

Responses	Frequency	%
Strongly disagree	37	66.1
Disagree	19	33.9
Total	**56**	**100.0**

Table 2.10 Baby showers are only found in towns

Responses	Frequency	%
Strongly disagree	21	37.5
Disagree	28	50.0
Agree	6	10.7
Strongly agree	1	1.8
Total	**56**	**100.0**

Nonetheless, there is evidence that urban-based showers in Botswana are shifting the public communal roles along the lines of age and marital status. The traditional practices of giving advice and guidance to the bride or the bride-to-be are based on experience and age. It is exclusively married women (in the Southern part of Botswana), and mostly elderly ones (in the northern region), who would sit around the bride (during the wedding day or the day before) normally in a closed room and speak to her about marriage, its challenges and its maintenance. The session is usually a heavy, somber, and serious moment where the bride/bride-to-be's job is to listen carefully and silently as one woman after another shares her experience of what it takes to successfully maintain a marriage. They candidly share stories on the difficulties that are most likely to come along – thereby underlining endurance. Brides are known to weep during these traditional counselling sessions, for while the speakers underline the need to maintain the marriage institution, most shared experiences highlight that marriage is a bed of thorns.

In the urban spaces of Gaborone bridal showers, this approach has changed. Moral guidance and advice are given by all participants who wish to, regardless of their marital status and age (Setume et al., 2017:173-191). The single, married, divorced, widowed, young, middle-aged and senior citizens are all welcome to bring their word of wisdom to the bride-to-be. The setting of giving advice and guidance is also markedly different, since it is joyful, playful, open (outside) and celebratory. The bride-to-be is expected to participate, especially when she is asked to share the story of how she met her fiancé. Save for the Naomi/Laban shower, directed to parents-in-law, hence featuring elderly participants, the age of bridal and baby shower, is markedly youthful. As the analysis above indicated, the age range of bridal shower participants is predominantly youth-oriented, for 90.4% are between 20–40 years, while only 9.6% participants were 41 years and above. Moreover, the marital status of the bridal shower indicates that the majority of participants are single (76.8%) while only 20.7% are married and 2.4% widowed. In terms of building community, the bridal shower was notable for its inclusiveness of participants in the area of *go laya* (counselling the bride-to-be). In the Gaborone bridal showers, adult women of all ages and all marital status are allowed to participate in *go laya,* thus being inclusive and subverting patriarchy that measures women's worth or wisdom by their heterosexual marital status. Indeed, the requirement for marriage to participate in the communal activity of *go laya* in the southern region has been tantamount to shaming and discrimination of the single adult women. In gratitude and appreciation of the open space of the bridal shower, one participant narrated how in her counselling for marriage she was surrounded by strangers since no woman in her family was married and hence, they were all excluded. The strict requirement of marital status in the southern region's counselling session has resulted in the creation of a new marriage named "*oa inyala*", that is, she "marries her-self". In the *oa inyala* ritual, a single adult woman who wishes to be recognised as married among the married women, throws up a big *oa inyala* party for herself to upgrade her status to married, although without a partner. Thereafter she is allowed to participate in *go laya.*

Gender: cultural base and cultural reconstructions in Gaborone showers

The project research question of this section is: "How does *Botho/Ubuntu* in the urban space construct and reconstruct gender?" The rate at which *Botho/Ubuntu* creates liberating spaces and movements takes different forms and levels among the three showers. To start with parental showers, Naomi/Laban showers focus on Naomi and Ruth, to the near exclusion of Laban – by default and by design (this was probably because men were supposed to be there to facilitate the Laban side of the shower but, more often than not, were not there). Their focus on Naomi and Ruth seeks to create a smooth and supportive relationship between daughter-in-law and mother-in-law. Women are trained for solidarity rather than competition. This solidarity allows them to subvert patriarchy that socialises women to compete with each other. The mother-in-law need not see the daughter-in-law as a threat. Rather, she should see her as her own daughter and place her on the pedestal of power in the home, community and career to ensure her success. A very striking finding in the Naomi/Laban showers is that there is very little or no teaching on instructing the daughter to be reliant on her husband and there is hardly much emphasis, if at all, on the new wife to assume a submissive role to her husband. The new daughter-in-law must care for his parents as he must care for her parents. Both have been born into new families, but the thrust of Naomi/Laban is on the mother-in-law (mother of the bridegroom) and her relationship with the new daughter-in-law (Ruth and Naomi). The mother-in-law is to 'mother' her 'new daughter', support her professional success by taking care of her children, and ensure that her daughter's professional pursuits are not hindered by mothering (Ruth 4:16). The mother must introduce her to the larger community and train her on how to move and participate in it knowledgeably and in an acceptable way. The Naomi/Laban shower notably constructs marriage as the marriage of families – not just the couple – thereby staying away from the westernised nuclear family model that often forces most mothers to remain at home. The Naomi shower deals with child rearing as involving not just the biological mother, but the grandmothers as well.

The Naomi/Laban showers also subvert patriarchy by almost ignoring the man and his role in the new family and community. Naomi/Laban facilitators subvert the centrality of men by shifting their importance through omission. In other words, the centrality of building family, raising children, participating in communal activities, and succeeding professionally is moved to women – who are being trained for successful performance and visibility. The Naomi/Laban shower attacks patriarchy, which leads women to compete with each other, by promoting a spirit of self-reliance among women. Women who are self-reliant need not compete for a man (son/husband) who would be their breadwinner. This is evident in the content of their teaching, their garments of ordination and the minimal role assigned to the father-in-law. The result is almost to relegate the man's role to irrelevance through empowering the woman (Ruth/daughter-in-law) to be a social and professional success, without giving the same attention to men (fathers, and new husband). The Naomi/Laban facilitators hardly read Laban's story in Genesis 29–32, for example, in comparison to the time spent on the book of Ruth. If they refer to the Laban story, it is in passing when they say: "Laban was a good father-in-law. He trained Jacob to be a successful and influential man in history, for he became Israel." If present, the father will be counselled to cease using his wife to communicate his messages to the children (married couple), for the father plays hide and seek behind his wife, while pretending to be a non-aggressive parent and leading his wife to a conflict-laden relationship with the married couple. Often when the ritual of ordaining new mothers-in-law as 'mothers' to the new daughter and new son is carried out as described above, the available male parent is given nothing. The mothers, on the other hand, are garbed with new white shawls and counselled to receive their new children with happy and welcoming hearts.

The bridal shower is possibly the most complex shower, for there were conflicting voices for and against patriarchy in this shower, more than in the other showers (Setume et al., 2017; Gabaitse et al., 2018:79-95). Data from observations and the interview guides highlight that participants are aware of the traditional stance and acknowledge it and try to subvert it. For example, one participant noted that "all women of age – single and *bomme ba ba nyetsweng* (married women), all have something to contribute to *go laya* (advice and guidance)". Since there are younger married women, the space of challenging gender roles is opened by refusing to peg a woman's capacity to speak and be heard to her marital status. Part of the change may be linked with geographical context, namely that most elderly people are in villages, but it may also be linked to the origin of showers as foreign and youth-oriented events. Hence, they were not patronised by elders. Be that as it may, this is a major shift towards inclusivity. It is radical because it does not measure a woman's worth and wisdom by her heterosexual marital status or age. In doing so, there is some form of unshackling from patriarchy.

This shift is also evident in the content of their teaching. While Setswana culture teaches the new bride that *monna gaa botswe kwa a tswang* and that *monna ke poo ga a agwele lesaka*, namely a married man should remain free to see other women and should not be interrogated about his whereabouts, the Gaborone bridal shower participants sought to rewrite this cultural script. They countered that "in the village it is advised that *monna ke selepe* (a man is a cutting axe that is freely borrowed by other users, meaning that a married man can still see other women). This is not said in urban settings, where people do not believe this. ...In bridal shower flexibility, they give the bride advice that in as much as you are getting married, you have a voice ... *Emang Basadi* maybe [*Emang Basadi* is Botswana's national feminist movement]. Yes, at times the bride-to-be is advised to demand that the husband must share in household roles." There is consciousness, therefore, that their teaching borders on feminism.

The findings of the study, however, indicate that it is the bridal shower, in particular, where traditional gender roles are also underlined the most; for while elderly married women may not be there, a keynote speaker, who is often an elderly married woman, will be featured, and young people will feel obliged to listen quietly. Indeed, in just one of the showers, out of the total of 14 bridal showers attended, the organisers had brought four elderly married women for counselling. When that part of the programme arrived, they took the bride-to-be inside and left the rest of the single participants outside. Some respondents also definitely held on to patriarchal cultural perspectives (cf. Montemurro, 2005). As one respondent underlined: "We are here because of our culture. People [referring to bridal shower participants, i.e., women] should humble themselves. They need to understand their purpose. You are a woman. He is a man." Yet another participant, dismissing its feminist edge, said: "*Ke dilo tsa dibuka fela tsa tekatekanyo ya banna le basadi*", namely the bridal teaching is nothing but just book-centred feminism, which speaks about "men and women being equal". These resistant voices indicate that not all bridal shower participants were subversive to patriarchal oppression. Many others counteracted this stance, calling for the maintenance of the status quo. Most importantly, these resistant voices do attest that bridal showers of Botswana are shaking the boat of patriarchy through challenging the age and marital status of participants; through changing the mood of advice and through rewriting the content that overtly embraced patriarchy (Dube et al., 2020).

Turning to the baby showers, they are the most aggressive and most explicit in subverting patriarchy. There is more insistence that babies are not only for women and that men (fathers) should be more involved – at the shower level and in the whole process of raising children. A statistical survey indicates that there are more men involved in baby showers than in bridal showers. Figure 2.6 below indicates that baby shower participants are challenging Batswanan men to be more involved in preparing for the well-being of the expected baby. In other words, only a small fraction disagreed that men should attend baby showers. The figure indicates that about three quarters were of the conviction that both men and women should attend baby showers.

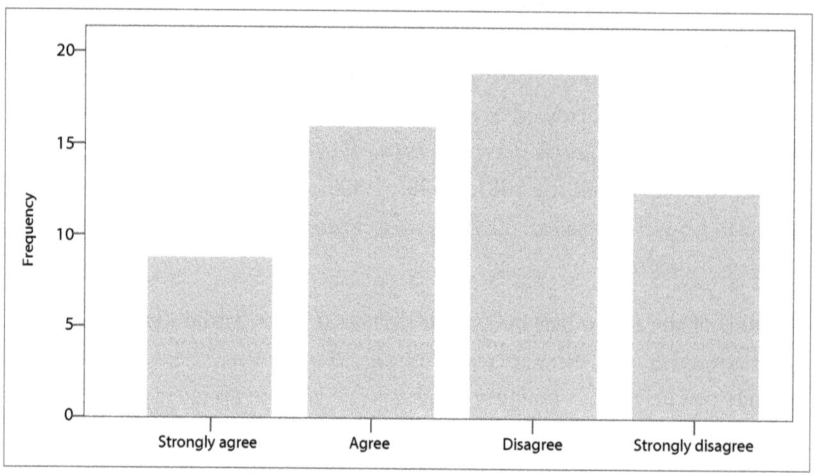

Figure 2.6 Baby showers are for women only

Such insistence is amply attested by qualitative data as well. When we asked the question of who should attend baby showers and why, the following collated answers indicated the shift towards holding men responsible for the arrival and raising of the new baby:

> Everyone should attend, men inclusive especially the father as people socialize at times ... Currently it's mostly restricted to women, but I feel even men should attend as they have a role in upbringing and nursing a child ... The Father should attend with his friends. ... Also ladies without babies should attend since for most of them it is the first time to attend such an event and to learn. First, there was a belief that it is exclusively women who should attend, but nowadays it is advised that men should also attend baby showers in order to make them aware of responsibilities as well. I attended this event to support the mother

> to be as I would also expect her to do the same for me. *Bomme le borre gonne ele boikarabelo legone ba imile balebabedi* (It should be attended by both the expectant mother and father, because they are both expecting a new baby).

Undoubtedly baby showers create female-centred spaces that celebrate birth, and empower the mother and the child. But as the above findings indicate, baby showers are widening (agitating for) the space to include men and younger women in the event. In so doing, they are breaking the gendered expectation that children are the responsibility of women and their mothers. Their inclusive move creates spaces of communal mothering, thereby affirming that it takes a village to raise a child. Its insistence on presence (community) for the mother and her forthcoming child and on gifts for the forthcoming child is an important intervention in counteracting possible poverty for mothers. It is a model for mother-centred economies.

In general, the Gaborone showers are female-centred events that are organised by women for other women and all that women care about. They are spaces for cultivating and maintaining mother economies, for they plan, gather and act in the service of empowering women to be able to live their best and to give their best in all aspects of their lives. The Botswana shower movement does not expect women to choose between being stay-home mums or wives and being professional women. Their subversive stance lies in creating female-centred movements, in promoting self-agency among women and in accompanying women to play their roles as mothers, wives, professional women and community members. Perhaps, the stance of insisting (from all three showers) that every mother and wife is to be supported to be a professional woman as well might be the most subversive stance that is informed by *Botho/Ubuntu* in the mother economies space, for it disburses with women who are economically dependent on men – a factor that fuels competition between the mothers-in-law, daughters-in-law and sister-in-laws, who are dependent on sons, brothers and husbands. Thus, this sense of community is supportive and guards against isolation, poverty, and competition among women.

Conclusion

To reiterate, the working definition employed in this study is that *Botho/Ubuntu* equates one's human identity with the capacity to respect, welcome, care for and empower the 'other'. An important expression of *Botho/Ubuntu* is the capacity to welcome the people – friends, neighbours, relatives, strangers, everyone. Welcoming means the capacity to receive people in one's own space in such a manner that they are comfortable. It involves opening one's space, to make room for the 'other'. It involves giving – giving space, time, food, respect, resources – where you have been challenged in your own zone to reach out to the 'other' and share your resources at your own volition, to live beyond yourself to the other. In other words, the host holds all the power and is at ease to exercise their welcome, fully, partially or to withhold it. Such a person may be a neighbour, stranger, pauper, rich person, clean, dirty, beautiful, old, young, middle-aged or a senior citizen; it may be a person of different religion, colour, ethnicity, sexuality or a person with disability. It is in this space and moment that one's *Botho/Ubuntu* is demonstrated – the capacity to make your guest feel welcome and respected, with their dignity upheld. Their welcome is the recognition of their human and God given dignity. It is a recognition of our membership to our common home – Mother Earth. This capacity to give one's welcome to the 'other' is the practice of *Botho/Ubuntu* by the host. Failure to welcome the 'other' is not a statement about the guest, but the host – it is the expression of their own inhumanity and ungodliness. Of course, as said, *Botho/ Ubuntu* is to be given everywhere, on the roads, in community level, national level, structural, institutional and global levels – where all members are welcome because their dignity and safety is guaranteed by the relationships we create and maintain in our families, public space, communities and national and international institutions and structures. *Botho/Ubuntu* is to be given and received by all.

Botho/Ubuntu is and should be justice par excellence; it is and should be the spirituality of worshiping the God who created all members of creation sacred. *Botho/Ubuntu* is, and should be, commitment to justice, liberation and goodness in all our relationships. *Botho/Ubuntu* spirituality is recognition of the God who has welcomed us on Mother Earth. Consequently, *Botho/Ubuntu*, as LenkaBula underlines, recognises community as beyond human, but inclusive of animals, plants, mountains, trees, plants – the whole creation (2008:375-394). Accordingly, most black Bantu people of the Southern African region identify themselves with an animal (totem). They hold these animals to be sacred members of their communities, whom they do not kill or eat or wear their skins. In so doing, the Bantu people's concept of community embraces the non-human members of the Earth (Dube et al., 2016:1-21). The *Botho/Ubuntu* environmental ethic is also attested by the rituals of cleansing the land just before the rainy season and thanksgiving rituals after the harvest (Kenosi, 2020:53-64). The Earth is held to be the host of the living and the dead (ancestors) and care should be taken to avoid polluting the environment and upsetting its balance (Dube, 2014:157-182).

Where *Botho/Ubuntu* is withheld and not generously given to all members of creation, then we have foundations of all forms of oppression, exploitation, discrimination, and wounds that hurt all of us. *Botho/Ubuntu* gives us an opportunity, daily, to evaluate our relationships, examine if we dwell in the space of *Botho/Ubuntu*, and interrogate if we are creating, giving, and maintaining *Botho/Ubuntu* in all levels of our relationships. Whenever we speak of gender discrimination, we are referring to the failure of our institutions to extend *Botho/Ubuntu* to women on the basis of gender; when we refer to racism, we are describing a situation where certain groups of people are not welcomed in our worlds on the basis of their darker skin colour; when we speak of the global environmental crisis, we are referring to the failure of humans to recognise and respect their host, the Earth. The list goes on – ethnic cleansing, classism, homophobia, Islamaphobia, religious intolerance, health-based stigmas, exploitation and marginalisation, among many other exclusions. They are all testimonies of our failure to create welcoming spaces for all members, and of withholding *Botho/Ubuntu*.

The Gaborone women's shower movement, with their agenda to welcome a new daughter-in-law, a new son-in-law, a new mother-in-law, a new father-in-law, a new bride, a new bridegroom, a new mother and a new baby, embody and model the spirit of *Botho/Ubuntu*. Their agenda is to create empowered families, empowered members of the community and empowered professionals; in so doing, they become co-creators with God in the management of God's resources. In their spirituality of maintaining and giving *Botho/Ubuntu*, they are imitators of God, for the God who created the Earth and everything in it was and is a welcoming God. The Creator God, who made sure that all was good and interconnected, catered for all members of the Earth community (Dube, 2015:1-17). In the scheme of the divine space of *Botho/Ubuntu*, there is no poverty, save as testimonies of our unwelcoming cultures and institutions. To practise *Botho/Ubuntu* is to allow the image of God in us to light the Earth community. By occupying the space of *Botho/Ubuntu*, the women of the Gaborone shower movement are keepers of the sacred space and sacred fire that seek to give a warm welcome to everyone.

The women of the Gaborone shower movement are therefore foot soldiers of the Creator God and all God's creation community. They take the responsibility to create welcoming spaces against urban isolation and poverty in the urban spaces. An isolated person is a person who is cut off from interconnectedness. Isolation is a violation of divine purpose, for Godself created humanity in fellowship (Genesis 1:26). Poverty is the epitome of the violation of the human dignity and their sacred identity, for in poverty there is shaming, dehumanisation, suffering, alienation from the Earth community, disease and the death of the impoverished. Sequentially, more often than not, poverty bleeds into the oppression and exploitation of the Earth. Poverty is thus not only dehumanisation and Earth oppression, but is also violence against the creator God who created all people in God's image, provided them with resources and pronounced the goodness of all creation in its interconnectedness. When the Botswana women spend months collecting money to empower the 'other' and to build *Botho/Ubuntu* communities, they stand in the gap against the festering wounds of isolation, poverty, patriarchy and exploitative national and international economic structures. They are seeking justice for all, against all sorts of evil that mars the image of God in the face of creation. Their small acts seek to keep the flickering flame of *Botho/Ubuntu* spirituality burning and lighting the way where many winds of structural injustice reduce the Earth and humanity of many on the basis of their gender, race, ethnicity, sexuality, disability, class, age and other differences.

It is in their struggle to sustain all life against all odds that African women become the cradle of *Botho/Ubuntu,* the art of being human through respecting, welcoming, caring and empowering the 'other'. As Mercy Amba Oduyoye observes, African women's struggle to raise children in the midst of amazing adversaries, remain a beam of the resurrection hope, underlining that 'another world is possible', a world where our human, economic, political and environmental relations are characterised by consistently seeking to maintain the sanctity of the creation community. *Botho/Ubuntu* as embodied by African women can and should be the model of liberation for all of us. It should be, as Oduyoye maintains, a model for economic, political and social structures that seek to maintain the sanctity of all life: for she underlines that we should not ignore "the humanity of women as persons made in God's image and mothers as co-creators with God and imitators of God's management of creation" (ibid.:62). Mercy Amba Oduyoye argues that we are better off recognising that these women model for us something bigger and better, namely a *Botho/Ubuntu* Earth community that seeks to recognise the image of the Creator and welcome God in all members and spaces.

References

Amadiumbe, I. 1987. *Male daughters, female husbands*. London: Zed Books.

Bless, C. & Higson-Smith, C. 1995. *Fundamentals of social research methods: an african perspective*. 3rd Edition. Lusaka: Juta Education (Pty).

Brigilia, B. 2005. 'Women and the church in (South) Africa: women are the church in (South) Africa'. In: I.A. Phiri & S. Nadar (eds). *On being church: African women's voices and visions*. Geneva: WCC. 8-15.

Bryman, A. 2001. *Social research methods*. New York: Oxford University Press.

Chitando, E. 2015. 'Do not tell a person carrying you s/he stinks: reflections on *ubuntu* and masculinities in the context of sexual and gender-based violence and HIV'. In: E. Mouton, G. Kapuma, L. Hansen & T. Togom (eds). *Living with dignity: African perspectives on gender equality*. Stellenbosch, South Africa: African Sun Media. 269-284.

Creswell, J.W. 2009. *Research design: qualitative, quantitative and mixed methodology approaches*. 3rd Edition. London: Sage Publications.

Dube, M.W. 1999a. 'Divining the texts for international relations (Matt.15:21-28)'. In: I. Kirtzberger (ed). *Transformative encounters*. Leiden: A.J. Brill. 315-328. https://doi.org/10.1163/9789004497665_018

Dube, M.W. 1999b. 'The unpublished letters of Orpah to Ruth'. In: A. Bremmer (ed). *A companion to the books of Ruth and Esther*. Sheffield: Sheffield University Press. 145-150.

Dube, M.W. 2001a. 'Divining Ruth for international relations'. In: K.A. Adam (ed). *Postmodern interpretations of the Bible*. St Louis, MO: Chalice Press. 67-80.

Dube, M.W. 2001b. 'Postcoloniality, feminist spaces and religion'. In: L. Donaldson & Kwok Pui-Lan (eds). *Postcolonialism & feminism religion*. New York: Routledge. 100-120.

Dube, M.W. 2005. Rahab is Hanging Out a Red Ribbon: One African Woman's Perspective on Future on the New Testament Scholarship. In: K. O'Brian. *Feminist New Testament studies: global and future perspective*. New York: Routledge. 177-202. https://doi.org/10.1007/978-1-137-11204-0_15

Dube, M.W. 2006. 'Looking back and forward: postcolonialism, globalization, gender and God'. *Scriptura*, 2:178-193.

Dube, M.W. 2009. 'I am because we are: giving primacy to African indigenous values in HIV&AIDS prevention'. In: M.F. Murove (ed). *African ethics: an anthology of comparative and applied ethics*. Pietermaritzburg, South Africa: UKZN Press. 178-188.

Dube, M.W. 2010. 'Intercultural Biblical interpretations'. *Svensk Missionstidskrift*, 98:361-388.

Dube, M.W. 2014. 'Translating Ngaka: Robert Moffatt rewriting the Indigenous Healer'. *Studia Historiae Ecclesiasticae*, XL(1):157-172.

Dube, M.W. 2015. 'And God saw that it was good! An earth-friendly theatrical reading of Genesis 1'. *Black Theology*, 13(3):1-17. https://doi.org/10.1179/1476994815Z.00000000060

Dube, M.W., Gabaitse, R.M. & Kgalemang, M. 2021. '*Botho/Ubuntu* and "unsettling patriarchy": *go laya* in Gaborone bridal showers'. *Journal of the Interdenominational Theological Center*, 50(Spring/Fall):1-45.

Dube, M.W., Modie-Moroka, T., Setume, S.D., Ntloedibe, S., Kgalemang, M., Gabaitse, R.M. & Sesiro, D. 2016. '*Botho/Ubuntu*: community building and gender construction in Botswana'. *Journal of the Interdenominational Theological Center*, 40(1):1-22.

Dube, M.W., Modie-Moroka, T., Setume, S.D., Ntloedibe, S., Kgalemang, M., Gabaitse, R.M. & Sesiro, D. 2021. 'Mother economies: *Botho/Ubuntu* and community building in the urban space: a focus on Naomi/Laban, bridal and baby showers'. In: L.C. Siwila & F.A. Kobo (eds). *Religion, patriarchy and empire: festschrift in honor of Mercy Amba Oduyoye*. Pietermaritzburg: Cluster Publications. 61-112.

Ebert, T. 1988. 'The romance of patriarchy: ideology, subjectivity and postmodern feminist cultural theory'. *Cultural Critique*, 10:19-57. https://doi.org/10.2307/1354105

Ellece, S.E. 2011a. 'Agency and gender in Setswana marriage ceremonies: "*patlo*" and "*go laya*" rituals'. *NAWA Journal of Language and Communication*, 4(2).

Ellece, S.E. 2011b. 'Be a fool like me: gender construction in the marriage advice ceremony in Botswana: a critical discourse analysis'. *Agenda: Empowering Women for Gender Equity*, 25(21):43-52. https://doi.org/10.1080/10130950.2011.575584

Fedele, N.M. & Harrington, E.A. 1990. *Women's groups: how connections heal* (work in progress no. 47). Wellesley, MA: Stone Center Working Paper Series.

Gabaitse, R.M., Dube, M.W., Kgalemang, M. & Madigele, T. 2018. 'Reproducing or creating a new male: bridal showers in the urban space of Botswana'. *Journal of Gender and Religion in Africa*, 24(1):79-95. https://doi.org/10.14426/ajgr.v24i1.42

Gaie, J.B.R. & Mmolai, S. (eds). 2007. *The concept of Botho and HIV&AIDS in Botswana.* Kenya: Zepf Chancery Publishers Africa. https://doi.org/10.2307/j.ctvgc61hd

Kanyoro, M. 2001. 'Cultural Hermeneutics: An African Contribution'. In: M.W. Dube (ed). *Other ways of reading: African women and the Bible.* Atlanta, GA: Society for Biblical Literature. 101-113.

Kyalo, P. 2012. 'A reflection on the African traditional values of marriage and sexuality'. *International Journal of Academic Research in Progressive Education and Development*, 1(2).

Leckey, R. 2013. 'Two mothers in law and fact'. *Feminist Legal Studies*, 21:1-19. https://doi.org/10.1007/s10691-012-9206-9

Le Grange, L. 2015. '*Ubuntu/Botho* as ecophilosophy and ecosophy'. *Journal of Human Ecology*, 49(3):301-308. https://doi.org/10.1080/09709274.2015.11906849

LenkaBula, P. 2008. 'Beyond anthropocentricity: *Botho/Ubuntu* and the quest for economic and ecological justice in Africa'. *Religion and Theology*, 15:375-394. https://doi.org/10.1163/157430108X376591

Livingston, J. 2005. *Debility and the moral imagination in Botswana.* Bloomington, IN: University of Indiana Press.

Magesa, L. 1998. *African religion: moral tradition of abundant life.* Nairobi, Kenya: Pauline Publications.

Magubane, P. 1998. *Vanishing cultures of South Africa: changing customs in a changing world.* Cape Town, South Africa: Struik Publishers.

Maluleke, T.S. 1998. 'Contesting *ubuntu*'. *The Natal Witness Echo*. 29 October.

Maluleke, T.S. 1999. 'The misuse of *ubuntu*'. *Challenge*, 53:12-13.

Manyonganise, M. 2015. Oppressive and liberative: a Zimbabwean reflection on *ubuntu. Verbum et Ecclesia*, 36(2):1-7. https://doi.org/10.4102/ve.v36i2.1438

Masenya, M. 1998. '*Ngwetsi* (bride): the Naomi-Ruth story from an African-South African woman's perspective'. *Journal of Feminist Studies in Religion*, 14(2):81-90.

Mertens, D.M. 2014. *Research and evaluation in education and psychology:*

integrating diversity with quantitative, qualitative, and mixed methods. 4th Edition. Thousand Oaks, CA: Sage.

Metz, T. & Gaie, J.B.R. 2010. 'The African ethic of *ubuntu/botho*: implications for research on morality'. *Journal of Moral Education*, 39(3):273-290. https://doi.org/10.1080/03057240.2010.497609

Mmualefe, D. 2004. 'Towards authentic Tswana Christianity: revisiting *botho*'. Master's thesis, Eden Theological Seminary, Missouri.

Mmualefe, D. 2013. '*Botho* and HIV and AIDS: a theological reflection'. In: J.B.R. Gaie & S.K. Mmolai (eds). *The concept of Botho and HIV/AIDS in Botswana*. Eldoret, Kenya: Zapf Chancery Research Consultants and Publishers. 1-29. https://doi.org/10.2307/j.ctvgc61hd.4

Mnguni, B. 2019. *Vital statistics report 2017*. Gaborone: Statistics Botswana.

Modie-Moroka, T., Dube, M.W., Setume, S.D., Kgalemang, M., Kebaneilwe, M.D., Gabaitse, R.M., Motswapong, E. & Madigela, T. 2019. 'Pathways to social capital and the *Botho/Ubuntu* ethic in the urban space of Gaborone, Botswana'. *Global Social Welfare: Research, Policy and Practice*, 7:231-243. https://doi.org/10.1007/s40609-019-00152-5

Molato, K. 2020. 'The role of rainmakers in awakening environmental consciousness: a postcolonial ecocritical analysis'. In: N.G. Penxa Matholeni, G. Kwanima-Boateng & M. Manyonganise (eds). *Mother earth, mother Africa and African indigenous religions*. Stellenbosch, South Africa: African Sun Media. 53-64. https://doi.org/10.18820/9781928480730/04

Montemurro, B. 2005. 'Add men; don't stir": reproducing traditional gender roles in modern wedding showers'. *Journal of Contemporary Ethnography*, 34(1):6-35. https://doi.org/10.1177/0891241604271332

Montemurro, B.2006. *Something old, something bold: bridal showers and bachelorette parties*. New Brunswick, N.J.: Rutgers University Press.

Motswapong, E.P., Kebaneilwe, M.D., Madigele, T.J., Dube, M.W., Setume, S.D. & Moroka-Modie, T. 2017. '"A little baby is on the way": *Botho/Ubuntu* and community building in Gaborone baby showers'. *Gender Studies*, 16(1):5-70. https://doi.org/10.2478/genst-2018-0006

Munyaka, M. & Mokgethi, M. 2009. '*Ubuntu* and its socio-moral significance'. In: F. Murove (ed). *African ethics: an anthology of comparative and applied ethics*. Pietermaritzburg, South Africa: UKZN Press.

Nadar, S. 2001. 'South African Indian womanist reading of the character of Ruth'. In: M.W. Dube (ed). *Other ways of reading: African women and the Bible*. Atlanta, GA: Society for Biblical Literature. 159-178.

Oduyoye, M.A. 2004. 'Poverty and motherhood'. In: M.A. Oduyoye (ed). *Beads and strands: reflections of an African woman on Christianity in Africa (vol. 3). Oxford Centre for Mission Studies*. New York: Orbis Press.

Penxa Matholeni, N., Boateng, G.K. & Manyonganise, M. (eds). 2020. *Mother earth, mother Africa and African indigenous religions*. Stellenbosch, South Africa: African Sun Media. https://doi.org/10.18820/9781928480730

Ramose, M.B. 2009. 'Ecology through *Ubuntu*'. In: F.M. Murove (ed). *African ethics: an anthology of comparative and applied ethics*. Pietermaritzburg, South Africa: UKZN Press. 308-314.

Setume, S., Gabaitse, R.M., Dube, M.W., Kgalemang, M., Modie-Moroka, T., Madigele, T., Kebaneilwe, M.D., Motswapong, E. & Matebekwane, A.K.M. 2017. 'Exploring the concept of *Botho/*

Ubuntu through bridal showers in the urban space of Gaborone, Botswana'. *Managing Development in Africa*, 2(3): 173-191.

Vision 2016. 2013. *Vision 2016: Towards prosperity for all.* Botswana Government.

Wagner, C., Kawulich, B. & Garner, M. 2012. *Doing social research: global context.* London: McGraw-Hill Higher Education.

PART ONE

Botho/Ubuntu, Bridal Showers and Marriage

EXPLORING THE CONCEPT '*BOTHO/UBUNTU*' THROUGH BRIDAL SHOWERS IN THE URBAN SPACE, GABORONE, BOTSWANA

Abstract

The purpose of this chapter[1,2] is to explore how women in the urban space express *Botho/Ubuntu* at bridal showers. We explore *Botho/Ubuntu* using the lens of agency. Agency aids in understanding how women in the urban space navigate and create their own space that would allow them to empower, help and support each other. In the rural areas in Botswana, *Botho/Ubuntu* is the basis of all social relations as reflected in economic cultural practices such as *mafisa*[3] and *molaletsa*.[4] While in the village, the space for exercising ubuntu is given; in the urban space it has to be created. The research shows that women in the urban space express *Botho/Ubuntu* through 'creating new family', presence at bridal showers, giving advice and presenting gifts to the bride-to-be. The study also found that through bridal showers in the urban space the traditional gender roles/ideologies are reproduced and marginally deconstructed.

Introduction

Bridal shower without the bride-to-be

"Ladies! Ladies, we have a problem! We have been waiting for the bride-to-be for over six hours now. She called to say she just left Mafikeng.[5] Let us support her even in

1 The article, 'Exploring the concept *Botho/Ubuntu* through bridal showers in the urban space, Gaborone, Botswana' by Setume, S.D. et al., was first published in 2017 in *Managing Development in Africa*, 2(3):173-191. It is republished in this volume by permission.

2 This work was supported by the John Templeton Foundation under Grant 2016-TH170.

3 '*Mafisa*' refers to a Setswana socioeconomic structure that allowed the lending of cattle by the rich to the poor. The poor would take care of the cattle on behalf of the rich; in the meantime, he would use the cattle for milk and draught power (Rankopo, Osei-Hwedie & Modie-Moroka, 2007).

4 '*Molaletsa*': a mutual self-help system to enable people to provide the much-needed labour to each other in a reciprocal way. Through this system the communities were productive and self-reliant (Rankopo, Osei-Hwedie & Modie-Moroka, 2007).

5 Mafikeng (now Mahikeng) is a town in South Africa, very close to the Botswana border. Some Batswana visit the town for shopping.

her absence. Let the shower continue", says the chief organiser as she addresses guests at the shower. Most ladies in attendance agree with the idea. The shower starts. A few excuse themselves and leave. We then started with an introductory game: "Introduce yourself to the person that you are sitting next to. Tell them something unique about yourself. I am giving you five minutes to do so. The next stage would be that your partner would introduce you to the house." The introductions start. We pick from the introductions and the laughter that most partners are making new creations as they introduce one another. The shock displayed by the one being introduced was overwhelming. After that very interesting introductory game, it was time to give presents to the absent bride-to-be. Each guest that had come with a present explained what the present was and how the bride-to-be was to use it. However, presents were not opened, because the bride-to-be was absent. We were then served food and the shower was dismissed. All these activities take about 45 minutes. Most people left. We (researchers) stayed behind to continue our interviews with the organisers who were waiting for the bride-to-be.

Botho/Ubuntu is reflected in the decision to proceed with the shower in the absence of the bride-to-be. Friends, relatives and church mates of the bride-to-be had waited patiently for her to arrive for many hours. The patience and love of guests at this shower demonstrated what it means to put the needs of the other person before one's own. Cornell and Marle (2013:2) explain that *Botho/Ubuntu* is a feeling of "obligation to others and others obligated to us".

Botho/Ubuntu is an important concept that underlines human social relations in most African communities. This is reflected by the existence of the concept in different African languages: Nguni languages: *ubuntu* (Dolamo, 2013); Shona languages: *unhu* (Manyonganise, 2015) and Tswana-Sotho languages: *Botho* (Dube, 2009; Mmualefhe, 2004). Cornell and Marlie (2015:2) conceive of *ubuntu* as "an African principle encapsulating what it means to be human and how social relations are necessarily embedded in a beginning that starts at birth. *Botho/Ubuntu* in Setswana traditional setup is lived through various forms of economic cooperation such as *molaletsa* and *mafisa* (Rankopo, Osei-Hwedie & Modie-Moroka, 2007). However, it has been observed that due to rural-urban migration, social fabrics such as *Botho/Ubuntu* have been eroded (Dolamo, 2015; Ng'weshemi, 2002). For instance, Schapera (1947) describes how rural-urban migration had contributed to changes in family life. Migration is perceived to have contributed to the loss of the authority of parents over their children. This resulted in lack of *Botho/Ubuntu* by the younger generation. This is because in the urban places the youth participate in the money economy and hence become economically independent from their parents (Gulbrandsen, 1986).

For Batswana in rural areas, as elsewhere in Africa, *Botho/Ubuntu* is a concept of acceptable social relations with other members of the society. When Mbiti (1969) explains the *Botho/Ubuntu* ethic, he clearly expresses its inherent recognition of the individual. However, with time, this strong social fabric seems to have been changed or distorted with the arrival of Christianity, colonisation, modernity and urbanisation in general (Dolamo, 2013). For instance, urbanisation led to more women moving into urban areas. At these centres, women find themselves away from the social environment of parents, aunts and uncles and other significant relatives that usually offer them social support (Ndlovu & Hove, 2015). A common African saying explains that in rural areas *it takes a village to raise a child.* However, since this 'village' in the urban space does not exist, how then do women in the urban spaces find support systems? Through the study of bridal showers in the urban space of Gaborone, this chapter explores how women create new ways through which they express *Botho/Ubuntu* in order to empower, support and help one another. However, before delving into details about the bridal shower under investigation, we will explore existing literature on *Botho/Ubuntu* and bridal showers.

Literature review

Understanding the concept of *Botho/Ubuntu*

Botho/Ubuntu has always been an important ethic in African society, shaping the varied interpersonal and social relations. *Botho/Ubuntu* has been defined by many scholars (Mbiti, 1969; Mugumbate & Nyanguru, 2013; Mawere, 2012; Manyonganise, 2015). *Botho/Ubuntu* is "an African philosophy that places emphasis on being human through other people" (Mugumbate & Nyanguru, 2013:82; Gade, 2012:487). For instance, Mawere (2012:3) explains ubuntu as:

> ...a multi-faceted philosophical system that involves logic, metaphysics, epistemology and ethics; it is a philosophy of life that is concerned with the reinforcement of unity, oneness and solidarity among the Bantu people.

Therefore, a person with *Botho/Ubuntu* is the one who fulfils their moral and social expectations. This is a person that Pearce (1990:147) describes as one who has morally worthy human qualities. Shutte (2001:2) notes regarding *Botho/Ubuntu*:

> The concept of UBUNTU embodies an understanding of what it is to be human and what is necessary for human beings to grow and find fulfilment. It is an ethical concept and expresses a vision of what is valuable and worthwhile in life. This vision is rooted in the history of Africa and is at the centre of the culture of most South Africans.

While some scholars have praised the concept of *Botho/Ubuntu* (Shutte, 2001), others have called for a more critical analysis of the concept (Manyonganise, 2010) as it perpetuates certain gender stereotypes that discriminate against women. For example, Manyonganise in her paper, 'Oppressive and liberative: A Zimbabwean woman's reflections on ubuntu', explains the positive and negative aspects of ubuntu. She found out that, by its nature, as an African philosophy, it is embedded in patriarchy – an oppressive system that already disadvantages women. She further explains some Shona proverbs, e.g., *chakafukidza dzimba matenga* (what covers houses are roofs), which are meant to silence married women from disclosing any abuse by their husbands. On a similar note, some scholars have expressed how *Botho/Ubuntu* has been changing or become distorted over time (Dolamo, 2013).

Erosion of *Botho/Ubuntu*

Dolamo (2013:2) explains that "the industrial revolution, urbanisation and modernisation in general have led to the erosion of *ubuntu*" (2013:2). He further explains that after the arrival of colonists, traders and missionaries, the "sense of *ubuntu* became altered and distorted" (ibid.). In particular, Christianity is viewed as having contributed to this distortion, since it isolated the converts from their communities. Eventually, "these converts adopted an individualistic approach to life, as Christianity itself was conceived as a private, inner and personal affair between God and the individual" (Dolamo, 2013:6). Communities in rural areas were largely communal and the differences between the rich and poor were minimal. This enabled the expression of *Botho/Ubuntu* more effectively as compared to modern societies. The new developments have created more individualistic attitudes that are not so conducive to the expression of *Botho/Ubuntu*. For instance, while in the past a farmer would dispose of surplus from his field, by assisting the poor, modernisation and urbanisation have created commercial markets where surplus goods are sold for profit. This creates fertile grounds for individualistic attitudes. The challenge posed by modernisation to the exercise of *Botho/Ubuntu* is that it has altered or distorted what it means to have it. By describing a report that had gone viral on social media, Matolino and Kwindingwi (2013:197) explain how generally in South Africa, for example, the concept of *Botho/Ubuntu* has died. They explain that a taxi driver

> ...diverted his vehicle from the road and darted into the pavement where he knocked a pedestrian down. He reversed and alighted to check the impact of his unique driving skills. Upon realising that his vehicle has not exerted discernible damage to the pedestrian, the driver unleashed a powerful kick to the abdomen of the poor pedestrian who was struggling to raise himself to his feet. ... other healthy-looking males standing around this shocking scene appeared either unbothered or too scared to come to the aid of the hapless pedestrian. The Minister of Police appeared on the eNews *Channel Africa* television [show] to bemoan the lack of reaction to this incident.

The lack of sensitivity to such a heinous act symbolises a diminished/distorted sense of *Botho/Ubuntu*. The ideal *Botho/Ubuntu* reaction would have been to restrain the taxi driver and help the poor pedestrian. The observation that people at the scene acted indifferently to the act is not consistent with the spirit of *Botho/Ubuntu*. One could probably add that this lack of action by the observers may be due to issues of security/safety; intervening while serving a stranger could cost them their lives.

After discussing what *Botho/Ubuntu* means, it is then important to have a common understanding of what is known about bridal showers in order to appreciate how women in the urban space organise themselves.

Understanding bridal showers

Origin of bridal showers

Bridal showers are ritual activities that prepare a woman for marriage. According to Montemurro (2005:7), a bridal shower is "a ritual that dates back to the 16th century Western Europe as a gendered ritual organised by women for women". According to Clark (2000:7), Jenkins (2000), and Montemurro (2005), the origins of bridal showers are traced to a legend in Holland. According to the legend, "a woman wanted to marry a poor man who her father feared would not be able to support her, and thus her father would not provide a dowry. Sympathetic to the love between the two, the would-be bride-to-be's friends gathered gifts so that she was able to wed" (Montemurro, 2005:13). This practice has since been adopted by women across the world in order to celebrate one another as one makes a milestone in their life through marriage (Solway, 2016). Montemurro explains that initially bridal showers were practised in urban areas. They were given by wealthy women "who had access to shops that carried items suitable for setting up a household" (Montemurro, 2005:13). Though they started in urban areas, a similar trend was later observed in rural areas as well. In Botswana, bridal showers are practised in urban areas more than in rural areas. Bridal showers are correctly described as highly gendered activities for women regardless of marital status that intentionally exclude men (Montemurro, 2005; Cott, 2000). Of particular interest to this study is how women understand the purpose of a shower for a bride-to-be.

Purpose of bridal showers

- ***Gifts to the bride-to-be***

A study that has been carried out in America (Montemurro, 2002; 2005) suggests that the main purpose of a bridal shower is to present gifts to the bride-to-be. Montemurro (2005) explains how the purchasing of gifts for the bride-to-be was very important. Gifts are important since "the shower centres on the accumulation of gifts" (Montemurro, 2005:83). Women would stress over the right gift for the bride-to-be. She further explains how the bridal shower's "invitation frequently includes information about where the couple is registered and guests are expected to purchase items from the registry" (ibid.:82). According to Montemurro, the gifts also reflect this giver's social status and their relationship with the bride-to-be. An "expensive gift implies generosity".

■ *Care*

Bridal showers offer women an opportunity to show that they care. Studies have shown that women are socialised to care (Gilligan, 1998). Therefore, since women feel that they have the obligation to care (Montemurro, 2005), bridal showers allow them an opportunity to live up to this obligation. Bridal showers serve as a site where women as family members and friends can express care for the bride-to-be not only through their gifts, but also their presence at the shower.

Solway (2016:315) investigated marriages in Botswana and observed that bridal showers in Botswana "have appeared as a new form of ritual combining both the consumerist driven allure of modern Botswana with aspects of didactic function of older instructional rituals and social connectedness they promoted". For Batswana women, bridal showers are not just about Western practices of presenting the bride-to-be with gifts, but she is also presented with wisdom, such as how she needs to behave in relation to the in-laws (ibid.). Women present at the shower would discuss and share views, experiences, and opinions with the bride-to-be as a way of preparing her for married life. Bridal showers in Botswana offer women of all ages, including friends and kin [the chance] to share advice for the bride-to-be and indeed for themselves as she explains that "bridal showers offer a new way in which non-kin are incorporated into the marriage process, this illustrating a 'social' expansion that contradicts the tendency of contraction (Solway, 2016:315).

The next section discusses different ways that Batswana used to prepare a woman for marriage before the arrival of bridal showers.

Cultural ways of preparing a woman for married life

Bridal showers are a contemporary way of preparing a woman for marriage. The concept of preparing for marriage is as old as societies. It has been observed that in most African societies, marriage is a process and not an event (Schapera, 1939; Comaroff, 1960; Radcliffe-Brown & Forde, 1950; Parkin & Nyamwaya, 1987).The process starts very early in life. For instance, the names given to children were imbued with specific expectations of how the society intends the child to conduct themselves in adult life, including married life (Ellece, 2002; Rapoo, 2010). A woman was prepared for marriage in different ways. The preparation for marriage would start from the names given to children, to the gendered roles in which they took part (Ellece, 2002; Rapoo, 2010; Schapera, 1939; Karambani, 2006) through puberty rituals and *go laya* (the giving of advice to the bride at marriage). This refers to laws for good conduct and behaviour, which are *Botho/Ubuntu* laws. The occasion of *go laya* is used as an opportunity to teach the bride that she is completely under the control of her husband and his family. The consequences of failure on her part to portray *Botho/Ubuntu* could be dire for her family as it means that the *bogadi* could be returned to the family of the husband (Shropshire, 1970) causing embarrassment to herself and her family. This will be an indication that her parents have failed to teach her proper ways of conducting herself. Unfortunately, most ways of socialisation "help to maintain dominant traditional discourses and ideologies" (Ellece, 2010; 2007).

The practice of *go laya*/giving of advice to the bride-to-be at marriage is very important since the practice has been incorporated into the Western concept of bridal showers. The practice is discussed in more detail below.

On the wedding day: *go laya* (giving of advice)

The climax for the process of preparing a woman for marriage is *go laya*/*tao* (Ellece, 2010). *Go laya* is the advice given to a woman, usually at the moment she is being handed over to her husband's family by her parents. This *go laya* is done by her relatives/parents in the presence of her in-laws. Ellece (2010:86) explains that *go laya* is a form of ritual advice that is very essential in order for a marriage to stand, and that it "prepares the bride-to-be for married life by prescribing the rules of how to behave in marriage". Ellece (2010:96) describes the setting of the ritual as follows:

> The bride-to-be is brought out of the house and made to sit in the middle position facing the groom's family. She is presented to the groom's family, and this is done by giving her advice on her new role as a married woman, after which she gives water in a cup to all the women from the groom's family in acceptance of her new roles and status.

This is the cultural rite that has been adopted and adapted by women at the bridal showers. The bride-to-be would be taken out of the house and made to sit by herself or with her best lady in a position where she will be seen by all in attendance. The main purpose will be to give advice, counsel and share experiences with the bride-to-be. A typical *go laya* session will take a format such as the following:

> The greatest thing is love. That love is going to breed and breed. As you have been told that you are now the child of this family, that is the way it is. You are going to live with your husband – a man my child (inaudible words)! Make sure that this time (i.e., evening) of the day you are in the house. In a house like this, you are the one who turns on the lights. About our mother-in-law, you

> must see to it that in the morning before you go to work, you have brewed her a cup of tea. Make sure that you have made a little porridge for her. A man should be cleaned. You are the one who makes him clean and handsome. All the handsome clean men you see around, they are clean because they are cared for by their wives. If you don't take care of him, they (other women) will take him from you....
>
> These are the parents we give you to. You are no longer a child of this household. You are their child. You now are going to find cripples and blind people and elderly people. All of them you are going to look after them. You do not discriminate against anyone. You do not look at the status/state of a person. You treat them equally. We give you to them. (Ellece, 2010:96)

Such pieces of advice are great, but they also reproduce dominant gender stereotypes of the position of a woman as a nurse, caregiver and hard worker around the homestead, especially if the same is taught to men.

Theoretical consideration: agency

As explained earlier, in this work we use 'agency' to understand how women in the urban space of Gaborone create their social space at bridal showers. Agency is the capacity of individuals to act independently and to make their own choices. This concept is usually 'deployed in debates over the relationship between individuals and social structure' (Rapport & Overing, 2000:1). Other scholars have conceptualised agency as a "property of individual" as well as "in terms of collectives as groups" (Morris, Menon & Ames, 2001:169; Keane, 2003). In this study, agency is looked at in terms of 'women' as a group and how they navigate their space as they cross socio-cultural boundaries. The following section briefly discusses the data collection methods that were employed in this investigation.

Methodology

Approach to the study

The study was carried out in Gaborone, the capital city of Botswana. The target group were women who attended bridal showers. Purposive sampling was used to identify key participants. Participants were identified through a list from the District Commissioners' office in Broadhurst office, through churches and snowballing. This was largely a qualitative study that was complemented by quantitative data. The principal data-collection techniques were in-depth interviews with the bride-to-be and her organisers, participant observations and a closed-ended questionnaire. Quantitative data were collected through closed-ended questionnaires that were administered to participants at the shower, usually at the beginning and end of the shower in order to avoid interrupting the shower proceedings. Qualitative data were collected through voice recorders and field notes. The researchers observed such things as setting, off camera conversations and the nature of gifts given.

Data analysis

Qualitative data that were collected through voice recorders was transcribed verbatim after which a thematic analysis was used to navigate data. Data are presented through narrative passages and verbatim quotes of the respondents. Quantitative data were analysed using SPSS.22 frequencies and are presented in summary tables.

Data presentation and interpretation

Bridal showers and agency

Women at bridal showers reflect agency in two ways. First, they create a social network that is largely based on friendship and church membership as compared to blood and marital ties. Secondly, since bridal showers are mainly organised and attended by single women, at bridal showers single women offer pieces of advice to the bride-to-be, a role that is usually reserved for married women. Data show that, of 110 women who responded to a questionnaire, 73 (65%) were single and 31 (28%) were married. This shows that women who organise, attend and give advice at bridal showers are mostly single.

In order for a bridal shower to be successful, it is important to have a good social network: without guests there cannot be a successful shower. In order to establish which category of women attend bridal showers, participants were asked: "Who should attend bridal showers and why?" The following are some of the responses that were given:

> Her friends who are single to learn from her how she got her man, and married women to give the bride-to-be advice. Sw 4 (12)

> Friends, relatives, church mates, etc.; only women, whether married or not. Sw 4 (17)

> Close relatives, cousins, workmates, and church mates – youths, married and single – everybody related to the bride-to-be. Sometimes our friends are not married ... and at bridal showers they are welcome. Sw 5 (21)

> Friends of the bride – friends of friends *le di-divorcee tota* (even divorced women). They come for different reasons: to celebrate the blessing; to see what is happening, and some to know how the couple met. Sw 5 (23)

> Ladies that the bride can understand: it excludes parents to avoid cultural/value clash. I feel this compromises[6] the atmosphere as unmarried *laya* (give advice), which is against our culture *'bana' ba a laya* ('children' giving advice). Males are excluded.
> Sw 8 (30)

> Close friends and relatives, not enemies. It's unfortunate that parents are excluded. They might not have patience with the discussion of feminist issues. If I am here and my mother is also here, I will not be free to say exactly what I want to the bride-to-be. They will be bored or offended.
> Sw 8 (34)

The narratives above indicate that elderly women (parents) and men are consciously excluded from bridal showers. There are different reasons why parents and men are usually excluded from bridal showers: parents might not like some things that might be said at bridal showers. However, as shall be discussed later, contrary to the idea that the content of what might be said at bridal showers might not be consistent with the traditional ways of counselling, the study found that traditional counselling content is also reproduced at bridal showers, although voices of change are also there. The study established that friendship and church membership are very important networks for women in the urban space. This was captured in a questionnaire that sought to establish how participants at the shower were related to the bride-to-be. The results are shown in Table 3.1.

Table 3.1 Relationship with the shower participants

Participant relationship	Frequency	%
Sister	11	10.0
Sister-in-law	2	1.8
Colleague at work	4	3.6
Church mate	32	29.1
Friend	37	33.6
Neighbour	6	5.5
Other	15	13.6
Offspring	1	.9
Subtotal	**108**	**98.2**
Missing	2	1.8
Total	**110**	**100.0**

Table 3.1 shows how participants are largely not related to the bride-to-be. The majority of women who attend showers are either friends of the bride-to-be or her church mates. Of the 230 participants who attended showers, 32 (29%) were church mates and 37 (34%) friends of the bride-to-be, making a total of 69 (63%). Bridal showers

6 The first person to express the exclusion of parents at a bridal shower as problematic.

in the urban areas are an expression of how women create significant relationships not based on blood and marital bonds. Church membership and friendship become very important determinants of the support system. This observation is consistent with new ways of relatedness as captured by Carsten (2000). Carsten (ibid.:2) points out that "we can no longer take for granted that our most fundamental relationships are grounded in biology or nature". She explains that such an approach in explaining how people become related is "deceptively simple" (ibid.), since there are some forms of relatedness that are not necessarily genealogical, such as friendship, but which are very meaningful and important. She further explains that as people, we are always conscious of our connections to other people. Through the study of bridal showers this chapter demonstrates how friendship and church membership form new family and relatedness ties. Furthermore, through bridal showers, the agency of women plays out in different forms. Over and above expressing agency by creating different social networks, women in the urban space create social spaces that single women are denied of in a traditional setup.

As mentioned earlier, in the traditional setup, the practice of *go laya* (giving advice to the bride-to-be) is done by married women only and mostly relatives. Throwing a bridal shower for a bride-to-be is done mainly by friends and church mates without much consideration to marital status. Peo, a participant, expresses her view as to why they allow women who are not married to perform a task at the bridal showers, which is otherwise reserved for the married in Setswana cultures:

> The experience of living with a man is not exclusive to women in marriage. The advice also includes how to raise children, and this [is] also not exclusive to married women only. (Peo)

Tumelo is a married woman who was an organiser at one shower. In support of the idea that single women gave advice at bridal showers, she narrates her experiences at the traditional *go laya* session and says:

> In my case there was no one who was already married in my family: like my aunt and my mother, no one was married. Even my mother's sisters, cousins ... nothing. I was the first to get married: It was for the first time in a long time when I got married. Now when it got to counselling at home, they are not allowed to advise, but at showers they are free to advise. So, when it got to counselling at home, I was left with 'strangers' – people I was not close with at all. No one was close to me *ka gore go tile go tsena batho baba nyetsweng fela* (because only the married can do traditional counselling). (Tumelo)

Bridal showers give close unmarried relatives an opportunity to participate in the process of advising their loved ones. As discussed above, the purpose of the bridal shower is mainly to give advice to the bride-to-be. This task is usually reserved for the married women in most Setswana cultures. However, this study found that women who attend bridal showers are, in the majority, educated and unmarried. To this extent, bridal showers deconstruct some cultural practices and allow unmarried women to share their experiences.

Purpose of bridal showers

Studies have shown that the origin and purpose of bridal showers in Europe centres on gift giving (Montemurro, 2005). The findings of this study show a different emphasis on the purpose of having a bridal shower. Extracts below express what participants at bridal showers regard as the purpose of bridal showers.

> Bridal showers are important, in my own opinion, because *difa ditsala* (they give friends) close friends and relatives an opportunity to be in contact with the bride-to-be *gore* (so that) in some sort of way to comfort themselves or *laela* (bid farewell) the bride-to-be as she takes up the new title to their name. And the showers are important for us brides-to-be because during a bridal shower, the language that is used is usually more explicit/straightforward as compared to that used during the traditional/customary counselling, *go laya*. (Neo)

Organiser Mpho had this to say about the purpose of bridal showers:

> *Nna* according to me the main purpose of bridal showers ke *go laya* (give advice) to the bride-to-be in a calm environment filled with friends and family. Because *ko taong ya Setswana tota tota* (during traditional counselling sessions). It will be tense, and the bride just has to listen. But with bridal shower the environment is more relaxed. (Mpho)

Selonyana also captures the same view that physical presence at the shower is more important than just bringing gifts:

> Okay, for me, the purpose of bridal shower is to ... it's more of a well-wisher for the new bride-to-be especially if that person is close to you and you have both been single for a very long time. And your friend telling you now I'm about to start a new life, it's a celebration ... my friend we have been single together, it's been nice and we just want to wish you well as you start a life with your husband ... let us come together and talk and reminisce our single days for one last time and probably give you advise from the little that we know, from God or from the experiences we have on how to live the next life as you start with your husband. (Selonyana)

Clearly, the main purpose of bridal showers among Batswana women is to give advice to the bride-to-be. As discussed earlier, in a traditional Setswana setup, the final stage of preparing the bride for married life is to give her some advice, referred to as *go laya/tao*. This concept of giving advice has been adopted at bridal showers and has taken precedence over the giving of gifts. Though presents are wanted, they are not as important as the physical presence of guests at the shower. Physical presence at the shower allows for more people to share their experiences with the bride-to-be in the process of giving her advice. Tables 3.2 and 3.3 summarise findings that the giving of advice at bridal showers is more important than presents.

Table 3.2 Purpose of the bridal shower is to give presents

Participant response	Frequency	%
Strongly disagree	27	24.5
Disagree	33	30.1
Agree	36	32.7
Strongly agree	11	10.0
Subtotal	**107**	**97.3**
Missing	3	2.7
Total	**110**	**100.0**

Table 3.3 Bridal showers are meant to give advice / counselling to the bride-to-be

Participant response	Frequency	%
Strongly disagree	2	1.8
Disagree	-	-
Agree	75	27.3
Strongly agree	30	68.2
Subtotal	**107**	**97.3**
Missing	3	2.7
Total	**110**	**100.0**

Table 3.2 shows that of the 110 guests who responded to the item on whether the main purpose of bridal showers is to give presents to the bride-to-be, 60 (65%) disagree with the idea that the main purpose of the bridal shower is to shower the bride-to-be with presents. One hundred and five guests (95%) agree that the main purpose of bridal showers is to give advice to the bride-to-be. Since giving advice at bridal showers is important, the next section focuses on advice that is given at bridal showers.

The advice at bridal showers

Bridal showers offer an ambivalent social space in which traditional gender stereotypes are sometimes challenged and at other times perpetuated, constructed, and deconstructed. Most advice given at bridal showers reproduced to a large extent those traditional ideologies about marriage. However, such were challenged precisely by the fact that elderly women were intentionally excluded from the showers and that only a small percentage of participants were married women. Participant Kuhle captures how women in urban spaces perpetuate the patriarchal ideology that women must always be ready to serve and care for their husbands and says:

> Love your husband. Even when he comes with dirty socks, love him. Cook for him in the kitchen and in the bedroom. If you don't, someone will. You know that in Botswana we have more women than men. You must also respect him. Don't discuss your husband with friends – he loses dignity. They will hold the grudge. If there is an issue, report to God. (Kuhle)

This piece of advice portrays the role of a wife as that of serving the interests of her husband. The bride-to-be is advised to play such roles as cooking for the husband both in the kitchen and bedroom, i.e., serve him with food and sex.

Perhaps these single women are just women who wish they could get married some day; as a result, they idolise marriage. This kind of advice might be suggestive of competitive discourses surrounding marriage; a woman marrying has to count herself lucky and hold on to that lucky star lest some other woman takes it away from her. Marriage is culturally/socially valued and is sometimes a symbol of a woman brought up well. The same percetion of upbringing does not apply to males, whether they marry or not. Similar sentiments were expressed by Sihle:

> The Bible says every wife must submit to her husband – *fela jaaka o nyalwa go nale batho ba ba fetogang bare 50/50, le nna kele mosadi ke na le sengwe ... ditlhogo ga di nke di nna pedi. Mo fe lerato le tlotlo*, that's all, *o tlaabo o ikagetse lelwapa*. As you get married, some (women) will tell you it is 50/50 (equal rights) – as a woman I have something too. You will never have two heads in the family. Just give him love and respect, that's all. That way you will build your family. Even when you are successful, don't ever think you cease to be submissive to him. He remains the head and father of the house. Don't ever think you are equal. He is not your business associate. (Sihle)

Sihle seems to have some understanding that there are unequal powers with marriage between men and women. The fact that she advises against the exercise of such rights betrays the ambivalence of bridal showers. There were many voices that advocated for equal rights in Gaborone bridal showers (see Chapters 5 and 7), which remained in competition with participants who advocated for traditional norms. Some women focused on the man/husband who is absent at the shower, and not on the bride-to-be who is present to receive such advice. Some pieces of advice given at the showers advocate for the interests of the man and his family more than those of the woman and her family. Self-sacrifice is emphasised throughout the shower as a strategy to protect the marriage. In some instances, the bride-to-be is urged to be more assertive, take care of herself and demand sexual gratification from her husband – these instances represent dissenting voices, which we shall explore further in the following chapters. Women are traditionally perceived as asexual and not looking for own sexual gratification during intercourse, but looking to please the man. Bridal showers offer new ways through which one creates their social support system.

Discussion and conclusions

Bridal showers reconstruct and reproduce gender roles in the process of preparing a bride-to-be for marriage. The content of the message that is given to the bride-to-be, to a large extent, asks her to conform to the roles traditionally played by women in Setswana societies. The roles that are reproduced include her role as a caregiver (for her husband and his people). These pieces of advice instil in the mind of a women who is about to get married that she must care for and serve her husband to be. However, the organisation of showers reflects agency on the part of women. As explained by Carsten (2000), women in the urban spaces of Gaborone find new ways through which they form their circle of social support where church membership and friendship become very important. While in the traditional counselling setup, only married women do the counselling, giving advice at bridal showers is given by all guests who are able and willing to do so. This in a way expands notions of 'kinship' beyond blood and marriage, thereby attesting to *Botho/Ubuntu*.

In summary, we have encountered changes and maintaince of traditional norms in the Gaborone bridal showers. However, this is not all in our data. What of those resisting voices and the changes noted above? How do we read them together with the consenting voices? In Chapter 4, on 'Unsettling Patriarchy: *Go Laya* in Gaborone Bridal Showers', we revisist the concept of agency in Gaborone bridal showers and how they create a new space within traditional and oppressive structures.

References

Carsten, J. 2000. *Cultures of relatedness: new approaches to the study of relationships*. Cambridge, MA: Cambridge University Press.

Cheal, D.J. 1989. 'Women together: bridal showers and gender membership'. In: B.J. Risman & P. Schwartz (eds). *Gender in intimate relationships: a microstructural approach*. Belmont, CA: Wadsworth. 87-93.

Clark, B. 2000. *Bridal showers*. Carpinteria, CA: Wilshire.

Comaroff, J.L. 1960. *The meaning of marriage payments*. New York: Academic.

Cornell, D. & Van Marle, K. 2015. 'Ubuntu feminism: tentative reflections'. *Verbum et Ecclesia*, 36(2). https://doi.org/10.4102/ve.v36i2.1444

Cott, N. 2000. *Public vows: a history of marriage and the nation*. Cambridge, MA: Harvard University Press. https://doi.org/10.4159/9780674029880

Dolamo, R. 2013. '*Botho/Ubuntu*: the heart of African ethics'. *Scriptura*, 112(1):1-10. https://doi.org/10.7833/112-0-78

Dube, M.W. 2009. 'I am because we are: giving primacy to African indigenous values in HIV&AIDS prevention'. In: M.F. Murove (ed). *African ethics: an anthology of comparative and applied ethics*. Pietermaritzburg, South Africa: UKZN Press. 178-188.

Emirbayer, M. & Mische, N. 1998. 'What es agency?' *The American Journal of Sociology*, 103(4):962-1023. https://doi.org/10.1086/231294

Gilligan, C. 1995. 'Hearing the difference: theorizing connection'. *Hypatia*, 10(2): 120-127. https://doi.org/10.1111/j.1527-2001.1995.tb01373.x

Gulbrandsen, Ø. 1986. 'To marry – or not to marry: marital strategies and sexual relations in a Tswana society'. *Ethnos*, 51(1&2):7-28. https://doi.org/10.1080/00141844.1986.9981311

Jenkins, J. 2000. *The everything wedding shower book*. Holbrook, MA: Adams.

Kambarami, M. 2006. 'Femininity, sexuality and culture: patriarchy and female subordination in Zimbabwe'. *Africa Regional Sexuality Resource Centre: Understanding Human Sexuality Seminar Series – September 2006.* University of Fort Hare, South Africa.

Matolino, B. & Kwindingwi, W. 2013. 'The end of *ubuntu*'. *South African Journal of Philosophy*, 32(2):197-205. https://doi.org/10.1080/02580136.2013.817637

Mbiti, J. 1969. *Introduction to African religion*. 2nd Edition. Nairobi: Heinemann.

Meekers, D. 1992. 'The process of marriage in African societies: a multiple indicator approach'. *Population and Development Review*, 18(1):61-78. https://doi.org/10.2307/1971859

Metz, T. & Gaie, J.B.R. 2010. 'The African ethic of *Botho/Ubuntu*: implications for research on morality'. *Journal of Moral Education*, 39(3):273-290. https://doi.org/10.1080/03057240.2010.497609

Mmualefe, D.O. 2004. 'Towards authentic Tswana Christianity: revisiting botho'. Unpublished Master's thesis, Eden Theological Seminary, Missouri.

Montemurro, B. 2002. 'You go 'cause you have to: the bridal shower as a ritual of obligation'. *Symbolic Interaction*, 25:67-92. https://doi.org/10.1525/si.2002.25.1.67

Montemurro, B. 2005. 'Add men, don't stir: reproducing traditional gender roles in modern wedding showers'. *Journal of Contemporary Ethnography*, 34(1):6-35. https://doi.org/10.1177/0891241604271332

Ndlovu, S. & Hove, E.F. 2015. 'Old wine in new wineskins: revisiting counselling in traditional Ndebele and Shona societies'. *Journal of Humanities and Social Science*, 20(1):101-105.

Ng'weshemi, A.M. 2002. *Rediscovering the human: the quest for a Christo-theological anthropology in Africa.* New York: Peter Lang.

Parkin, D. & Nyamwaya, D. (eds). 1987. *Transformations of African marriage: international African seminar series.* Manchester, UK: Manchester University Press.

Rankopo, M.J., Osei-Hwedie, K. & Modie-Moroka, T. 2007. 'Issues in service and volunteerism in Botswana'. A joint issue of *The Social Work Practitioner-Researcher* and the *Journal of Social Development in Africa, Special Issue on Civic Service in the Southern African Development Community.* 24-38.

Schapera, I. 1939. *Married life in an African tribe.* London: Faber and Faber.

Schapera, I. 1947. *Migrant labour and tribal life: a study of conditions in the Bechuanaland protectorate.* Oxford: Oxford University Press.

Schapera, I. 1978. 'Some notes on Tswana bogadi'. *The Journal on African Law*, 22(2):112-124. https://doi.org/10.1017/S0021855300009608

Setume, S.D., Gabaitse, R.M., Dube, M.W., Kgalemang, M., Modie-Moroka, T., Madigele, T., Kebaneilwe, M.D., Motswapong, E.P. & Matebekwane, A.K.M. 2017. 'Exploring the concept *Botho/Ubuntu* through bridal showers in the urban space, Gaborone, Botswana'. *Managing Development in Africa*, 2(3):173-191.

Shropshire, D.W.T. 1970. *Primitive marriage and European law: a South African investigation.* London: Frank Cass.

Shutte, A. 2001. *Ubuntu: an ethic for a new South Africa.* Pietermaritzburg, South Africa: Cluster Publications.

Solway, J. 2017. 'Slow marriage, fast bogadi: change and continuity in marriage in Botswana'. *Anthropology of Southern Africa*, 39(4):309-322. https://doi.org/10.1080/23323256.2016.1235980

4

UNSETTLING PATRIARCHY

Go laya in Gaborone bridal showers

Abstract

This chapter's[1] analysis of data from Gaborone bridal showers used theories of agency propounded by Ashivat and Saba Mohammed, drawn from religious women. They highlight "agency as resistance" that might also appear as "negotiation with oppressive social structures, and partial compliance" thereby indicating that "docility does not necessarily compromise agency" (Ashivat, 2016:267). Gaborone bridal showers are undoubtedly about women encouraging and accompanying another woman to enter a very patriarchal institution: heterosexual marriage, hence its agentic an.gle has to be interrogated carefully. The analysis of data collected from Gaborone bridal showers asked the following questions from interview guides: How does *go laya* (counselling of a bride) in the cultural setting and the urban-based bridal showers of Gaborone construct and reconstruct gender? How do they create new female spaces? Granted that they still buy a woman household items and that some voices are outright conservative, there is sufficient evidence-based conclusions that Gaborone bridal showers are still embracing patriarchy. Yet the analysis of the context and content of the Gaborone bridal shower, with its insistence on 'outright freedom' and that every woman is welcome and must be free to talk, regardless of age and marital status, creates an inclusive space that resists equating women's full humanity with heterosexual marriage. Even the most conservative voices acknowledged radical inclusivity as a change brought by Gaborone bridal showers in the *go laya* female space. Content wise, evidence-based findings indicate iconoclastic twists in *go laya* – insisting that a married woman keep her voice, keep her friends, wear what she wants, hold the man financially accountable, insist on faithfulness, insist on shared household chores, watch out for intimate partner violence, enjoy her sexuality and pursue her profession.

Introduction: shower the bride!

As used here, the Setswana phrase *go laya* refers to the group counselling of the bride or bride-to-be by elderly married women in preparation for entering the

1 The article, '*Botho/Ubuntu* and "unsettling patriarchy": *go laya* in Gaborone bridal showers' by Musa, M.W. et al., was first published in 2021 in *Journal of the Interdenominational Theological Centre*, 50:1-45. It is republished in this volume by permission.

institution of marriage in Botswana. Traditionally, *go laya* is a ritual of crossing that either occurs the day before the marriage or during the afternoon of the wedding day. It is strictly carried by married or elderly women, speaking to a new bride about marriage. Gaborone bridal showers, hosted by younger generations for their friends, also undertake *go laya.* The aim of this chapter is to assess the content of *go laya* in Gaborone bridal showers so as to understand how it confronts, reconstructs or cohabits with patriarchal structures, as well as to note their agency. The data were part of a larger study[2] sponsored by the John Templeton Foundation. A group of University of Botswana researchers spent a year (2016–2017) collecting data from Gaborone, Botswana showers.[3] There were four different showers: The Naomi, Laban, bridal and baby showers. The Naomi/Laban showers are for parents and in-laws, who will be receiving new daughters- and sons-in-law in their families. Naomi/Laban showers originate from Botswana and are open to both men and women. They tend to be attended by elders, although in actual fact it remains predominately female. The bridal shower is for the bride-to-be, often held a few weeks before the wedding and is exclusively female (Setume et al., 2017:173-191). The baby shower is held for an expectant mother, to prepare for the forthcoming baby, to rejoice with the expectant mother and to prepare her for motherhood (Motswapong et al., 2018:3-13). It is also largely female, although increasingly, men are urged to attend.

As said earlier in the introduction, the overall aim of the study was to explore how *Botho/Ubuntu* is expressed in Botswana urban areas, using the case study of Gaborone showers. While there are several ways of defining *Botho/Ubuntu* (Munyaka & Motlhabi, 2009), the working definition used in the study is *Botho/Ubuntu* as a philosophical understanding that equates one's human identity with the capacity to respect, welcome, care for and empower another person.[4] Fieldwork was preceded by desktop research that investigated cultural practices and celebrations surrounding the preparations for a marriage and for a new baby – how they indicated *Botho/Ubuntu* and how they may be the foundations of current urban showers (Dube et al., 2016:1-22). Two of the four[5] specific objectives of the study sought to inves-

2 The project was named '*Botho/Ubuntu* and Community Building in the Urban Space'.

3 The project used a mixed method to collect data, but the study was primarily qualitative. First, we reviewed literature concerning the area of study, particularly to establish how traditional Setswana handled the arrival of the daughter-in-law, son-in-law, and a new baby. The project sought to establish both continuity, discontinuity, and hybridity. Our instruments for collecting data included an interview guide, self-administered questionnaire, recorded data in video and audio as well as an observation instrument.

4 In the chapter, 'Mother Economies: *Botho/Ubuntu* and Community Building in the Urban space, a Focus on Naomi/Laban, Bridal Showers in Gaborone', we dwelt much on defining the concept and assessing how the showers may be driven or may express *Botho/Ubuntu*. To avoid repetition in this chapter, we shall not dwell on this aspect of the study, since it is already covered.

5 The rest of the objectives sought to: (1) Explore the theological and spiritual base of *Botho/Ubuntu* values/ethics; (2) examine how *Botho/Ubuntu* was understood and manifested in traditional Batswana

tigate how shower participants construct and reconstruct gender and how they contribute towards building and maintaining "justice loving communities" that counteract the encroachment of poverty in the urban space. Mixed methods were employed to collect data in Gaborone using such instruments as observation form, interview guide, self-administered questionnaire, and video and audio recording. Altogether, 31 showers were covered, 14 of which were bridal showers. This chapter focuses on the Gaborone bridal shower, particularly on the above-stated specific objectives of the study, including how they contribute towards building justice-loving communities. The chapter, therefore, seeks to analyse the agency of Gaborone women in undertaking self-initiated communal projects to empower one another and how such an act may be reconstructing or maintaining patriarchal gender roles, and in the process counteract poverty and contribute towards building justice-loving communities. The structural process of the chapter involves defining and discussing gender, Gaborone bridal showers participants, theories of agency, processes and content of Gaborone bridal showers, and highlighting the creation of a liberative space for Batswana women in the midst of a patriarchal institution – marriage.

Gender as a social construct

In her article, 'We should all be Feminists', C.N. Adichie writes that "gender matters everywhere in the world" (2014:25), and that "gender as it functions today is grave injustice" (ibid.:21). According to Susan Archer Mann (2012:69), "a major contribution of the second wave liberal feminists was to make gender a core concept in feminist analysis. By highlighting the distinction between biological sex and socially learned gender, they focused on how gender roles could be transformed through conscious social and political action to foster a more egalitarian society". Similarly, Musa W. Dube (2003:86) argues: "The fact that gender is culturally constructed needs to be underlined. This means that gender is not natural; is not divine; has to do with social relationships of women and men; can be reconstructed and transformed by the society for it is culturally constructed [... and] gender overlaps with other social, cultural, economic and political factors."

The 2017 report on 'Progress towards Sustainable Development Goals' features gender and poverty concerns and the need for empowerment. Goal Number 1 of the Sustainable Development Goals (SDGs) is: 'End poverty in all its forms everywhere'. It is an imperative voice underlining urgency. Thus the 2017 report states:

communities; (3) analyse how the *Botho/Ubuntu* ethic is expressed in contemporary urban settings in Botswana; and (4) highlight how *Botho/Ubuntu* spirituality can inform the building and maintenance of justice-loving communities. These objectives are covered in the various chapters of this special volume and in previously published articles of the study.

> Social protection systems are fundamental to preventing and reducing poverty and inequality at every stage of people's lives, through benefits for children, mothers with newborns, persons with disabilities, older persons and those persons without jobs. Preliminary data show that in 2016 only 45% of the world's population was effectively protected by a social protection system and the coverage varied widely across countries and regions. (2017:3)

Concerning the Africa region in particular, it is noted that "42% of people in Sub-Saharan Africa continued to subsist in conditions of extreme poverty in 2013", hence the report underlines that "intensified efforts are required to boost the incomes, alleviate the suffering and build the resilience of those individuals still living in extreme poverty in particular in Sub-Saharan Africa" (ibid.:2). Goal 5 of the SDGs is on gender. With an imperative voice, it states that nations should seek to "achieve gender equality and empower all women and girls", again underlining urgency and a call for action. The 2017 report notes that "gender inequality persists worldwide, depriving women and girls of their basic rights and opportunities. Achieving gender equality and empowerment of women and girls will require more vigorous efforts … to counter deeply rooted gender-based discrimination that often results from patriarchal attitudes and related social norms" (2017:5).

According to the SADC *Gender Protocol Barometer Botswana*: "The proportion of female-headed households living in poverty is higher than that of male-headed households, on average 33% and 27% respectively" (SADC, 2012:39). The *Barometer* continues to note: "According to the 2007 National Population Policy Review, almost 50% of households are female-headed, and they make up the majority of poor households … There are no special policies for women to access credit" (ibid.:46). Gaborone showers are not formal social systems that are government imitated; rather they are community-based initiatives that become some form of social capital to participating members. Since they are community initiatives, they suggest agency among participants, which may contribute towards mitigating pockets of poverty, and they may provide a space where "gender-based discrimination that often results from patriarchal attitudes and related norms" may be discussed and possibly reconstructed – or embraced strategically. Consequently, two objectives of our study sought to investigate how *Botho/Ubuntu* activities in the urban space construct and reconstruct gender, and if they contribute towards mitigating poverty.

Gaborone bridal showers participants

Although Gaborone bridal showers are open to women of all ages, our data indicate that the age range of bridal shower participants is predominantly youth oriented. Of the total, 90.4% were between 20 and 40 years, while only 9.6% participants were 41 years and above. Educationally, they ranged from Form 3 to PhD, with the highest number of participants having a degree and post-graduate qualification (41.4%). The marital status of the bridal shower indicates that the majority of participants are single (76.8%), while only 20.7% are married and 2.4% widowed. The bridal showers are dominated by youths who are mainly friends and non-relatives such as workmates, church mates and neighbours of the bride-to-be (89%), while blood relatives constitute only 11% (mostly sisters), which is statistically significant because it highlights that bridal showers are driven by the *Botho/Ubuntu* community-building spirit than by blood relations.

This chapter's analysis will dwell particularly on the responses given in the interview guide to two questions. The first one sought to assess the production of cultural roles and efforts to reconstruct them. This question asked respondents to compare bridal showers to traditional activities surrounding preparation for marriage. Participants were asked to share what they think is the unique contribution of bridal showers. Lastly, in a more specific way, participants were asked how roles of men and women have changed from the traditional ones.

The second thematic question drawn from the interview guide concerns community building, and it asks how bridal showers "build or divert from African ways of community building". Some data are also drawn from the theme of character building, where respondents were asked to discuss how bridal showers build the characters of participants. The overall picture of Gaborone bridal showers as an exclusively female's space is that there is an unsettling of patriarchy. It is a space of women on the margins of society making movements in and out of the cultural boundaries of patriarchy – unsettling patriarchy, in small and big ways.

Unsettling patriarchy

If Gaborone bridal showers have become such strong female-centred movements and spaces dominated by largely younger women who are relatively educated, how do these showers unsettle patriarchy? How do they construct and reconstruct gender in the content of their *go laya*? To be unsettled can be described at various levels. First and foremost, it means to be uneasy – to be out of one's comfort zone. Second, it can refer to that eerie feeling that comes with the uncanny knowledge that something is no longer what it used to be, or not what it seems to be. It is the state of detecting threats of change. Lastly, it is to be uprooted, moved from the comfort zone to some strange space where one is forced to see things anew. To be unsettled is to be disturbed.

The ever-growing Gaborone bridal showers have been unsettling to some men. One often hears that, "*Kante dishowera tsa lona, go tholwa go etswe teng ruri* (complaint and suspicion – you women why are you always going to these showers)?" or "*dishowera tseo tsa lona dithuba malwapa* (outright accusations – your showers destroy marriages)" or "*Nna wame mosadi ke mmoleletse gore ga a ye ko dishowereng* (taking control – I have told my wife/girlfriend that she will not go to the showers)". In these comments there are some fears, suspicions and attempts to stop women from going to the showers, for they are thought to be dangerous.

In the rest of this chapter, we shall analyse some of the findings from the interview guides, highlighting how bridal showers as exclusively female spaces are 'unsettling patriarchy'. We will investigate how they construct and reconstruct gender by focusing on the content of their act of *go laya* in the data collected from interview guides. Initial data analysis has uncovered the unsettling encounter with patriarchal persistence in an exclusively female space. Consequently, the analysis on 'mother economies', points out that the "bridal shower is possibly the most complex shower in reading the nuanced spaces that are created to subvert patriarchy. Age conflicts between speakers and participants, their different ethics as well as how new spaces of liberation are created need to be explored closely".

In short, we may not always find an outright rejection of patriarchal marriage and its patriarchal norms and values because the purpose of a bridal shower is to prepare "the bride-to-be" for her new role as a new wife, and to be a good one for that matter – one who will manage to maintain the marriage despite its well-acknowledged challenges. However, many respondents call for change, bringing bridal showers into the creative and continuous tension of cultural norms and the call for transforming gender roles, as one respondent said, "We teach old ways and new ones". Another respondent captures this in-between space by saying the purpose of bridal showers is, "*go laya*, though with a modern twist". She went on to say, "so we teach a woman to ask her husband where he was and what he was doing. We teach mutual respect". She compared the cultural and urban Motswana man, stating: "Yes, the roles are the same, but in cities men cook, buy grocery, change nappies because at times the wife is busy at work, has travelled for a meeting, etc. But a woman is still a man's helper, and the man is still the head of the household." The creative tension and its seemingly contradictory stance towards gender reconstruction is endlessly attested in the data. The material gifts, for example, that are given to brides-to-be seemingly suggest that she must accept her gendered role as a homemaker. One respondent stated: "Gifts give tips about marriage, e.g., a plate means 'serve a decent meal', and all gifts have a meaning." She added: "*Mosadi o bonwa ka dilwana*", that is, a wife is identified through her utensils. Clearly there are seismic moves upon the patriarchal cultural rock upon which the Setswana marriage is based in Gaborone bridal showers. It is a troubled, cracking rock for there is a 'twist'; there is asking about a husband's whereabouts, which is a direct affront to the cultural constructions of a Motswana man as a free bachelor, married or not; and there is acceptance that a married Motswana woman is also a professional woman whose duties must be attended to. Be that as it may, the "man is still the head of the household" in Gaborone bridal showers. Thus, the question of agency and empowering women in the bridal shower space becomes central and requires a nuanced theoretical framework to appreciate the twisting of gender roles and its magnitude.

Agency, empowerment and bridal showers

According to Ian Buchanan, "agency is the degree to which a subject is able to determine the course of their actions", but points out that Karl Marx held that "people make history, but not in conditions of their own choosing" (2010:10-11). Karl Marx puts suspicion into our so-called choices, as choices to do what we have already been socially constructed to choose and to do, according to our class, gender, race and ethnicity as subsequent studies have shown. According to Joseph Childers and Gary Henzi, "the term is often used interchangeably with the similar yet distinct concept of the subject ... the subject is capable of thought and critique, and thus is also capable of choice and action" (Childers & Henzi, 1995:6-7). However, they note that

> The difficulty with this concept of agent and agency has to do with theorizing change, especially political and social change. If the individual is always subjected to ideological and discursive constraints, and all his or her actions – even the ones that seem oppositional – are always accountable in terms of those ideologies and discourses, how then is it possible that anything can change? Some new historicists, like Louis Montrose have argued that agents and their concomitant agency are both constrained and enabled by the interaction of these power structures.

These definitions of agency and subjectivity, imply two opposing but also intersecting perspectives about Botswana women of the bridal shower movement. First, it highlights that we cannot rule out that Batswana women of the bridal shower movement are indeed constructed by patriarchy that they fully embrace and serve, although not without resistance. They have been taught that a woman must grow up and be married and that a married woman should try to please her husband, cook and clean – and so they buy her household items, teach her to respect her husband and to sexually satisfy him. At the same time, we cannot rule out that the same subjugation is the seed of possible resistance. That is, women in patriarchal relationships, whether married or not, experience the oppressive structures that govern such relationships and, consequently, they seek to empower the bride-to-be with skills of survival, perhaps subtle resistance, and at times overt resistance. It is this range of resistance that we seek to articulate or tease out and how such agency functions through embracing patriarchal roles at the same time subverting them.

In her article, 'Theorizing gender from religion cases', Orit Avishai writes that

> Agency, a key concept in social thought, has challenged feminist theorists to discern its limits when individuals interact with oppressive social structures. What kind of agentic action, decisions, preferences, and choices can be expected from subjects who are constrained by their environments? ...The late 1990s are a turning point from emphasis on resistance, empowerment, and negotiation within oppressive social structures to frames that unmasked secularist biases and expanded the definition to include self-authorship. (Avishai, 2016:265)

Avishai points out that the first feminist understanding of agency has been highly critisised for being "steeped in secularist, liberal, Western biases that disregard local, national cultural arrangements" (ibid.:267). Using an example of Muslim women who remain within their patriarchal religion while remaining as "thinking, strategising and planning individuals" has led to an expanded understanding of agency as "resistance, negotiation with oppressive social structures, and partial compliance making many subtle ways of resistance", indicating that "docility did not necessarily compromise agency" (ibid.:267). Citing Saba Mahmood, Avishai says that "Women may be agentive in ways that do not align with feminist expectations – such as choosing not to resist unequal social arrangements; embracing the family, nation, or other social structures that feminism sees as a location of oppression or even contributing to the subjugation of others" (Avishai, 2016:268).

And so it is with Gaborone bridal showers. One can easily get away feeling that there is no particular change towards oppressive structures of patriarchal marriage – that women are still being taught to cook, clean, submit to, respect their husbands, and to live for their children. Such a conclusion may indeed be justified, especially after listening to some invited keynote speakers and some other commentators, but it is not the whole story. Rather, a closer reading of the data using the lens of generative agency reveals a range of movements between those who seem to maintain the status quo; those who inhabit the in-between spaces and those who are seemingly calling for outright change. While we may seem to be presenting these as three separate perspectives, it is more of a continuum, it is a more ambiguous agency characterised by ambivalence towards the patriarchal institution of marriage, but one which is undoubtedly unsettling patriarchy.

Outright freedom! The Gaborone bridal shower female space

Accordingly, the Gaborone showers are 100% female spaces that have almost developed into an urban female movement due to their frequency and their ongoing state. It may not be an exaggeration to say that if Gaborone women are not attending one shower or another, they are busy preparing for a forthcoming bridal, baby or Naomi/Laban shower. As underlined in the introductory chapter, preparations for one shower may stretch from two to six months, depending on the type of shower the organisers wish to hold, as well as the class of organisers. A series of meetings are held by organisers: identifying friends, church mates, workmates, relatives and other associates of the targeted recipient. The organisers decide on contributions to be made by the closest associates and on presents to be bought. They decide on the dress code and venue. They design the invitation cards, state the required gate pass, and send them out. They draw the programme for the day and invite speakers. They buy core presents, which may be in consultation with the recipient or a close friend of the recipient who knows her needs, taste and wishes – if it is a surprise shower. For the rest of the invitees, the recipient of the shower selects one or two gift shops for household related-items and writes her wish list. One organiser captured the energy that goes with the process thus:

> Yes! Since Baitse is getting married, what can we do for her? From the group, some suggested we make a surprise bridal shower for her. From there, we formed a solid group taking into consideration the number of members. Sometimes we can reach up to forty people. Then we would consider the contribution fee and reach a consensus on popping P300 per member. We then contribute our shares towards the stipulated date of the shower. We then approach the bride-to-be to enquire about the gifts. The bride-to-be can suggest a sofa, for example, or a stove. Organisers will then meet to purchase the desired gifts. After purchasing the gift, we would buy meat, sorghum meal, voerwoers and other foods needed to have fun with family and friends. Decorations are then taken care of as you can see nice deco on the tables!

As the above quote points out, when the day of the shower finally comes, the organisers decorate the venue, cook elaborately, and welcome all the invitees to a great and joyful celebration of the 'bride-to-be'. The organisers have their core gifts all wrapped up – they may include a washing machine, refrigerator, stove, coffee table, sofa – depending on the class or ties of the recipient and her friends' financial capacity. They may also give hard cash to the bride-to-be from their collected contributions for her to use wherever need arises. The rest of the invited guests bring items such as household utensils of sorts, drawn from the recipient's gift list or from other areas. Many others without material gifts come along, bringing the gift of their presence and verbal advice. Although programmes differ, there is usually music and great fun and laughing as the programme begins casually and playfully. Such a mood of the event is indeed intended, desired and created, for the respondents state that every attendant "must participate and MUST never make the shower boring by behaving like a guest – *moeng ko showereng*!" (emphasis original). The Setswana expression underlines that members should not carry themselves as guests in a shower. It is a welcoming space, a home for all women regardless of their social status – whether they are carrying a present or not – what is important is that they must feel free and actively participate in the celebration. Hence the respondents underlined that we expect "laughter, joy, outright freedom" and every participant to "speak their minds" and "have all the fun!"

And in this mood of playful seriousness, the bridal shower begins. They surround her, or sit her in front on a princess chair, pray, play games, dance, sing loud and laugh a lot. They finally ask, "where and how did you meet this man – your husband to be?" It is a story that is heard and told with much fun as the listeners become participant listeners, interjecting with laughter, questions, commentary and co-telling. They seem to be having much fun. The mood is that of joyful playfulness. This item is followed by words of advice, *go laya*, to the bride-to-be about all things concerning marriage. The theme of *go laya* is definitely the core business of the showers as almost all participants define the purpose of bridal showers as *go laya* while others express it in English phrases saying, "to give advice", "to give moral support", "to encourage", "motivate", "share experiences" and "give tips about marriage", among others. Repeatedly, the participants underline *go laya* as the main purpose of the bridal shower. Out of 24 answers, 20 identified *go laya* as the primary purpose. Quantitative data collected from a self-administered questionnaire also indicated that only 40.2% thought that the main purpose of the bridal shower was to give presents while 59.8% disagreed, placing emphasis on moral support, giving advice, guidance, and social networking, that is, *go laya.* In some cases, there might be an invited speaker, but in almost all cases, all attendants participate, either after the speaker has spoken, or before she speaks. These collated words of four respondents illustrate the point, underlining that bridal showers seek to

> bid the bride farewell, bring gifts, advise her, *go laya* ... sort of ...[to] come together and create friendships ... [to] give presents to the bride, share advice with the bride, *go mo laya* and to socialise ... [to] share a moment with a friend before marriage, [to] encourage and motivate her, share experience from the married, single and divorced ... to make the bride feel special; celebrate her; help her have a glimpse of what to expect in marriage ... to come together as women and support the other, share ideas on marriage to make it work ... [to] make the bride feel supported with women encouraging her, without them there is no way, there is no joy!

These answers, which are thematically typical, indicate that the Gaborone bridal shower movement is more than just focused on the recipient of the shower. It is rather a female-centred movement and a deliberate creation of a female space which brings women 'together' to 'create friendships', 'socialise' and 'share'. A Gaborone bridal shower is therefore women's attempt to accompany one woman on her journey into marriage through presence, presents and words of wisdom. Without these women walking along with her, helping her to cross the bridge from single life into marriage (Kebaneilwe et al., 2018), they insist, "there is no way, no joy for her". In so doing bridal showers build community in the urban space, show *Botho/Ubuntu*, and create a female space and female movement.

Go laya: woman-to-woman talk

Asked if the main drive behind holding a bridal shower is to give the bride-to-be material gifts or verbal advice, the respondents underlined the latter, namely *go laya* (Setume et al., 2017:12). Out of 24 answers given to the question of similarities of purpose between the Gaborone bridal showers and the cultural one, 20 said it is all about *go laya*. How does *go laya* in the cultural setting and the urban-based bridal showers of Gaborone construct and deconstruct gender? How do the Gaborone bridal showers problematise gender? How do they create new female spaces? And how do they maintain the status quo while they are remaking their world? According to Musa W. Dube (2003:87):

> Gender does not distribute power equally between men and women. Men are constructed as public leaders, thinkers, decision-makers, and property owners. Women are constructed primarily as domestic beings, who belong to the home or the kitchen, the mothers, wives. They are constructed to be dependent on the property of their husbands, brothers, or fathers. Women are constructed to be silent, non-intelligent, emotional, well behaved, non-questioning, obedient faithful to one partner – be they husbands, boyfriends or live-in partners. And so, we think of a good woman as one who takes very good care of her home, children, husband, one who hardly questions or speaks back to her partner and one who remains faithful to her partner.

Go laya is a cultural practice, held either during the wedding day or the day after (Ellece, 2007). Culturally, *go laya* occurs primarily in the afternoon, after the new wife has taken off her white Western gown and has been dressed in a cultural dress and wrapped in a shawl (*tshale/mogagolwane*) and given a head gear (*tukwi*) that marks her new status as a married woman. Garbing the bride with these two items (the shawl and head gear) is sometimes performed to start the counselling session by *Mmamalome* (maternal uncle's wife); at other times they dress her up in private then bring her out to the counselling group. *Go laya* is held in *lolwapa*, a woman's cooking and sitting veranda or in a closed room. The married women all sit down on the floor with outstretched legs – not on chairs. This sitting on the floor with outstretched legs symbolises a well-founded, relaxed and calm woman. She does not move a lot and shall not be easily moved by the storms that come along in the marriage institution.

In this strictly woman-only session, characterised by a heavily somber mood, married and elderly women with covered heads (*ditukwi*) and wearing their traditional blanket shawls (*ditshale/megagolwane*) that reflect their marital status, surround the new wife and counsel her strictly and painfully about her new role and marriage challenges and how she must endure to maintain it. They draw primarily from their experiences. There is some observed order, since *go laya* begins with *mmamalome* (wife to her maternal uncle), followed by *rakgadi* (sister to her father), grandmother,

other relatives and married women – they will all individually give their word of wisdom. The newly married woman has no say, save to occasionally say: "Yes. Yes. I am listening" to some counsellor who might ask her: "*A wa nkutlwa ngwanaka*" (Are you listening to me, my child?), or to look down quietly and respectfully as they speak to her.

Rewriting the space of *go laya* in the Gaborone bridal showers

Asked about differences and similarities, Gaborone bridal shower participants agree that they share the same purpose, namely *go laya*. They are also an exclusively female space. However, they point out that there are differences in terms of timing of the event, the mood, the participants, the attire, and the content of *go laya*. Timewise, bridal showers are deliberately scheduled a few weeks before the actual wedding, for the participants say they know that once the wedding comes, they would not have the authority or space to speak to their friend, who would by then be a new wife. One respondent stated that during the cultural counselling done by married women, they are relegated to the kitchens (cooking and serving guests) noting that "*kana gatwe rona bo ma singili le go feta gaufi re seka ra leka!*" (that is, during the counselling session, we the single ladies should not even be seen passing close to the counselling place!). Another respondent, grateful for the opportunity provided by the bridal shower, pointed out "bridal showers are more accommodative of marital status – "*bo rona nko re se fa*" (otherwise some of us would not be here for *go laya*). While some bridal showers are held in the afternoon, many are also held during the evening or during the night, a fact the participants believe the Setswana elderly married women would most likely problematise as sessions for unruly behaviour.

Speaking of the mood, participants described their bridal showers as 'more relaxed', 'flexible', 'jovial', 'more casual', 'less stressful', 'socially welcoming', 'counselling fun', while they described the cultural sessions as 'strict', 'too formal', 'too rigid and secretive' and characterised by 'serious protocol', and 'orderly', in terms of who participates, who begins to speak and who follows in the process of *go laya*. In the village, the counselling 'done by elders', they say, is 'too intense'. Monyadi (the bride), "even cries" underlined one participant. Gaborone bridal shower respondents acknowledge that they are aware that in terms of participants, *go laya* the bride-to-be or the new wife, is culturally an exclusive role of married women – so much so that if the mother of the bride and some other relatives are not married, they are excluded from the counselling of their daughters. One participant who had such an experience during her wedding said:

> Bridal showers offer close relatives who are not married an opportunity to advise. For instance, in my case, there was no one who was already married in my family: like my aunt and my mother, no one was married. Even among my

> mothers' sisters, cousins, nothing ... I was the first to get married, so, when it got to counselling at home, they were not allowed to advise, but in the showers, they are free to advise. I was left with strangers, people I was not close with at all ... because only the married can do the traditional counselling.

In some Botswana cultures, where there is some flexibility (in the northern region), they include elderly women in the counselling session of the bride even if they are not married. Here age, namely seniority, becomes an additional criterion to marital status for admission into counselling the bride. In the Tswapong and Bobirwa regions, they do open advice, with every guest standing up to give both a gift and advice at the same time. But in such a practice, the counselling is directed to both the bride and the groom.[6] In the Southern region in particular, the *go laya* session is strictly for and by married women. An adult single woman is excluded from *merero ya lenyalo* (communal discussions of marriage), even if it includes her own children.

In the Gaborone showers, as indicated by the quote above, all participants, regardless of their age and marital status, are free to bring words of wisdom from their life experience or from what they know about heterosexual relationships. The openness to all women, regardless of age and marital status is well attested and strongly underlined from the collected data. Under the section where the interview guide invited respondents to state the "Differences between traditional cultural ways of preparing for marriage and bridal showers", out of the 24 answers, 17 named the inclusiveness of bridal showers, while the rest identified time, attire, and the mood of the counselling. Again, when participants were invited to talk about "Changes brought by bridal showers versus traditional ways", of the 23 answers rendered, 17 respondents identified "participation of unmarried women at showers", pointing out that "traditional counselling is exclusive (only attended by married women) while bridal showers are more inclusive. Therefore, bridal showers have an impact on the attendees, that is, even the character of some other girls/women is moulded and changed". Collected data concur here that "marital status does not matter" because "even those not married counsel".

This is a major departure from the cultural space of counselling, *go laya*; and it is a very significant one. Not only does it open a space for younger women to listen and be moulded and changed as stated above, but it also dismantles patriarchal gender constructions that present unmarried women as inadequate, hence incomplete persons – a myth and a social device that serves to perpetuate the patriarchal institute of marriage. As Adichie (2014:30) points out: "Our society teaches a woman at a certain age who is unmarried to see it as a deep personal failure. While a man at the same age, who is unmarried, has not come around to making his pick."

6 It is unclear to us if they still carry out an exclusive counselling session for the new wife or if age still matters, even in the open counselling.

A single woman is thus characterised as incomplete, that is, a 'Miss', as the English language graphically labels every single woman, thus creating pressure for women to seek marriage to become Mrs So-and-So (Dube, 2003:94). In addition, the exclusion of unmarried women is also a dismissal of the diversities of families that exist in Botswana. For example, it is statistically attested that the Botswana family is primarily made of single-headed families who make up 50% (SADC, 2012:16). Gaborone bridal showers' dispersal with marital and age requirement in *go laya* is thus a subversive twist and an iconoclastic move, as it knocks away a major patriarchal pillar from a woman's space by saying "women need not become married in order to be recognised as successful and wise adults". Dispensing with the requirement for marriage also opens the space for recognising and affirming varieties of families in the landscape of Botswana. In so doing, Gaborone bridal showers create room for a wider transformation.

Rewriting the contents of *go laya* in Gaborone bridal showers

Turning to the content, cultural counselling of the new wife includes taking care of the husband, her in-laws, the disabled, the house, the children, endurance, and respecting and serving her husband. The new wife is counselled to forgo her friends and to keep the secrets of her house to herself and to avoid discussing them with her friends. If she needs a listening ear, she must go to *mmamalome* or *rakgadi*. This secrecy includes hiding violence where it occurs. Since the counselling of the new wife is an ancient oral tradition, certain counselling messages have become codified sayings (Dube, 2003:91). These include, "*monna ga a botswe kwa a tswang*" (do not ask your husband where he is coming from, whenever he arrives home); *monna selepe o a amogwana* (a man is an axe that we all use and pass around); *monna poo ga a agelwe lesaka* (a man is a bull, so do not build a kraal for him). In these Setswana cultural teachings, a man is never married, only his wife is married to him. He remains a free roaming "bull" that mates with many cows; a communal cutting axe that services several other women; and one who does not need to account for his whereabouts and movements. Sexual faithfulness of a husband to his wife is not to be expected and his unfaithfulness is not a reason for leaving the marriage, the elderly married women tell the new wife. She must focus on building her home and raising her children; she must respect and submit to her husband without fail and not allow anything to destroy her marriage.

Bridal showers' space and content are suspicious of the cultural counselling held by married women and seek to counteract it both by action and content. As described above under the section "Outright Freedom!", the bridal shower mood of playfulness, laughter, joy and casualness counteracts the rigid, secretive cultural approach and seeks to free every woman to speak and to hear. Participants of the bridal shower sit on chairs and tables decorated according to the theme's colour. The married women counsellors embody marriage authority and status through their attire (*leteisi, ditsale le ditukwi*), while they welcome the bride into the club by garbing her with the same attire that they come wearing. With bridal showers, casual wear such as short skirts, hot pants and jeans are fine. The bride-to-be sits on a princess chair and is treated to much laughter, games and joy. Her participation is expected such as, for example, sharing how she met the groom-to-be. The shower recipient wears a dress of her choice, although several times they had a salmon silk banner across her shoulder with 'bride-to-be' written on it.

Then there is much attestation that the content of the teaching is also delivered with a 'twist'. Let us take, for example, the classic Setswana sayings about a husband's freedom from accountability about his whereabouts and his freedom to see other women. The respondents say:

> In the village, they advise that *monna ke selepe* (a man is a freely used cutting axe). This is not said in urban settings, where people do not believe this ... traditional counseling *monna oa apeelwa, monna gaa botswe dipotso, monna ke tlhogo* (traditional counselling that says a husband must have his food cooked; he should not be asked any questions and he is the head). In the bridal shower flexibility, they give the bride advice that as much as you are getting married, you have a voice. in-laws must not *tshwenya* (oppress) you. Wear trousers if you want ... Emang Basadi may be (Botswana feminist movement). Yes, at times the bride is advised to demand that the husband must share roles.

Similarly, the discussion under the topic, "What roles have bridal showers changed or reproduced", indicates a subversive twist to the content. One respondent saw the overall goal of bridal showers as a feminist movement, holding that "at showers women encourage each other not to be docile. There is a bit of feminism – a peaceful feminism". This perspective is underlined by other respondents who held that

> Time has changed. House chores are now 50/50 for men and women. The bride should continue to hang out with friends ...[to] demand, to expect a man to account financially and for his whereabouts, a man must help share tasks ... women should hold men accountable for their whereabouts ... women are empowered; namely be the woman you want to be. Women can now work and have the same status as men. Monna (your husband) must be your friend, not your father – *gase rrago* (he is not your father). We need to overcome gender stereotypes.

The above responses indicate the 'modern twist' at work in the content of *go laya* in the bridal showers. They rewrite the content of cultural teaching insisting that a husband must account for his movements and should be faithful. In addition, they insist a woman must remain a 'speaking voice'. "She must have a voice" and "she must be empowered". They try to reimagine family headship, suggesting friendship between wife and husband than a fatherly authoritative figure. They suggest that household chores should be shared. Moreover, they insist a woman must wear what she wants. Critiquing the cultural content of silence and secrecy, they point out that in traditional counselling, "a woman is told to be quiet even in the face of abuse. Emphasis is on the woman respecting the man". Bridal showers problematise this teaching of silence, of tolerating violence, for "a woman is told to look out for signs of cheating or abuse, while in the village the woman is told to look away when the husband cheats".

The *2010 Gender-Based Violence Indicators Study of Botswana* found that "over two-thirds of women in Botswana (67%) have experienced some form of gender violence in their lifetime, including partner and non-partner violence. A smaller but still high proportion of men (44%) admit to perpetrating violence against women" (2010:11). Similarly, *Gender Protocol Barometer Botswana* points out: "Up to two in three women in Botswana have experienced gender-based violence at some point in their lifetime. Sixty per cent of women in Botswana reported experiencing intimate partner violence in their lifetime" (SADC, 2012:51). The recent *Botswana AIDS Impact Survey 2013* (BAIS IV) results showed that "24.8% of females with early sexual debut reported not giving consent at the time of intercourse" (NACA, 2013:15). Gaborone bridal shower insistence that intimate partner violence must be exposed rather than swept under the carpet is, therefore, an important part of dismantling patriarchal pillars in marriage and contributing towards national health (2017:39-57).

The Setswana cultural construction of a married man as a free bachelor (bull, axe) who is free to see other women is counteracted in the Gaborone bridal showers. In the context of HIV and AIDS, Batswana married women and women in heterosexual relationships, be it cohabitation or at dating stage, were highly vulnerable to HIV infection with a patriarchal construction of a Motswana man as a perpetual bachelor (Dube, 2016:161-180). Indeed, HIV and AIDS statistics overwhelmingly indicate their vulnerability. The *Gender Protocol Barometer Botswana* points out: "Women and girls are more vulnerable to HIV infection than men and boys due to biological and socio/cultural factors. These include multiple concurrent relationships, intergenerational relationships, unequal gender and power relations, early marriages and teenage pregnancy among girls" (SADC, 2012:71). Indeed, the BAIS 1V report indicates that females are continuing to be the most adversely affected by HIV and AIDS in all its aspects, 36 years after the first discovery of the disease (NACA, 2013:8-10, 17, 19).

Multiple concurrent partners, voicelessness and powerlessness of women contribute towards their vulnerability. The Gaborone bridal shower twists in *go laya* – their subversive take towards culturally tolerated unfaithfulness of husbands; their insistence that the married woman must retain her voice and hold her husband accountable to faithfulness is a very important one in the HIV and AIDS context. While research has shown that married women tend to be more vulnerable to HIV infection than their single counterparts due to gender-based disempowerment (Browning, 2014) – Gaborone bridal showers insist that being a married Motswana woman should not translate into signing oneself to death due to tolerance for multiple-concurrent partners in her husband's life. In the Gaborone bridal showers *go laya*, a woman is counselled to hold a man accountable for his movements and must look out for signs of cheating. The teaching that *monna ga a botswe kwa a tswang* is not acceptable.

In addition, bridal showers discuss new topics that are not normally discussed in the cultural setting, namely sexuality and finances. On sexuality, they do not only discuss and exchange ideas about bedroom tactics, but they also encourage a woman to enjoy herself – as an active participant rather than only serving at the pleasure of her husband. In other words, "there is fun in marriage – sex is important for both and styles of doing sex are many", observed one participant. The subject of finances comes up several times in the content of Gaborone bridal showers. They encourage the woman to hold the husband accountable in the finances of the home, partly because the wife is herself a working woman who contributes to the family finances. This contribution of the woman becomes a lever for negotiating for more power, for the held that "women offer financial support in the family", which legitimates "equal partnership". Clearly the Gaborone bridal showers make great efforts to stand up to their desire to create a space of 'outright freedom" by rewriting gender roles – they underline that if a woman becomes a wife, she must be a free wife – a woman with a voice.

The in-between spaces of Gaborone bridal showers

Nonetheless, while the chapter may run the risk of sounding as if it was all subversive in the Gaborone bridal showers, and that the cultural counselling done in the villages and the Gaborone urban showers are two opposites, this should be best seen as a strategy of presentation. Just as they both take up the role of *go laya*, they overlap. Just because in the cultural setting they teach a woman to be docile does not necessarily mean she is not resisting patriarchy in some way. Consequently, there are two more perspectives from Gaborone bridal showers that need our brief attention:

1. those who stand in the in-between space, oscillating between the cultural end and the new boundaries created in the bridal shower, and
2. the skeptical and critical voices against the subversive twists of the bridal shower.

To start with those who stand in-between, they likely represent the majority, for by giving household gifts, most bridal showers somewhat embrace the construction of a woman, as one who belongs to the kitchen and manages the home. In the two-themed focus of this chapter's analysis, namely similarities and difference with *go laya* in the cultural space and changes brought by bridal showers; there were 46 answers altogether, five of which qualify as occupying in-between spaces. The latter perspective maintains a creative tension, oscillating between the cultural perspectives and the new ways inaugurated by urban bridal showers. So, concerning the theme of changes brought by bridal showers versus traditional ways, there were two answers that occupied this space. Here, the respondents held that, in Gaborone bridal showers a major change lies in opening an inclusive space for all women, but insisted that concerning the content of *go laya*, it is the same. On the question of "What roles have bridal showers changed or reproduced?" there were three out of 24 answers whose response took the in-between space. They insisted that in bridal showers it is taught that "women should hold men more accountable on their whereabouts, but in most cases roles do not change". This creative tension is perhaps best captured by the following response:

> [The] bride adopts new things during these showers. She learns about bedroom tactics. She is still the wife, but she has to take action in bed. Thus, her role is changed – no passivity now. She has to cook for him and take care of him as well. Traditional counselling speaks of the obvious roles, but we teach her to be a contemporary wife (take charge in the bedroom), but also to cook, iron, so that you (a wife) have the Setswana that is upgraded. In so doing we don't live like *makgoa* (white people). Women's roles have changed a bit. A woman is still a woman, but she should take charge a bit in finances. Women work and have money.

In-betweeners are go-betweeners – chameleons who change colours as they cross various boundaries to trick the system. They are not what they seem or say they are. They are tricksters (Dube, 2015:890-902; Dube, 2016b:54-75). Tricksters seek to subvert structures of power.

Hence these respondents repeatedly underline that she is still a wife, but her role has changed. If there is one thing in-betweeners surely attest to, it is the 'unsettling' power of the Gaborone bridal showers, as well as the unsettling power of persistent patriarchy.

Critical and sceptical voices within the Gaborone bridal showers

There are some participants who are critical and sceptical of the changes inaugurated by bridal showers. Their sympathies lie with the traditional ways of *go laya.* Again, when invited to speak of the differences and similarities, one respondent said apart from the inclusivity of the bridal showers, their content of *go laya* is the same as the cultural one. The second critical respondent did not appreciate that single women are allowed to participate in counselling, pointing out that "*kana* this person *o bua fela ga a na* evidence. You need to talk from experience" (8:34). Her main criticism of single people's participation in *go laya* is that they do not have the necessary experience to counsel the bride-to-be. Experience here is equated with married women's experience. Women in cohabitation, divorced ones and single women in other heterosexual relationships are dismissed.

Concerning the question about changes inaugurated by Gaborone bridal showers, there were several critical respondents. Out of the 24 answers, 10 denied that there were any significant changes introduced by bridal showers. Their answers to this question were characterised by 'none', 'not much' or '*go tshwana fela*' (i.e., it is just the same/they make no difference), and that there is 'no initiative' to bring change. Others asserted that "women should take care of their husbands; women are taught how to cook and to clean", while another held that "not much – women still must cook, take care of children and husband". Two respondents defended culture against the desire to seek change. She underlined: "We are where we are because of our culture. People (women) should humble themselves. People need to understand their purpose; you are a woman; he is a man." Dismissing the proposed changes as unpractical bookish feminist myths, another asserted that "most of the time we affirm cultural activities", while the rest is "*ke dilo tsa dibuka fela tsa bo tekatekanyo ya banna le basadi*" (8:36), that is, unproven feminist theories of equality. This respondent is backed by another who says, "*Ga rona fa ke ditoro*", that is, changes proposed in bridal showers are nothing but daydreams. For another respondent, the problem was that bridal showers do not have the last word; rather the latter lies with the elderly married women who will do *go laya* during the wedding day. She asserted: "None [no changes are made]. *Kana* here at the shower we can say what we want to say but *kwa ba ya go mo apesa kobo le sekopelo*, that is what is going to work in their home. *E bile kana monna wa laiwa, rona fa re laya mosadi fela.* This cannot work *ko lapeng.*"

These critical voices are a very important attestation to the unsettling of patriarchy in Gaborone bridal showers. The hard critic who says, "*ga rona ke ditoro fela*", namely that bridal showers teachings and activities are tantamount to daydreaming, desires to see change in the teaching and act of Gaborone bridal showers. She certainly does not like what she hears and what is happening in comparison with the cultural space of *go laya* – but her critical words attest to the 'unsettling of patriarchy', which she chooses to dismiss as mere daydreaming because it is too radical. So does the critic who says there is much bookish feminism which, according to her, is impracticable theory – "*ke dilo tsa dibuka fela tsa bo tekatekanyo ya banna le basadi*". Her comment testifies that the content of Gaborone bridal showers does upset the patriarchal status quo. It unsettles patriarchical ideology. The despair of the other critic is not the content itself, but rather that elderly married women will have the last word and even dress her up with the garb of married Motswana women (*baya go mo apesa kobo le sekopelo*), and that their words will prevail over the Gaborone bridal showers' subversive ways. Her comment does not deny that Gaborone bridal shower content and process unsettle patriarchical ideology. Although the elderly married will drill the bride in silence, her silence is not equal to compliance. In her paper, 'The Liberative Power of Silent Agency', Alice Yafeh-Deigh (2012) insists that we should be aware that there is silent agency, namely that subjects who remain silent without verbally expressing their dissent should not be taken to be unresisting subjects. Whether or not elderly married women's *go laya* overrides the words of urban showers is really a subject of another research, namely to evaluate the impact of Gaborone bridal showers on its recipients. A follow-up longitudinal study will be in order.

Conclusion

Our analysis of data from Gaborone bridal showers used theories of agency propounded by Avishai and Mahmood, drawn from religious women. They highlight "agency as resistance that might also appear as 'negotiation with oppressive social structures and partial compliance', thereby indicating that docility did not necessarily compromise agency" (Avishai, 2016:267). Bridal showers are undoubtedly about women encouraging and accompanying another woman to enter a very patriarchal institution, namely heterosexual marriage, so its agentic angle had to be examined carefully. The analysis of data asked the following questions from interview guides: How does *go laya* in the cultural setting and the urban-based bridal showers of Gaborone construct and deconstruct gender? How do they create new female spaces? How do the Gaborone bridal showers problematise gender? And how do they maintain the status quo while they are remaking their world? There are sufficient evidence-based conclusions that Gaborone bridal showers are unsettling patriarchical ideology. The context and content of the Gaborone bridal shower, with its insistence on 'outright freedom' and that every woman is welcome to talk regardless of age and marital status, creates an inclusive space that resists equating women's full humanity with heterosexual marriage. Even the most conservative voices acknowledged radical inclusivity as a change brought by Gaborone bridal showers in the *go laya* female space.

Content wise, evidence-based findings indicate iconoclastic twists in *go laya*, insisting that a married woman keep her voice, keep her friends, wear what she wants, hold the man financially accountable, insist on faithfulness, insist on shared household chores, watch out for intimate partner violence, enjoy her sexuality and pursue her profession. It is, therefore, not an exaggeration that Gaborone bridal showers are unsettling patriarchy. In their own words, they even refer to what they do as some form of feminism. For example, one respondent used the phrase "*Emang Basadi*" (literally meaning 'stand up, women'), which is the name of the Botswana national women's/feminist movement. Gaborone bridal showers also counteract poverty and contribute towards building justice-loving communities through their 'peaceful feminism'. By accompanying a young woman entering marriage materially and wisdom wise, they counteract poverty and lay foundation for a different family. A young woman starting a new family has household items for beginning a new home, including hard cash for other arising needs. In so doing, the Gaborone bridal showers generate *Botho/Ubuntu*-centred families and communities that are intolerant to injustice. Indeed, where *Botho/Ubuntu* exists there should not be discrimination and oppression. The Gaborone bridal showers practically demonstrate feminist perspectives of *Botho/Ubuntu* as the understanding that equates one's human identity with the capacity to respect, welcome, care for and empower the other.

References

Adichie, C.N. 2014. *We should all be feminists*. London: Fourth Estate.

Avishai, O. 2016. 'Theorizing gender from religion cases: agency, feminist activism and masculinity'. *Sociology of Religion: A Quarterly Review*, 77(3):261-279. https://doi.org/10.1093/socrel/srw020

Browning, M. 2014. *Risky marriage: HIV and intimate relations in Tanzania*. New York: Lexington Books.

Buchanan, I. 2010. 'Agency'. In: *Dictionary of Critical Theory*. Oxford: Oxford University Press. 10-11.

Childers, J. & Gary H. 1995. 'Agent'. In: J. Childers & H. Gary (eds). *Columbia Dictionary of Modern Literary and Cultural Criticism*. New York: Columbia University Press. 6-7.

Dube, M.W. 2003. 'Culture, gender and HIV/AIDS: understanding and acting on the issues'. In: M.W. Dube (ed). *HIV/AIDS and the curriculum: methods of integrating HIV/AIDS in theological programmes*. Geneva: WCC. 84-100.

Dube, M.W. 2015. '*A luta continua*: towards trickster interllectuals and communities'. *Journal of Biblical Literature*, 134(4):890-902. https://doi.org/10.1353/jbl.2015.0049

Dube, M.W. 2016. 'Let there be Light! Birthing ecumenical theology in the HIV&AIDS apocalypse'. In: E. Chitando, E. Mombo & R.G. Gunda (eds). *That all may live: essays in honour of Nyambura J. Njoroge*. Bamberg, Germany: Bamberg University Press. 161-180. https://bit.ly/3ptaOfp

Dube, M.W. 2016a. 'The sub-altern can speak: reading the Mmutle way'. *Journal of Africana Studies*, 4(1):54-75. https://doi.org/10.5325/jafrireli.4.1.0054

Dube, M.W. 2017. 'Dinah (Genesis 34) at the contact zone: shall our sister become a whore?' In: J. Claassen & C. Sharp (eds). *Feminist frameworks*. London: T&T Clark. 39-57.

Dube, M.W. 2020. 'On becoming a change agent: journey of teaching gender and health in an African crisis context'. *Journal for Interdisciplinary Studies*, 2(1):13-28.

Dube, M.W., Gabaitse, R.M. & Kgalemang, M. 2021. '*Botho/Ubuntu* and "unsettling patriarchy": *go laya* in Gaborone bridal showers'. *Journal of the Interdenominational Theological Centre*, 50(Spring/Fall):1-45. https://bit.ly/3pIDeCb

Dube, M.W., Modie-Moroka, T., Setume, S.D., Ntloedibe, S., Kgalemang, M., Gabaitse, R.M., Madigele, T., Mmolai, S., Motswapong, E.P., Kebaneilwe, M. & Sesiro, D. 2016. '*Botho*, community building and gender constructions in Botswana'. *Journal of the Interdenominational Theological Centre*, 4(Spring):1-22.

Economic and Social Council. 2017. *Progress towards sustainable development goals*. June. New York: United Nations.

Ellece, S.E. 2007. 'Gendered marriage discourses in Botswana'. PhD thesis, Lancaster University, Lancaster, UK.

Gammage, S., Naila, K. & Van der Meulen Rodgers, Y. 2016. 'Voice and agency: where are we now?' *Feminist Economics*, 22(1):1-29. https://doi.org/10.1080/13545701.2015.1101308

Mann, S.A. 2012. *Doing feminist theory: from modernity to postmodernity*. Oxford: Oxford University Press.

Motswapong, E.P., Kebaneilwe, M.D., Madigele, T.J., Dube, M.W., Setume, S.D., Modie-Moroka, T. 2017. '"A little baby is on the way": *Botho/Ubuntu* and community building in Gaborone baby showers'. *Gender Studies: A Journal of West University of Timisoara*,

16(1):3-13. https://doi.org/10.2478/genst-2018-0006

Munyaka, M. & Motlhabi, M. 2009. '*Ubuntu* and its socio-moral significance'. Pietermaritzburg, South Africa: UKZN Press. 63-84.

NACA. 2013. *Botswana AIDS Impact Survey 2013*. Gaborone: Ministry of Health.

SADC (Southern African Development Community). 2012. 'Gender protocol barometer Botswana'. *Gender Links*. https://bit.ly/42AyNb9

Setume, S.D., Gabaitse, R.M., Dube, M.W., Kgalemang, M., Modie-Moroka, T., Madigele, T., Kebaneilwe, M.D., Motswapong, E.P. & Matebekwane, A.K.M. 2017. 'Exploring the concept of *Botho/Ubuntu* through bridal showers in the urban space in Gaborone, Botswana'. *Managing Development in Africa*, 2(3):173-191.

Yafeh-Deigh, A. 2012. 'The liberative power of silent agency: a postcolonial afro-feminist-womanist reading of Luke 10:38-44'. In: M.W. Dube, A. Mbuvi & D. Mbuwayesango (eds). *Postcolonial perspectives on African biblical interpretations*. Atlanta: SBL. 417-440.

5

REPRODUCING OR CREATING A NEW MALE?

Bridal showers in the urban space in Botswana

Abstract

Each society has specific constructed images of acceptable maleness and femaleness, and these constructions can happen within social groups that share a common identity and purpose such as bridal showers.[1] This chapter[2] is based on findings of a research conducted by women researchers from the University of Botswana,[3] who sought to explore how the African philosophy of *Botho/Ubuntu* is manifested through bridal showers in the urban space in Botswana.[4] Although masculinities were not necessarily part of our main objective for carrying out the study, it was nevertheless one of the themes that emerged. Bridal showers are gendered spaces where masculinities – old, new and in competition – are constructed, reproduced and questioned. This chapter, therefore, seeks to establish whether bridal showers reinforce or reproduce hegemonic masculinities or whether they offer space to construct newer forms of masculinities. The analysis of the data is guided by feminist theories of power and masculinity studies globally.

Introduction

Although bridal showers are not indigenous to Batswana, women in Botswana have embraced them as part of their subculture. While the main purpose of bridal showers

1 A bridal shower is a pre-wedding party held in honour of a bride-to-be mainly to give her presents before her wedding. Bridal showers have their roots in Western culture. Our findings reveal that bridal showers gained popularity in Botswana in the 1990s through American television programmes.

2 The article, 'Reproducing or creating a new male: bridal showers in the urban space of Botswana' by Gabaitse, R.M. et al., was first published in 2018 in *Journal of Gender and Religion in Africa*, 24(1). It is republished in this volume with permission.

3 The research was sponsored by the Nagel Institute in America. Apart from bridal showers, it also focused on baby showers, and Naomi/Laban showers, which we discuss in separate chapters.

4 *Botho/Ubuntu* refers to "an African philosophy that places emphasis on being human through other people" (Tutu, 1999). Ubuntu/Botho embraces values of caring, generosity and sharing, respect and mutual existence. Botho is revered in Africa and Botswana as an indigenous 'text' and as a value system. *Botho/Ubuntu* has been expressed as 'I in You and You in I', 'I am because we are', and 'I exist because you exist'.

might be to shower brides-to-be with gifts, they achieve more than that.[5] They provide spaces for women to talk among themselves and forge friendships. For the purposes of this chapter, bridal showers are gendered spaces where masculinities, old, new and in competition are constructed, reproduced and questioned. The media, church, sports and men are actively engaged in constructing masculinities. Bridal showers demonstrate that women are actively engaged in shaping, co-producing, normalising and even fetishising masculinities (Talbot & Quayle, 2010:256). The existence of any form of masculinity needs women's approval, encouragement, endorsement and performance. In all the showers we attended, women emphasised during *go laya*[6] that understanding what a man is, his ego, sexual needs, and understanding his role as the head of the household, were important. When the women devoted much of their time discussing these aspects about a man, they were actively shaping and co-producing and co-creating some form of masculinity. Therefore, women are not just 'consumers' of masculinities. But which masculinities are reproduced, negotiated or even constructed in the bridal shower space in Gaborone, if any?

Methodology

The study followed a cross-sectional survey design, supported by a combination of qualitative and quantitave data collection instruments/techniques.[7] The data were collected using a triangulation of one-to-one in-depth interviews, open-ended

5 Bridal showers have been used to raise funds to be used for necessities on the day of the wedding, such as paying for the venue of the wedding and for food.

6 *Go laya* is a Setswana word that means to give advice on good and acceptable behaviour. However, its meaning is deeper. It is a lifelong process of giving sets of rules that govern good behaviour in order to avoid bad and unacceptable behaviour. It is also a rite, a counselling process, and a form of socialisation where expectations and attitudes are communicated. It usually happens during some form of transition, such as children growing up, transitioning from childhood to teenagedom, during the transition from singledom to marriage, following the death of a loved one, when one enters university, when a person starts a new job, among others. In the contexts of marriage and bridal showers, it is a cultural process, a ritual, a ceremony, where only married women intentionally come together in one place in the 10s and 20s, gather around the bride, and give her advice on marriage. During *go laya*, no chairs are allowed; all women sit on the floor of a house veranda or a private room with outstretched legs, wearing traditional dresses with headscarves and shawls around their shoulders. The bride is dressed in traditional attire too, and sits in the middle with her head bowed. She does not say anything except to nod her head occasionally when asked if she understands the advice given.

Bridal showers have adopted *go laya*, but in a more relaxed manner. *Go laya* assumes different shapes depending on the bridal shower; however, it is never scripted and it is spontaneous as women stand up and talk freely to the bride about topics such as how to treat her husband and in-laws, money and sex, among other matters. In the context of this chapter, *go laya* is critical for the construction of masculinities because it is through this process that patriarchal prerogatives and gender stereotypes are communicated to the bride. Unfortunately, since we did not want to interrupt the flow of the bridal showers, we never got to get the ages and educational qualifications of all the women who were engaged in this process. However, from the demographics, we know that the bridal shower attendees were mostly younger than 40 years of age.

7 This was largely qualitative research with the quantitative aspect used for demographics.

questionnaire, participant observation, field notes, audio and video recordings, and informal focus groups discussions. In addition to these 'social science approved' methods, we obtained massive data on masculinities through the session on *go laya.*

The study was conducted among women over a period of 15 months, focusing on Gaborone, the capital city of Botswana, following arrangements to carry out the research. We applied for ethical clearance from the University of Botswana and the government of Botswana. The participants were selected by way of purposive availability sampling. We made randomised calls to numbers on the publicised list from the marriage registry at the District Commissioner's office and churches, and accompanied those who accepted our requests to research during their showers. Some brides-to-be invited us after we made announcements on Facebook and radio about our research intentions. Whenever we attended a shower, one of us introduced the study objectives, research ethics and methods at length. The women asked questions for clarity, after which they gave us permission to carry out the research, record and audiotape conversations in writing and signing consent forms. Since issues of confidentiality and anonymity are critical in research, we assured the respondents that we will quote them verbatim in our analysis, but we will not disclose their real identities.

We attended 14 bridal showers, distributed self-administered questionnaires and received 110 of them back. One hundred women volunteered for one-to-one in-depth interviews. In total, 40 interviews were conducted. Of the women who participated in our study, 90.4% fell within the 20–40 age groups, while 9.6% fall within the 41–45 bracket, which means the bridal showers were attended by young people according to the Botswana standards. The women's educational qualifications ranged from Form 5 certificates to PhD, with many women holding bachelor's degrees. We used both Setswana (the local language) and English during our research. Digressions from English to Setswana happened and it is normal in Botswana for speakers to mix English and Setswana in their conversations. The data collected through tape recorders were transcribed as accurately as possible, pausing where the respondents paused and leaving some sentences incomplete as they left them. We tried as much as possible to capture the laughs, the giggles, and the hesitancy in answering questions because these are also forms of communication and form part of a greater narrative about womanhood and manhood in Botswana. We use verbatim quotations from our participants interspersed throughout the chapter and they are in italics. The numbers in brackets at the end of each indicate the shower number. If the quotations have a mix of both English and Setswana, and the Setswana bits are short, we interpret those parts within the quotations. If the quotations in Setswana are longer, we provide a full translation in English in the footnotes.

The bridal shower

A month or two before the day of the bridal shower, the chief organiser contacts the close friends and relatives of the bride-to-be, who form an organising committee. With almost all the showers, the organisers used social media, especially WhatsApp, to communicate among themselves in addition to sending invitations to guests stating the date, venue, time of the bridal shower and the 'gate pass'; the gate pass is a small gift, such as a litre of juice, a dish cloth, or liquid soap, which all guests are expected to bring for them to be admitted into the bridal shower venue. The organisers agree on the amount of money they have to contribute in order to buy the bride-to-be gifts and food for the day. We observed that the organisers' monetary contribution, the kind of gifts the bride-to-be receives, and number of guests was guided by her wish list, status, and network of friends and relatives, hence the number of attendants differed in each context.

On the day of the bridal shower, women arrive at different times to a well-decorated venue with food and drinks prepared by the organisers beforehand. The women socialise in small groups, before the director of ceremony takes over and informs them of the programme for the day. Generally, the programme for the day involves opening prayer, introductions of each participant and their relationship to the bride-to-be, games such as, 'what is under my skirt' and 'how well do you know the bride-to-be?' When women are settled, the important businesses of the day, which are *go laya* and presenting the bride-to-be with gifts begin. The attendees who are single, married or divorced are given an opportunity to stand up and give advice to the bride-to-be. Each woman is free to give advice on any theme/topic, such as money, intimacy, how to treat their in-laws and entertainment, to name a few. There is no time allocated and women speak for as long as they are comfortable, with occasional interjections from other women. This process is taken seriously and is never rushed. In some showers, the organisers invite married women who have close connection with the bride-to-be to *go laya* (advise) her before all other invited guests do so. In all the showers, the keynote speakers were married women in their forties. When *go laya* is complete, the bride-to-be is presented with her gifts after which the women eat together, engage in conversation or dance until late.

Gender: masculinities and femininities

Masculinities and femininities are central aspects of gender performance, and how they function must be understood within the gender spectrum.[8] Raewyn Connell

8 Talbot, K. & Quayle, M. 2010. 'The perils of being a nice guy: contextual variation in five young women's constructions of acceptable hegemonic masculinities'. *Men and Masculinities*, 13(2): 255-278.

(2005:829-859) identifies four types of masculinities, namely hegemonic, subordinate, marginalised and complicit. This chapter largely references the hegemonic type because it is the dominant, idealised, culturally privileged and socially accepted version of masculinity. It is often manifested through the domination of women, children and other men who perform other masculinities (ibid.). The hegemonic masculinity framework elevates males to a status higher than that of females. Males are privileged as leaders; strong, powerful and devoid of emotions. In addition, males should distance themselves from what is considered feminine and instead practise aggression, risk taking and high sexual energy (Fausto-Sterling, 2010).

Within this spectrum, gender is understood as "a set of socially constructed relationships which are produced and reproduced through people actions" (Gerson & Peiss, 1985:327). In addition, 'gender' refers to the assigning of roles, attitudes, traits and behaviours that emphasise difference between males and females.[9] Scholars of gender studies argue that women and men are born, but females and males are created and constructed through social interactions. Awareness of the social constructed-ness of gender assists in understanding that femininity and masculinity, the terms that denote one's gender, refer to a complex set of characteristics and behaviours that are prescribed for a particular sex by a society and learned through the socialisation process (Peterson & Runyan, 1993:17).

Thus, through the socialisation process, boys and men are conditioned to be males and girls and women are conditioned to be female. Boys and men learn acceptable ways of being a male through proverbs, music, imitation, and role-playing (Dube, 2003). The community, family, media, friends, government systems, men and women are all involved in teaching boys to be males and girls to be females. These institutions constantly weave norms of behaviour, attitudes, expectations, and culture typical of and ascribed to male and female within a society (Connell, 2005). This process never stops; it continues even when men are grown because manhood evolves and social groups such as bridal showers are constantly constructing images of an ideal male.

Masculinities and bridal showers in Gaborone

There are three main responses or attitudes towards hegemonic masculinity that emerge from bridal showers in Gaborone which, in this chapter, we refer to as types or forms of masculinities. However, in one bridal shower, some women affirmed one or two forms of masculinities at the same time, holding them in tension and contradictions. In the following section we discuss the different forms of masculinities emerging out of bridal shower narratives.

9 Hughes, M. & Paxton, P. 2014. *Women, Politics and Power: A Global Perspective*. London: Sage. 24.

Conformity to hegemonic masculinity

Some women conform and reproduce Botswanan hegemonic masculinities as the idealised form of masculinity.[10] Here, heterosexual males are elevated and celebrated as heads of households and in charge of economic and spiritual success of the home. This group of women endorses hegemonic masculinity as *normal*, because it is *our tradition* and *the way we have been doing things* (Keynote speaker 9). Other women who challenged hegemonic masculinity were accused of being *modernised* and betraying Setswana cultural norms where *mosadi remains under the authority of the man* (Keynote speaker 5).[11] Hegemonic masculinities are reproduced in two main ways during bridal showers. First, the bride-to-be is instructed in the art of submission towards her husband and second, the bride-to-be is domesticated through the gifting process. We will discuss these in turn.

Reproducing hegemonic masculinity through submission

One of the recurring themes within the bridal showers is that the bride-to-be must submit to her husband's *leadership and vision* because he is the *head of the household*, and the wife is *molala* (the neck).

> He is the head – he comes with the vision, your job is to pray and support him. Sometimes you should be silent. Be careful when and how to speak ... Career; even if you succeed, don't ever think you cease to be submissive to him. He remains the head and father of the house. Don't ever think you are equal. He is not your business associate. (Keynote speaker 4)

> *Tiro ya mosadi is to help – ke molala hubby ke tlhogo*[12] ... but finances are controlled by wife; women must be in charge of her sexuality. A man comes with a vision and a woman implements it. (Keynote speaker 5)

10 Most of the women who attended bridal showers were young, educated and financially independent. We had expected more latitude with questioning hegemonic masculinities, but they still spoke of the man as the provider, as though women's salaries are not useful in the household. It is possible that they were perfoming a public transcript because of the presence of the researchers. However, because of the carefree natures of bridal showers, this is unlikely. If the women could talk about their sexual encounters, their experiences of drinking too much and not remembering what they did the night before in our presence, then they should not have difficulties discussing their beliefs about masculinities.

11 '*Mosadi*' means female, woman or wife.

12 Translation: "The job of the wife is to help. She is the neck and the husband is the head. But finances are controlled by the wife; women must be in charge of their sexuality. The man comes with a vision and the woman implements it." This extractly demonstrates the inconsistency between belief and practice.

The respondent believes that the husband is the head of the household, suggesting that he should be in charge of the finances and his wife's sexuality, yet in the same sentence, she says that the wife has control over the family finances and owns her sexuality. Control of wealth and female sexuality by husbands is important in maintaining hegemonic masculinity. If the wife has power to control these, the headship of a man is useless. Whether this plays out in marriages exactly as it is said in bridal showers needs another chapter and research. But it may demonstrate that although hegemonic masculinity requires male dominance and female submission, women are not as powerless within

The above quotations endorse husbands as visionaries in the home; the role of the wife as the *helper*, as *molala* (neck), is to honour the husband's leadership through submission, silence and prayer. The bride-to-be is cautioned that a well-paying job does not make her equal to her husband because the husband is not a *business associate*, but the head of the household. If she has to speak, she must be careful *when and how she speaks*, because silence is a marker of submission, but also a strategy of maintaining one's home by allowing a man to be a man. The bride-to-be's mode of operation in affirming hegemonic masculinity is silence. She has to be silent, even if she is not clear of her husband's whereabouts. Instead, she should just submit to him through sex, even if *she has a headache*.

> *Gape monna ga a bodiwe gore o tswa kae monna, o tshwanetse gore ere ha a batla ... waitse gore ke bua ka eng akere, o seka wa re tlhogo e a opa jaaka mme a ne a bua, mo neele di tsa gagwe ka nako tsotlhe.* (Shower 5)[13]

James Amanze, writing within the context of Botswana, states that "if a wife asks the husband where he has been, it is a sign of disrespect" (Amanze, 2002:184), and some women endorse this characteristic of hegemonic masculinity. Therefore, the silent and submissive wife, the husband as the head of the household whose whereabouts cannot be questioned, and the affirmation of his high sexual libido are all markers of hegemonic masculinity in Botswana, and this masculinity is affirmed and reproduced by women in the bridal showers in the urban space.

Reproducing hegemonic masculinity through the domestication of the bride-to-be

The second way in which hegemonic masculinity is reproduced in bridal showers is through the gifting process, which entrenches female domesticity. The bride-to-be's gifts consisted of household items such as pots, plates, microwave ovens and bed sheets. In the Botswana context, the home is the domain of women, and the girl child is socialised from a very young age to emulate her mother in taking care of domestic chores, such as cleaning the house and sweeping the yard (Dube, 2003). Bridal showers solidify and confirm the bride-to-be's understanding of her domestic responsibilities; she will cook and clean for her family. Through the gifts the bride-to-be receives, the house is thoroughly feminised (Williams, 1995). This entrenches female domesticity in as much as it safeguards hegemonic masculinity, which thrives on demarcating spaces for men and women.

relationships. This ambiguity and contradiction are a demonstration of cognitive dissonance at its best.

13 Translation: A husband's whereabouts should not be questioned ... but when he comes home you give him sex. You do know what I mean right? Don't say you have a headache; give him sex when he wants.

> Put your house in order since you are the chief of the house[14] ... Let your house be clean at all times, be patient with your husband, even when he's messing up the house, make sure it's always clean ... take care of your husband's dressing, making sure that his clothes are neat and ironed ... be in charge of the cooking and cleaning of the house. (Shower 3)[15]

Whether the domestic role of the wife is exaggerated and does not mirror reality is not much of a concern at this moment. What is critical is what the exaggeration achieves; the absent groom and the bride-to-be are taught to draw boundaries of what is feminine and to respect boundaries that emphasise the masculine so that hegemonic masculinity is preserved.[16] Therefore, endorsing the submission of the wife to the husband and entrenching female domesticity are the two main ways in which hegemonic masculinity is entrenched by women's narratives within bridal showers in Gaborone.

Subversive masculinities

The second narratives of women within bridal showers endorsed subversive masculinities that challenge gendered social hierarchies perpetuated through hegemonic masculinities. The masculinities produced here emphasise mutuality and egalitarian existence between husbands and wives. The following verbatim quotations capture these constructions. We use several of them in order to allow the women to 'speak' for themselves as well as to capture their depths and intensity:

> Yes, at times the bride-to-be is advised to demand that the husband must share roles. (Keynote speaker 6)
>
> In villages they advice that monna ke selepe – this is not said in urban setting- where people do not believe this. (Keynote speaker 4; see also Keynote speakers 5, 6, 8 and 9)[17]
>
> Times have changed. House chores are now 50/50 for men and women. Demand to share household chores. (Keynote speaker 4)

14 Being the chief of the house in its own way explodes the very rhetoric of hegemonic masculinity, where women are perceived as powerless.

15 One of the recurring themes in the bridal showers is how the wife needs to take care not only of the house, but of the husband as well (get Vaseline and apply it to his lips, upgrade his hygienic status, buy him new stuff, pick up his clothes when they are lying on the floor, etc). This is ironic; it seems the husband/male is disorganised, chaotic, cannot dress himself and cannot take care of himself. He is not so much in control and the wife should take control of his life, yet he is supposed to be the head of the household, coming up with a vision. Isn't a hegemonic male supposed to preserve his own status? Does this chaotic man deserve the high status that the women give him?

16 These are the women who have professions, and it can be exhausting and unrealistic for women to do the household chores on a daily basis after a full day's work. Yet, it seems this is a reality for some women in this community.

17 Translation: In the village, they advise that a man is an axe. This is not said in the urban setting, where people do not believe this.

> Women are empowered: be the women you want to be; women now can work and can have same status as men. (Keynote speaker 5)

> We say you are going to work on the 9 to 5 pm job, you need to ask your man *gore o tswa kae* (where he comes from), we do not see a relationship unlike *bogologolo* (in the old times) where you kept quiet, also as the breadwinner of the family, you need to know *gore o tswa kae* (where he comes from) and everything. We also advise the bride that her husband should assist with the children. You need a time off as a wife ... so we definitely do change the roles here and there. Help the wife with the kids, clean the dishes, *o feele* because *lotlhe le tswa ko tirong* (husband and wife sweep the floor), you are both tired, since you are both coming from work, you must take turns in doing household chores. (Keynote speaker 4)

> Men in towns are held accountable by their women. Women expect their men to participate in household chores. They carry babies around. Look around and see how men take babies to clinics etc. (Keynote speaker 5)

> ...work together as a team and contribute towards the upbringing of a healthy and happy family ... you have to be transparent to each other; you should know the salary of your partner and know the expenses. (Keynote speaker 3)

We can draw several conclusions about the masculinity celebrated in this group. First, the demand is on husbands to cross gender boundaries and participate in what are generally characterised as feminine roles, such as cleaning the house and taking care of the children. Second, this kind of masculinity demands fidelity and accountability from husbands. Men are expected to be faithful to their wives in order to preserve their health and minimise chances of contracting sexually-transmitted infections and HIV. Language that encourages husbands to have multiple partners in order to prove their manhood is rejected.[18] During one of the off-camera conversations, some women articulated the importance of language in shaping masculinities. One of them argued that women create dogs out of their husbands by consistently naming them *dogs*, *axes* and *gourds*.[19] She said that men behave like dogs because they know that is what is expected from them anyway. She concluded the conversation by saying, "*my husband is not a dog*". Third, the proposed masculinity demands transparency between wives and husbands. Hence this masculinity thrives on mutuality and equal existence between spouses towards building a healthy and happy home. Fourth, this masculinity affirms female libido and sexual desire. The following extracts are profound in celebrating female sexuality:

18 These women reject sayings such as *monna ke selepe* (a man is an axe), which means, like an axe that cuts many trees, a man can be shared by many women. These women deconstruct male promiscuity by rejecting language that normalises male promiscuity.

19 There are sayings making rounds in Botswana, such as *monna ke ntsa* (a man is a dog), *monna ke phafana* (a man is a gourd). These sayings normalise male promiscuity (Gabaitse, 2012; Dube, 2003; Mookodi, 2000).

> There is fun in marriage. Sex is important for both, and styles of doing sex are many. I don't think these things are said in the village. (Keynote speaker 5)
>
> It's okay to ask for sex whenever you want it as much as your husband may ask for it. Also avoid going to bed with your clothes on. (Keynote speaker 3)
>
> Taking a bath with your husband is very good because you can continue the fun all the way from the bathroom to the bedroom. (Keynote speaker 3)

The bride-to-be is encouraged to seduce her husband; to give and demand sexual pleasure, because she is a sexual being. Not only is the recognition of female libido subversive, but women discussing sexual desire in Botswana in a public gathering cross boundaries of traditional hegemonic masculinities, because "sex talk is masculinized" (Montemurro et al., 2015:139). Yet, this kind of masculinity unambiguously acknowledges that women are sexual beings and should participate together with their husbands in creating a conducive atmosphere for the enjoyment of sex. Lastly, this new masculinity encourages a new male to be in touch with his emotions and to be available and present for his wife – *men must be friends and mates of the wife* (Keynote speaker 7). Friendship demands companionship, intimacy, dependability and care, and this encourages egalitarian existence.

Fractured and complicit masculinities

The third type of masculinity that emerges from bridal showers in Gaborone demonstrates that masculinities are fractured, forever shifting and full of ambiguities (Suttner, 2009). The new kind of male constructed by the narratives here has one foot in the world of hegemonic masculinity and the other foot in some kind of counter-hegemonic masculinity, giving way to complicit masculinity. Complicit masculinity is a form of masculinity in which a man does not fit into all the characteristics of hegemonic masculinity, but does not intentionally challenge hegemonic masculinity, because they look the part of fitting into hegemonic masculinity (Connell, 2005:79, 82).

Such men "enjoy and reap the hegemonic masculinities' dividends" (Connell, 2005: 116), and so they are not bothered to actively and overtly challenge it, although they do not subscribe to most of its characteristics. The ambiguities and ambivalence in the women's weaving of this masculinity comes from the resentment and defiance towards hegemonic masculinity, while they are still guarding and endorsing it. Our data are littered with numerous ambiguous articulations of this masculinity:

> Don't be a silent woman. I think also that's why I love bridal showers ... there's a bit of feminism ... the peaceful feminism ... there's nothing wrong with your husband hiding money from you, but you as a wife you don't need to attack him, you can humble yourself ... you are not against him.[20] (Keynote speaker 4)

20 Do not be silent as women. Bridal showers encourage a bit of peaceful feminism, an encouraging sort of feminism, the kind that does not encourage women to be against men. Even when the husbands

> Be a man, but not that kind of a man, be a contemporary man. Being a contemporary man doesn't mean you are weak. It means you know you are not *mo lenyalong ole one* (not alone in marriage), there is nothing wrong with the wife being dominant, a provider in the house, but as a woman, *ole ko* bridal shower (at the bridal shower) you know there is an aspect of pride, an ego and everything else *mo monneng* (in a man). You are giving him that pride and respect *le ha ele wena o tshwereng* the title of the provider in the house. (Allow him to be a proud man, respect his ego even if you are the provider in the home.) (Keynote speaker 4)

> At showers women encourage each other not to be docile; there is a bit of feminism. Bridal showers give the bride insight on how to do things – peaceful feminism. They conscientise each other of the men ego. (Keynote speaker 5)

> A woman is submissive, and a man is the leader of the house. But in the bridal showers, ladies advise the bride that she has the power to take care of her husband, meeting his basic needs ... I think so because with traditional *go laya* it says '*Tsoga o feele jarata*' (wake up and sweep the yard), whereas with showers it's 'Tsoga o lebege' (wake up and smarten yourself). So, there is an element of taking care of yourself as a woman but yet being submissive to your husband. (Keynote speaker 5)

On the surface, these extracts are subversive; the wife speaks, she is in control, she is assertive in demanding the right treatment from the husband; she is not silenced, and she is not docile. While the bride-to-be is advised to be assertive, the demand is on the husband to be a *contemporary man*. The *contemporary man* is the one who acknowledges that marriage is a *partnership*. He understands that *there is nothing wrong with the wife being dominant and a provider in the house*. This *contemporary man* engages in domestic duties such as *cleaning the dishes, feeding children and cooking*, yet these should not be expected from them because *men do it out of love and not expectation* (5). When asked if she will be comfortable finding her married brother washing the dishes, the young married woman in her late twenties with a university degree, who responded:

> I'd feel okay; yes ... [the yes is prolonged; she giggles and laughs here] especially because I'm the only girl *ko lapeng* (in my parents' house) so my brothers grew up helping me with the dishes. (Keynote speaker 4)

Another one in the same age group from another shower said:

> Husbands cook as well ... but when the mother is around, he doesn't do this (she giggles). (Keynote speaker 5)

Here lie the contradictions: the wife can assert herself, however, subversiveness is contradicted in the same breath, within the same conversation. The bride-to-be has to engage in *peaceful feminism*, where she must constantly be mindful of the *male's*

hide the money from the wife, the wife will not attack the husband, but the wife humbles herself as she asks the husband about it so that the husband does not feel attacked.

ego and *pride*. Maintenance of male ego, pride and encouraging women to be demure keep hegemonic masculinity flourishing. Husbands can participate in domestic roles, yet they cannot do so in the presence of their mothers, for the latter are guardians of traditional norms. The giggles from our respondents communicate discomfort and the tensions surrounding the performance of this kind of masculinity, because it is under surveillance from family members such as mothers-in-law and married female relatives. While some women desire the performance of this egalitarian masculinity, they as the weavers and custodians of masculinities discourage its performance in the presence of family members in order to maintain their husbands' status as 'real' men. The men are happy to pretend to subscribe to hegemonic masculinity by avoiding 'feminine' roles when their mothers are around. The tensions between daughters and mothers-in-law are discussed in the Naomi/Laban showers, covered in Part 2 in Chapters 7, 8 and 9.

Discussion of findings

Bridal showers reinforce hegemonic masculinities as much as they construct and nurture other forms of counter hegemonic masculinity. However, the subversive and fractured/complicit masculinity narratives, which are less rigid operate within the hegemonic masculinity framework in their failure to unreservedly denounce it. The subversive masculinity narratives dismiss most characteristics of hegemonic masculinity. The new man constructed by these narratives ideally values equality, mutuality, coexistence and faithfulness within marriage. However, the construction of this masculinity is negotiated within the hegemonic masculinity paradigms. While there is a demand for partnership and equal sharing of roles, the gifts from the women who produced this masculinity did not reflect that. Instead of presenting the bride-to-be with a mix of kitchen and farm equipments such as wheelbarrows and shovels to change the narrative of domesticity communicated by the gifting process within bridal showers, these women did not do that. In addition, while the bride-to-be is advised to be proactive on issues of romance and seduction, the counsel is partly driven by the need to ensure that the husband will not have extramarital affairs. In so doing, they still entrench narratives of hegemonic masculinity that affirm men's high sexual energy, which needs to be contained by the wife and not by him. They also embrace an unhealthy ideology of blaming women; that is, when the husband cheats, the wife is supposedly failing to contain her husband's libido. This pits women against each other as rivals who seduce each other's husbands. It normalises male infidelity, because men are perceived as helpless victims of their own actions.

Finally, the third narrative endorses hegemonic masculinity through ambivalence. Men and women are demanded to dismiss hegemonic masculinity, while they still subscribe to and honour it. Clearly, the women destabilise most of the brutal characteristics of hegemonic masculinity, such as male infidelity and violence against women. However, pressure to conform to dominant norms of traditional Botswana masculinity renders performance of this masculinity challenging. The construction of the *contemporary man* within this group of women demonstrates that masculinities are ever-changing, and men can subscribe to different forms of masculinities at the same time.

In conclusion, bridal showers destabilise the performance of hegemonic masculinities. Although they have not produced a clear and unambiguous new masculinity without traces of qualities of hegemonic masculinity, the subversiveness of the second and third narratives constructing newer masculinities should be celebrated. Bridal showers offer a space for conversations to nurture these subordinate masculinities going forward. The conversations demonstrate that a change in social norms, mind-sets, language and more needs to take place for these masculinities to be entrenched in schools, churches and society as a whole. Bridal showers have the potential to transform and influence the construction of less rigid masculinities where violence against women and children, male infidelity and homophobia is not tolerated. The construction of these masculinities goes a long way in influencing religious communities' construction of maleness, which currently focuses on the supremacy of the male, instead of equality between men and women. This could form part of the religious groups' premarital counselling in the future. It is already evident in very small ways within bridal showers as the Bible is used to instruct young women to know that God desires partnership in marriage using such text as Genesis 3. Contrary to the popular reading that blames Eve for causing Adam to sin, the keynote speaker in bridal shower 4, for example, stated that the text can be used to demonstrate that Adam and Eve were partners who influenced each other in eating the forbidden fruit. The texts can teach modern families that women and men can listen to each other and exist as partners. In addition, we have already presented some of the data to the churches and government in an effort to transform policies and mindsets about unhealthy masculinities and as a way of sharing our findings with communities outside the academy.

References

Connell, R.W. 2003. 'Masculinities, change and conflict in global society: thinking about the future of men's studies'. *Journal of Men's Studies*, 11(3): 249-266. https://doi.org/10.3149/jms.1103.249

Connell, R.W. 2005. *Masculinities*. Berkeley, CA: University of California Press.

Connell, R.W. & Messerschmidt, J.W. 2005. 'Hegemonic masculinity: rethinking the concept'. *Gender and Society*, 19(6):829-859. https://doi.org/10.1177/0891243205278639

Dube, M.W. 2003. 'Culture, gender and HIV/AIDS: understanding and acting on the issues'. In: M.W. Dube (ed). *HIV/AIDS and the curriculum: methods of integrating HIV/AIDS in theological programmes*. Geneva: WCC. 84-100.

Fausto-Sterling, A. 2010. *Sexing the body: gender politics and the construction of sexuality*. New York: Basic books.

Gabaitse, R. 2012. 'Passion killings in Botswana: masculinity at crossroads'. In: E. Chitando & S. Chirongoma (eds). *Redemptive masculinities: men, HIV and religion*. Geneva: WCC. 305-312.

Gabaitse, R.M., Setume, S., Dube, M., Lefa, M., Kgalemang, M., Madigele, T. & Modie, T. 2018. 'Reproducing or creating a new male? bridal showers in the urban space of Botswana'. *Journal of Gender and Religion in Africa*, 24(1): 79-95. https://doi.org/10.14426/ajgr.v24i1.42

Gerson, J.M. & Peiss, K. 1985. 'Boundaries, negotiation, consciousness: reconceptualizing gender relations'. *Social Problems*, 32(4):317-331. https://doi.org/10.2307/800755

Hughes, M. & Paxton, P. 2014. *Women, politics and power: a global perspective*. London: Sage. https://doi.org/10.4135/9781452275482

Montemurro, B., Bartasavich J. & Wintermute, L. (eds). 2015. 'Let's (not) talk about sex: the gender of sexual discourse'. *Sexuality and Culture*, 19(1):139-156. https://doi.org/10.1007/s12119-014-9250-5

Mookodi, G. 2004. 'Male violence against women in Botswana: discussion of gender uncertainties in a rapidly changing environment'. *African Sociological Review*, 8(1):118-138. https://doi.org/10.4314/asr.v8i1.23240

Peterson, V.S. & Runyan, A. 1993. *Global gender issues*. Oxford: Westview Press.

Talbot, K. & Quayle, M. 2010. 'The perils of being a nice guy: contextual variation in five young women's constructions of acceptable hegemonic masculinities'. *Men and Masculinities*, 13(2):255-278. https://doi.org/10.1177/1097184X09350408

Tutu, D. 1999. *No future without forgiveness*. Doubleday: New York. https://doi.org/10.1111/j.1540-5842.1999.tb00012.x

Williams, C.L. 1995. *Still a man's world: men who do women's work*. Berkeley, CA: University of California Press. https://doi.org/10.1525/9780520915220

6

PATHWAYS TO SOCIAL CAPITAL AND THE *BOTHO/UBUNTU* ETHIC IN THE URBAN SPACE IN GABORONE, BOTSWANA

Abstract

Botswana has experienced rapid urbanisation and industrialisation since independence, with people consequently moving from the rural to the urban areas. The quality of family and peer relationships and the spirit of community have also deteriorated significantly over the years. However, few studies have investigated how people forge or reproduce significant values from the rural areas/traditional practices in the urban space. This study[1] investigated the *Botho/Ubuntu*-driven practices of building community in the urban space in the form of Naomi/Laban, bridal and baby showers in Gaborone. Showers are gendered celebrations organised by women for a mother or father, who will either receive a daughter- or a son-in-law; a woman who is engaged to be married, or one who is about to become a mother respectively. Themes such as social networks, social norms of mutuality, reciprocity, social support, collective efficacy, informal social control, mutual trust, empathy, and reciprocity appeared in the study. Results show that participation in the showers could bring satisfaction, improved social relations, and an increased sense of control and empowerment.

Introduction

The historical legacies of colonialism and slavery, colonisation and globalisation threatened the social and economic prowess of the developing world and negatively affected its populace (Rodney, 1981). The effects of rural-urban migration in Botswana have been well-documented (Brown, 1983; Mookodi, 2004; Schapera, 1939). Through the process of rural-urban migration, societies moved from reliance on the kinship system, mutual loyalty, and ascriptive values to a 'modern' mode of life characterised by marginalisation and exclusion. Rural-urban migration in Botswana started with the growth of the mining industry in South Africa (Schapera, 1939).

1 The article, 'Pathways to social capital and the *Botho/Ubuntu* ethic in the urban space in Gaborone, Botswana' by Modie-Moroka, T. et al., was first published in 2019 in *Global Social Welfare: Research, Policy and Practice*, 7:231-243. It is republished in this volume with permission.

When Botswana gained independence, the migration patterns redirected to urban places. Modernisation of the colonies was based on the notion that traditional societies impeded the process of developing efficient relations of production via a market. The modern state, with its cold, detached and indirect associations, would make market relationships possible. The rural family was seen as multi-functional and responsible for reproduction, emotional support, production (usually on the family farm but not for profit), education (usually through informal parental socialisation), welfare (care of the elderly, disabled and sick), and religion (usually ancestral veneration). It is accepted that most of the community-building activities are lost in the urban space. However, few studies have investigated how people forge or reproduce significant values from the rural areas/traditional practices in the urban space. The question of how these female-centred movements express the *Botho/Ubuntu* ethic; construct and reconstruct gender, as well as articulate an African acculturated Christianity were best highlighted in this chapter by a collection of data from the field.

The project sought to investigate how the *Botho/Ubuntu*-driven practices of building community are expressed in the urban space in the form of Naomi/Laban, bridal and baby showers. These showers are gendered celebrations organised by women, for a mother or father who will either receive a daughter or son-in-law; for a female who is engaged to be married or one who is about to become a mother respectively. The showers have become a standard female-centred practice in Botswana's significant cities expressing the *Botho/Ubuntu* ethic and spirituality in urban areas. Botswana cities are a result of rural-urban migration, where the community spirit can give way to individualism and pockets of dehumanising poverty. The objectives of the *Botho/Ubuntu* research were to explore and examine the theological and spiritual base of *Botho/Ubuntu* values/ethics; how the *Botho/Ubuntu* ethic is understood and manifested in traditional Botswana communities; to analyse how the *Botho/Ubuntu* ethic is expressed in urban settings of Botswana, and to investigate how *Botho/Ubuntu* activities in the urban space construct and deconstruct gender. The project was intended to highlight further how *Botho/Ubuntu* spirituality can inform the building and maintenance of justice-loving communities. The chapter uses data collected in Gaborone throughout six months, using both qualitative and quantitative methods of inquiry.

Methodology

The study combined both quantitative and qualitative methods of inquiry. The study first carried out secondary desktop analysis and, second, conducted fieldwork-based research. The last two objectives were constituted by the analysis of the findings. The quantitative approach of the study was used to explain the relationship between the central study variables, such as socio-demographic characteristics, and *Botho/Ubuntu* and other participants' behaviours at showers. Quantitative data were collected through a self-administered questionnaire from individuals who were attending the different showers. The qualitative approach enabled the researcher to solicit in-depth descriptions, explanations, and narrations of the experiences of the respondents as regards the *Botho/Ubuntu* ethic and other behaviours at showers. Qualitative methods emphasise naturalistic, interpretative, phenomenological methods and data collection and analysis (Creswell, 1994) and are concerned with learning from people's perspective, the point of view, vision, and reality of the world. Qualitative methods are based on the belief that people are capable of experiences, reflection, and formulation of thought. The qualitative data methods helped enrich the variables under study by linking them to specific case histories, incidents and observations and the meanings attached to those observations.

The interactive nature of variables necessitated a combination of quantitative and qualitative methods of inquiry for cross-fertilisation and to allow the strengths of one method to compensate the other. Mixed methods are the third research movement, a movement that offers a logical and practical alternative (Creswell, 2007; Johnson & Onwuegbuzie, 2004; Mertens, 2010; Creswell, 2009; Tashakkori & Teddlie, 1998). The themes were captured by the words of the participants, hence helping to illuminate the central issues. In this chapter, exact quotations were used to maximise understanding of the respondent's experiences. Qualitative content analysis of the interviews revealed concepts important for understanding the experiences of showers attendees. Conclusions were then drawn based on this analysis.

Procedures

Ethical approval for the study was obtained from the University of Botswana Internal Review Board (UB IRB). The UB IRB analysed the proposal and determined whether it was fit for the study to be conducted, looking at the different aspects of the proposal. Informed consent to take part in the study was obtained from each participant. The researchers made sure that every participant understands the consent clearly and answer questions about the consent. In this manner, the participant was able to know what to expect. Participants were also informed that information that concerns them would be kept confidential and none of their names will be revealed to anyone or expressed in the study and the responses of the respondents will be kept separate from their demographic variables to make linkages between them and the research. Participation in the study was voluntary, and participants could withdraw from the research for whichever reason they may have wanted.

Sampling participants and setting

Convenience sampling was used to choose Gaborone as a site in which to carry out the study. A lot of bridal showers take place in Gaborone, thus making it an ideal site. The target population was people attending the bridal showers. The sampling for different categories of respondents is described below. Shower event sampling was done by attending the bridal shower events by invitation as they occur during six months. All attendees were eligible for participation. Purposive sampling was used to identify potential recipients of the different showers. Therefore, the researchers visited specific areas where such are likely to be camera identified. Participants were recruited from showers in Gaborone. The researchers attended the showers and recorded the events and teachings that went with them. Interviews allowed researchers to collect data about "ideas, experiences, beliefs, views, opinions, and behaviours of the participants" (Kawulich & Gardener, 2012:133) at the showers about *Botho/Ubuntu* and community building in an urban setting.

Data collection processes

The questionnaires were distributed by the researchers themselves at the Naomi/ Laban, bridal and baby showers. The researchers personally attended the showers to observe; conduct the interviews using voice recorders, and, where permission was secured, utilised video cameras to capture data from the participants. The researchers took notes during showers and the interviews. Qualitative data were collected through participatory observations (Bryman, 2001) and in-depth interviews with key informants from each shower, such as organisers and the recipient of the shower.

Instrument(s)

The study used two instruments: the questionnaire and the in-depth interview guide, together with participatory observation, to collect quantitative and qualitative data, respectively. The instruments were prepared beforehand and piloted before the study was carried out. Data were gathered through in-depth interviews using a semi-structured interview guide. The researchers recorded the events and the teachings on video and audio. Interviews allowed researchers to collect data about ideas, experiences, beliefs, views, opinions, and behaviours of the shower participants.

Botho/Ubuntu shower observation instrument

The shower observation instrument included a description of the location of the shower, the setting, how the organisers received and greeted the guests; off-camera conversations before and after the shower; an indication of who was invited, and the mode of invitations; activities, games, refreshments, gifts that were given to the recipient during the shower. Some of the items tapped in on who the designated speakers were and reasons for their selection and the content of their counselling. Theory-driven questions included power dynamics at the shower; positive and negative community building and *Botho/Ubuntu* features; the presence of relational and controlling images and strengths; messages that influence capacity to create and maintain mutually empathic, growth-fostering relationships; evidence of connections and disconnections (cultural relational theory), and strategies that encourage engagement in the shower witnessed during the shower (social capital).

Shower observation checklist

A shower observation checklist was developed, consisting of 14 items to which the researcher indicated with a 'Yes' or 'No' if they observed a particular behaviour during the shower. The items addressed 14 specific areas, such as the behaviour of shower organisers, guests, and other socio-demographic variables such as age, sex, church membership, kin/relation, ethnicity, the guests' behaviour and the types of gifts that were brought to the shower. The mean was 7.4 (SD = 2.3). The scores ranged from 0 to 14, which shows a wide variation in the checklist.

Bridal shower participants' questionnaire

A bridal shower participants' questionnaire was developed to establish respondents' understanding of the bridal showers: the purpose of the shower, whether it assists in community building and whether the shower furthers the cultural tradition of *Botho/Ubuntu* or offers a new social gathering altogether. The survey instrument asked respondents to indicate their sex, marital status, educational status, their role in the shower and their relationship to the shower recipient. The scale consisted of 18 items to which respondents indicated their level of agreement or disagreement with statements on bridal showers. These items were scored on a five-point scale, labelled at the endpoints with 'Strongly Agree' to 'Strongly Disagree'. Higher scores indicated more adherence to statements on bridal showers. Scores range from 40 to 200, with high scores reflecting more stringent cultural beliefs. Some of the items on this scale are "Bridal showers offer moral and social support", "I usually have a long-term relationship with people that I have attended their bridal showers".

Reliability of the scale was coefficient alpha = .67. For this study, the reliability of the scale was alpha = .94. Items in the study ranged from 18 to 90, suggesting that on the whole, respondents adhered to most sociocultural beliefs on the item list. The mean score in this study was mean = 50.03 (SD = 5.6). The median was 49, and the mode was 46. Scores ranged from 36 to 72. Results from higher mean scores show that bridal showers offer moral and social support (mean = 3.78; SD = .42), that they are intended to give advice/counselling to the bride-to-be on being a wife and mother (mean = 3.78; SD = .42); that bridal showers are important (mean = 3.71; SD = .50);

that bridal showers demonstrate *Botho/Ubuntu* (mean = 3.45; SD = .58); that they are a modern development (mean = 3.07; SD = .80); and that they are for women only (mean = 3.09; SD = 1.1).

Data analysis

Upon receipt, the quantitative questionnaires were examined for correctness and completeness; data were coded and entered into SPSS version 26. The study uses Pearson's r-correlation to measure the strength of association among variables. All reports of significance are at least at the level of $p < .05$. Data were analysed per research question. For each research question, descriptive statistics using measures of central tendency and dispersion were used. We present quantitative results of socio-demographic characteristics, and the respective instruments used in data collection, followed by bivariate correlations. Using a concurrent transformative design under the mixed methods approach, we collected both qualitative and quantitative data during the same phase, and nested the quantitative data collection second, under the themes of the qualitative data for purposes of triangulation. We then present findings in an integrated and interpretive manner making sure that the quantitative results are used to interpret the results of the qualitative phase. In this study, the social capital theory and *Botho/Ubuntu* were used to conceptualise the research problem, to guide the investigations on the truthfulness of theoretical propositions. We applied the core concepts or principles to collect, analyse, and interpret the data, such as drawing connections. We then articulated the theoretical framework that fits the phenomenon being studied. We used the identified theoretical perspective of the researcher to guide the analysis and interpretation.

Results of the study

Respondents ranged in age from 20 to 50 years, which suggests a wide variability in the age of the sample. All respondents were women (N = 110). Sixty-eight per cent of the respondents were single (N = 73), 29% were married, 2.5% were separated, 2% were widowed, and 2% were divorced. Two respondents did not indicate their marital status. Table 6.1 shows the socio-demographic characteristics of respondents. All respondents had some form of formal education. More than half of the respondents (76%) had more than a Form 5 level of education: certificate and diploma (20%); bachelor's (33.3%); master's (3%), and doctorate (2%). Two respondents did not indicate their levels of education.

Bivariate correlations were computed among all items in the bridal shower participants questionnaire's scale. Most correlations were significant and in the expected direction. Respondents who planned to visit the new family after marriage also believed that bridal showers were important ($r = .20$, $p < .05$); that counselling is given is only provided by women who are married ($r = .33, p < .001$); that counselling should be offered by the married adults during counselling "*go laya mosadi*" ($r = .24$, $p < .05$); that bridal showers demonstrate *Botho* ($r = .28$, $p < .001$); that the bridal shower gives the bride-to-be the privilege to receive presents from members of the community ($r = .23$, $p < .05$). People who tended to attend showers of people with whom they had a long-term relationship also believed that bridal showers allow for the opportunity for community building in the urban space ($r = .28$, $p < .001$); and that after a bridal shower they would visit to see the new family after marriage ($r = .43$, $p < .001$). Respondents who believed that bridal showers were a modern development ($r = .20$, $p < .05$) also tended to think that giving presents to the bride-to-be was the most important part of the shower ($r = .21$, $p < .001$). Those who felt that bridal showers were a modern development also thought they were found in towns only ($r = .27$, $p < .001$). Respondents who associated bridal showers with rich people also believed that bridal showers were a modern development ($r = .20$, $p < .05$); and that giving presents to the wife-to-be was very important to the shower ($r = .21$, $p < .05$); that after a bridal shower they would visit to see the new family after marriage ($r = .22$, $p < .05$); that they are similar to *go laya ngwetsi* during the marriage ceremony ($r = .30$, $p < .001$).

Table 6.1 Socio-demographic characteristics of the bridal shower respondents

Marital status	Frequency	%
Married	31	28.2
Single	73	66.4
Divorced	2	1.8
Widowed	2	1.8
Subtotal	**108**	**98.2**
Did not indicate	2	1.8
Total	**110**	**100.0**
Educational qualifications	**Frequency**	**Valid %**
Form 3	7	6.4
Form 5	17	15.5
Certificate	16	14.6
Educational qualifications	**Frequency**	**Valid %**
Diploma	27	24.5
Degree	36	32.7
Master's	3	2.7
PhD	2	1.8
Subtotal	**108**	**98.2**
Did not Indicate	2	1.8
Total	**110**	**100.0**

Age	Frequency	Valid %
20–25	15	14.0
26–30	37	34.6
31–35	22	20.6
36–40	22	20.6
41–45	7	6.5
46–50	4	3.7
Total	107	100.0

Qualitative data analysis

The qualitative data collected through the observations and voice recorder were first transcribed into text. The transcribed data and notes were then coded to bring a new coherence to them. Interviews were tape-recorded, transcribed verbatim and analysed through qualitative content analysis. The process of data analysis involved searching for meaningful units of data that could stand independently and were associated with the overall purpose of the study. Investigators read all of the interviews, discussed each interview, and noted themes. Where comments were addressed in more than one category, they were cross-referenced. Coding allowed the data (the transcripts) to be broken down and conceptualised. Information obtained from the survey provided a general description and profile of the women. The descriptive phase, which is provided through quantitative data, provides a broad context of the characteristics and profiles of the sample. Information collected from the quantitative data includes correlations and other relationships between variables. The qualitative phase comprised exploration of the emerging themes, patterns, explanations, flows and propositions and from the open-ended interviews with survivors and stakeholders (Miles & Huberman, 1974).

This study used the data analysis plan by Miles and Huberman (1994), which consists of three components, namely data reduction, data display, and drawing and verifying conclusion. Data reduction is the process through which data are selected, focused, simplified, abstracted and transformed to appear in field notes or transcriptions. To reduce data, one may identify themes or carry out activities such as summary writing, coding, and clustering of chunks of data (Daniel, 2010). The researcher identifies themes of the research and all the other processes that are needed for data reduction. A synthesis of the themes emerging from the interviews shows several pathways in the *Botho/Ubuntu* showers study. The psychosocial pathways presented here may not be exhaustive, though they converged and overlapped, reflecting the process of showers as building and instilling a spirit of *Botho/Ubuntu* ethic on the shower recipient and in the attendees in general. There were recurring themes such as social networks, social norms of reciprocity, social support, collective efficacy, informal social control, mutual trust, and empathy. Therefore, the results of this research are organised under these themes.

Social capital driving bridal showers for the collective good

Social capital was one of the dominant themes that emerged as a critical factor that drives the shower agenda, instituting a spirit of family and community with the *Botho/Ubuntu* ethic. The subthemes under social capital include social networks and connectivity, norms of reciprocity and obligation, norms, beliefs, and standards, the need to develop trusting relationships, social support, a sense of security and social capital, meeting specific needs and showers as pathways to *Botho/Ubuntu*, and relationship differentiation and togetherness. We will address them in the section below.

Social networks and connectivity

Social networks represent social interactions in a society. The embeddedness of social networks is a major driver in bridal showers. To tap into social networks as building blocks of showers, respondents were asked to indicate their relationship to the shower recipient (Table 6.2). Quantitative data confirmed that showers were indeed an outcome of one's network. Results showed that most attendees were friends (34%), church mates (30%), sisters (10%), neighbours (6%), colleagues at work (4%), or other (15%). Social connections tend to depend on who we know, and who has value to both the person and the community.

> Like I said, I think it is an individual thing of whether you put much effort into making sure you fulfil your promise. Regarding organisers, some did not contribute at all, whereas some did not bring the plates as they pledged. So, one can question the relationship between these people and the bride...

When members of the network member fail to conform to the expectations, other network members jointly react to bring the individual to order. Off-camera conversations could be heard when members were asking others different questions such as:

> Where were you all this time?
>
> We expected you to come early, but you are arriving now ... this is not fair ... if it were your shower, you would have wanted people to arrive early, *gakere*? *Ga lo dire sentle* (you are not doing the right thing).

When shower organisers do not meet their obligation to contribute, they threaten the mutual benefits of participating in the social network. A respondent stated:

> I would say it differs for each because some would attend out of obligation or expectations since they are church mates. At this point, I am a bit disappointed because only two mates from church came and the church is not in Francistown, its right here in Gaborone. People not showing up makes me wonder, "where is the humility in their absence?" Also, it starts off with the purpose of bridal

showers, i.e., if one of us is getting married, there's an expectation that we should hype up for that in a celebratory mood for it. Moreover, if you are invited, for someone who may not know the bride, you will start thinking of free food and entertainment you will naturally come with no pressure of bringing a present.

Table 6.2 Relationship to the shower recipient and role in the shower

Relationship to the shower recipient	Frequency	%
Sister	11	10.0
Sister-in-law	2	1.8
Colleague at work	4	3.6
Church mate	32	29.1
Friend	37	33.6
Neighbour	6	5.5
Other	16	14.6
Subtotal	**108**	**98.2**
Did not indicate	2	1.8
Total	**110**	**100.0**
Respondent's role in the shower	**Frequency**	**Valid %**
Shower organiser	34	30.9
Chairperson	2	1.8
Bride	5	4.6
Family member	3	2.7
Guest speaker	2	1.8
Invitee	1	0.9
Bridesmaid	1	0.9
Other	6	5.5
No special role, just attending	54	49.1
Subtotal	**108**	**98.2**
Missing data	2	1.8
Total	**110**	**100.0**

From the data, social capital is inherent in the network structure but is activated by the individual's role, primarily decisive, in the network. In the process, the person and the social network both benefit. Bridges built through co-workers and church mates provide access to different kinds of individuals, which in turn give access to various kinds of information, support, and resources. The erosion of strong social support is particularly troubling considering that social capital is both self-reproducing and self-reinforcing. Social capital makes more social capital, but it takes social capital to make other forms of capital in its diversity. Thus, the diminishment in mutual obligation not only threatens their social capital reserve, but it also influences their ability to get other forms of social capital as well. Much of their participation revolved around joining with those with similar interests, such as their neighbours or people with whom they shared a religious belief or some other unifying characteristic, and may be an indication of one's connection to the immediate network of the shower recipient. It is possible that the immediate people in an individual's network provide connections to other networks, hence the people that came to the shower, yet had no direct relationship with the recipient through the network. Information about a shower is passed through one's network to all the nodes connected to that individual, and when sharing is understood, networks grow rapidly becoming greater in size. Ideally, through this growth, social trust and mutual obligation deepen, norms are strengthened, and values are shared more, all of which sustain bonds among family, friends, co-workers, church mates and the community as a whole did.

Norms of reciprocity and obligation

Showers are built on a bed of social networks and interactions. A bridal shower event exemplifies a network, and that interpersonal communication among individuals resembles a relationship between a node and another nesting in the network. One respondent asked about the role of showers stated:

> Back then, it was a close support system, your family and in-laws only. These days the system is broadened to include friends, former schoolmates, and anyone can be part of the preparations for the wedding. They can offer you advice, all sorts of support you might need for your wedding.

Quantitative data confirmed that there were positive correlations associated with items that typify norms of reciprocity. Respondents who believed that if they have attended a bridal shower for X, they would expect X to attend their shower as well, also believed that they would feel offended if they organised a bridal shower for X and then X would refuse to organise their bridal shower ($r = .65$, $p < .001$). A surprising finding was that people who would feel offended if they organised a bridal shower for someone who would later refuse to organise their bridal shower was also likely to feel that it was okay to attend a bridal shower without bringing a present ($r = .25$, $p < .001$). People who thought that bridal showers are necessary also believed bridal showers offer moral and social support ($r = .67$, $p < .001$); that bridal showers are meant to give advice/counselling to the wife-to-be on being a wife and mother ($r = .63$, $p < .001$); that bridal showers demonstrate *Botho* ($r = .48$, $p < .001$); and that bridal showers allow for the opportunity for community building in the urban space ($r = .28$; $p < .001$).

Social networks of family, friends, church members, and co-workers provide resources that are needed in times of need, to protect married couples and their families from marital conflict and divorce. Social networks embedded in showers allow access to instrumental, spiritual, financial and emotional support. Information sharing may be beneficial for individuals who need help on marriage and family life, living with in-laws, to name but a few. Intergenerational and inter-household exchange networks have a long history in Botswana. In this study, we note that the ability of these networks to assist has remained stable, and norms of mutuality and reciprocity have become more possible to maintain.

A recurring theme in the study was the emphasis on norms. Several participants saw showers as not only a mode through which they could demonstrate their *Botho/ Ubuntu* and sense of togetherness values. Showers were perceived as a conduit for enacting those values in their network. Asked about who should attend showers, respondents showed that both married and single women should participate, as they occupy different spaces in their experience or lack thereof. Single women should attend to learn so that they know what to expect from married life. Married women should attend to share their experiences, because they know the 'hardships'. The following quote illustrates this:

> All women of all ages, single and *bomme ba nyetsweng* (married women), all have something to add, to contribute towards *go laya* (to provide counsel). Married women know what is; they can advise her with authority. Single women also learn how to behave well so that they can also catch a husband; we also learn why couples are not always happy, why when they are driving in the morning, they do not hold hands as they used to.
>
> (Bridal Shower Interview B)

Another respondent also shared her views:

> Married women and single ... married women to groom the new bride from experience, they are in it. With a single woman, we hope to get married. We are learning now so that one day we will be there. In traffic we see couples looking sad, we ask why, so we learn, they might scare us as well.
>
> (Bridal Shower Interview C)

Showers are therefore a primary source and a producer of social capital, as they involve developing connections that provide instrumental, informational, and emotional support to members of the network.

The need to develop trusting relationships

Another subtheme in the study was the need to develop trusting relationships. Participants of this study reported that confidence in a person was a prerequisite of being a shower organiser. Thirty-two per cent of the respondents were shower organisers, suggesting the level of trust the recipient had for those individuals. However, trust was important to participants; but rather than feeling the need to trust others within their community, their focus on trust tended to be internal. Trust was a consequence of prolonged successful involvement with networks and associations.

Quantitative data show that respondents who believed that bridal showers offer moral and social support also tended to think that bridal showers are necessary ($r = .68, p < .001$); that bridal showers demonstrate *Botho/Ubuntu* ($r = -.54, p < .001$); that bridal showers allow for the opportunity for community building in the urban space ($r = .32; p < .001$) and that it was okay to attend bridal shower without bringing a present and that after a bridal shower they would visit to see the new family after marriage ($r = .24$, $p < .001$). Respondents who believed that bridal showers demonstrate *Botho/Ubuntu* also believed that those bridal showers are meant to give advice/counselling to the wife-to-be on being a wife and mother ($r = .55, p < .001$). Another statistically significant finding was that respondents, who believed that showers offer the same counselling as that provided by the married adults during the counselling *go laya mosadi* session, also believed that counselling should be given and is only provided by women who are married ($r = .35, p < .001$). Another aspect reflected in the showers was the communal tradition reflected through the appreciation of the worth of importance of each other, family, and the community. The importance of a human being is reflected in norms of hospitality, sharing, generosity, and compassion, often reflected in the manner of greeting each other and giving of food.

Social support, a sense of security and social capital

Social support and social capital may be a reflection of the same concept operating at different levels. In the process, certain behaviours are promoted and enabled to diffuse in the community.

> We do bridal showers for various reasons; to support the bride and groom because at times they get married at an early age, at the beginning of their courtship; to support the bride and groom who have already been together for some time and we do the showers to advise the woman on how to handle herself, 3. To support for the celebration, maybe when there are insufficient funds for the celebration we 'meet her halfway', also to give her some love. In short, I would say for support, education, love, and affection. ... I think us Batswana we believe in supporting each other and it is essential to work together, '*Ipelegeng*'.

Another respondent stated:

> To unite as sisters, married and to enlighten in the process of marriage; not just for the bride. Make bride feel supported, women encouraging her, without them there is no way there is a joy. (Bridal Shower Interview D)

Social support reflects the totality of positive micro-level relationships, including what may serve as buffers to adverse influences in one's immediate environment.

Social capital, however, encompasses developing customary local norms, patterns of discipline or support that serve to counterweigh unhealthy behaviours. It may also appear as if social capital extends to the community, while social support is often restricted to a close group of people, who at times are aware that one is going through some distress. While the two may appear to serve seemingly mutual goals, the levels at which they operate are different, with social support operating more at the micro level and social capital at the macro level. The literature on social capital at the family level is still undeveloped and often reflects the same notions operating at the community level (Alvarez, Kawachi & Romani, 2016; Lüscher, 2002; Donati & Prandini, 2007; Widmer, 1999, 2000; Widmer & La Farga, 2000; Widmer, Giudici, Le Goff & Pollien, 2009). The study below shows that the two variables may act at different levels in the ways through which they influence individual well-being. Social support at the micro level may be a building block for social capital at the macro level.

Meeting specific needs

Organising and participating in showers helps to address the needs of the recipients, but in the process, they also benefit from the counselling and advice during the proceedings, such as in this case:

> Showers are *matshelo* – it was done in the past (*Motshelo* is a social engagement event where families would take turns helping each other during ploughing, weeding, harvesting and thrashing seasons. The host would provide food and traditional beer as a way of returning the favour). People shared each other's burden in the fields, cattle post and through other *metshelo* (plural for *matshelo*) initiatives. Bridal showers have modernised the *magadi* (payment of bride price) events, where the community gathered to help each other during the preparations for a wedding. (Bridal Shower Interview B)

Access and participation in the showers were also seen as a way to strengthen social inclusion and offset social isolation. Asked about how bridal showers develop women, one respondent stated:

> The purpose of bridal showers is to learn from each other ... To advise married people. Showers help to give gifts and financial support to the bride and to celebrate with her with gifts from friends and organisers. ...
>
> I think ladies develop by learning from each other and they can learn possible solutions from others. (Bridal Shower Interview A)

Another respondent stated:

> To contribute money towards the gifts as well as to celebrate with the bride. Ideally, they are there to appreciate the bride; to show that we are happy for the bride, appreciate her; an opportunity to buy something for the bride. However, some showers have lost meaning; people (brides) want to get the

> stuff they cannot afford. This puts organisers under pressure. For example, a bride can mention an exact item; this might need more money: people fight and argue. They are pressured. Nna, I think presence should be more important than presents. It's ok to come to a shower without a present.
>
> (Bridal Shower Interview B)

Other respondents stated:

> They should be fair enough to open up and share their experiences and knowledge that can benefit the bride. Some women enter the marriage as virgins, so it is good, to be honest with her and share the experiences.
>
> It is a free, flexible and calm environment. The setting allows the bride to be comfortable to express herself. Everything can be laid out on the table; provided people are willing to share. The language used in bridal showers make it easier for everyone to relate for example in referral to sex, we use the term 'bedroom', but with the traditional one they use profound and confusing terms like '*go dirisa mogagolwane*' in [reference] to sex. Batswana tend to be reluctant to express themselves freely.

According to another respondent:

> To unite as sisters, married and to enlighten in the process of marriage; not just for the bride. Make bride feel supported, women encouraging her, without them there is no way there is a joy. (Bridal Shower Interview D)

Showers have the potential to act as a protective buffer for some of the threats posed by socio-demographic factors such as poverty, material hardship, and lack.

Showers as pathways to *Botho/Ubuntu*

Several times during counselling, counsellors would say:

> *O se ka ya re o tsena ko bagwagwading wa re tlhabisa ditlhong ka boitshwaro jwa gago. O itse gore sengwe le sengwe se o se dirang kwa, se a re ama.* (When you get to the in-laws, do not embarrass us with your unacceptable behaviour. Know that whatever you do there affects us as well.)

To tap in on the concept and practice of *Botho/Ubuntu* ethic, respondents were asked how showers reflect *Botho/Ubuntu*. One of the interviewees stated:

> Botho is sharing and caring. We demonstrate botho here by donating money; we accept help from each other. We teach botho/*maitseo*, we teach [the] bride to respect her new family, love the sisters of the groom, to exist peacefully with her husband. We teach obedience and submission these are all contributing to the character. A wife must have good character otherwise the whole collapses.
>
> (Bridal Shower Interview A)

The assertion suggests that an individual is an embodiment of their family, church, and workplace. Therefore, they have to behave in a way that brings honour to their whole body, not just themselves. For example, the Tswana proverb, which asserts that *motho ke motho ka batho*, means that one can only be a person in the community with others. Showers showed us that even when people live in urban areas, they still identify strongly with the ways or customs of their respective ethnic groups, or they may face sanctions. Reflecting on the relationship between *Botho* and showers, some respondents stated:

> I think there is a connection between showers and botho even though sometimes it is not as it should [be] regard[ing] commitment, responsibilities, and accountability from the organisers. However, those who are there maintain a good relationship because we all want to please the bride; we want things to be perfect for that day. The bride is taught to behave well, give gifts, and participate in the shower. We expect them to bless the bride and pray for her. (Bridal Shower Interview A)

> Yes, they are, we teach each other botho/*maitseo* here; one cannot build a home *a sena maitseo*. Showers demonstrate our ability to care for each other although we are not related by blood, so caring is botho. We are also interested in building each other so that we succeed in our lives; showers build the bride and the guests. ... We teach botho/*maitseo*, we teach [the] bride to respect her new family, love the sisters of the groom, to exist peacefully with her husband. We teach obedience and submission; these are all contributing to the character. A wife must have good character otherwise the whole collapses ... To behave well, give gifts and participate in the shower. We expect them to bless the bride and pray for her. (Bridal Shower Interview B)

> The bride is groomed to keep calm and behave well in marriage. She is taught botho, *monna wa apeelwa, mo* kitchen, and bedroom. We teach botho so that the bride knows that she respects her in-laws, a bride is taught to love the mother of the groom for a man to love her, in that way botho is core, you can be close to your in-laws. Good behaviour to teach the bride botho – we too expect advice that build *monyadi*, not the one that tells *monyadi* to leave a marriage when it is tough. Presents to show their support of the bride, we do not want spectators. We do not want gossips – we want those who build, we want good advice to build the bridge. (Bridal Shower Interview C)

Asked to give examples of what might be identified as character building during bridal showers, a respondent said:

> ... *Setho*. Sometimes for other people, it is like an outing, they will just hang out and by so doing it loses the meaning of being a bridal shower. For example, having a formal session requires low key behaviour, but instead, some people do not care much, they tend to disrupt the event. So, respect is necessary during the event.

Another also stated:

> There are some negative issues regarding bridal showers; some of them are done mainly to show off, like spending lots of money on decorations, hiring expensive venues and equipment. In short, spending much on [the] occasion

> [rather] than helping the bride financially. Youth these days enhance the behaviour of attendees by adding drugs in drinks and food for the event, and they eventually lose themselves and botho along the way.

Botho is also related to existing customs and traditions that prescribe togetherness and oneness of purpose, as shown in this case:

> ...we have a culture of botho, and even in our villages, botho is well taught in the community. Even though we live in a modern world at times, the culture gets compromised. However, at the bridal showers, the culture is revived because the preparations and proceedings are diligently done with botho and love.

Reflecting on another aspect of anti-*Botho* behaviour, a respondent stated:

> People not showing up on time delay the whole process and inconveniences the proceedings of the shower. Merely be courteous, maintaining a quiet environment, but when you are given the floor, you can speak freely. It is not a formal setting, but we expect people to be casual but attentive at the same time.

It is also possible that within close-knit neighbourhoods, social affiliation might enhance the well-being of those individuals living in it. At the same time, social harmony and cohesiveness may be achieved through social ostracism. People are socialised to abide by this value or face sanctions from immediate family members and the supernatural (such as displeased ancestors). Uka (1985) shows that individuals, who do not behave by these expectations, may be ostracised through non-attendance of showers, not participating in the arrangement, in cooking and in distributing food and in buying presents. The differences in the types of presents, the density of social networks and the level of participation during games, could be interpreted regarding ostracism tendencies. Off camera, people would say:

> *Le ene ga a nke a tla dilong tsa batho* (She also doesn't attend other people's showers).
>
> *Kana sharwara e tswa hela gore le wena o tsenelela di shwara tsa babangwe o bo thusa go le kae mo dishawareng tse dingwe* (Showers also depend on whether you ever attend other people showers and help).

Batswana rely on proverbs, which prescribe how one can relate to others. Within the culture and traditions of Botswana, there are some proverbs that denote working together, humanism and caring for one another. Another nuance of the Setswana *motho ke motho k aba bangwe* means a person cannot make themselves by themselves; it is others in the family and community who shape and sculpt him/her to a level where they are deemed acceptable.

Relationship differentiation and togetherness

Of note in the bridal showers was the cord that runs through *Botho*, differentiation, and togetherness. Differentiation involves balancing the drive for independence and the drive for devotedness, togetherness, closeness, and inseparability. Showers noted that though it was difficult to leave one's family and go and live with in-laws, marital problems are not a result of failure to separate, but rather the difficulties she would experience in trying to maintain connections while also asserting her needs and desires, a principle of differentiation. Individuality propels us to follow our advice and instruction to create a unique identity. Norms of togetherness push us to be part of a group. One is taught during showers that the drive for individuality should be balanced with "living together and in harmony with" others in a healthy, mutually reinforcing transaction that does not depreciate one as they blend into life with the in-laws. Most brides were warned that behaviours that suggest that one is estranged or separated from the in-laws would result in one being less of a person with less of a relation.

Based on this discussion, it would follow that one would expect to find some closely knit family units that are reciprocal in the urban areas. Wafawanaka (1997) suggests "the young look up to the elders for nourishment, wisdom, instruction, and knowledge. The elders look to the young for protection, caring and the continuation of the family name" (ibid.:56). Rural-urban linkages have served to strengthen the bonds and raise rural incomes and maintain the stability of these living in the urban areas (Krüger, 1995; Riddell & Harris, 1985). The study further shows that women are the backbone because they often occupy strong positions within African families and are the drivers of *Botho/Ubuntu* social capital, and community building. They are responsible for educating themselves and others about moral, ethical, and social values. The study showed the importance of women in socialisation, in providing financial, providing moral support, and in helping others.

Discussion

Social capital draws from the works of Coleman (1988, 1990), Sampson and Groves (1989), Sampson, Raudenbush and Earls (1997), and Putnam (1993, 1995). Examining the literature on social capital, one finds a robust field of scholarship. Paxton (1999), for example, came up with the concept of "physical capital" to explain the ways that physical implements (tools or machines) could facilitate agricultural production. Gifts, presents, and money that are brought to the showers may fall under the category of physical capital. Becker (1964), building on the work of Schultz (1961), introduced the idea of "human capital" to illustrate how individuals, through education or job training, may have within themselves the ability to facilitate production. Analogous to physical and human capital, social capital has a long history in the social sciences, drawing from the works of several theorists (Bourdieu & Wacquant, 1992; Burt, 1992; Coleman, 1988, 1990; Fukuyama, 1995; Hanifan, 1920; Jacobs, 1961; Loury, 1977; Modie-Moroka, 2003, 2009; Narayan, 1999; Portes & Sensenbrenner, 1993; Sampson, 1989, 1997; Paxton, 1999; Putnam, 1993, 1995; Edwards, 1997; Woodcock, 1998). Mignone (2003b:132) notes that social capital

> characterises a community based on the degree that its resources are socially invested, that it presents an ethos of trust, norms of reciprocity, collective action, and participation, and that it possesses inclusive, flexible and diverse networks. The social capital of a community is assessed through a combination of its bonding (within community relations), bridging (intercommunity ties), and linking (relations with formal institutions) dimensions.

Social capital therefore refers to the presence of both thick and thin, or embedded or autonomous networks, the levels of social and civic trust, the binding norms (including of reciprocity), the density of civic associations, and civic involvement in the community, which facilitate cooperation and equip participants with the power to produce a desired result, both at the individual and collective level. Implicit in this definition is the fact that social capital is determined to smooth facilitation and coordination of community efforts for mutual benefit. Social capital, therefore, is the glue that holds societies together. It would follow that showers are dependent on civic engagement, a sense of interpersonal trust and tolerance, community integration, formal and informal networks, norms based on obligations of mutuality, information potential, and informal social control.

The philosophy of *Botho/Ubuntu*, defined as "an African worldview that is based on values of intense humanness, caring, sharing, respect, compassion and associated values", in essence promotes social cohesion and peaceful living within the family and community (Broodryk, 2002:19). *Botho/Ubuntu* is the groundwork of support structures, where everybody needs other people to be able to adapt and survive. *Botho/Ubuntu* plays a major role in people's lives through reciprocity – an expectation that good deeds will be rewarded by a higher entity or by other people. *Botho/Ubuntu* as the 'inner being' of a person, the 'Setho' that connects with humanity. The *Botho/Ubuntu* ethic states that one needs to have care, compassion and empathy towards each other for other people to strengthen the community's spirit. The ethos of *Botho/Ubuntu* embodies reciprocity, mutual assistance, and a sense of responsibility, respect, recognition to all. Participants depend on selected individuals for showers to run to enable the recipient to cope with the burdens, demands, and stresses of a marriage. *Botho/Ubuntu* culture is believed to result from harmonious relationships among individuals, between individuals and society, and between people and their environment. The negotiated spaces with their social ties, bonds, and relationships are where members find comfort, relief, and strength to continue with their lives. For example, a community that has high levels of social capital may also have exclusionary practices and be distrustful of other people who are not from their same community.

Social network is a structure of nodes, an aggregation of personal networks that are individuals and organisations that represent relationships between family, friends, and acquaintances and work colleagues (Barnes, 1954). The behaviour of an individual towards others and of others towards them shapes the structure of their social network. Virtually all definitions of social capital include references to interlocking associations or networks of relationships between individuals or between individuals and groups (Portes, 1998; Putnam, 1993; Woolcock, 1998). In this study, social networks were central to putting together the shower, its execution, and its outcomes. Social networks were an important part of getting things done, building relationships, and developing useful information.

Social norms are the rules or standards shared within a particular culture or group. It is possible from the study that norms impact the form that social capital takes, and also facilitate the social capital stock. This research found strong support for the influence of social norms on both the production and sustainability of relationships. When participants were asked to explain why they became involved in the showers, they often described themselves as having responsibility or as the manifestation of a set of values or beliefs. The general notion is that when a group of people has a shared group of norms, there is also a shared understanding of the expectations. Individuals are more likely to go along with them, thus fulfilling one another's expectations. So, the individual behaviour must be viewed within the context of a much larger system of rules and traditions that are shared within that person's community. Many of the investments that participants brought to the showers reflected the level of integration with others into their lives in a way that made them both transparent and obligated. That is, many of the participants did not think of their participation as forced, but rather as just another part of their routine. Social norms of obligation, collective efficacy is already knitted in their being that they did not stand out as something extra. This result is consistent with Haley's (2004) notion that social norms are often unconscious because they are deeply embedded into a shared point of view within a particular context.

Informal social control is a subtheme of social capital, measured by the community's ability to monitor each other's behaviour and to intervene for the common interest. Mutual trust and solidarity among kin and neighbours enhance informal social control. According to Wafawanaka (1997), the family is the primary unit of socialisation in African society. It is in the family that children are introduced to social norms, traditions, and customs around kinship, a religion that become the guiding principles through their lives (Mtutuki, 1976). According to Gyekye (1996:3), "religion enters all aspects of African life so fully, determining practically all aspects life, including moral behaviour – that it cannot be isolated". Since time immemorial, they have served as the 'glue' that holds communities together.

The importance of informal social networks that provide social control in the forms of instilling norms and values are worth noting in this study. We point out that in the showers, morals, and ethics are regulated through different social institutions, such as the family through morally laden folktales, fables, riddles, proverbs, songs, myths, and legends, age-grade systems, totems, and *mephato* (regiments). The showers were a fertile avenue for communicating these expectations. The bonds that exist enhance behavioural expectations and result in members making trust and obligation claims among individuals in the network. This study shows that webs of trust are built through a process by which people become cooperative and public-spirited as they work together for the betterment of the community and themselves. As a result, one is taught that one cannot exist as an individual outside a community and one can carve out a new behaviour outside the confines of established rules. Kinship ties are an essential building block of the community, controlling social relationships and binding people together.

Botho/Ubuntu ethical and moral sentiment is an important traditional cultural norm that has been associated with solidarity community building through its force to enable the empowerment of members of the community to live dignified lives. At the core of *Botho* is the belief that one's behaviour affects others. The ethic thus urges individuals to define their identity by developing a sense of humanness, an ethic of care, welcoming others and hospitality affirming and respecting the 'other' (Livingstone, 2008). The *Botho/Ubuntu* ethic plays a significant role in day-to-day lives of people and builds community relations among Batswana. Since time immemorial, *Botho/Ubuntu* practices have permeated all aspects of individual African culture and is seen as a product of inner peace, which propelled an ideal and meaningful life, where there is a sense of respect in the treatment of all people, recognising their inherent dignity and worth. The practice is strengthened by a culture of cooperation between individuals, sharing, caring, and living in harmony with all creation. The expressions of *Botho/Ubuntu* are affirmed in acts of sociability such as hospitality, kneeling and shaking or wringing of hands when greeting each other to show respect, visiting neighbours, participating in weddings, funerals, and parties of neighbours, family members, and friends and sharing food during festive seasons. Other expectations include a person who exhibits good character and manners, courtesy and discipline.

Conclusion

All human experience is personal, subjective and collective. We depend on significant others of our membership in the human community. Women are often encouraged through gender socialisation processes to adopt relational schemas related to how to create and maintain intimate relationships, silence feelings, thoughts, and actions in meaningful relationships. Bridal showers are a model of human development that emphasises growth-fostering relationships as building blocks of wellness. The study has shown that women are active participants in the development of themselves and other people. The goal of development is the ability to build and enlarge mutually to enhance relationships in which each person can feel an increased sense of well-being. A key lesson is that bridal showers are a basis for a woman to self-empathise in a mutual, interactive process, suggesting a way of joining in which each person is emotionally available, attentive, and responsive to other in the relationship. The space created in showers allows a woman, through the spirit of *Botho/Ubuntu* and social capital, to be relationally authentic and to emotionally real, connected and recognised for one who is, to vital, transparent, and purposeful in their relationships with one another. The dialogues between the friends, church mates, family members and the rest of the crowd allow relational authenticity, and responding to each other, creating truth and cementing togetherness. The study further showed that there are opportunities for people who live in urban areas to have community networks, informal social control, a sense of responsibility and care, adapting one's needs to those of others and using one's relational strength to enhance other people's well-being and nurturing others.

References

Alvarez, E.C., Kawachi, I. & Romani, J.R. 2016. 'Family social capital and health: a systematic review and redirection'. *Sociology of Health & Illness*, 39(1): 5-29. https://doi.org/10.1111/1467-9566.12506

Broodryk, J. 2002. *Ubuntu: life lessons from Africa*. Pretoria, South Africa: National Library.

Broodryk, J. 2004. *Ubuntu: life lessons from Africa*. Pretoria, South Africa: Ubuntu School of Philosophy.

Chuller, T., Baron, S. & Field, J. 2000. 'Social capital: a review and critique'. In: S. Baron, J. Field & T. Schuller (eds). *Social capital: critical perspectives*. Oxford: Oxford University Press. 1-38.

Coleman, J.S. 1988. 'Social capital in the creation of human capital'. *American Journal of Sociology*, 94(1)(Suppl.): 95-120. https://doi.org/10.1086/228943

Coleman, J.S. 1990. *Foundations of social theory*. Boston, MA: Harvard University Press.

Donati, P. & Prandini, R. 2007. 'Family and social capital: European contributions'. *International Review of Sociology/Revue Internationale de Sociologie*, 17(2):205-208. https://doi.org/10.1080/03906700701356770

Hanifan, L.J. 1920. *The community center*. Boston, MA: Silver, Burdette & Co.

Kawachi, I., Kennedy, B.P. & Lochner, K. 1997. 'Long live community: social capital as public health'. *The American Prospect*, November/December:56-59.

Kawachi, I., Kennedy, B.P., Lochner, K. & Prothrow-Stith, D. 1997. 'Social capital, income equality, and mortality'. *American Journal of Public Health*, 8(9):1491-1498. https://doi.org/10.2105/AJPH.87.9.1491

Krishna, A. 2002. *Active social capital: tracing the roots of development and democracy*. New York: Columbia University Press. https://doi.org/10.7312/kris12570

Livingston, J. 2008. 'Disgust, bodily aesthetics and the ethic of being human in Botswana'. *Africa*, 78(2): 288-307. https://doi.org/10.3366/E000197200800017X

Lüscher, K. 2002. 'Intergenerational ambivalence: further steps in theory and research'. *Journal of Marriage and Family*, 64(3):585-593. https://doi.org/10.1111/j.1741-3737.2002.00585.x

Midgley, J. & Livermore, M. 1998. 'Social capital and local economic development: implications for community social work practice'. *Journal of Community Practice*, 5(1-2):29-40. https://doi.org/10.1300/J125v05n01_03

Mignone, J. 2003a. *Measuring social capital: a guide for first nations communities*. Ottawa, Ontario: Canadian Institute for Health Information.

Mignone, J. 2003b. 'Social capital in first nations communities: conceptual development and instrument validation'. Doctor of Philosophy thesis, University of Manitoba, Canada.

Minkoff, D.C. 1997. 'Producing social capital: national social movements and civil society'. *American Behavioural Scientist*, 40(5):606-619. https://doi.org/10.1177/0002764297040005007

Modie-Moroka, T., Dube, M.W., Setume, S.D., Kgalemang, M., Kebaneilwe, M.D., Gabaitse, R., Motswapong, E. & Madigele, T. 2019. 'Pathways to social capital and the *Botho/Ubuntu* ethic in the urban space in Gaborone, Botswana'. *Global Social Welfare: Research, Policy and Practice*, 7:231-243. https://doi.org/10.1007/s40609-019-00152-5

Narayan, D. 1997. 'Voices of the poor: poverty and social capital in Tanzania'. *Environmentally and socially sustainable development studies and monographs series*. Washington, DC: The World Bank. 1-80.

Narayan, D. 1999. *Bonds and bridges: social capital and poverty*. Washington, DC: The World Bank.

Narayan, D. & Cassidy, M. 2001. 'A dimensional approach to measuring social capital: development and validation of a social capital inventory'. *Current Sociology*, 49(2):59-102. https://doi.org/10.1177/001139210 1049002006

Narayan, D. & Pritchett, L. 2000. 'Social capital: evidence and implications'. In: P. Dasgupta & I. Serageldin (eds). *Social capital: a multifaceted perspective*. Washington, DC: The World Bank. 269-295.

Paxton, P. 1998. *Capitalizing on community: social capital and the democratic society*. Chapel Hill, NC: The University of North Carolina at Chapel Hill.

Paxton, P. 1999. 'Is social capital declining in the United States? A multiple indicator assessment'. *American Journal of Sociology*, 105(1):88-127. https:// doi.org/10.1086/210268

Portes, A. 1995. 'Economic sociology and the sociology of immigration: a conceptual overview'. In: A. Portes (ed). *The economic sociology of immigration: essays on networks, ethnicity, and entrepreneurship*. New York: Russell Sage Foundation. 1-41.

Portes, A. 1998. 'Social capital: its origins and applications in modern sociology'. *Annual Review of Sociology*, (22):1-24. https://doi.org/10.1146/annurev. soc.24.1.1

Portes, A. 2000. 'The two meanings of social capital'. *Sociological Forum*, (15):1-12. https://doi.org/10.1023/ A:1007537902813

Portes, A. & Landolt, P. 1996. 'The downside of social capital'. *The American Prospect*, 7(26):18-21.

Portes, A. & Landolt, P. 2000. 'Social capital: promise and pitfalls of its role in development'. *Journal of Latin American Studies*, 32(2):529-547. https://doi.org/10.1017/S0022216X 00005836

Portes, A. & Sensenbrenner, J. 1993. 'Embeddedness and immigration: notes on the social determinants of economic action'. *American Journal of Sociology*, 98(6):1320-1350. https://doi.org/10.1086/230191

Putnam, R.D. 1995. 'Tuning in, tuning out: the strange disappearance of social capital in America'. *Political Science and Politics*, 28(4):664-683. https:// doi.org/10.2307/420517

Putnam, R.D. 2000. *Bowling alone: the collapse and revival of American community*. New York: Touchstone. https://doi.org/10.1145/3589 16.361990

Putnam, R.D., Leonardi, R. & Nanetti, R.Y. 1993. *Making democracy work: civic traditions in modern Italy*. Princeton, NJ: Princeton University Press. https://doi.org/10.1515/97 81400820740

Sampson, R.J. 2003. 'Neighborhood-level context and health: Lessons from sociology'. In: I. Kawachi & L. Berkman (eds). *Neighborhood and health*. Oxford: Oxford University Press. 132-146. https://doi.org/ 10.1093/acprof:oso/9780195 138382.003.0006

Sampson, R.J. & Groves, W.B. 1989. 'Community structure and crime: testing social disorganization theory'. *American Journal of Sociology*, 94(4): 774-802. https://doi.org/10.1086/ 229068

Sampson, R.J., Morenoff, J.D. & Earls, F. 1999. 'Beyond social capital: spatial dynamics of collective efficacy for children'. *American Sociological Review*, 64(5):633-660. https://doi.org/10.2307/2657367

Sampson, R.J., Raudenbush, S.W. & Earls, F. 1997. 'Neighborhoods and violent crime: a multilevel study of collective efficacy'. *Science*, 277(5328):918-924. https://doi.org/10.1126/science.277.5328.918

Wafawanaka, R. 1997. *Perspectives on the problem of poverty in traditional Africa and in ancient Israel.* Boston, MA: Boston University School of Theology.

Wellman, B.A., Quan-Haase, A., Witte, J. & Hampton, K. 2001. 'Does the internet increase, decrease, or supplement social capital? Social networks, participation, and community commitment'. *American Behavioural Scientist*, 45(3):437-456. https://doi.org/10.1177/00027640121957286

Widmer, E.D. 1999. 'Family contexts as cognitive networks: a structural approach to family relationships'. *Personal Relationships*, 6(4):487-503. https://doi.org/10.1111/j.1475-6811.1999.tb00205.x

Widmer, E.D. 2006. 'Who are my family members? Bridging and binding social capital in family configurations'. *Journal of Social and Personal Relationships*, 23(6):979-998. https://doi.org/10.1177/0265407506070482

Widmer, E.D., Giudici, F., Le Goff, J. & Pollien, A. 2009. 'From support to control: a configurational perspective on conjugal quality'. *Journal of Marriage and Family*, 71(3):437-448. https://doi.org/10.1111/j.1741-3737.2009.00611.x

Widmer, E.D. & La Farga, L. 2000. 'Family networks: a sociometric method to study relationships in families'. *Field Methods*, 12(2): 108-128. https://doi.org/10.1177/1525822X0001200202

Woolcock, M. 1998. 'Social theory, development policy, and poverty alleviation: a comparative-historical analysis of group-based banking in developing economies'. Doctor of Philosophy Sociology, Brown University, Rhode Island.

Woolcock, M. 1999. 'Managing risks, shocks, and opportunity in developing economies: the role of social capital'. Unpublished Work.

World Bank, The. 2000. *Let's talk social capital* #25, 26, 27, 32.

PART TWO

Botho/Ubuntu, Naomi/Laban Showers and In-Laws

7

EMERGENT 'RITES OF PASSAGE' IN BOTSWANA

A case study of Naomi/Laban showers

Abstract

As already discussed in the preceding chapters, a multi-disciplinary group of researchers from the University of Botswana carried out research on '*Botho/Ubuntu* and Community Building in the Urban Space: An exploration of Naomi/Laban, Bridal and Baby Showers in Gaborone', which was generously funded by the John Templeton Foundation. The aim of the research was to explore how the African/Setswana concept of *Botho/Ubuntu* drives the showers in urban and peri-urban spaces in Botswana. Our observation on these showers is that the beneficiaries are assisted, oriented and reorientated, taught, advised, and supported materially, emotionally, and morally by the community as they enter new stages and statuses of their lives. The study was carried out within Gaborone, the capital city of Botswana, and the surrounding villages. This chapter[1] is limited to two of the four showers studied, namely the Naomi/Laban showers. The said showers are the newest in the country. The project employed a mixed-method design, which combined quantitative and qualitative research methods. The chapter explores how and to what extent the two showers constitute emergent rites of passage. The main findings of the study were that the four showers studied were fostered by the *Botho/Ubuntu* ethos and spirituality, which encourage communal life and individual responsibilities that work together for the common good.

Introduction

In 2016, a group of scholars from across faculties at the University of Botswana conducted empirical fieldwork research under the title, '*Botho/Ubuntu* and Community Building in the Urban Space: An exploration of Naomi/Laban, Bridal and Baby Showers in Gaborone' (hereinafter '*Botho/Ubuntu* Project'). The research was made possible by the generous funding of the John Templeton Foundation through the

1 The article, 'Emergent Rites of Passage in Botswana: The Case of Naomi/Laban Showers' by Kebaneilwe, M.D. et al., was first published in 2019 in *Pula: Botswana Journal of African Studies*, 33(1):62-79. It is republished in this volume with permission.

Nagel Institute. It focused on four showers, namely Naomi, Laban, bridal and baby showers. The fieldwork was carried out in Gaborone and the peri-urban villages of Tlokweng, Mmopane, Mogoditshane, Ramotswa, Kanye and Molepolole.

This chapter presents the findings of an investigation on the Naomi/Laban showers as possible emergent rites of passage in Botswana. We interpret these rites of passage within the framework of *Botho/ Ubuntu*, a Tswana/African ethos best captured in the words of Desmond Tutu (2004:25):

> A person is a person through other persons. None of us comes into the world fully formed. We would not know how to think, or walk, or speak, or behave as human beings unless we learned it from other human beings. We need other human beings in order to be human.

The term 'emergent' seems appropriate, because baby and bridal showers are common practice in Botswana, as in many other parts of the world. For instance, Montemuro (2005, 2006) maintains that bridal showers (also known as kitchen parties) can be traced back to sixteenth- and seventeenth-century Western Europe as pre-wedding activities organised by women for women. Baby showers too have a long history, as scholarly literature indicates that they originated in ancient times and have continued to evolve to the present-day baby showers. In contrast, Naomi/ Laban showers are relatively new in Botswana and, as far as we are aware, are practised nowhere else. Before we continue, we would like to briefly explain the concept of *Botho/Ubuntu*, which is at the heart of the research project from which this chapter emerges.

The *Botho/Ubuntu* ethic

Defining the *Botho/Ubuntu* ethic and spirituality is not easy because, as observed by one scholar, the essence of *Botho/Ubuntu* is elusive and difficult to pin down (Gaie, 2007:32). However, we provide an overview of the concept, insofar as it expresses that which gives society the thread that connects and unites it. John Mbiti is known for having popularised the saying "I am because we are, and since we are, therefore I am" (Mbiti, 1970:141). At the heart of the *Botho/Ubuntu* ethic, therefore, is the communal ideal. *Botho* expresses the shared African philosophy that emphasises the importance of human relationships and values (Mmualefhe, 2007:3). The concept is founded on the African understanding that the existence and well-being of an individual person cannot be separated from the well-being and existence of others. Thus, one's well-being is defined by that of others in the spirit of "I relate, therefore, I am" (cf. Mmualefhe, 2007:3, following Mbiti, 1970:282). According to Gaie (2007:30), in Setswana, "*Botho* is simply human-being-hood or the essence of being a human person". He explains further that society expects certain behaviours from individuals that reflect the metaphysical reality called *motho* (a human being) as a being who "captures the moral concept of *Botho*" (Gaie, 2007:32). Therefore, without trying to provide an exhaustive definition of *Botho/Ubuntu*, we want to point out that *Botho* recognises the rights and responsibilities of all people individually and collectively; it promotes the social wholeness of all (Dube et.al., 2018:6). This is the force (as we shall see shortly) that drives initiatives such as Naomi/Laban showers that are the object of the study we carried out.

First, we will describe our understanding of rites of passage in order to situate the Naomi/Laban showers within the framework of rites of passage as they emerge in the context of Botswana.

Understanding rites of passage in Botswana: a historical background

Rites of passage are "ceremonies that mark important transitional periods in a person's life such as birth, puberty, marriage, having children, and death. The ceremonies usually involve ritual activities and teachings designed to strip individuals of their previous roles and prepare them for new ones".[2] Rites of passage, therefore, are rituals and/or ceremonies that accompany major personal transitions as individuals move from birth to death (Fischer & Gainer, 1993:320). A famous folklorist, Arnold van Gennep (1960) found that virtually all rituals share or follow the same tripartite, sequential structure of separation, transition and incorporation. According to Walter Gmelch (2000:3), the first phase consists of separating a person from the familiar social context; the second phase represents a gap between the old way of being and the new; the final stage is when the inner changes have happened, and the person re-enters the social order on a new basis. Thus, rites of passage mark a process by which an individual is separated from their old self or status to transition into a new self and status, and to be incorporated into a new position and stage in life. The process, which is necessitated by growth and development, begins at birth and spans a person's life, marked at every stage by rites of passage enacted in ritualised activities or ceremonies.

We now briefly discuss rites of passage in the context of Setswana culture and in Botswana generally. This is the backdrop against which the Naomi/Laban showers may be understood. As noted by Denbow and Thebe (2006:181), Batswana mark important stages in life with ceremonies and rituals. These stages include the naming of a newborn baby, puberty, marriage, and death. During such significant stages in the life of an individual, the community comes together to recognise and provide support to families and individuals as they assume new roles and responsibilities (Denbow & Thebe, 2006:181).

2 https://www.dictionary.com/browse/rites-of-passage

Birth and naming rites

Denbow and Thebe (2006) further explain that, according to Setswana culture, after a woman has given birth to a newborn baby, she undergoes a period of confinement (*botsetsi*), which ranges from three to six months (cf. Amanze, 1998:19). After the seclusion period, a ceremony takes place to reconnect her and the baby with the rest of the family and society. During such a ceremony (known as *mantsho*, which literally means 'the taking out from the house'), certain rituals are performed to welcome and usher the mother and the new baby into the community. During this time, the baby is also given a name, which would traditionally make reference to and connect the child to some event(s) surrounding the baby's birth. For instance, a child born during a rainy period was most likely named *Mmapula* (rain woman), *Rapula* (rain man), *Motlalepula* (one who comes with rain), *Pule* (Mr Rain), *Mpule* (Ms Rain), etc. (Denbow & Thebe, 2006:181-182).

Puberty rites

Traditionally, puberty was also marked by ritualistic activities – a practice that is no longer as popular in contemporary Botswana as it used to be (Denbow & Thebe, 2006). For girls, appropriate rituals were performed during the first menstrual period. They were confined for some time when they had their first menstruation, and older women would teach them about the stage of womanhood they were entering. They would be taught how to handle themselves hygienically every time they had their periods, how to become good wives, and the dangers of engaging in (premarital) sexual activity (Denbow & Thebe, 2006:182).

Another important ritual performed at puberty was the initiation ceremony, which marked an important transition from infancy to adulthood (Amanze, 1998:20). In Tswana culture, there were separate ceremonies for boys and girls; these were *bogwera* and *bojale* respectively. It is not clear what was taught to the initiates during the ceremonies, as they were very secretive ceremonies (ibid.:21). However, it is thought that the initiates underwent rigorous and intense training, which was considered important and necessary to train them for their responsibilities in the society as men and women. For instance, boys were taught their responsibilities as heads of families and how to effectively perform the duties entrusted upon them by the society (*morafe*). They also learnt important skills, such as dancing, carpentry, and making shields (ibid.:22). Girls were taught mothering and nurturing skills, cooking, as well as how to be respectful to their husbands and generally take care of their households. At the end of their initiation schools, the now-trained men and women were welcomed into the society as full citizens with certain rights, duties and responsibilities (ibid.:22). It was at the stage of puberty, with its accompanying rites, that gender roles were instilled into individuals so that there were clear demarcations between masculine and feminine roles. Men were taught to be tough as heads of their families and women to keep their lowly ranks as domestic workers, child bearers and servants of their master husbands.

Marriage rites

Amanze (ibid.:22) maintains that marriage is regarded as a very important passage in traditional Setswana culture, because it not only forms the basic unit of society, namely family, but it also ensures the continuity of the group, lineage and tribe. Ellece (2011:43) has noted that a ritual called *go laya* (ritual advice), is perhaps the most important of marriage ceremonies, in traditional as well as contemporary Botswana. Before a bride is presented to her in-laws, her married female relatives gather and take turns to advise her on how to be a good wife. Ellece maintains that recently even the groom is subjected to the *go laya* ritual, further pointing out that there are differences in the content that each is given (2011:43). During this ritual, gender roles are accentuated. Further still, Ellece (2011) argues that while the ritual is intended to foster a harmonious relationship between married couples, often it is self-defeating, given its patriarchal nature that eventually perpetuate inequality in marriages in Botswana.

Amanze points to another important ritual that accompanies marriage ceremonies in the country. According to him, payment of *bogadi* (bride price/dowry) is a ritual that transfers the labour of a woman and her childbearing properties to her husband and his family (1998:22).[3] This is a ritual in which the man, who wants to marry, pays cattle to the parents of his wife-to-be. *Bogadi* has sometimes functioned to legitimise the oppression and abuse of women. In many instances, it has given some men the excuse to behave as owners of their wives, claiming that they bought them for a price (cf. Masenya, 1997; Dube, 2003; Gichaara, 2008). Nonetheless, this chapter focuses on how Naomi/Laban showers are emergent rites of passage in Botswana. In what follows, we briefly outline the objectives and research questions that informed our research before expounding on the methodology that was used.

Objectives and research questions

Our study, the *Botho/Ubuntu* Project, had several objectives and research questions. The objectives were to:

1. explore the theological and spiritual basis of *Botho/Ubuntu* values/ethics;
2. examine how the *Botho/Ubuntu* ethos was understood and manifested in traditional Botswana communities;

3 See also Masenya, 1997; Chirawu, 2006; Ellece, 2012.

3. analyse how the *Botho/Ubuntu* ethos is expressed in contemporary urban settings of Botswana;
4. investigate how *Botho/Ubuntu* activities in the urban space construct and reconstruct gender; and
5. highlight how *Botho/Ubuntu* spirituality can inform the building and maintenance of justice-loving communities.

The research questions were as follows:

1. How is the *Botho/Ubuntu* ethos spiritually founded and manifested in the indigenous Botswana communities?
2. How does the *Botho/Ubuntu* ethos drive the Naomi/Laban, bridal and baby shower events in the urban space?
3. What cultural traditions and roles are produced, reproduced, or deconstructed in the urban space through the Naomi/Laban, bridal and baby showers?
4. How do these *Botho/Ubuntu*-driven showers forge an African-founded spirituality?
5. How can *Botho/Ubuntu* spirituality foster justice-loving communities that rally against the encroachment of poverty in urban spaces and empower women?

The idea of Naomi/Laban showers as emergent rites of passage is derived from research question number three of the *Botho/Ubuntu* Project, as outlined above. The question is: "What cultural traditions and roles are produced, reproduced or challenged in the urban space through the Naomi/Laban, bridal and baby showers?" As indicated above, this chapter focuses on the Naomi/Laban showers only. We have already shown that Setswana culture had and still has rituals and ceremonies to mark important transitions in an individual's life, and that these were and are known as rites of passage. Consequently, Naomi/Laban showers are similar to some of the traditional rites of passage, especially those related to marriage. This shall be demonstrated later in this chapter. But before that, we discuss the method(s) used in the data collection stage of the study. Our aim was to find out how the Naomi/Laban showers support our claim that they are emergent rites of passage in Botswana.

Methods

The mixed-design method of the research employed multiple data collection techniques that played a supportive role for each other (Mertens, 2014; Creswell, 2009). A combination of qualitative and quantitative methods (as used in the project) had advantages of convergence through the illustration of points, which brings in flexibility and verification of results. It also ascertains that facts are observed within the context and perspective of the respondent. The qualitative methods enrich the variables under study by linking them to specific incidents and observations. The research design is, therefore, both descriptive and exploratory in nature. The interactive character of the showers necessitated such a combination of methods. As noted by Jick (1979:608), the importance of such integration has been advocated by many scholars (cf. Reiss, 1968; Diesing, 1971). In summary, combining different methodologies in the study of one phenomenon, or triangulation as noted by Jick (1979:604) and others (cf. Denzin, 1978), is important in that the weakness in each method is compensated for by the strengths of another. The study, therefore, integrated fieldwork and survey methods. We collected quantitative data from the attendees through a self-administered questionnaire. Qualitative data were collected through participatory observation (cf. Bryman, 2001) coupled with extensive interviews of the organisers and beneficiaries. These methods were outlined in-depth in the proposal of the research project. We had used social media and other personal networks to get our informants, who in turn invited us to the showers. We took turns to attend the showers and our focus was on showers in Gaborone and other urban or peri-urban areas of Mogoditshane, Tlokweng, Kanye, Molepolole, Ramotswa and Mmopane. In total, 12 Naomi/Laban showers were attended by the research team. The two showers are almost always held concurrently. This is probably due to the nature of the showers themselves. That is, the Naomi shower is for the prospective mother-in-law and the Laban is for the prospective father-in-law, in which case the two parents may be a married couple – hence, the showers are held simultaneously.

Naomi/Laban showers: what are they and where do they come from?

According to our research findings, the Naomi/Laban showers are organised specifically for women and men who are about to become mother-in-law and father-in-law respectively. However, it was observed that during these showers, the bride- and groom-to-be were also invited and expected to attend. The showers can be traced to the biblical characters of Naomi in the Book of Ruth, and Laban in the book of Genesis. This section will begin with a history of each of the showers, which will be followed by a narrative description of the showers in order to orientate the reader to what really happens at the two ceremonies. After the narrative description, we will move onto a discussion of the data on the two.

The two showers started in Botswana, founded by a group of Christian women of Pentecostal background. The women, who now act as leaders, teachers, facilitators, and organisers of the Naomi/Laban showers, further revealed that they saw the need to teach – especially other women – the importance of being an in-law. These women asserted that one of their friends was preparing to receive a daughter-in-law, but the woman was worried about how she was going to accept the new member of the family. Thus, her friends organised a counselling session for her. The idea behind this initiative was to foster a harmonious relationship between the mother-in-law to-be and her prospective daughter-in-law. The ritual was intended to set a social platform to share ideas and experiences on the issue. They named the ceremony 'the Naomi shower'. As time went on, the founders realised that there was need to further their services to include prospective fathers-in-law, as well as to bring the prospective brides and grooms into the showers. The question now is "What do the showers have to do with the biblical characters branded after them?" Thus, we shall provide condensed summaries of the narratives of Naomi and Laban from the Bible.

The biblical Naomi character: Ruth 1-4

Naomi is a female character in the biblical book of Ruth, which can be summarised as the story of women who struggle to survive in a man's world (Masenya, 2004:46). The story begins with a tragedy in which a migrant family of four, namely Naomi and her husband Elimelech and their two sons Mahlon and Kilion, who originated from Bethlehem in Judah, and who were now in Moab, were struck by death. All the men, i.e., Elimelech and their two sons, died and left behind three childless widows, namely Naomi and her widowed daughters-in-law, Ruth and Orpah. The grieving Naomi decided to return home to Bethlehem, and she asked Ruth and Orpah, who were from Moab, to also return to their maiden families. While Orpah heeded Naomi and returned home, Ruth made a vow to Naomi thus:

> Do not urge me to leave you, to turn back and not follow after you. For wherever you go, I will go; wherever you sojourn, I will sojourn; your people shall be my people and your God my God. (Ruth 1:16)

The pledge has been described by Athalya Brenner (1993) as a memorable and poignant statement of loyalty. Another scholar, Patricia Tull (2003:56), describes the commitment as 'fierce fidelity'. Sharing similar sentiments, Carolyn Pressler (2002:256) asserts that Ruth's loyalty to Naomi "crosses ethnic and religious boundaries and flies in the face of social conventions". It is an example of what true loyalty entails (cf. Fewell & Gunn, 2009; Meyers, 1993). By so pledging, Ruth was not only selfless and loyal, but also trustworthy. Importantly, she and Naomi returned to Bethlehem together, where they lived in a loyal, loving partnership as mother- and daughter-in-law. Thus, the Naomi shower envisages that mothers-in-law and their daughters-in-law should learn from the example of Naomi and Ruth and endeavour to imitate them.

Nonetheless, the biblical narrative does not hide their imperfections. Naomi instructed Ruth to seduce Boaz (Ruth 3:3-4) and Ruth did as directed. For that, Naomi has been described as a crafty old woman (Campbell, 1974). Ruth herself can be faulted for agreeing to seduce Boaz and acting like a harlot (cf. Ruth 3:7).

It is such details and more that make the Naomi shower a deconstructive strategy to the biblical text. Notably, the founders are only interested in the dimension of the narrative that portrays its two female characters as exemplary to mother- and daughter-in-law relationships.

Generally, the relationship between mothers-in-law and their daughters-in-law can be the most difficult of all the in-law relationships (Jackson & Berg-Cross, 1988). Lucy Fischer (1983) contends that mothers-in-law and daughters-in-law have a potentially competitive relationship when compared to fathers-in-law against sons-in-law. It is on the understanding of such social conventions that the Naomi shower was conceived.

The biblical Laban character: Genesis 29-31

The narrative of Laban and Jacob is recorded in Genesis 29-31. Jacob wanted to marry Laban's youngest daughter, Rachel, but instead was tricked by the girls' father into marrying her elder sister, Leah. As the story unfolds, it is clear that the girls (Rachel and Leah) had no say in the entire play involving their getting married to one man, and that their husband had to work hard for their father. Laban further sought to dispossess Jacob of his hard-earned possessions (Genesis 31:7-12). Ultimately, the inevitable break-up between the two men occurred. Jacob fled with his wives and livestock, and Laban followed him. Finally, they made a contract to go their separate ways and to never harm each other.

David Petersen (2005) maintains that the Jacob and Laban story represents a time of difficulty. Their relationship was characterised by deceit and theft. The only realistic option was a separation expressed in religious terms as Laban swore by the god of Nahor, while Jacob swore by the fear of the god of his father Isaac. According to Petersen (2005), Laban's household was no longer viewed as part of the immediate family of Jacob. All that was left for Jacob was to hope for pardon and remission of legal consequences. In the context of Botswana, the Laban shower seeks to curb such possible tragedies between fathers-in-law and sons-in-law, and it serves as a deconstruction of the biblical Laban narrative.

A narrative description of the Naomi/Laban showers

Naomi/Laban showers are held in a home setting. The home where the shower is held is prepared so that tables and chairs are set up nicely for the ceremony, with tents for shade. The atmosphere is similar to a wedding ceremony in Botswana. See Figure 7.1 below.

Figure 7.1 The typical setting of the Naomi/Laban showers

What we observed is that the showers are organised by close friends and relatives and usually hosted by a friend to the one who is being showered. The attire resembles that of a traditional wedding ritual of *go batla* and *go laya* (the premarital counselling). Women are dressed in blue German prints known as *leteisi*, shawls and head scarves as shown in Figure 7.2.

Figure 7.2 Sitting arrangement and dress code at a Naomi shower. The two women seated in front on the floor are the prospective daughter- and mother-in-law. The rest are the attendees and facilitators.

The showers begin with a prayer and one or two Christian songs typical of a Christian gathering. One such song goes like this: *Modimo o re file sebakanyana se*, which means "God has given us this little opportunity". All the guests are greeted and welcomed by the leader of the ceremony. The prospective mother- and father-in-law and their prospective daughters- and sons-in-law are introduced. The facilitators of the showers take turns in the teaching. The Bible, especially the narratives of Naomi and Laban, form the basis of the teaching at the showers. However, any scripture deemed relevant can be used. For instance, at one shower, the teaching began with the reading of Titus 2:2-5, which states:

> Teach the older men to be temperate, worthy of respect, self-controlled, and sound in faith, in love and in endurance. Likewise, teach the older women to be reverent in the way they live, not to be slanderers or addicted to much wine, but to teach what is good. Then they can urge the younger women to love their husbands and children, to be self-controlled and pure, to be busy at home, to be kind, and to be subject to their husbands, so that no one will malign the word of God. (New International Version)

While the focus is on the prospective parents-in-law, all the attendees are reminded that they too should receive the teaching so that they can use it to better and foster their own relationships with their in-laws. The beneficiaries of the showers are advised to get ready to receive a new child, who is about to be born into their family as either a daughter- or son-in-law. They are also cautioned to let go of their child, who is to be given away in marriage to another family where s/he will be adopted through marriage. Prospective parents-in-law are further cautioned that once married, their children are no longer under their custody as they have become one with their marriage partners (Genesis 1:24). That is, parents are taught to let go completely and not try to 'remote control' their married children. The metaphor used is that, at this stage, the woman (Naomi) who is about to receive a daughter-in-law is expectant and on the wedding day she will be giving birth to a child. She is to love, care for and nurture this new child. The same teaching is given to the man (Laban). He is expected to love, teach, and impart his culture to the young man who is coming into his family. He is urged to treat him like his own son.

A special ritual that is characteristic of the Naomi and Laban showers is one in which the two families, who are about to become in-laws, are asked to join hands and unite as demonstrated in Figure 7.3 below.

Figure 7.3 A uniting ritual in Naomi/Laban showers

Ideally, there should be six people in the ritual, comprising three couples, namely the mother and father of the bride-to-be, the mother and father of the groom-to-be and the bride- and groom-to-be. In Figure 7.3, the women in the middle are the bride-to-be's mother on the left, and the groom's mother on the right. Still on the left are the bride-to-be's father, with the bride-to-be facing the groom and his mother. It is worth noting that in the above picture, the groom's father is missing and hence it is just him and his mother. This is typical of families that are single-headed. What happens here is that the two families face each other. The fathers on both sides hold onto their wives from behind while the two women at the front also hold each other and the bride- and groom-to-be hold hands embracing all their parents who are standing between them. The teaching is that not only are the two families becoming united through their children's marriage, but as the bride-to-be faces her mother- and father-in-law, they are now her parents, and vice versa. The bride- and groom-to-be then swap places in that he becomes a son to his wife's parents and his wife becomes a daughter to his parents. That is, while a daughter is born into one of the two families as a daughter-in-law, a son is born into the other family as a son-in-law. This is like the Setswana culture that says to the bride-to-be concerning her prospective in-laws during the premarital counselling (*patlo*) ceremony: "[T]hese are the parents we give you. You are no longer the child of this household. You are their child" (Ellece, 2007:234).

Naomi/Laban shower interview data

As indicated in the methodology section of this chapter, data were collected using various tools; the interview data chosen here are a sample to highlight what transpired at the showers. The data were chosen in an ad hoc fashion for the limited purpose of this discussion, which is to show how the Naomi/Laban showers are a reconstruction of the traditional *go laya* and *patlo* rituals, and in turn have become emergent rites of passage. The data cannot be exhaustively analysed, given the substantial amount that was collected during the research project. The questions are only a part of the interview guide that was used.

Question 1: Please explain in detail the purpose of the Naomi/Laban showers in the urban space.

Answers:

a. *Ke go aga motho ka bo ene* (it is to build an individual self).

b. *Go nale thuto ee tseneletseng. Go na le kgakololo mo batsading* (there is intense teaching. There is advice to the parents).

c. To build a relationship between mother-in-law and daughter-in-law.

d. It is educational and very important in teaching *Botho.*

e. Offers counselling to the new in-laws.

f. To shower the mother with gifts and advice from the word of God and from Setswana culture.

g. It is to share and give advice to the new in-laws.

h. To educate, build the community and assist each other.

i. To develop healthy relationships between bride/groom and their in-laws.

j. To assist the mother-in-law of the groom to know how to handle the groom as a new child in her family. It also assists her financially through contributions.

Question 2: How did Naomi/Laban shower(s) originate?

Answers:

a. *E tsamaelana le go laya ngwetsi* (it is related to the *go laya* (to advise) rite of passage. *Ngwetsi le matsalaagwe ga ba tshele sentle* (there is usually tension and conflict between mother-in-law and daughter-in-law).

b. *Baebele. Ga go fose kgolagano ya rona ya Setswana gope, ke gore gone go na le kgakololo ee tseneletseng e eseng sephiri* (Bible: it is similar to the Setswana tradition of *go laya* except that it is done intensely and openly – not in secret).

c. *Ke bona e simolotswe ke bomme, gape e tswa mo baebeleng. Ke selo se se siameng thata* (I realise it was founded by women and it is based on the Bible. It is something very good).

d. Having observed conflicts between daughters-in-law and mothers-in-law, it was designed to build relationships.

e. Before I did not know where it came from but after attending, I realised it is biblical.

f. No idea except I read it in the Bible.

g. A friend's daughter was getting married, and friends organised a session for her (the friend) to encourage her and contribute towards wedding expenses.

h. I do not know.

i. Some Christian women gathered together and saw the need to teach each other.

j. There was this lady who was preparing for her daughter's marriage ceremony and kept asking herself how she was going to accept the new member of her family and her friends organised a counselling session for her.

k. No answer.

Question 3: How do you compare and contrast Naomi/Laban showers with traditional cultural activities of welcoming a bride?

Answers (similarities):

a. *Go tshwana ka go laya* (the counselling is similar).

b. *Go nkgopotsa ngwana a batlwa* (it reminds me of the traditional *patlo*).

c. They are not different at all. However, note: I feel incompetent to answer this question since I am single and Ngwaketsi culture excludes unmarried women from attending *patlo*.

d. *Go tshwana le go laya ngwetsi le go laya mogwe* (it is similar to *go laya* the bride and the groom.

e. *Go laya le go rutubatsa* (to counsel and to calm).

f. Counselling.

g. *Go laya* (to give advice). *Dimpho* (gifts). Unity and oneness.

h. Dress code. Respect. Different counsellors are invited.

i. They all aim at character building. Advice. Encouragement. Financial support. Gifts. Attendance by friends, colleagues, relatives, church mates, etc.

j. Done by women only as organisers.

Answers (differences):

a. *Go laya ga batsadi eseng banyalani fela* (to give advice to the parents and not just the bride and the groom).

b. *Naomi e bua puo phaa…patlo ya Setswana e sephiri* (Naomi shower speaks openly while the Setswana *patlo* ceremony is secretive).

c. It exposes what culture keeps secret. *Naomi e ya aga* (Naomi shower builds) and does not tolerate oppression and unhappiness.

d. Naomi demonstrates that it can build families and the nation.

e. No answer.
f. *Matsale le batsadi botlhe baa laiwa* (the mother-in-law and all the parents are given advice/counselling).
g. It involves both parents.
h. Naomi/Laban gives spiritual support to the parents-in-law.
i. Traditionally, only married people attend.
j. Both women and men are mixed while culturally they do it separately.
k. Some cultural teachings can be based on cultural beliefs. Naomi/Laban showers are based on biblical principles. Cultural activities can be gender biased. There is a gate pass to attend, and money contributions are made immediately. There are some selected organisers. The Naomi shower allows unmarried women and youth to attend. The Naomi shower is more transparent. It encourages relationship building and openness. Men are allowed to attend.

Question 4: What changes do Naomi/Laban showers bring in the urban space when compared to the traditional activities in villages?

Answers:

a. No answer.
b. *E ka tokafatsa botsalano fa gare ga ngwetsi le matasale* (it can improve or foster a better relationship between daughter-in-law and mother-in-law).
c. *Go tshwaraganya* (uniting). *Go bua boammaaruri* (to tell the truth). *Go bua puo-phaa* (to say it openly) and explaining the Bible.
d. I am not sure. It is the first time I attended.
e. No answer.
f. Present giving.
g. In urban areas people are not related and friends come together to give support.
h. Cannot think of any.
i. Christian women gather from different denominations and share the activity.
j. The showers gather us and bring us together in the urban space where we would otherwise have remained separated.
k. The showers include both men and women and can bring mutual understanding between the two.
l. They are not restricted to traditional values handed down from generation to generation.
m. They include teachings from the Bible.
n. Provide both spiritual and financial support.

Question 5: Give examples of what might be identified as character-building in the Naomi/Laban showers.

Answers:

a. No answer.

b. *Matsale o rutwa go amogela ngwetsi le ngwetsi e rutwa go amogrla matsale* (mother-in-law is taught how to receive a daughter-in-law and vice versa). *Ha ba tshwaraganngwa go supa bokopano* (during the uniting ritual, unity is demonstrated).

c. By telling people what really happens, the Naomi/Laban shower tells it as it is; what may happen and what may cause it; they are better than pastors. They assist people to build their characters.

d. Teaches all parties to be tolerant of and accept each other in their differences.

e. Provide social support.

f. The advice given during the showers helps build characters, not only of the recipients but all those attending.

g. Biblical characters and biblically discussed.

h. Even the dress code shows respect and *Botho* is all about respect. In Setswana culture, we show respect through dress code and the same is done in the showers.

i. Accepting an in-law is the individual's responsibility and it contributes to community building. The mother-in-law is to serve as a steward to the couple and to mentor them throughout.

Naomi/Laban showers: emergent rites of passage in Botswana

We deduce that the Naomi/Laban showers are emergent rites of passage in Botswana. This is because while these showers re-produce and/or reconstruct some Setswana traditional rites of passage to some extent, especially those of *patlo* and *go laya* rituals, they are also different from *patlo* and *go laya*. During the traditional *patlo* ceremony in Botswana, women and men take part in separate counselling of the bride- and groom-to-be – women do it inside the house with the bride, while the men and groom sit in the front yard (*kgotla*). As proposed by Ellece (2011:44), the advice given to brides and grooms is based on a network of traditional discourses that perpetuate unequal power relations between spouses. The separate sitting arrangements during the ceremony clearly point to a segregation of gender in traditional Setswana culture. Gender roles are assigned and emphasised, and as further explained by Ellece (2011:44), the advice given perpetuates gender stereotypes. On the contrary, the Naomi/Laban showers, provide a joint counseling and teaching session with every attendee present regardless of marital status or gender. Thus, the showers allow for transparency compared to Setswana culture, which thrives on secrecy. They further deconstruct the *patlo* and *go laya*, which discriminate against unmarried women and men by excluding them from participating in the rituals (Ellece, 2011:45). For instance, when asked to compare the Naomi/Laban showers with traditional cultural *patlo*, one of the participants asserted:

> I feel incompetent to answer the question because I am single, and the Setswana culture excludes unmarried people from attending the ritual. Naomi/Laban showers are more relaxed and open. They involve both parents. Men and women are mixed while culturally they are separated. The showers allow unmarried women and youth to attend. They are more transparent; the advice and teaching are not done in secret. They encourage relationship building that is based on openness. Parents are given counseling and not just the bride and groom as in traditional rituals. The basis of the teaching is biblical although some cultural aspects are also apparent.

The Naomi/Laban showers appropriate the *patlo* and *go laya* rituals and recontextualise them so that the focus is not on the bride- and groom-to-be, but on the mother- and father-in-law, who are on the verge of receiving an in-law child. Thus, the Naomi/Laban showers acknowledge the importance of parents-in-law for the success of their children's marriage. Character building is intended for both parents and their children who are entering into marriage.

The Setswana culture is further deconstructed, appropriated, and adapted for biblical teachings. For instance, when the Setswana proverb asserts that *monna selepe oa fapaanelwa*, meaning "a man is an axe to be passed around" (Dube, 2003), the Naomi/Laban teaches that *wa rona ga se selepe*; that is, "ours is not an axe". The message here is that while the Setswana culture allows men to be promiscuous, the shower advice explicitly proscribes sexual immorality and infidelity. The bride-to-be is told to be faithful to her husband and vice versa. They use the metaphor of a 'well' – *sediba*, which means that the woman's body is like a 'sacred well' to her husband. In like manner, they teach that the husband must drink exclusively from the same well in reciprocation for his wife's fidelity.

Consequently, the showers are characteristic of rites of passage in that they are meant for a mother and father who are about to make a transition into the realm of being mother- and father-in-law. They are also inclusive of the bride- and groom-to-be, who are transiting into the statuses of wife and husband, as well as daughter- and son-in-law. The new roles and statuses of the beneficiaries of the Naomi/Laban showers are celebrated by the community of close family and friends who give moral, financial, and material support. Importantly, the community, much as in traditional rites of passage, offers guidance concerning the new ranks to be assumed. The teachings aim at building character in all individuals concerned. This in turn is in line with the spirit of *Botho/Ubuntu*, which, as we have seen, was the overarching objective of the *Botho/Ubuntu* Project.

Conclusion

The data explored throughout the chapter indicate that the Naomi/Laban showers have invested in the traditional rituals surrounding marriage new meanings and significance. The showers bring together all important parties, namely parents from both sides, and the bride- and groom-to-be, so that they are supported and ushered into their new phase of life, which are to be in-laws. The showers recontextualise traditional Setswana rituals and meanings, giving them new contemporary inflections. For instance, the Naomi/Laban showers are open to both men and women, married and unmarried, and the teaching and advice are done in an open and inclusive space. The spirit of *Botho/Ubuntu* is the driving force behind the initiative as it encourages the community spirit where individuals show love, care and support for their fellow human being. We have demonstrated that individuals who are to become parents-in-law are assisted by the community to transition into their new positions and responsibilities. Finally, Naomi/Laban showers are evolving as 'emergent rites of passage' in Botswana. However, because the chapter does not constitute an exhaustive study of the Naomi/Laban showers, there is more that the overarching research has shown, but is not covered in this chapter. The *Botho/Ubuntu* research has yielded quite a substantial amount of data from which a lot can be learnt, and which forms part of the content of other chapters and articles emanating from the research.

References

Amanze, J.N. 1998. *African Christianity in Botswana: the case of African independent churches*. Gweru, Zimbabwe: Mambo Press.

Brenner, A. (ed). 1999. *A feminist companion to Ruth and Esther.* Sheffield, UK: Sheffield Academic Press.

Bryman, A. 2015. *Social research methods.* New York: Oxford University Press.

Campbell, E.F. 1974. 'The Hebrew short story: a study of Ruth'. In: H.N. Bream, R.D. Heim & C.E. Moore (eds). *A light unto my path: Old Testament studies in honor of Jacob M. Meyers.* Philadelphia, PA: Temple University Press. 83-102.

Chirawu, S. 2006. 'Till death do us part: marriage and the law in Zimbabwe'. http://law.bepress.com/expresso/eps/1419 [Accessed 14 May 2023].

Coquery-Vidrovitch, C. 1997. *African women: a modern history*. Colorado: Westview Press.

Creswell, J.W. 2009. *Research design: qualitative, quantitative and mixed methodology approaches.* 3rd Edition. London: Sage.

Denbow, J.R. & Thebe, P.C. 2006. *Culture and customs of Botswana.* London: Greenwood Publishing.

Denzin, N.K. 1978. *The Research Act: a theoretical introduction to research methods.* New Brunswick, NJ: Aldine Transaction.

Diesing, P. 1979. *Patterns of discovery in the social sciences.* New Jersey: Transaction Publishers.

Dube M.W. 2003. 'Culture, gender and HIV/AIDS: understanding and acting on the issues'. In: M.W. Dube (ed). *HIV/AIDS and the curriculum: methods of integrating HIV/AIDS in theological programmes.* Geneva: WCC. 84-110.

Dube, M.W., Modie-Moroka, T., Setume, S.D., Ntloedibe, S., Kgalemang, M., Gabaitse, R.M. & Sesiro, D. 2016. '*Botho/Ubuntu*: community building and gender constructions in Botswana'. *Journal of the Interdenominational Theological Center*, 42(1):1-21.

Ellece, S.E. 2008. 'Gendered marriage discourses in Botswana: a critical discourse approach'. PhD thesis, Lancaster University, Lancaster, UK.

Ellece, S.E. 2011. 'Be a fool like me: gender construction in the marriage advice ceremony in Botswana – a critical discourse analysis'. *Agenda*, 25(1):43-52. https://doi.org/10.1080/10130950.2011.575584

Ellece, S.E. 2012. 'The "placenta" of the nation: motherhood discourses in Tswana marriage ceremonies'. *Gender and Language*, 6(1):79-103. https://doi.org/10.1558/genl.v6i1.79

Fewell, D.N. & Gunn, D.M. 2009. *Compromising redemption: relating characters in the Book of Ruth.* Louisville, KY: Wipf and Stock.

Fischer, E. & Gainer, B. 1993. 'Baby showers: a rite of passage in transition'. *Advances in Consumer Research*, 20: 320-324.

Fischer, L.R. 1983. 'Mothers and mothers-in-law'. *Journal of Marriage and Family*, 45(1):187-192. https://doi.org/10.2307/351307

Gabaitse, R.M., Dube, M.W., Kgalemang, M. & Madigele, T. 2018. 'Reproducing or creating a new male: bridal showers in the urban space of Botswana'. *Journal of Gender and Religion in Africa*, 24(1):79-95. https://doi.org/10.14426/ajgr.v24i1.42

Gaie, J.B.R. 2007. 'The Setswana concept of *Botho*: unpacking the metaphorical and moral aspects'. In: J.B.R. Gaie & S.K. Mmolai (eds). *The concept of Botho and HIV/AIDS in Botswana.* Eldoret, Kenya: Zapf Chancery. 29-43. https://doi.org/10.2307/j.ctvgc61hd.5

Gangoli, G. & Rew, M. 2011. 'Mothers-in-law against daughters-in-law: domestic violence and legal discourses around mother-in-law violence against daughters-in-law in India'. *Women's Studies International Forum*, 34(5):420-429. https://doi.org/10.1016/j.wsif.2011.06.006

Gichaara, J. 2008. 'Women, religio-cultural factors and HIV/AIDS in Africa'. *Black Theology*, 6(2):188-199. https://doi.org/10.1558/blth2008v6i2.188

Gmelch, W.H. 2000. *Rites of passage: transition to the deanship*. Opinion Papers. https://files.eric.ed.gov/fulltext/ED439094.pdf [Accessed 22 June 2019].

Jackson, J. & Berg-Cross, L. 1988. 'Extending the extended family: the mother-in-law and daughter-in-law relationship of black women'. *Family Relations*, 37(3):293-297. https://doi.org/10.2307/584565

Jick, T.D. 1979. 'Process and impacts of a merger: individual and organizational perspectives'. PhD thesis, Cornell University, Ithaca, New York. https://bit.ly/3o0mDcF

Kebaneilwe, M.D., Motswapong, E.P., Setume, S.D., Dube, M.W., Gabaitse, R., Modie-Moroka, T., Kgalemang, M. & Madigele, T.J. 2019. 'Emergent rites of passage in Botswana: the case of Naomi/Laban showers'. *Pula: Botswana Journal of African Studies*, 33(1):62-79.

Mabee, C. 1980. 'Jacob and Laban: the structure of judicial proceedings (Genesis XXXI 25-42)'. *Vetus Testamentum*, 30(2):192-207. https://doi.org/10.2307/1517524

Masenya, M.J. 1997. 'Proverbs 31:10-31. In a South African context: a reading for the liberation of African (Northern Sotho) women'. *Semeia*, 78:55-68.

Masenya, M. 2004. 'Struggling with poverty/emptiness: rereading the Naomi-Ruth story in African-South Africa'. *Journal of Theology for Southern Africa*, 120:46-59.

Mbiti, J.S. 1970. *African religions and philosophies*. New York: Doubleday.

Mertens, D.M. 2014. *Research and evaluation in education and psychology: integrating diversity with quantitative, qualitative, and mixed methods*. California: Sage.

Meyers, C. 1993. 'Returning home: Ruth 1.8 and the gendering of the Book of Ruth'. In: A. Brenner (ed). *A feminist companion to the Book of Ruth*. Sheffield, UK: Sheffield Academic Press. 85-114.

Mmualefhe, D.O. 2007. '*Botho* and HIV/AIDS: a theological reflection'. In: J.B.R. Gaie & S. Mmolai (eds). *The concept of Botho and HIV/AIDS in Botswana*. Eldoret, Kenya: Zapf Chancery. 1-27. https://doi.org/10.2307/j.ctvgc61hd.4

Montemurro, B. 2005. 'Add men, don't stir: reproducing traditional gender roles in modern wedding showers'. *Journal of Contemporary Ethnography*, 34(1):6-35. https://doi.org/10.1177/0891241604271332

Montemurro, B. 2006. *Something old, something bold: bridal showers and bachelorette parties*. New Jersey: Rutgers University Press.

Petersen, D.L. 2005. 'Genesis and family values'. *Journal of Biblical Literature*, 124(1):5-23. https://doi.org/10.2307/30040988

Pressler, C. 2002. *Joshua, Judges, and Ruth*. Louisville, KY: Westminster John Knox Press.

Reiss, A.J. 1968. 'Stuff and nonsense about social surveys and observations'. In: H.S. Becker, B. Geer, D. Riesman & R.S. Weiss (eds). *Institutions and the person*. Chicago: Aldine. 351-367. https://doi.org/10.4324/9780203788448-26

Rezeanu, C.I. 2019. Introduction to the phenomenological approach to urban, residential, and domestic space. *Logos Universality Mentality Education Novelty: Philosophy & Humanistic Sciences*, 6(2):42-56. https://doi.org/10.18662/lumenphs/10

Tull, P.K. 2003. *Esther and Ruth*. Louisville, KY: Westminster John Knox Press.

Tutu, D. 2004. *God has a dream: a vision of hope for our future*. London: Rider.

Van Gennep, A. 1960. *The rites of passage*. M.B. Vizedom & G.L. Caffee (transl.). Chicago: University of Chicago Press. https://doi.org/10.7208/chicago/9780226027180.001.0001

8

NAOMI/LABAN SHOWERS AND THE CREATION OF A WOMANIST-*BOTHO/UBUNTU* ETHIC OF COMMUNAL LIVING SPACES

Abstract

Marriage in Setswana culture is a community of relationships. One of these important relationships is the mother-in-law and her daughter-in-law. This relationship has historically been wrought with tensions and difficulties. In 2014, a group of Pentecostal Christian women formed the mother-in-law and father-in-law showers. They chose biblical eponyms, Naomi and Laban, to name parental showers. In this chapter,[1] we explore Naomi/Laban showers. Our exploration is based on data collected in Gaborone and surrounding areas over a period of eighteen months (2016–2018). We examine critically how Naomi/Laban showers build community. We also investigate how the showers construct and reconstruct gender. Our analysis of the data is framed by the intersectionality of womanist (or womanism) social theory and *Botho/Ubuntu* African philosophy. We conclude that Naomi/Laban showers create a womanist-*Botho/Ubuntu* ethic of communal living in which the mother-in-law must un-other her daughter-in-law to create a harmonious relationship between them.

Introduction

Women adorned in blue traditional *mateisi*,[2] their shoulders garlanded in either blue-checked mini-blankets or white scarves, own the veranda space. Their garb is the Setswana symbol of their marital statuses. The women are gathered for a new urban celebration: the mother-/father-in-law shower. The celebrated mother-in-law is either a mother, a sister, an aunt or a friend to any of the gathered women. Either her daughter or son is getting married. The women gathered are an important cloud of witnesses. Their gathering demonstrates the gendered and women centredness of the mother-in-law shower. Moreover, the congregated women are a gathered

1 The article, 'Naomi/Laban showers and the creation of womanist-*Botho/Ubuntu* ethic of communal living spaces' by Kgalemang, M. et al., was first published in 2022 in *Journal of the Interdenominational Theological Centre*, 51:1-54. It is republished in this volume by permission.

2 Sometimes called Shweshwe attire. It is common traditional attire for weddings and celebrations.

community of women seeking to assist, prepare and advise the mother-in-law on the values of receiving either a *ngwetsi* (daughter-in-law) or *mogwe* (son-in-law).

Traditionally, socially and historically, we are accustomed to women organising rites of passages such as bridal and baby showers. However, there is currently a new addition called the 'mother-in-law shower'. Similar to the bridal and baby showers, the mother-in-law shower is a new gendered ritual. It traces its origins to the year 2016, when four church women founded what they signified as Naomi/Laban showers. The shower was a product of their particular context; one of the founding women's son was getting married. According to the founders, she was a towering figure in her son's life. The co-founders articulated that she fitted the stereotypical image of the unwelcoming and domineering mother-in-law. The founders viewed her role as fundamental in her daughter-in-law's relationship with her husband's relatives.

Therefore, their goal was to prepare her for the mother-in-law role, so she "welcomes and fosters a healthy mother-in-law and daughter-in-law relationship" (Naomi Laban Data, 2016 – hereinafter NL). The founders created the Naomi/Laban shower spaces to socially recreate and reconstruct a new mother-in-law identity. Their decision to host a shower in honour of the future-mother-in-law reflects what Beth Montemurro calls a "collective conscience, a feeling that they belong to the community and thus are morally obligated to it" (2002:70).

Unlike the bridal and baby showers, the mother/father-in-law shower is not signified by its adjectival noun. It is, instead, signified by biblical character names, Naomi and Laban. Naomi is a mother-in-law to Ruth and Laban is Jacob's father-in-law. Naomi and Ruth's narrative are told in one of only two biblical books named after women, the book of Ruth. Naomi was an Israelite woman from Bethlehem, whereas Ruth was a foreigner, a Moabite. When famine hit Bethlehem, Naomi, along with her husband and sons moved to Moab for better productive lives. While sojourning in the foreign land of Moab, her sons married Moabite women. Soon, tragedy struck. Her husband died. Her sons followed suit. She, then, was left with her Moabite daughters-in-law, Ruth and Orpah. The three widows were, according to Amy-Jill Levine (1992), now defined by lack of husbands and offspring. However, while in Moab and seasoned with a poor, bitter and tragic life, Naomi learns that God had remembered Bethlehem with a bountiful harvest.

Naomi decides to journey alone back to Bethlehem. She urges her daughters-in-law to return to their respective homes. She blesses and releases them to find new husbands. However, they instantly do not share Naomi's sentiments. They insist on accompanying her back. Naomi refuses. They all wail. Naomi makes her case. Orpah relents. She goes back to her mother's house to remain with her people. We will not hear about Orpah again. Her decision exits her from the Naomi-Ruth stage (McKinlay, 1999:151). Ruth, however, insists on accompanying Naomi to Bethlehem. Naomi is still hesitant. Ruth makes a vow to Naomi. Naomi gives in. Ruth poetically declares:

> Do not urge me to leave you or to return from following you. For where you go, I will go, and where you lodge, I will lodge. Your people shall be my people, and your God my God. Where you die, I will die, and there I will be buried. May the LORD do so to me and more also if anything but death parts me from you.
> (Ruth 1:16-17)

The vow Ruth makes to Naomi sets the foundation of their future relationship. Ruth makes a commitment to accompany Naomi when she returns to her people. She will not allow Naomi to sojourn alone, so she makes a claim upon Naomi. She and Naomi will bond forever, Ruth promises. Ruth will build a life with Naomi, she vows. She leaves her people and her gods to be joined with Naomi's people and their God. Naomi becomes Ruth's mother-in-law and also her mentor in the ways of her people and of her God (McKinlay, 1999; 2004). McKinlay further states that, "for the Moabite herself, there will be no return; her bones will not lie in the soil of Moab" (1999:152). Only death can separate them. These claims reaffirm the bond between the two. They both return to Bethlehem where they will live together.[3] In the end, Ruth's mother-in-law, Naomi, organises for Ruth to marry a man. Ruth bears Naomi a son, and the community calls Naomi the blessed one.

The Laban shower is derived from the narrative of Jacob and his father-in-law, Laban, in Genesis 29-31. By the well, Jacob meets Laban's daughter, Rachel and falls in love with her. He decides he wants to marry her. In order to allow him to marry Rachel, Laban sets for Jacob a seven-year *lobola* labour requirement. On the day of his wedding to Rachel, Laban tricks Jacob into marrying Rachel's elder sister, Leah. When Jacob discovers and confronts Laban, he informs Jacob that the younger cannot marry first. Jacob again labours seven more years to marry Rachel, the love of his life. In the end, Jacob succeeds and marries both sisters. Thereafter, Jacob continues living with his wives and Laban's family while breeding goats and sheep that Laban gifted him. Laban continues to cheat Jacob by breaking his promises concerning the domestic animals that he allocates to him.

The biblical narratives of Naomi, Ruth, Laban and Jacob are key stories of value and importance to the Naomi/Laban shower founders. They set the background to the Naomi/Laban showers. The narratives are pertinent in establishing and building in-law relations, community, and knowledge. The narratives partly construct the values and belief systems of the Naomi/Laban shower practices.

3 McKinlay (1999:152): "... the two of them. Naomi returns; Bethlehem, home of plenty, is home to Naomi, but Ruth, despite her speech, is explicitly the Moabite, the daughter-in-law."

On the one hand, Naomi/Laban showers are produced and function in a Setswana social marriage setting along with its norms and values. On the other hand, the Naomi and Laban narratives are paradigms reading the Setswana contemporary world of in-law relations. In fact, Naomi/Laban narratives are used to think and write (or think with) mother-in-law and fathers-in-law relationships in Setswana marital relationships. Thinking with Naomi and Laban biblical narratives is an analytical and critical endeavour. To think with Naomi and Laban biblical in-law narratives is to conceptualise biblical narratives into modern contexts. For Naomi/Laban showers are sources of practical theology to the founders. After all, the church women define themselves as Pentecostal Christians who find solace and strength in the Bible as the Word of God. Thinking with Naomi and Laban biblical narratives assists in excavating and making meaning and knowledge. It conceptualises new socio-religious meaning.

In their appropriation of the biblical narratives, or thinking with Naomi and Laban narratives, new values, norms, ideas, beliefs, and constructions of in-law relationship are created. Therefore, the biblical Naomi and Laban narratives assist the shower facilitators to hypothesise liberating in-law relations. Thinking with Naomi and Laban biblical narratives creates a Christian-religious-social meaning. It assists in creating discursive spaces that have culturally been ignored. Naomi/Laban Showers use biblical narratives to articulate, and construct informed and idealised social and religious relationships. The Naomi and Laban narratives are a mirror held to the mothers- and fathers-in-laws and their relationship with their daughters- and sons-in-law. It is used to challenge prevailing oral norms, values, and tensions traditionally governing in-law relations.

Second, Naomi/Laban showers are intersectional practices. Intersectionality, coined historically to address the interaction of gender, race and class categories, also implies the amalgamation of multiple identities. Intersectionality, initially formulated to scrutinise what black feminists called the "interlocking systems of oppression"[4] helped to identity a combination of oppression, domination, exploitation and privilege. In this chapter, we locate Naomi/Laban showers as practices of intersectionality in that Naomi/Laban showers intersect with Setswana marriage values, norms and belief systems. Therefore, the significance of intersectionality is the interconnecting of systems, categories and practices central to women's lives. Intersectionality reveals that Naomi/Laban showers occupy multiple locations where the interlocking systems can

4 The concept of interlocking systems of oppression emerges in the work of three black women thinkers, namely Hooks, B. 2000. *Feminist theory: from margin to center* (3rd Edition). New York: Routledge; Crenshaw, K. 1991. 'Mapping the margin: intersectionality, identity politics, and violence against women of colour', *Stanford Law Review*, 43(6):1241-1299; Hill-Collins, P.H. 1990. *Black Feminist Thought: knowledge, consciousness, and the politics of empowerment*. Boston: Unwin Hyman.

either be liberating or oppressive. We, therefore, establish that not only is the Naomi/Laban shower categorised as a religious group with Christian values, belief system and practical theology, but it is categorised through (or by) traditional Setswana marriage with its culture/tradition and gender constructs.

A Setswana marriage is both a nuclear and an extended family affair. According to Isaac Schapera, a Motswana woman or man marries into the family of their spouse. Schapera writes about a "mutual agreement between the two families concerned, as reflected in the formalities of betrothal" (Schapera, 1970:118). The litany of Setswana marriage rituals and practices such as *patlo*, *bogadi*, *lenyalo* and *kgoroso*[5] are observed. For this chapter, we are more interested in the latter, namely the Setswana marriage practice of *kgoroso*. *Kgoroso* takes place after wedding celebrations at the bride's place, normally known as the first leg of the wedding. Once the first leg is completed, the bride is taken to her new home, which is her husband's parents' homestead. At her parents-in-law's homestead, another marital practice, *go laya* is conducted. However, the *kgoroso* practices of *go laya* is replicated in different forms within Naomi/Laban showers.

According to James Denbow and Phenyo C. Thebe (2006), *go laya* is "one of the traditional customs that occur for the bride and groom to be given advice" (ibid.:149). Similarly, Sibonile Ellece asserts that *go laya* in Setswana weddings is premarital advice or counselling (2011:44). It is a wedding ritual for the bride. Bakadzi Moeti and Hilda Mokgolodi write that premarital counselling is viewed as vital for instilling values of perseverance, tolerance, patience, and sacrifice in women entering into marriage (2017:65). Denbow and Thebe note that *go laya* consists of the bride and groom's "obligations and responsibilities to one another by the married members of their families" (2006:149). Further, Ellece asserts that the responsibilities of *go laya* lie with the bride's aunt and other married female relatives (Ellece, 2011:45; Moeti, 2018:82). *Go laya* forbids unmarried women participation. However, the *go laya* process does not solely lie with the bride and her married female relatives – the groom is also counselled by his uncles and married male relatives (2011:45). Nonetheless, there are challenges and issues pertaining to the process of *go laya*, which are often gendered and implicated in "unequal power relations in the family" (Ellece, 2011:45). Our focus is not on the production and implications of *go laya* by married persons. Our proposal, rather, is that Naomi/Laban showers appropriate the Setswana practice of *go laya* to counsel and advise the mother- and father-in-law.

The Naomi/Laban showers' appropriation of *go laya* of the mother-in-law and father-in-law was constructed parallel to *go laya* of the bride and groom. Realising that

5 Some scholars call it *Go isiwa ga Ngwetsi*. I prefer the more formalised name, *kgoroso*, and will use it throughout.

there are no cultural practices or counsel to prepare the mother-in-law in receiving her *ngwetsi*, the founders created Naomi/Laban shower to complete this dearth. Their objective was to create a space for a harmonious transition and to welcome the bride into her mother-in-law's space and homestead. Given that Naomi/Laban showers appropriate Setswana marital practice of *go laya*, we posit that Naomi/Laban showers are doubly embodied. On the one hand, they are driven by their biblical appropriation, and on the other, by the appropriation of Setswana practice of *go laya*. Through the Naomi/Laban showers' appropriation of the biblical mother-in-law, the utilisation of Naomi as a model of a good mother-in-law is intersected with the Setswana marriage concept of *go laya*. Given this background, this chapter analyses data from the ethnographic study of *Botho/Ubuntu* Community Building in Naomi/Laban showers, which was carried out in Gaborone and its surrounding areas in 2016-2018.

Methodology and data collection

During the period from 1 August 2016 to 31 March 2017, a group of researchers from the University of Botswana undertook fieldwork and collected data on Naomi/Laban, bridal and baby showers. We were divided into three groups according to the showers. Ours, as the preceding discussion demonstrates, collected data on Naomi/Laban showers. We initially concentrated our data collection in the city of Gaborone. However, due to the newness of Naomi/Laban showers, we chose to extend our collection of data to the surrounding semi-urban villages. The villages were Kanye, Thamaga, Molepolole, Ramotswa and Mochudi. We collected Naomi/Laban shower data from a total of 12 showers.[6]

Our focus group were people invited and attending Naomi/Laban showers. There was no sampling conducted as we did not have an existing available list of Naomi/Laban shower participants. We used the observation-survey-participant-questionnaire. Specific questions guided our observation. A self-administered questionnaire for individual participants addressed participants' biographical data. Moreover, in-depth interviews were given to the Naomi/Laban shower honourees and organisers. Our collection of data was driven by five objectives.The objectives were:

a. Explore the theological and spiritual base of *Botho/Ubuntu* values/ethics.
b. Examine how the *Botho/Ubuntu* ethic was understood and manifested in traditional Botswana communities.
c. Analyse how the *Botho/Ubuntu* ethic is experienced and expressed in contemporary urban settings of Botswana.

6 This study was made possible through the generous funding of the Nagel Institute.

d. Investigate how *Botho/Ubuntu* activities in the urban space construct and reconstruct gender.
e. Highlight how *Botho/Ubuntu* spirituality can inform the building and maintenance of justice-loving communities.

This chapter, therefore, draws and works on only two of the aforementioned objectives, namely:

a. Examine how the *Botho/Ubuntu* ethic was understood and manifested in traditional Botswana communities.
b. Investigate how *Botho/Ubuntu* activities in the urban space construct and reconstruct gender.

In order to examine and explore how the above objectives are met and fulfilled, we focused on the following two objective questions from the data:

a. How do Naomi/Laban showers build on or divert from African ways of community building?
b. How do Naomi/Laban shower activities in the urban space construct and reconstruct gender?

We argue that the focus on the *Botho/Ubuntu* ethic of the mother-in-law and father-in-law shower locates and places the woman at the centre of community building. In fact, the focus on the mother-in-law creates the mother-in-law subjectivity, a Naomi/Laban shower constructed identity of women while also enabled by the *Botho/Ubuntu* community logic. We frame our investigation of the mother-in-law's subjectivity, women building and creating spaces of *Botho/Ubuntu* harmonious community with womanist social theory and *Botho/Ubuntu* philosophy. We explore how Naomi/Laban showers' facilitators' counselling and teaching construct the practice and philosophy of *Botho/Ubuntu*. In the next section, we map the concept of *Botho/Ubuntu* African philosophy and the womanist social theory.

On the African philosophy of *Botho/Ubuntu*

The African philosophical concept of *Botho/Ubuntu* was the driving objective of our research and data collection. Since our goal was to investigate how Naomi/Laban showers demonstrated or cultivated the essence of *Botho/Ubuntu* and community building, this section will map the logic of *Botho/Ubuntu*.

Botho/Ubuntu's genealogy is traced to the Sotho and Nguni language groups of Southern Africa. According to Dumi Mmualefe (2007:1), "*Botho* and *Ubuntu* can be used interchangeably". It is rendered in Setswana as *motho ke motho ka batho ba bangwe* and in Nguni as *umuntu ngumuntu ngabantu* (2007:1). *Botho/Ubuntu* is a philosophical understanding that equates one's human identity with respecting, welcoming, caring and empowering the 'other'.

In his essay, '*Botho/Ubuntu*: The Heart of African Ethics', Ramathate Dolamo (2013:1) defines *Botho/Ubuntu* as "an agent or an instrument factor in human relationship and interaction". He holds that *Botho/Ubuntu* is an "ethical concept and expresses a vision of what is valuable and worthwhile in life" (2013:2). Dolamo asserts that *Botho/Ubuntu* is a "vision rooted in the history and centre of the culture of most African countries" (2013:2-3). He argues that the secret in *Botho/Ubuntu* is "for individuals to realise that they would become human only by becoming members of their respective communities" (2013:1). According to Dolamo, the axiom "I am, therefore we are" (ibid.) embodies an "understanding of what it is to be human and what is necessary for human beings to grow and find fulfilment" (ibid.).

Dolamo references Shutte's *Botho/Ubuntu* definition, which we quote at great length below:

> Our deepest moral obligation is to become more fully human, and this means entering more and more deeply into community with others. So, although the goal is personal fulfilment, selfishness is excluded.
>
> The concept of *Botho/Ubuntu* embodies an understanding of what it is to be human and what it is necessary for human being to grow and find fulfillment. It is an ethical concept which expresses a vision of what is valuable and worthwhile in life. This vision is rooted in the history of Africa. (Dolamo, 2013:1, 3)

Shutte's definition recognises *Botho/Ubuntu* with both moral and ethical principles. Its "moral obligation" (Dolamo, 2013:1) has no room for selfishness but is driven by and towards "personal fulfilment" (ibid.). According to Shutte, *Botho/Ubuntu*'s ethical concept is marked with an important and worth life pursuing vision. In essence, *Botho/Ubuntu* is relational at its core. It encompasses relational principles in which social beings form a community with the 'other'.

We understand *Botho/Ubuntu* as a community-building ethic, therefore we cannot speak of *Botho/Ubuntu* 'outside community' (see Dube et al., 2016). From '*Botho/Ubuntu*: community building and gender construction in Botswana' (2016:3), we noted that for Batswana of Botswana, *Botho/Ubuntu* is a "concept of acceptable relational living". We assert that "it was measured by one's relationship to family, community, the environment and the divine powers (ancestors and God)" (ibid.). *Botho/Ubuntu* has also a theological aspect. Mmualefhe captures *Botho/Ubuntu*'s theological function thus: "*Botho* is what constitutes God's image in us, and that … according to the *Botho* worldview, one can never be a Christian or attain salvation without *Botho*" (2008:22).

We discovered further that *Botho/Ubuntu* pervaded all aspects of individual and communal human relations. These included "local governance … ethic of valuing community" (2016:9) and welcoming and giving land not only to members of the community but to strangers as well. We defined "community" to include the "living, the divine powers, and the environment in an interconnected fashion" (2016:2). Dube et al. reveal that "the *Botho/Ubuntu* concept of communicating includes non-human members of the Earth" (2016:3). Puleng Lenka-Bula underlines that "relationality and respect for humanity is explicit in the understanding that human life cannot be full unless it is lived within a web of interactions of life, which include creation" (2008:380). Augustine Shutte, in his article '*Ubuntu* as the African Ethical Vision' (2009), locates *Botho/Ubuntu* as the conception of community. Shutte says it is "the insight that persons depend on persons to be persons; … It is this insight that gives the African conception of community its distinctive character" (ibid.:93). Community lies at the centre of *Botho/Ubuntu*. According to Shutte, community is an integral space where *Botho/Ubuntu* is practised. In his discussion, he references Leopold Senghor's concept of 'communalism' (2013). The value of *Botho/Ubuntu* is for "individuals to realize that they become human only by becoming members of their respective communities" (Dolamo, 2013:2). Thus, *Botho/Ubuntu* tells the story of humans as intertwined.

Botswana's *Vision 2016* provided a definition of *Botho/Ubuntu*, which became the national principle of the country. The vision defined *Botho/Ubuntu* as the "process of earning respect by first giving it and of gaining empowerment by empowering others" (Vision 2016, 2013). This vision also defined relationality as humanity to others. It holds that our humanity is only realised through other human beings. We can only exist through relations to the other. We are all others, and we exist as others to others. It is "an integral part of African ethics that is steeped in issues of liberation, development, identity, etc. It has to do with a person's integrity and dignity" (Vision 2016, 2013:2). Social beings understand the world through "an ethicality that inheres in our being with inescapable obligations" (Dolamo, 2013:3). This social bond demands then "that since it is an ethical one, this social bond is always demanding the rethinking of what the ethical and therefore, politico-ideological demand" (ibid.). They also see *Botho/Ubuntu* as a philosophy on "how human beings are intertwined in a world of ethical relations from the moment they are born" (Dolamo, 2013:2).

Botho/Ubuntu defines how the individual social can become fully human through relational practice with other individuals. Cornell and Van Marle (2015) signify this relational practice of *Botho/Ubuntu* as relational philosophy in their article '*Ubuntu* Feminism'. They assert that *Botho/Ubuntu* marks "how human beings are intertwined in a world of ethical relations from the moment they are born" (2015:3). Human are born as social beings. They are born, according to Cornell and Van Marle, into "a language, a kinship group, a tribe, a nation, and a family" (2015:3). They note further that we are mutually obligated to support each other on our respective paths to becoming unique and singular persons" (2015:3). The secret here is for individuals to realise that they can only become fully human by becoming members of their respective communities.

Having provided the various definitions and understandings of *Botho/Ubuntu*, we conclude that marriage, as we discuss elsewhere, is also a communal practice of the "philosophy of *Botho/Ubuntu* specifically in its practice of families uniting and continuing a lineage" (2016:9). We asserted also that since marriage is the "uniting of two families, the practice and ethics of *Botho/Ubuntu* were at the forefront of this union" (2016:9). Therefore, the Naomi/Laban showers build *Botho/Ubuntu* communities and relations between in-laws. It does this through an empowering and supportive community to the mother-in-law and her relationship with her daughter-in-law. However, the origins of Naomi/Laban showers by church women compels a gendered analysis of the data. We, therefore, locate our theoretical framework within womanism or womanist[7] social theory, which we discuss below.

Theoretical framework

Since this research is woman-centred and focused, a woman-focused theory is relevant to frame the Naomi/Laban showers. Therefore, this chapter is framed with womanist social theory. This theory is relevant because the objectives of our research and collection of data are attuned to the social and philosophical thought of African women's lived and material experiences. Womanist social theory incorporates particular cultural practices.

Womanist theory

Womanism is historically traced to the work of Alice Walker, a writer and philosopher. Walker details womanism in her book, *In Search for Our Mothers' Gardens: Womanist Prose* (1983), where she provides a number of definitions. Subsequently, other black women took up womanism and expanded its meaning and agenda. This section explores the work of two womanist scholars in addition to Walker's womanism. They are Chikwenye Okojo Ogenyemi and Clenora Hudson-Weems. Both Ogenyemi and Hudson-Weems slightly depart from Walker's womanism, while keeping the overlaps between them clear.

7 'Womanist' and 'womanism' will be used interchangeably throughout our discussion.

From *In Search for Our Mothers' Gardens,* Walker (1983) provides the following definitions:

1. From womanish (opposite of 'girlish', i.e., frivolous, irresponsible, not serious). A black feminist or feminist of colour. Interested in grown-up doings. Acting grown-up. Being grown-up. Responsible. In charge. Serious.
2. Also: a woman who loves other women, sexually and/or nonsexually. Appreciates and prefers women's culture, women's emotional flexibility (values tears as natural counterbalance of laughter), and women's strength. Sometimes loves individual men, sexually and/or non-sexually. Committed to survival and wholeness of entire people, male and female. Not a separatist, except periodically, for health. Traditionally universal. Traditionally capable.
3. Loves music. Loves dance. Love the moon. Loves the Spirit. Loves love and food and roundness. Regardless.
4. Womanist is to feminist as purple is to lavender (1983:xi).

Walker's first definition relies on the particularities of black American women and ties gender and race to reveal womanism as both a raced and gendered theory. It provides a certain quality of maturity and consciousness. Walker's second definition is about love (the epitome of womanism) and black women. Not only is the love filial but also sexual. Love is not only about a black woman's self-love, rather loving herself, her relatives, loves nature, but she has permission to also love other women sexually. However, the second definition's highlight is its last sentences in which Walker articulates and accentuates communal relationship, cooperation, and emphasis on relationship with men. Walker's succinct point that a womanist is "committed to survival and wholeness of entire people, male and female. Not a separatist…" (1983:xi) is an important value to Naomi/Laban showers. The last definition lays the relationship and point of departure between womanism and feminism. It insists the difference between the two are shades more than anything else: "Womanist is to feminist as purple is to lavender" (ibid.). This now famous axiom foregrounded the multiple voices of women of colour by their demand for seats at the theoretical table of women's rights and quest for freedom.

Monica A. Coleman (2013:3) asserts that Walker's definitions set the flame for a theoretical development of womanism as a social theory and philosophical analysis. Coleman, however, argues that Walker's definition raises "two significant challenges" (ibid.). First, that Walker's 'definition' is not really a definition (ibid.), even though Coleman appreciates Walker's 'poetic in nature' (ibid.) definitions. Coleman says Walker's definitions create resonance and rhetoric that is appealing to women of colour's sensibilities. Moreover, Coleman notes that Walker's definition is a "point of departure" (2013:4) to a distinct black or women of colour's own untangling of gender and race politics and intersectionality. This is a response against the history of feminism. Womanist was, therefore, historically set against the narrow political and social constructs of white feminism. Womanism argued against white feminism's sole focus on gender as a category of analysis. It argued that race and other categories are important too.

African women, African American women and womanist social theory

Ogunyemi is another womanist who articulates an African womanism similar to Walker's. In her essay, 'Womanism: The Dynamics of the Contemporary Black Female Novel in English' (1985), Ogunyemi holds that she came up with 'womanism' (1985:38) independently of Walker though both she and Walker see womanism as a "departure from white feminism" (ibid.:35). While Walker describes a distinctive African American woman experience (that perhaps does not cater per se for African women), Ogunyemi uses womanism to describe both the African American and African female experiences, which she identifies as black womanism (ibid.:38-44). She defines black womanism as an "ideology created and designed for all women of African descent" (ibid.:36). Its foundations are 'African culture' (ibid.). And its concentrations are the "unique experiences, struggles, needs and desires of African women" (ibid.). Furthermore, black womanist is celebratory in motive and drive. It is a "philosophy that celebrates black roots, the ideals of black life, while giving a balanced presentation of black womanhood" (ibid.:37). Not only is it celebratory, but its goal seeks a totality of black womanhood in the "dynamism of wholeness and self-healing that one sees in the positive, integrative endings of womanist novels" (ibid.:35).

Ogunyemi demonstrates black womanism by reading African and African American women's creative novels. She argues that, in comparison to white feminist novels, black womanist's creative novels are an articulation of (a purely) African womanist ethos. Ogunyemi asserts the following: "many black female novelists writing in English have understandably not allied themselves with radical white feminists, rather, they have explored the gamut of other positions and produced an exciting, fluid corpus the defies rigid categorization" (1985:26). Ogunyemi writes that the African womanist "incorporates racial, cultural, national, economic and political considerations into her philosophy" (ibid.:25) and that is why she is not "limited to issues defined by their femaleness but attempts to tackle questions raised by their humanity" (ibid.).

Similarly, Hudson-Weems creates a form of Africana womanist literary theory in a number of books and articles. In *Africana womanist literary theory* (Hudson-Weems, 2004a), Hudson-Weems sees Africana womanism as separate and different from all other women-based outlooks. She asserts that Africana womanism is "an endemic paradigm, separate and distinct from all other female-based perspectives" (ibid.:35). She traces the tenets of womanism to Africa as signified by the prefix: Africana. Africana womanism is a theoretical construct that unapologetically restores meaning within the African and African diaspora's women's experiences. According to Hudson-Weems, the Africana woman, "perceives herself as the companion to the African man and works diligently toward continuing their established union" (ibid.:41).

Hudson-Weems follows a similar trajectory to Ogunyemi by creating a womanist theory that strictly departs and is not informed by the theoretical framework of 'feminism' (ibid.:39). Hudson-Weems, however, differentiates her Africana womanism from Walker's. Hudson-Weems argues that Africana womanism should not be confused with Walker's womanist. Focusing on Walker's third definition, which is "almost exclusively in the women, her sexuality and her culture" (1983) and Walker's "affinity between the womanist and the feminist" (1983:ix) are not how Hudson-Weems postulates her Africana womanism. Hudson-Weems defines Africana womanism as "an ideology created and designed for all of African descent grounded in African culture, and therefore, it necessarily focuses on the unique experiences, struggles, needs and desires of African women" (1994:24). Hudson-Weems still asserts one other common thread between herself, Walker and Ogunyemi, which African women have "historically demonstrated that they are dramatically opposed to the concept of many white feminists who want independence from family responsibility" (2004b:38).

For Hudson-Weems, the Africana woman's role and opinions are critical to the overall community. She outlines about 18 features important to Africana womanism and its community building. These include self-definition, family centredness, wholeness, role flexibility, adaptability, black female sisterhood, struggling with male oppression, male compatibility, recognition, ambition, nurturing, strength, respect for elders, mothering and spirituality (1994:40). These form and create African womanism's first category (ibid.).

The characteristics are paramount to understanding the Naomi/Laban shower community building. Some of the defining characteristics are to be "family-centered; in concert with males in the struggle, spiritual, adaptable, mothering and nurturing" (1994:40). These are important in the translation and understanding of African womanists. Therefore, womanism is a theoretical framework that is viable to read and analyse the Naomi/Laban shower's *Botho/Ubuntu* creation of community.

Common to the three thinkers, Walker, Ogunyemi and Hudson-Weems, is their insistence on the multiplicity of women of colour's particular contexts. They note also that women of colour are conscious of their ever-shifting identities. Their reading of culture and society should incorporate the politics of gender, politics of sexuality, racial, cultural, and national issues affecting black women and women of colour. Womanism (or womanist) social theory as already noted is, therefore, a theoretical analysis for this chapter. Walker's "committed to survival and wholeness of an entire people, male and female. Not a separatist" (1983:xi) is poignant and relevant to Naomi/Laban shower's concerns and goals. Ogunyemi's "foundation of African culture" (1985:26) the celebratory practice, balanced presentation of womanhood and Ogunyemi's search for the "dynamism of wholeness and self-healing that one sees in the positive, integrative endings" (ibid.:35) are African womanism tenets apt and relevant for Naomi/Laban showers. The aforementioned are relevant for articulating Naomi/Laban showers as female spaces where meaning and community building of male and females is paramount. Thus, commitment to the flourishing and survival of black people is important to the framing and analysis of the Naomi/Laban shower. The Naomi/Laban shower forms of facilitation, goals and objectives reveal an exclusive negotiation and articulation of the African female experience, which in this case is the Motswana Pentecostal Christian woman's experiences.

Data analysis of Naomi/Laban showers

The creation of the womanist-*Botho/Ubuntu* community

From the *Botho/Ubuntu* and womanist discussion above, this chapter proposes that Naomi/Laban showers create a *womanist-Botho/Ubuntu ethic of communal living.* To demonstrate this proposition, we examine the Naomi/Laban showers' data to show how the *Botho/Ubuntu* ethic was understood and has manifested in traditional Botswana communities. Second, we investigate the data for *Botho/Ubuntu* activities in the urban space and how they construct and reconstruct gender. The following answers from Naomi/Laban shower participants are analysed to demonstrate the womanist-*Botho/Ubuntu* ethic of communal living.

When asked, "how do Naomi/Laban showers build or divert from African ways of community building?", the Naomi/Laban participants provided the following answers:

> Understanding each other through the teaching of Naomi/Laban showers adds to the community building and the African spirit of *Botho*. (NL11)

> The shower strengthens the prevailing value and cultures, e.g., ways of dressing, respect of family and marriage. (NL12)

Although it was not clear what ways of dressing ultimately meant, its function in the "prevailing value and cultures" of "respect of family and marriage" were palpable.

> The stakeholders begin to know and understand themselves better as they open to a wider spectrum of people, friends, colleagues, etc. (NL13)

> In African culture, people support one another in every way. When one family is in need, financially or needing food or clothes, other families provide. Therefore, the showers are similar, in that family needing support, are supported by well-wishers. (NL14)

NL11, 12, 13 and 14 (2016) articulate Naomi/Laban showers as spaces of community building. They asserted also that Naomi/Laban shower teachings "added to community building and the spirit of *Botho/Ubuntu*" (NL12, 2016) and stated the showers as spaces to share, learn and teach each other. Mabogo More, cited in Cornel and Van Marle (2015:3), notes that *Botho/Ubuntu* is a "philosophical concept forming the basis of relations … a traditional politico-ideological concept referring to sociopolitical action". The communal gathering reveals the *Botho/Ubuntu* ethical relations, which form the basis of unity and inscribes participatory obligation "to others and those others who are obligated to them … and ontologically narrated social being are actually intertwined" (2015:3).

Data for NL13 reveal the participants' own learning process when they observe themselves as beginning "to know and understand themselves better as they open to a wider spectrum of people, friends, colleagues, etc" (2016). This consciousness is well noted by Masolo's discussion of "participatory difference", again cited in Cornell and Van Marle (2015). A concept that "recognizes that each one of us is indeed different from all other people. The crucial part of this difference, however, is that we are also called to make a difference by contributing to the creation and sustenance of a human and ethical community" (2015:2). The participants stipulated that the Naomi/Laban showers teaching enabled them to play a role in the "creation and substance of a human and ethical community" (ibid.:2).

Participants responded variously regarding the creation of harmonious relationships. They noted the support people gave each other in African culture. One participant noted: "When one family is in need, financially or needing food or clothes, other families provide" (NL16, 2016). Another observed that Naomi/Laban showers "…add to the African ways of bringing people together as a team-encouraging *tirisanyo mmogo* (*communal practice*)"[8] (NL15, 2016). The participants recognised the Naomi/Laban showers as a social force at work in creating harmonious relationships that are non-stereotypical but affirming. Dube et al. cite Jean-Miller, Gillian and Jordan who assert women's communitarian harmony as instances where "women organize themselves around relationships and the ethic of responsibility care, and nurturing others" (Dube et al., 2016:9). According to these researchers, "women are involved in other people live through empathy, caring, and capacity for intimacy" (ibid.). This is womanist-*Botho/Ubuntu* ethic communal living in its practice, logic and value.

8 Phrase and emphasis added.

Again, Dube et al. (2016) assert that Naomi/Laban showers practise the all-encompassing spirit of women from various walks of life. They note that "a significant indicator of *Botho/Ubuntu*" (2016:9) is marked by being a "driver and community builder in the shower movements of Botswana" (2016:9). This sentiment was highlighted by Naomi/Laban showers participants. They note that not only are Naomi/Laban showers spaces of women communal gathering, but are open and inclusive to women of different marital statuses. Naomi/Laban showers operates the womanist-*Botho/Ubuntu* ethic of communal living with its emphasis on the value of every woman participant. Naomi/Laban shower participants noted that though marrige is the uniting of marrying families, Naomi/Laban showers extend the unity of marrying families through the creation of a non-blood related community. These non-blood families are self-created and self-chosen. This, we note, reflects a womanist-*Botho/Ubuntu* communal ethic in which "self-definition, family centeredness and commitment to family are major African community values" (Hudson-Weems, 2004b:45). In addition, the inclusive gathering of women produces a social bond that narrates and emphasises the ontology of *Botho/Ubuntu* in which women, through a womanist logic, are socially united for a womanist-*Botho/Ubuntu* ethic of communal existence.

Go laya and the production of the mother-in-law

> The showers' focus on *matsala* (mother-in-law) is to be commended. For a long time, things have been concealed and not spoken about. It is good since it chastises the mother-in-law and sisters-in-law, and we hope they hear. Therefore, it can build a nation. For a war within the family starts when a woman marries their breadwinner, so the wife is going to be seen as the one who uses their breadwinner's money. Note: it should be advertised, well known, and used. (NL15)

In one of the first preceding discussions of this chapter, we proposed that Naomi/Laban showers appropriate the Setswana concept of *go laya*. Following Ellece, we defined *go laya* as premarital advice or counselling practice (2011:44). Similarly, Denbow and Thebe (2006:149) note that *go laya* is a traditional custom of 'advice' to the bride and groom. Naomi/Laban showers appropriate this Setswana traditional custom of premarital advice and instruction. NL15 participant demonstrates that Naomi/Laban shower's focus on the mother-in-law is an appropriation of the Setswana ethic of *go laya* or counselling. The participants note that the "focus on the mother-in-law" (NL15, 2016) is a wise move, because the role and representation of the mother-in-law was historically hidden if not ignored, yet she held an important role. Another participant noted that the "mother-in-law was hardly advised on how to treat her daughter-in-law" (NL15, 2016). We propose that one of Naomi/Laban showers' goals is to reproduce the mother-in-law. With this point, we note Naomi/Laban showers' communal spaces as sites of the mother-in-law production.

Participants at NL15 articulate that the "focus on *matsale* (mother-in-law) is to be commended" (2016), thus making the mother-in-law the protagonist of the showers. Her well-being and that of her social relations are given priority through the guided, envisioned, organised social, ethical and spiritual teachings dominating the showers. Apparently, social, cultural, and traditional practices of Setswana marriage had historically concealed information regarding the role of the mother-in-law. Schapera writes that when the *ngwetsi* (daughter-in-law) went to live with her in-laws, "her lot is notoriously difficult, for her conduct will be closely scrutinized. She is expected to be humble and respectful, work hard and in effect be the general servant of the household" (1994:149). The mother-in-law's role in making "her lot notoriously difficult" (1994:149) is one element Naomi/Laban showers sought to undo and deconstruct.

The incessant practice to produce Naomi/Laban showers as sites of the production of the mother-in-law is not to produce as per Angelo Nicolaides "ideology of radical individualism" (2015:5), but to reproduce her in relation to her daughter-in-law. Her community is "not abstract and outside" (ibid.), but is "part of who and how we are with others" (ibid.), that is, part of who the mother-in-law is and how she is with others. This *Botho/Ubuntu* logic and practice realised in Naomi/Laban showers reflects "an intertwinement that makes *Botho/ Ubuntu* transformative as there is always more work to do together in shaping" in-law future relations (ibid.).

Participants noted that Naomi/Laban showers performed forms of preparation and advice in resolving and addressing conflicts. They note that often tensions exist between the mother-in-law and her daughter or son-in-law. For example, tensions can brew when a daughter-in-law marries a man who is closely tied to his family because her in-laws will expect or demand the right to full financial support from their son. If a woman marries their breadwinner-son, "a war within the family starts, for the wife is going to be seen as one who uses their breadwinner's money" (NL16, 2016). Therefore, Naomi/Laban showers' goal is to empower, or *go laya*, in-law relations by reimaging and reconfiguring a new harmonious and communal relations of family in-laws.

Furthermore, it is important to note that when Naomi/Laban showers appropriate *go laya* or counsel the mother-in-law, they do not replace the original Setswana practice. Instead, they differently build on the *go laya* concept. Furthermore, they do not replicate its tenets but reproduce its logic. They deconstruct and reshape the cultural expectation (or assumption) and construction of the difficult and unwelcoming mother-in-law. Through *go laya* of the mother-in-law, Naomi/Laban showers seek to achieve a smoother effect of community building and transition. The showers shape *go laya* with Naomi/Laban logic of values, beliefs system and communal living ethic. Therefore, the decision to counsel/*go laya* the mother-in-law and daughter-in-law reconfigures what was culturally a difficult in-law-relationship between the daughter-in-law and the mother-in-law. This reconfiguration is affirmed with Mmualefe's assertion that *Botho/Ubuntu* "emphasizes relationships; it is about concern for others. *Motho* is a 'relating thing'" (Mmualefe, 2007:3; see also Dube, 2018).

The theme of inclusivity recurs in a deconstructive move in the Naomi/Laban showers' *go laya* practice. Naomi/Laban participants noted that the Setswana *go laya* marital practice is exclusive to married people. They alone qualify *go laya.* According to Ellece, "the duty of counselling the bride lies with her married aunts and other married female relatives. The groom is counselled by his married uncles and other married male relatives" (2013:45). However, Naomi/Laban showers are inclusive. Comparing and marking Naomi/Laban shower unique from Setswana traditional marriage activities, participants articulated openness and inclusivity "to a wider spectrum of people, relatives, friends, colleagues, unmarried individuals, etc. Setswana traditional marriage practices limit attendance to specific groups" (NL, 2016). The Naomi/Laban showers include all women, be they single, married, divorced, or widowed. Its logic is that the community of Setswana marriage includes single, married, divorced and widowed relatives of the mother-in-law and daughter-in-law.

This practice, according to Dolamo (2013:1), demonstrates that "*Botho/Ubuntu* is an agent or a factor in human relationship and interaction". Dolamo further argues that the secret in *Botho/Ubuntu* is "for individuals to realize that they would become human only by becoming members of their respective communities" (ibid.). Therefore, this inclusion thinks and writes a *Botho/Ubuntu* "ontology and epistemology" (ibid.:3) of an inclusive community that is determined by every individual forming a community of "I am, therefore, we are" (Mmualefhe, 2007:7). *Botho/Ubuntu* "always entails a social bond, but one that is always in the course of being shaped and reshaped by the heavy ethical demands it puts on all its participants" (Dolamo, 2013:3).

The Naomi/Laban shower narratives and the creation of the mother-in-law womanist-*Botho/Ubuntu* subjectivity

This section investigates how *Botho/Ubuntu* activities in the urban space construct and reconstruct gender. We closely read and critically analyse the Naomi/Laban showers' facilitators' narratives for the following objective as initially stated: How the Naomi/Laban shower facilitators' data narratives construct and reconstruct gender through the representation of the mother-in-law as a driver and builder of the community and how that representation is an example of manifesting community.

The narratives of the showers' facilitators are the foundational texts of the showers. The narratives can be signified as the arts and transcripts of reconstruction and reconfiguration.[9] The narrative transcripts forge and create Naomi/Laban showers as new cultural spaces. Olga Idriss Davis cites Martin and Nakayama who define cultural spaces as "both a particular location that has culturally constructed meaning and a metaphorical space from which we communicate" (Davis, 1999:365). Naomi/Laban showers create female "particular locations" (ibid.) that culturally construct and reconstruct gender meaning. Naomi/Laban showers are also "metaphorical spaces" (ibid.) located in the "experiences to focus on the relationship between communication and culture" (ibid.). Since gender is an important focus of the showers, the facilitators' narratives foreground the mother-in-law as the driver and builder of community. The facilitators' narratives emphasised her reign within the domestic space. There were instances where the mother-in-law was advised to seek her own independent space from her husband by not becoming the link between her daughter-in-law and husband.

Both womanist and *Botho/Ubuntu* have similar values and have the potential to enable more liberating and emancipatory experiences for women. The womanist ethic insists on turning a critical eye on culture and social images – Naomi/Laban showers turn a critical eye on negative cultural experiences of mothers-in-law and daughters-in-law. Through the narratives, the showers critically intervene in gender discourses of oppression.

The Naomi/Laban showers' facilitators' opening statements are reproduced below:

> We are here to explore how to receive daughters-in-law in our families and to build affirming relationships. We are holding this shower so that we can honour God the creator of marriage, so that we can avoid the curse of Miriam. We realise that while there are numerous bridal showers held for the soon to be brides, to prepare them for the marriage institution, no one, on the other hand, prepares the parents of the couples who about to marry. There is an assumption, rather, that these parents know how to receive a daughter-in-law or a son-in-law. Evidence on the grounds, however, indicates otherwise, since mothers-in-laws are known to oppress their daughters-in-laws leading to marriage break. Reading the book of Naomi gives us a good example on building a healthy relationship with our daughter-in laws. (NL17, 2016)

The facilitators' narratives indicate they are intentional in their *go laya*/counsel. The facilitators noted there was a dearth in premarital and marital practices such as

9 This art of reconstruction and reconfiguration is informed by James C. Scott's famous book, *Domination and the arts of resistance: hidden transcripts* (1990). Domination proposes that in any context, a public script be produced and displayed in the face of direct surveillance, while simultaneously a hidden transcript is spoken on stage. Naomi/Laban showers do not fulfil either. However, the idea of transcripts or arts is quite relevant to the work that the showers perform.

bridal showers or *go laya* marital practices. They observed that the brides are often thoroughly prepared. However, they pointed out that the parents of the marrying couple are hardly initiated into receiving and relating with their daughters- or sons-in-laws. They cautioned that this important relation is often left to unfold on its own. Their goal, therefore, was to prepare how mothers-in-law can receive their daughters-in-law and build life-affirming relationships.

They argued that mothers-in-law are historically instrumental in the in-law relationships and have often played a role in their children's marriage. The showers' facilitators indicated the tyranny of the mother-in-law was produced by the mother-in-law's unwelcoming domestic spaces and bad attitude towards her daughter-in-law. They disclosed that "evidence on the ground says the mother-in-law" (NL16, 2016) is the instigator of tensed relationship with and to her daughter-in-law. They noted that "mothers-in-laws are known to oppress their daughters-in-laws leading to marriage break" (NL16, 2016). They pointed also the difficulty of mothers-in-law letting go or releasing their sons for marriage. Using the metaphors of cutting, they asserted they want to cut "the chain of the mother-in-law revenge on their daughter-in-law", for the mothers-in-law have suffered "traditionally from their (own) mothers-in-law" (NL16, 2016).

Noting the mother-in-law as the instigator may perhaps be unfair particularly if looked through gender stereotyping. However, the fact that the mother-in-law can create difficult communal existence is because the showers acknowledge and recognise the domestic space as traditionally female. The mother-in-law occupies and controls the "container of social actions" (Rezeanu, 2015:10). The mother-in-law's gender control of the domestic space is where she wields her power. Low, referenced in Cataline-Ionela Rezeanu (ibid.:12), argues that "gender and space are produced in interactions influencing and being influenced by larger social structures and that gender identity and gender relations are produced in interactions that reproduce the cultural construction of gender differences". However, the mother-in-law should not be solely seen as the one and only actor. She is also an "actor influencing and being influenced by social interactions" (ibid.:10) such as her own in-law socialisation and experiences. Naomi/Laban Showers seek to reinvent the mother-in-law's domestic space and its social interactions from oppressive and tyrannical practices.

A womanist ethic's interaction with *Botho/Ubuntu* community building has the potential to present and initiate liberating communal spaces. Naomi/Laban shower facilitators articulate the following: "We the Naomi/Laban shower facilitators, focus on the mother-in-law (particularly the groom's mother)" (NL3, 2016) because the "mother-in-law is the most important person in the lives of her married son" (NL3, 2016). Since the mother-in-law is the central figure, or the showers' protagonist, we propose that her subjectivity is the driving power in building womanist-*Botho/*

Ubuntu ethics of communal living. We posit that Naomi/Laban showers create the *Mother-in-Law subjectivity*. Subjectivity simply means created identity. Identity can be socially, politically, culturally, and religiously constructed. Most importantly, subjectivity means "to take the perspective of the individual self, rather than some neutral, objective, perspective, from outside the self's experience" (Lewis, 2020:1). In the Naomi/Laban showers' context, the subjectivity of the mother-in-law requires social empathy towards her daughter-in-law. The mother-in-law's subjectivity as discussed in the preceding paragraphs often entailed tyrannical and oppressive mother-in-law subjectivities to her daughter-in-law; that is the subject acts on the object. After all, the mother-in-law was in her space and site of power and control. However, the shower facilitators take the lived experiences of both the mother-in-law and daughter-in-law seriously.

Naomi/Laban showers seek to create the mother-in-law's subjectivity as a non-domineering figure. Because the mother-in-law's subjectivity is ontologically her being, it constitutes how she sees and creates her social world (Gaie & Mmolai, 2007:30). In fact, their purpose is to deconstruct the (historically and socially) domineering mother-in-law subjectivity with an intention to create and reproduce domestic spaces of harmony, liberation, empowerment and resistance against tyrannical representations of the mother-in-law subjectivity. In simple terms, the mother should create an ethical relationship.

Botho/Ubuntu narrates that ontologically social beings are actually intertwined, while womanist insists on transformative women subjectivities. Since the mother-in-law's subjectivity is a recurring theme, if not the foundation of the showers, the mother-in-law's subjectivity is linked and connected to her daughter-in-law or son-in-law. The showers seek to reconstitute her subjectivity. Paola Rebughini says that subjectivity is "relational, when the subject is the result of the relationship he or she has with other subjects and with immediate environment…" (2015:2). As a womanist-*Botho/Ubuntu* subject, the mother-in-law's role is a social and religious subject engaged in *Botho/Ubuntu* relational processes with her daughter-in-law. Davies states that "Womanism is also a process of self-conscious struggle that empowers women and men to actualize a humanist vision of community" (1999:366).

How then does the mother-in-law's subjectivity function to perform and create affirming and conducive relationships? The mother-in-law's subjectivity is rebuilt and reconfigured from the traditional and gendered identities and practices of oppression and domination to a welcoming and liberating figure to her daughter-in-law. Two practices emerge in the subjectivity of the mother-in-law: first is the womanist consciousness of the mother-in-law's new subjectivity, and second is that the mother-in-law's subjectivity is one with agency.

The mother-in-law's agency is deployed through the practice of the "resisting subject" (1994:37). She (must) resist meddling in her son's marriage through initiating harmonious relationship with her daughter-in-law. But subjectivity is not an individual identity. It is an identity produced by articulating the *Botho/Ubuntu* logic about character and conduct of the mother-in-law. Her subjectivity is an important vehicle through which *Botho/Ubuntu*'s can build interdependence of persons for the development and fulfilment of their potential to be both individuals and community through the practice of 'un-othering'.

The 'un-othering' of the daughter-in-law is one of the key driving values of the Naomi/Laban shower. We appropriate the logic of othering to frame the daughter-in-law's identity in relation to her mother-in-law. Subjectivity in identity and culture has always developed through its interaction with the other. If the mother-in-law is the subject, the daughter-in-law is located in the other. She is, in essence, an 'other'. Othering is a term that expresses prejudice based on group or individual identities. It signifies the many various forms of prejudice and oppression. John A. Powell and Stephen Menendian define othering as "a set of dynamics, process, and structures that engender marginality and persistent inequality across any of the full range of human different based on group identities" (Powell & Mendendia, 2017). Othering captures "expressions of prejudice and behaviours" (ibid.) that are unwanted and undesired. The other is an identity that is the complete opposite of the subject. The other is often an anomaly. The other is a stranger to be known only through negativity and limitations. The other is often marginal. The other is unwanted, unwelcome and remains in the periphery. The mother-in-law's subjectivity is critical in the un-othering of the daughter-in-law.

When a woman marries into a family, she is an other and a foreigner to her husband's people, particularly to her husband's mother. Foreignness relates to strange, unknown, and un-belonging. Therefore, her foreignness and otherness is opposite to her mother-in-law. The Naomi/Laban shower facilitators rightly noted the daughter-in-law's foreignness. They pointed that she is a foreigner, because she "has been raised differently'; (the mother-in-law) does not actually know how her daughter-in-law was raised; therefore, (the mother-in-law) must receive her, and (the mother-in-law) and was often required, traditionally, to create a space for her demonstrated in famous songs, such as "*mosutele, mosutele, ke yoo fitlhile*..."[10] (NL15, 2016). Moeti and others claim this song is sung to welcome the bride to her husband's family. The song says: "Make space for your daughter-in-law. She has arrived." They say the song

10 This is a song that usually accompanies Setswana wedding celebrations. It goes like this: "*Mmatswale tlogela dipitsa tseo; Monnga tsona ke yo o fitlhile; Mosutele, Mosutele, ke yo o fitlhile*". This song translates as "the mother-in-law should refrain from cooking, as the owner has arrived; the mother-in-law should step aside for her daughter-in-law to take over".

underscores "communalism that the wife is coming to a place where the mother-in-law has been in control of the kitchen, so the mother-in-law has to create a space for the wife to participate in household duties so that together they may know each other better and hence build a relationship" (2017:69). The song's sentiment, however gendered, echoes the mother-in-law's welcoming of her daughter-in-law. However, Naomi/Laban showers are not so easily lulled. They insist on a visible real practice and ceremonial practice of receiving the daughter-in-law. Therefore, the mother-in-law should rework to un-other her daughter-in-law. Like the biblical Naomi, the mother-in-law should make a home for her daughter-in-law. She must create a harmonious social existence.

The following biblical allusions were used to emphasise the mother-in-law's role in 'un-othering' her daughter-in-law:

> Naomi took a daughter-in-law and they were not from the same place. Naomi was a mother-in-law from Bethlehem and her son married Ruth from Moab. Naomi called Ruth, "my daughter", and taught her how-to live in the Bethlehem culture. Her survival is [dependent on] her mother-in-law. The mother-in-law needs to be trained on how to receive her daughter-in-law. (NL17, 2016)

Insisting that the daughter-in-law should be un-othered, Naomi/Laban shower facilitators use pregnancy, labour pain and delivery metaphors. The Naomi/Laban shower facilitators insist that the mother-in-law should think herself delivering a new daughter through the practice of *kgoroso* (the official bringing in of a new wife to her husband's family). Since the husband is the head of the family in Setswana culture, the wife is usually taken or delivered to her husband's people. Even though the daughter-in-law and her husband live in a different geographical place, the husband's mother's homestead becomes the most important space of their lives. It is where the daughter-in-law will first make her home and will always remain part of his home, apart from the city (workplace) dwelling and her independent home that she builds with her husband. Therefore, the daughter-in-law's relationship with her mother-in-law is very important. The Naomi/Laban shower facilitators insist that prior to the *kgoroso*, the mother-in-law should begin to think with the idea of pregnancy, labour and delivery of a new daughter.

How then do these metaphors function in the un-othering of her daughter-in-law? On the day of *kgoroso*, the mother-in-law should receive her daughter-in-law with a mindset of delivery and imagine birth pangs. They suggested the following to one of the mothers-in-laws:

> Mrs Stella,[11] you are receiving a daughter on the 3rd of November 2016. We pray that you should be highly expectant and give birth to a daughter on

11 Not her real name.

> November 3rd. Deliver a daughter. After delivery, you can no longer call her *ngwetsi* or daughter-in-law. She is your daughter. If you fail to deliver her, you will not properly receive her.

The metaphor is a theoretical significance for the mother-in-law to think herself as giving birth to a daughter. The mother-in-law will birth her daughter-in-law through *kgoroso* marital celebrations. The metaphor of birthing or delivering a baby, rather a daughter-in-law, was appropriated to reframe her role and transfer her status from mother-in-law to mother proper. The mother-in-law will encounter her daughter-in-law in the "singularity of the other" (Rivera, 2007:65), and not in the opposition of the self and the other. The mother-in-law must "not only create inclusive structures, but (she) must foster new identities and inclusive narratives that can support all" (Barkey, 2017:40). After that, the daughter-in-law will no longer be othered. She, like her mother, is a subject, in fact, a daughter.[12]

Conclusion

This chapter explored womanist-*Botho/Ubuntu* ethic of communal living in Naomi/Laban showers in Gaborone and surrounding semi-urban areas. We drew from both womanist/womanism social theory and the African philosophy of *Botho/Ubuntu* to read gender construction and creation of *Botho/Ubuntu* community in Naomi/Laban showers. This study discussed how reading with and through biblical in-law narratives was essential to Naomi/Laban facilitators' counsel while simultaneously drawing on the Setswana marital practices of *go laya* to counsel the mother-in-law. We argued through a close reading and analysis of the Naomi/Laban shower data that the showers create and build inclusive womanist spaces and *Botho/Ubuntu* community living with the focus on the mother-in-law and daughter-in-law relationship. The mother-in-law as the protagonist of the Naomi/Laban shower is empowered to forge her own unique identity with her daughter-in-law. This unique identity is constructed against the deconstruction of negative scripts of a traditional Motswana mother-in-law, which may possibly be patriarchal constructs of women and their relations with each other. Given the above summation of our study, more questions can be posed to the nature of the showers such as, for example, their construction of womanist-centred spaces. Therefore, we have proposed and demonstrated that the Naomi/Laban showers are in the business of creating a womanist-*Botho/Ubuntu* ethic of communal living.

12 In fact, the new endearing labels are now mother-in-love and daughter-in-love, replacing mother-in-law and daughter-in-law.

References

Barkey, K. 2017. 'Contemporary cases of shared sacred sites: forms of othering or belonging?' *Othering and Belonging*, 3:30-49. https://www.otheringandbelonging.org/sharedsacredsites/

Coleman, M.A. 2006. Roundtable discussion: must I be womanist?" *Journal of Feminist Studies in Religion*, 22(1):85-134. https://doi.org/10.2979/FSR.2006.22.1.85

Coleman, M.A. 2013. *Introduction: ain't I a womanist too? Third wave womanist religious thought*. Philadelphia, PA: Fortress Press. https://doi.org/10.2307/j.ctt22nm936

Cornell, D. & Van Marle, K. 2015. *Ubuntu* feminism: tentative reflections. *Verbum et Ecclesia*, 36(2):1-8. https://doi.org/10.4102/ve.v36i2.1444

Davis, O.I. 1999. 'In the kitchen: transforming academics through safe spaces of resistance'. *Western Journal of Communication*, 63(3):364-381.

Denbow, J. & Thebe, P.C. 2006. *Culture and customs of Botswana*. London: Greenwood Press.

Dolamo, R. 2013. '*Botho/Ubuntu*: the heart of African ethics'. *Scriptura*, 112:1-10. https://doi.org/10.7833/112-0-78

Dube, M.W., Modie-Moroka,T., Setume, S.D., Ntloedibe-Kuswani, S., Kgalemang, M., Gabaitse, R.M., Madigele, T., Mmolai, S. & Sesiro, D. 2016. '*Botho/Ubuntu*: community building and gender constructions in Botswana'. *Journal of the Interdenominational Theological Center*, 41(Spring):1-20.

Dube, M.W. 2018. '"I am because we are": giving primacy to African indigenous values in HIV/AIDS prevention'. In: M.F. Murove (ed). *African ethics: an anthology of comparative and applied ethics*. Pietermaritzburg, South Africa: UKZN Press.

Dube, M.W. 2021. 'Postcolonial *Botho/Ubuntu*: transformative readings of Ruth in the Botswana urban space'. In: J. Claassens & F. Olojede (eds). *Transformative readings of the Bible.* T&T Clark. 161-183. https://doi.org/10.5040/9780567696274.ch-011

Ellece, S.E. 2007. 'Be a fool like me: gender construction in the marriage advice ceremony in Botswana – a critical discourse analysis'. *Agenda*, 87/25(1):43-52. https://doi.org/10.1080/10130950.2011.575584

Gaie, J.B.R. 2007. 'The Setswana concept of *Botho*: unpacking the metaphysical and moral aspects'. In: J.B.R. Gaie & S.K. Mmolai (eds). *The concept of Botho and HIV/AIDS in Botswana.* Eldoret, Kenya: Zapf Chancery. 29-44. https://doi.org/10.2307/j.ctvgc61hd.5

Gaie, J.B.R. & Mmolai, S.K. (eds). 2007. *The concept of Botho and HIV/AIDS in Botswana*. Eldoret, Kenya: Zapf Chancery. https://doi.org/10.2307/j.ctvgc61hd.5

Hollander, J.A. & Einwohner, R.L. 2004. 'Conceptualising resistance'. *Sociological Forum*, 19(4):533-554. https://doi.org/10.1007/s11206-004-0694-5

Hooks, B. 2000. *Feminist theory: from margin to center*. London: Pluto Press.

Hudson-Weems, C. 1994. 'Africana womanism: reclaiming ourselves'. Troy, MI: Bedford Publishers.

Hudson-Weems, C. 2004a. 'Africana womanism'. In: L. Phillips (ed). *The womanist reader*. New York: Routledge. 37-44.

Hudson-Weems, C. 2004b. *Africana womanist literary theory: a sequel to Africana womanism: reclaiming ourselves.* Trenton, NJ: Africa World Press.

Kgalemang, M., Modie-Moroka, T. & Dube, M.W. 2022. 'Naomi/Laban showers and the creation of womanist-

Botho/Ubuntu ethic of communal living spaces'. *Journal of the Inter-denominational Theological Centre*, 51(Spring):1-54. https://bit.ly/3o09alb

Kolawole, M. & Modupe, E. 1997. *Womanism and African consciousness.* Trenton, NJ: Africa World Press.

LenkaBula, P. 2008. 'Beyond anthropocentricity: *Botho/Ubuntu* and the quest for economic and ecological justice in Africa'. *Religion and Theology*, 15(3-4):375-394. https://doi.org/10.1163/157430108X376591

Levine, A.J. 1992. 'The Book of Ruth'. In: C. Newsom & S.H. Ringe (eds). *The women's Bible commentary.* Philadelphia, PA: Westminster. 78-84.

Lewis, J.J. 2020. 'Subjectivity in women's history and gender studies'. *ThoughtCo*. https://www.thoughtco.com/subjectivity-in-womens-history-3530472 [Accessed 11 February 2020].

McKinlay, J. 1999. 'A son is born to Naomi: a harvest for Israel'. In: A. Brenner (ed). *Ruth and Esther: A feminist companion to the Bible.* Sheffield, UK: Sheffield. 151-157.

McKinlay, J. 2004. *Reframing her: Biblical women in postcolonial focus.* Sheffield, UK: Sheffield Phoenix Press.

Mmualefe, D.O. 2007. '*Botho* and HIV&AIDS: a theological reflection'. In: J. Gaie & S. Mmolai (eds). *The concept of Botho and HIV/AIDS in Botswana.* Eldoret, Kenya: Zapf Chancery. 1-28. https://doi.org/10.2307/j.ctvgc61hd.4

Moeti, B. & Mokgolodi, H.L. 2017. 'Indigenous marital therapy: a case of Botswana'. *International Journal of Social Science Studies*, 5(11). https://doi.org/10.11114/ijsss.v5i11.2582

Montemurro, B. 2002. 'You go 'cause you have to: the bridal shower as a ritual of obligation'. *Symbolic Interaction*, 25(1):67-92. https://doi.org/10.1525/si.2002.25.1.67

Nicolaides, A. 2015. 'Gender equity, ethics, and feminism: assumptions of an African *ubuntu* oriented society'. *Journal of Social Science*, 42(3):191-210. https://doi.org/10.1080/09718923.2015.11893407

Ogunyemi, C.O. 1985. 'Womanism: the dynamics of the contemporary Black female novel in English'. In: L. Phillips (ed). *The womanist reader.* New York: Routledge. 21-36.

Olga, I.D. 1999. 'In the kitchen: transforming academics through safe spaces of resistance'. *Western Journal of Communication*, 63(3):364-381. https://doi.org/10.1080/10570319909374647

Powell, J.A. & Meniendian, S. 2017. 'The problem of othering: towards inclusiveness and belonging'. https://www.otheringandbelonging.org/the-problem-of-othering/

Rebughini, P. 2004. 'Subject, subjectivity, subjectivation'. *Sociopedia.isa.* https://bit.ly/3MqouRj

Rezeanu, C.-I. 2015. 'The relationship between domestic space and gender identity: some signs of the emergence of alternative domestic femininity and masculinity'. *Journal of Comparative Research in Anthropology and Sociology*, 6(2):9-29. http://compaso.eu/wpd/wp-content/uploads/2016/03/Compaso2015-62-Rezeanu.pdf

Rivera, M. 2007. *The touch of the transcendence: a postcolonial theology of God.* Louisville, KY: Westminster John Knox Press.

Schapera, I. 1970. *A handbook of Tswana law and custom.* London: James Curry.

Scott, J.C. 1990. *Domination and the arts of resistance: hidden transcripts.* New Haven, CT: Yale University Press.

Taylor, J.Y. 1998. 'Womanism: a methodological framework for African American women'. *Advances in Nursing Science*, 21(1):53-64. https://doi.org/10.1097/00012272-199809000-00006

Vision 2016. 2013. *Vision 2016: Towards prosperity for all.* Botswana Government.

Walker, A.C. 1983. *In search of our mothers' gardens: womanist prose.* London: Harcourt Brace Jovanovich.

Walker, A. 2006. 'Womanist'. In: L. Phillips (ed). *The womanist reader.* London: Routledge.

PREMARITAL PASTORAL COUNSELLING/*GO LAYA* ON ISSUES OF GENDER AND HUMAN SEXUALITY

Naomi/Laban showers in Gaborone, Botswana

Abstract

The purpose of this chapter[1] is to assess premarital counselling offered by the counsellors during Naomi/Laban showers. The study will also assess the content of counselling about gender roles and responsible sexual activity in Christian marriages in Gaborone, Botswana. The chapter proposes the use of African pastoral counselling in providing premarital counselling. This theory is suitable for Naomi/Laban bridal showers because it helps focus premarital counselling on issues that affect their counsellees (Barlow, 1999:6). It offers an opportunity for preventing marital conflicts and marriage failure (Antoine, 2012). The chapter utilised the data collected on 1 August 2016 to 31 March 2017 in Gaborone and its surrounding villages of Kanye, Tlokweng, Mochudi and Ramotswa. It aims at examining how Naomi/Laban showers might offer effective premarital counselling to couples intending to marry and their in-laws for the purpose of building strong marriages.

Introduction

Research conducted in Botswana reveals that divorce is on the rise (Ahmed & Letamo, 1989; Bakadzi, 2015). Chief Justice Maruping Dibotelo says divorce is a matter at the heart of the fabric of the society and indeed the cohesion of the family unit (Dibotelo, 2017). Statistics reveals that 1 301 divorce cases were registered at the High Court in the period between January and December 2016, of which 1 435 cases, including those carried forward from 2015, were completed, compared to the 971 cases recorded in 2012 (*The Midweek Sun*, 2011). During January and February 2011, 200 cases have so far been registered, stated the High Court Deputy

1 The article, 'Premarital pastoral counselling/*go laya* on issues of gender and human sexuality: Naomi/Laban showers in Gaborone, Botswana' by Madigele, T.J. et al., was first published in 2020 in *International Journal of African Catholicism*, 10(1):177-201. It is republished in this volume by permission.

Registrar Jacob Manzunzu who further indicated that in total there are 40 901 cases from 2006 to 2011 (*The Midweek Sun*, 2011). Due to a high rate of divorce, more often than not people in marriage seem to be experiencing certain challenges of how to keep stable marriages or relationships. Marital distress is one of the traumatic experiences one can encounter in their lifetime. Divorce is growing at an alarming rate and in the process are negatively impacting the lives of children (Bakadzi, 2015).

Throughout the world, divorce continues to ravage homes both inside and outside of the church, and the number of divorce cases is increasing at an alarming rate each year. Couples face many challenges to building and sustaining strong marriages. The overwhelming outcomes of divorce do not only affect the parties in the relationship but also the children involved, friends, the general well-being of both extended families, the church and society as a whole (ibid.:272).

This is a worrying experience to Botswana as a whole, especially given that just like in many societies, marriage in Botswana is considered a lifelong and consecrated union. The need for premarital counselling has been recognised by churches and family therapists for years. Several denominations have included instructions to pastors about the necessity of preparing couples for marriage, but detailed steps to follow are not provided. The wording in denominational policies is vague regarding the purpose and content of premarital counselling (Barlow, 1999:3).

Naomi/Laban showers were designed to provide space for married people to interact and provide premarital counselling to the new couple and parents to accept their children in their families. The first step of Naomi/Laban bridal showers is to inform the couple preparing for marriage about what to expect in marriage, followed by discourses on in-law relations with their children and as parents. The pastoral premarital counsellors, motivated by their experience in marriage and the Christian faith, address parents and the premarital couple publicly and emphasise on reconciliation, especially in areas where there are conflicts. During Naomi/Laban showers, premarital counseling is done by elderly women, most of whom have never gone to class to learn about it. Nonetheless, they have enough experience that enables them to give guidance to others. In so doing, they are following cultural structures of premarital counselling, which was always the avenue of either married women (southern region) or elderly women (northern region). Indeed, the church has a responsibility to prepare couples to build strong marriages from the beginning than mend broken ones. Barlow (1993:3) argued that

> Christians are slightly more likely to experience divorce than non-Christians. In fact, fundamentalist Christians have a higher percentage of being divorced than the others. In light of these statistics, the church has a responsibility to help prevent the increasing number of divorces. A preventative measure which seems to be overlooked in today's churches is premarital counseling.

Premarital counselling is a service offered to individuals engaged for marriage. This chapter focuses on premarital pastoral counselling services offered by Pentecostal pastoral counsellors during Naomi/Laban showers. The need for premarital counselling has been recognised by churches for years now. It can be observed that pastoral counsellors do more marriage counselling than other helping professionals. They work with District commissioners in Botswana to provide marriage counselling as well as premarital counselling. Just like most of the African societies, Naomi/ Laban shower counsellors view marriage as not a two-people affair, but as an inter-family affair.

Theoretical framework

This study is based on a model called 'African pastoral counselling'. The model proposes that counsellors should be able to understand human behaviour from different perspectives including psychological, spiritual and Biblical points of view (Kanokanga, 2002; Hove, 2007). It is more structured and focused on a specifically articulated need or concern. The model is effective because counsellors are expected to be equipped spiritually to systematically follow the therapeutic procedure in dealing with the root cause of the problem. Counsellors are also expected to know the Word of God and be able to interpret and recommend appropriate scriptural texts for each marital case. This is because the use of biblical teachings may actually assist in the alleviation of human suffering; the teachings and narratives may address existential challenges and problems (Schipani, 2003). In addition, counsellors should be contextual; in an African context, they should be able to appreciate the interconnectedness and the interrelatedness of human beings. In that regard, counsellors should facilitate that understanding and instil it in their counsellees (Mtetwa, 1996; Ackermann, 1993).

Methodology

The study used both quantitative and qualitative techniques, but the main approach was qualitative. The qualitative method allowed the researcher to investigate the phenomenon in detail within the participants' own context (Kombo & Tromp, 2006). Quantitative data wer collected through a self-administered questionnaire from individuals who were attending the different showers. Quantitative research involves the use of methodological techniques that represent the human experience in numerical categories, sometimes referred to as statistics. Conversely, qualitative research provides detailed description and analysis of the quality, or the substance, of the human experience. However, this study used both methods from Naomi/ Laban showers that was collected from 1 August 2016 to 31 March 2017 in the capital city Gaborone and the semi-urban surrounding villages of Kanye, Tlokweng, Mochudi and Ramotswa. Altogether, twelve Naomi/Laban showers were attended involving 145 participants. The methods of data collection included questionnaires, interviews, document review and observation. Data for this study were collected through in-depth, open-ended individual interviews, which took approximately 30 minutes per person. The interview guides were employed in order to ensure that the same general areas of information were collected from each respondent as proposed by Turner (2010).

The idea of using both interviews and observations was meant to allow the two methods to complement each other. The informants were the organisers of the showers, the recipients of the showers and the people who attended the Naomi/Laban showers. Data gathered through interviews allowed for the direct interaction between the interviewee and the interviewer. This facilitates data collection because the researcher can clear up obscurities and ask for more information if necessary. The researchers used a field notebook to comment and describe the respondents' unique behaviours. A questionnaire was also used to collect data. The questionnaire is a self-report data collection tool that each research participant fills out as part of a research study. The method is suitable for getting quantitative and qualitative information, depending on how the questions are phrased (Turner, 2010:34). The researchers made use of open-ended questions in order to give respondents the opportunity to answer in their own words and to express their thoughts and ideas.

Researchers started preparing for data analysis in the first quarter of 2017, with statistical analysis through using SPSS. Statistical data for the three showers were analysed and presented in tables and figures. In the case of interview data, the interviews were transcribed and stored electronically and on paper. The researchers analysed the data and identified themes that emerged from it. The next section deals with data analysis and discussions of themes that emerged from the data.

Findings and discussions

Table 9.1 demonstrates that the majority of people who attend showers are elderly women above the ages of 41–50. The youth are low in numbers, reflecting only 3%, compared to the 16.7+% of the elderly folks. The age variable is thus brought in so that the researcher may assess whether it had contributed to varying views on maintaining a healthy marriage. Among the varying ages, this research aims at establishing who were mostly vocal during counselling in and who were most liberal in the age groups. During Naomi/Laban showers, main counsellors were elderly women and were mainly the ones who were contributing during the counselling sessions.

Table 9.1 Age of participants

Age	Frequency	%
20–25	2	3.0
26–30	2	3.0
31–35	4	6.1
36–40	2	3.0
41–45	11	16.7
46–50	19	28.8
50+	26	39.4
Total	**66**	**100.0**

Table 9.2 shows that seven (10.6%) respondents were males, while 59 (89.4%) were females. This shows that Naomi/Laban showers are female dominated. Men and women were interviewed in order to establish whether gender plays a role in the differing views of maintaining a healthy marital relationship. Only seven men took part in the research because showers of this nature are known as a safe space of women in Botswana. However, the Naomi/Laban is a space for parents of premarital couples. It invites and welcomes both men and women even though men do not come. This is problematic though, since men have a potential in guiding their children to have strong marriages especially the man to model men who are exemplary both culturally and biblically.

Table 9.2 Gender of participants

Gender	Frequency	%
Male	7	10.6
Female	59	89.4
Total	**66**	**100.0**

Theme 1: Naomi/Laban showers bring people together

In the interview, participants were asked to explain in detail the purpose of Naomi/Laban showers in urban space. One of the participants responded: "To build a relationship between daughter-in-law and mother-in-law." Another one mentioned that the showers are supposed to develop a healthy relationship between a premarital couple and both of their parents. The results obtained from this study indicate that Naomi/Laban showers bring people together. They mould or build up the community as well as for families and the attendants to know each other. It is important for people to come together, share their experiences and stories in order to help the uniting families and the couple to avoid marital conflicts. Naomi/Laban showers give an opportunity for parents of premarital couples to gain knowledge on how to avoid being culprits of their children's marital conflicts. Premarital couples are also oriented on how have healthy relations with their parents for the sake of peace and unity.

During Ledumadumane shower, the first counsellor reflected on Genesis 2:24 (therefore, a man shall leave his father and his mother and hold fast to his wife, and they shall become one flesh) with an attempt of curbing conflicts between mothers-in-law and daughters-in-law. While reflecting on this Genesis text, it was advised that a couple "should stick together like superglue and should be inseparable. The word of God says they are bound together and the two shall become one". In another shower at Phakalane, parents were also advised to let go of their children. This relational pattern facilitates couples' independence from their respective parents. Notwithstanding this, counsellors also emphasised co-independence in the above shower: "They will honour you as they will come back to you to seek wisdom." With this advice, Naomi/Laban counsellors in Gaborone were trying to cultivate a healthy relationship between a mother-in-law and a premarital couple. As an elder, and as an experienced person, a mother-in-law should be able to guide, support and counsel her children.

Moreover, in Mochudi, a semi-urban area, the counsellors outrightly emphasised the need for a close and mutual relationship between parents-in-law and their children-in-law. A mother-in-law was advised: "You should go with her wherever you go. Introduce her as your daughter not as a daughter-in-law." A daughter-in-law was advised to cling to her mother-in-law, and a mother-in-law was advised to embrace her as her daughter. In reflecting on both urban and semi-urban showers, it could be concluded that a mother-in-law is the key to either successful or failing of marriages. For a sustainable marriage, the counselling advocated both independence and co-independence models for parent-in-laws and their daughters-/sons-in-law. Ampim (2003) advises that premarital pastoral counsellors should appreciate that the African worldview entails interdependence, collective sharing, and survival. In a traditional Setswana context, one should be informed or influenced by traditions, customs, beliefs, morals, values, and practices of the community. Therefore, counselling approaches should be in line with socio-cultural influences such as communalism for it to be efficient.

Theme 2: Showers are important because they reflect *Botho/Ubuntu*

The findings show that the majority of informants think that Naomi/Laban showers are important, because they reflect *Botho/Ubuntu*. *Botho/Ubuntu* is affiliated with the maxim that "a person is a person through other persons". Mbiti says: "I am because we are and since we are, therefore I am" (Mbiti, 1988:108). In Botswana, the concept of *Botho* derives from the Setswana saying *motho ke motho ka batho*, which translates into "a human being is a human being because of other human beings" (Gaie & Metz, 2010:273). A reflection on the concept of *Botho/Ubuntu* underscores the main objective of an African, which is to live a life of harmony with fellow humanity. Given that the *Botho/Ubuntu* ethic seeks to build positive relationships in the community and to empower all members to live in full human dignity, it is to be seen in the preparation and arrival of a new daughter-in-law and a new son-in-law.

Botho/Ubuntu acknowledges interconnectedness, interrelatedness and harmony of human beings (Venter, 2004:156). A community that has *Botho* emphasises the need for one to be aware of his/her responsibility towards the other (Beets & Le Grange, 2005). By and large, during Naomi/Laban showers, parents-in-law, especially mothers-in-law as reflected in Theme 1's data, were advised to be heralds of peace and harmony, not of discord. This is because as parents, they have the power to break up the marriages of their children.

Botho/Ubuntu also connotes principles of sharing and caring for one another (Ramose, 2002). This implies that everyone has a duty to his/her family. This includes many extended members such as in-laws, uncles and cousins (Gyekye, 1997; Masolo, 2004). During this age of the economic downturn, the Naomi/Laban group found it imperative to work together to lessen socio-economic problems collectively as a family of God. In the interview, the respondents were asked: "What is expected from those who attend?" In summary, the respondents answered that those who attend are expected to offer moral, physical, spiritual, material and financial support. Indeed, the showers promoted socioeconomic activities that combined social support with economic support to reflect *Botho* as well as building the community together. The people showed solidarity towards the other, by being there for those who were about to get married; they came with presents; they offered money; and they counselled those who were about to unite as a new family. Some of those presents were to be used during the actual wedding, while others were to be used by the newlyweds in their family.

Apart from material support, the informants also indicated that the showers offered moral support. They recommended counselling as a tool to building new couples and ensuring harmony, peace and acceptance of new couples with their in-laws.

Theme 3: Naomi/Laban showers are similar to Setswana traditional counselling

Informants stated that the Naomi/Laban counselling approach by facilitators borrows positive values from Setswana traditional culture and the Bible as a whole (Figure 9.1).

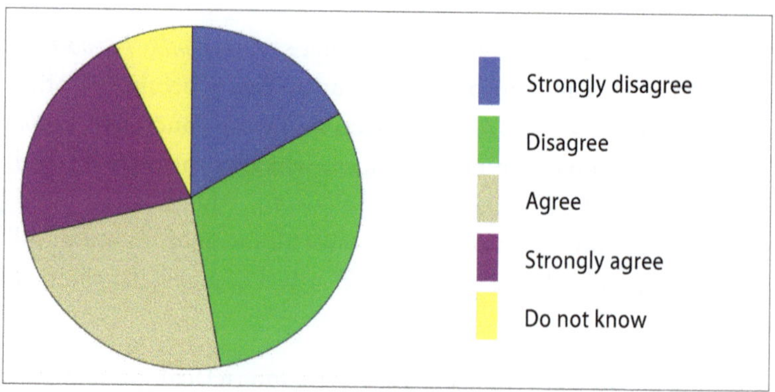

Figure 9.1 Naomi/Laban shower similarity question

Theme 4: Prerequisites for counselling during showers

Naomi/Laban facilitators and counsellors indicated that their approach to premarital counselling is different from the Setswana practice, which was strictly conducted by aunts/*rakgadi* and uncles/*malome*, who would tell the daughter-in law that *monna gaa botswe kwa a tswang kgona ke selepe oa adimanwa* (you should not ask your husband about his whereabouts; he is like an axe that can be shared). The Naomi/Laban premarital counselling underlines consultation and transparency as ingredients to a happy marriage. They argue that the husband is not an axe for sharing – faithfulness in marriage is encouraged for all god-fearing couples. In taking this stance, they depart from cultural perspectives.

Theme 5: Interference of siblings in marriages

During the Naomi/Laban showers, counsellors deliberated much on the interference of siblings in marriages. One of the counsellors in Phakalane suggested that it is the responsibility of the soon-to-wed couple to protect each other from any harm from either extended family. It was advised that a woman should have a relationship with her partners' siblings and parents. In that way she would reduce the amount of tension between her and her new family. One of the organisers, who was the first counsellor during a Kanye shower, read Numbers 12:1-8 to advise against interfering in siblings' marriages. "Siblings, do not be like Miriam and Aaron. You should not interfere in the marriage of your brother. Accept this woman as one of you." According to her interpretation, Miriam and Aaron attacked Moses for the wife he married. Miriam was consequently cursed with leprosy for interfering in her brother's marriage. The same text was used in Gaborone West to advise against the interference of both parents' laws and siblings in a new marriage.

Theme 6: Blaming the mother-in-law

All showers generally focus blame on the mother-in-law than on the father-in-law and siblings. When dealing with this kind of relational problem, Olutola (2012:12) suggests that it is important to understand that the behaviour patterns of the mother-in-law had developed over time; therefore, it cannot be easily changed. The mother-in-law should also accept that her son is with a new woman, and she should just let him go instead of being overprotective; the mother-in-law should cooperate with the daughter in-law for the good of her son.

The above suggestion holds water because, inasmuch as people have common problems that may be addressed in a communal setting, there are some problems that are unique to the one being counselled. Therefore, it is important for counsellors to understand and address their counsellees according to their needs. Pastoral counselling should offer an opportunity for guidance and healing. Knowing people's individual problems and adequately addressing them may consequently guide and heal the mother-in-law who has problems that may lead to conflicts within her children's marriage.

Theme 7: Sexuality, gender, age factors in Naomi/Laban counselling

Naomi/Laban counsellors discussed how a premarital couple should relate as sexual beings. The term 'sexuality' provides for a comprehensive understanding:

> A central aspect of being human throughout life encompasses sex, gender identities and roles, sexual orientation, eroticism, pleasure, intimacy and reproduction. Sexuality is experienced and expressed in thoughts, fantasies, desires, beliefs, attitudes, values, behaviours, practices, roles and relationships. While sexuality can include all of these dimensions, not all of them are always experienced or expressed. Sexuality is influenced by the interaction of biological, psychological, social, economic, political, cultural, legal, historical, religious and spiritual factors. (WHO, 2006a)

From this definition, it is clear that sexuality has to do with diverse combinations of physical, emotional, and relational interactions or how people express themselves as sexual beings within the concepts of biological sex, gender identity and presentation. Gender identities and roles make up a small component of sexuality.

The World Health Organization (WHO) defines gender as "socially constructed roles, behaviours, activities, and attributes that a given society considers appropriate for men and women" (WHO, 2017). Thus, males and females are considered as sex categories, while masculine and feminine are gender categories (WHO, 2017). Given that the definition of gender includes the types of behaviour that are deemed to be culturally and socially appropriate for men and women, it would seem likely that gender, or sex roles, could be linked to relational conflict.

Naomi/Laban premarital counselling facilitates conversations on gender expectations in an attempt to facilitate conflict resolution between parents, siblings and the premarital couple. In a traditional Setswana society, women had been held responsible for their husbands, children, parents, their husband's parents, or any other dependent member of their family. After marriage, the daughter in-law moves to her husband's home, where she is expected to take care of the household and caring tasks of course in collaboration with other women of the family if they are there (Poiret, 1996).

Some women had been culturally conditioned to think that being a daughter-in-law means to work, cook, wash clothes, and do other household chores for the in-laws. The family of the daughter-in-law would come in to examine if their daughter is pleasing the in-laws and if she is doing what is expected of her. "Failure to do this may lead to divorce or polygamy" (Sabalele, 2010:50).

Different speakers during Naomi/Laban showers advised against a tendency of abusing daughters-in-law. During the Gaborone West Naomi/Laban shower event, one of the counsellors advised the mother-in-law: "Do not treat her as your maid but as your daughter." The counsellors emphasised the godly instruction, which is that both husband and wife should cling together as one body. This biblical instruction as extracted from Genesis 2:24 is against any form of abuse by in-laws. In trying to address this problem, all mothers-in-law were advised to start calling their daughters-in-law their daughters instead of calling them *ngwetsi* (daughter-in-law).

Genesis 2:24 was also used at Phakalane by the first counsellor to advise against abuse of one's daughter-in-law. She mentioned that most people in Botswana are deliberately biased in their understanding of this text. They think the text means that a woman should go and join her in-law family where she is expected to do all chores in the family. She mentioned that Batswana have a tendency to abuse their daughters-in-law. They think having a daughter in-law is more like having a maid. She also used the Bible to reconstruct the following Setswana song:

> *Mmamosetsanyana* x2 (mother to the daughter)
> *Sala o di bona tsa lapa la gago se ile sephonono* (take care of the domestic chores in your home, the pretty lady is gone)
> *Se ile, se ile* x2 (she is gone, she is gone)
> *Se ile, se ile se ile sephonono* (she is gone, the pretty one is gone)

Although staying in a different world of modernisation, some mothers-in-law may expect their daughters-in-law to serve them as per the expectations of the traditional Tswana society, possibly leading to strained relationships. Naomi/Laban premarital counsellors emphasise that "she is a valuable addition to the family, a gift from God which should be welcomed wholeheartedly". The same was said about a son-in-law. Mothers-in-law were encouraged to take care of their daughters-in-law. They were advised to *cut the chain.* This means that they were not to take revenge on their daughters-in-law for oppression they suffered from their mothers-in-law. This form of abuse must stop with them.

One of the counsellors mentions: "*Sego se a tlhokomelwa, se a babalelwa*", literally meaning, "A calabash should be taken care of, cherished and protected". A calabash is a very important item in Setswana traditional society. It is used for different purposes, including storing milk, as a cup for drinking water and traditional beer, and even for decoration.

Figure 9.2 *Sego sa Setswana* (Setswana calabash) with traditional beer[2]

Even though a calabash has many purposes, it is a fragile item that is easily broken. Yet, if taken care of, it can last for a long time. It should be taken care of, because it plays a major role in the family. It unites people, because the family can drink from the same calabash. It is a beautiful item that attracts attention and is pleasing to the eye.

Just like the calabash, a woman has diverse roles; she serves her family, spouse, as well as the professional world. She has greater emotional involvement in the lives of all of her dependants and is likely to be emotionally affected more than men (Kessler & McRae, 1984). This means that diverse caring networks may leave a woman vulnerable to stresses such as illness, unemployment and divorce.

Counsellors in the Naomi/Laban shower tried to address the above problem by performing a ritual of white shawl wearing. A white shawl was wrapped around

2 https://www.google.co.bw/pictures [Accessed: 2020].

the waist of a mother-in-law who was made to embrace her daughter-in-law. The facilitator recites: "I put this white shawl around you so that you receive Maduo with a pure, loving heart. Welcome Maduo, receive her." Whiteness is a sign of purity. Therefore, a mother-in-law was advised to have a pure heart and receive her daughter-in-law with gladness.

At the Phakalane Naomi/Laban event, however, a mother-in-law's white shawl was interpreted as being clothed with a blanket. *Go apesa mosadi kobo* (clothing a woman with a blanket) is a symbol of taking a vow of silence about one's family matters. A mother-in-law was advised to learn to keep family secrets, not to share them with other people. Mothers were taught not to trust other people with their marital problems, but only God. Figure 9.3 shows a woman dressing the mother of the groom-to-be with a shawl at Phakalane.

Figure 9.3 A woman dressing a mother of the groom-to-be with a shawl at Phakalane

The narrator was reciting the following words as she was dressing her:

> *O mmaagwe bana. Otlile go nna nkuku wa bana. Mme kgang ya gago e tona, re go apesa tjale e gore ka ha teng ga tjale ena, diphiri tsa lelapa la ga Dipuo tse di tlisiwang ko go wena di helela hela ka ha. Wena o bo o diisa kae? Ko Modimong.* This means that as a mother, you are going to mother all children, and as a mother of all, you will be loaded with lots of secrets of those that you are mothering, including your grandchildren. You should take all those secrets to God. Therefore, wrapping the shawl or gathering it around her shoulder and locking it through a safety pin (*Sekopelo*) is a symbol of taking a vow of silence especially on family matters. Women are responsible for holding the family together, just like a shawl being gathered around her shoulder. They are expected to maintain unity and develop very strong relationships with their

children and other family members. Therefore, the mother-in-law to-be should develop a mature character.

The Ledumadumane shower placed more emphasis on the change of character; the bride was advised to be humble and have a godly character. In another instance, Kgalemang (personal communication, 2017/05/06) reported that during Naomi/Laban showers at Kanye, women made it clear that a woman who has gone through shawl wearing and pinning should *rutubala / imamela*. *Rutubala* means relax or take it easy or be calm and collected at all times. This means that as someone who has the responsibility of handling everyone's problems, she should be calm at all times, not only for the sake of playing her role effectively, but it should also be seen in her character.

McGoldrick mentions that as the keeper of family secrets, a woman, whether as a mother-in-law or mother is often put in the position of talking about the issues of other members of the family and then blamed again when things go wrong. She is likely to be blamed because she is emotionally attached to each and everyone one of the family. When something goes wrong, even if it has nothing to do with her, she remains a scapegoat. She therefore remains "a natural arena for displacing tensions in the couple or in the family of origin of each spouse" (2005:245).

This means that most couples are more likely to abuse their mothers emotionally. They run to them when they need help and blame them when things go wrong. Mothers-in-law are not always the guilty party; they are also exposed to emotional abuse by their children. A mother is normally regarded as a confidant, but she is human after all. Some of the secrets may slip out of her mouth during the process of counselling when she attends one of her children's problems. As the family's bag of secrets, she is exposed to more networks stresses and is much more emotionally affected (Kessler & McRae, 1984).

Therefore, to avoid this pitfall, as per the advice of Naomi women, she should take it to the Lord in prayer. Being able to be emotionally attached to members of one's family is a maternal gift – a gift that only mothers possess. This is one characteristic that could give a woman a central position of power. This degree of power could be reflected in the alliances mothers often build with children against strict fathers, who are perceived to be lacking in understanding of emotional issues. This is one area that was not touched during Naomi/Laban premarital counselling sessions, primarily because men hardly attended these showers. The topic of mothers having an emotional attachment to their children was addressed across all showers. Women were advised to let go of their children in order to avoid being the cause of conflict. The Naomi/Laban women also advised the soon-to-wed couple not to be extremely close to or at a great distance from either family of origin. The couple should always address each other's emotional needs since depending on external sources may create more marital problems or conflicts.

It could be argued that women are realising how inequalities in power structure limit the options of women for the rest of their lives (Dowling, 1996). This awareness may give a sense of liberation to women in marital relationships. Some of the concepts that are reconstructed through Naomi/Laban premarital pastoral counselling are gender roles and the traditional societal expectations of daughters-in-law.

During the Naomi/Laban premarital pastoral counselling session at Phakalane, the second counsellor of the day used John 4:16-18 in an attempt to address sex within marriage. This is basically an account of a Samaritan woman meeting Jesus at a well of water. Jesus and the encounter with the Samaritan woman, exposed/revealed her lifestyle of marital or sexually intimate sin and disregard, and imparted his message of hope for effectively changing her life for the better.

Figure 9.4 Jesus and the woman at the well[3] (John 4:16-18)

During counselling at Phakalane, a vagina was likened to a well and drinking from a well was figurative language used for sexual intercourse. While advocating for loyalty and warning against multiple sexual relationships, the counsellor was mainly using figurative language because traditional African cultures do not directly verbalise taboo subjects such as sex, disease and sexuality. One of the counsellors said that the well must be kept clean and safe; there should be one person to drink from her well (advising the premarital bride). Other counsellors, including the mother of the

3 https://stpaulsnorthandover.org/spiritual-resources/jesus-mafa-woman-at-the-well/ [Accessed 9 May 2017].

bride-to-be, also used an image of a well to address issues of sex in marriage. She was advised against the misuse of the well. Even though it is not clear how this image of a well is related to sex, it is only clear that the message behind the text underlines the need to abstain from sexual immorality.

Moreover, one of the counsellors during Naomi/Laban showers at Gaborone West referred to 1 Corinthians 6 in addressing issues of sex in marriage and faithfulness. She emphasised that the body of the wife is for the husband and the body of the husband is for the wife. The premarital couple was advised not to abuse their bodies: "Her body is yours and his body is yours. Take care of your bodies for one another."

The latter shower indeed came up with an image of equality in sexuality in order to develop sexually gratifying partnership relationships. McGoldrick (2005:243) advises that counsellors should do away with the usage of images of sexuality that are to do with a dominant and a submissive female. Couples should be freed from gender stereotypes by counsellors. Moreover, couples should share the experience of sexual pleasure and gratification. Dominian (2014) asserts that men and women should give themselves to one another. This means that there should be ultimate mutual devotion in all aspects of the couple's lives. Human sexuality by nature is communal. Nelson and Longfellow (1994:xiv) define human sexuality as the blend of emotions, passion, behaviours, and physical involvements of human beings related to their sexual nature. Human beings are sexual beings and only express their sexuality with the other.

Theme 8: Naomi/Laban showers and LGBTQIA+

Although the story of Naomi and Ruth could easily work for lesbian relationships, Naomi/Laban counsellors hardly talked about LGBTQIA+ unions, partly because their focus was heterosexual relationships. It is not clear if they would hold an LGBTQIA+ Naomi/Laban shower, since Botswana had not yet legalised such unions during our data collection. The Naomi/Laban shower is only held to complement a publicly announced forthcoming wedding, by uniting the parents-in-law with the new couple. Within all attended Naomi/Laban showers, there was silence, neither support nor condemnation, towards LGBTQIA+ relationships.

Be that as it may, one counsellor during the Phakalane shower used the Sodom and Gomorrah story in Genesis 18:16 to 19:29 to instruct against looking back. A daughter-in-law was advised not to look back where she comes from and let go of her history. Green (2012:157) defines homosexuality as a relational and sexual orientation towards a member of the same sex. Through their silence the Naomi/Laban counsellors can be exclusive in their dealings on this matter, since even those who are living in heterosexual relationships, are not necessarily heterosexual. They may be only claiming to be heterosexual because the Church in which they want to belong is against homosexuality.

Halpern argues that sexuality is a cultural production. He maintains that sexuality is determined and must conform to the expectations of a society. He says, "Masculinity is the aggregate combining the congruent functions of penetration, activity, dominance and social precedence [while] femininity signifies penetrability, passivity, submission and social subordination" (Halpern, 1990:130). It could therefore be maintained that as much as Naomi/Laban showers intend to reconstruct culture for the benefit of women, they should even advocate for the inclusion of all sexes and genders. *Botho/Ubuntu* advocates for the respect of human dignity, community and oneness, liberation, and justice as well as the assessment of our relationships for the sake of harmony (Dube, 2009:202).

We learn that each person is the image of the Lord who proclaims that "as you have done unto the least of these you have done unto me" (Mat. 25:40). In other words, there is an apophatic dimension to each person whose real being is "hid with Christ in God" (Col. 3:3) and ultimately remains beyond the experience of the counsellor. Therefore, Naomi/Laban counsellors could be advised against the use of exclusivitic language during their sessions and rather to use a holistic inclusive approach in their counselling. Counselling is pastoral if it respects and appreciates the complexity and uniqueness of each person.

Theme 9: Ruth portrays an ideal mother-in-law–daughter-in-law relationship

The book of Ruth was used across all showers in an attempt to cultivate the spirit of love, tolerance and unity between mothers-in-law and daughters-in-law. One of the facilitators during Naomi/Laban bridal showers at Block 6 used the Book of Ruth as a resource for mother-in-law relations. She underlined that although Naomi is the main character, the book's attention focuses on Ruth as a real daughter-in-law. In Ruth 1:16-18:

> 'Entreat me not to leave you or return from following you; for where you go I will go, and where you lodge I will lodge; your people shall be my people and your God my God; where you die I will die, and there I will be buried' ... And when Naomi saw that she was determined to go with her, she said no more.

Using the above text, Naomi/Laban counsellors emphasised that Ruth has taken a decision to be in solidarity with her mother-in-law; she has a new identity and has renounced her native religious affiliation. They mentioned that it shows massive commitment to the welfare of the family she has joined in marriage above her personal interest. It takes so much sacrifice to leave to a foreign country especially if you are not sure of security. Naomi took that risk, nevertheless. The story of Ruth is explicitly about a woman committing to another woman. As indicated,

Naomi/Laban showers are female-centred events that are organised by women for other women to rectify all that concern women in in-law relationships. As seen in Table 9.3, their counselling is still dominated by traditional views (that is married women are main counsellors), while indicating significant shifts.

Table 9.3 Counselling only given by married women

Responses	Frequency	%
Strongly agree	21	31.8
Agree	16	24.2
Disagree	15	22.7
Strongly disagree	9	13.6
Do not know	5	7.6
Total	**66**	**100.0**

Table 9.3 shows that 37 respondents agreed, while 24 disagreed with the given statement. Marital status is therefore the variable that was used to establish the main providers of premarital counselling during Naomi/Laban showers, which is a standard Setswana practice. However, it is notable that, unlike in some regions of Botswana, Naomi/Laban shower does not exclude single women as counsellors. In fact, among the founders of the movements there were widows and divorced women. This shift is subversive to patriarchy that forces women to define their human dignity through association with a man through marriage.

In her commentary on Ruth, Levine notes that, while Ruth vows to cling to her mother-in-law forever: "Naomi never acknowledges her daughter-in-law's fidelity" (1992:80). Naomi rather instructed her daughter-in-law to prepare herself (wash and anoint yourself, put on your best clothes) and follow Boaz to the threshing floor. Ruth's command to Boaz, "spread your cloak over me, for you are next of kin", is regarded as a marriage proposal. It takes a lot of courage to propose marriage to a man. Survival tactics of Ruth and Naomi should also be emulated. Even single woman who attends a Naomi/Laban shower could learn a lot from those. Naomi and Ruth were not solely dependent on men for their survival. They walked alone for miles without any male protection; they managed to survive despite their economic deprivation. All women – widowed, single and married, or transgendered – should emulate Naomi and Ruth during economic hardships. It is, therefore, imperative for Naomi/Laban counsellors to go through exegetical training to enable them to address all women who attend their showers.

Conclusion

Naomi/Laban bridal showers indisputably present an important forum where women primarily offer premarital pastoral counselling to parents-in-law prior marriage even though men rarely turn up to this event. This is crucial due to increasing high rates of divorce in Botswana, particularly in the church. This counselling intervention borrows from cultural and biblical tools in their dealings with the people. Their approach is largely inclusive, holistic, and communal hence relevant to our context in Botswana. African pastoral counselling provides ample time to thrash and address internal and external problems of parents-in-laws; it facilitates a systematic counselling process that prevents cultural, age and gender biasness in counselling.

References

Ahmed, G. & Letamo, G. 1998. 'Causes and consequences of current marriage and family transformation: what Botswana think about the changes'. Unpublished monograph. University of Botswana.

Ampim, M. 2003. 'Africana studies: the five major African initiation rites'. https://www.manuampim.com/AfricanInitiationRites.htm

Antoine, C.M. 2012. *Effective marriage mentoring*. USA: Liberty University Baptist Theological Seminary. https://bit.ly/3pBceoh [Accessed 15 May 2023].

Avis, L. 1985. 'Live in relationships and its impact on the institution of marriage in India'. *Westminster Law Review*, 3(1):12-24.

Babbie, E. 1992. *The practice of social research*. Belmont, CA: Wadsworth Publishing Company.

Bakadzi, M. 2015. 'Restoring marriages in church: a case study of four Pentecostal churches in Gaborone, Botswana'. *Academic Research International*, 6(4):272-285.

Barlow, J.L. 1999). 'A new model for premarital counseling within the church'. *Pastoral Psychology*, 48(1):3-9. https://doi.org/10.1023/A:1021998511250

Barna, G. 1993. *The future of American family*. Chicago: Moody Press.

Beets, P. & Le Grange, L. 2005. '"Africanising" assessment practices: does the notion of *ubuntu* hold any promise?' *South African Journal of Higher Education (SAJHE)*, 19:1197-1207. https://doi.org/10.4314/sajhe.v19i7.50216

Bible. 1984. *New King James version*. Nashville: Thomas Nelson.

Bryman, A. 2001. *Social research methods*. New York: Oxford University Press.

Carter, B. & McGoldrick, M. 2005. *The expanded family life cycle, individual, family, and social perspectives*. New York: Pearson and AB.

Choong, M.K., Galgani, F., Dunn, A.G., & Tsafnat, G. 2014. 'Automatic evidence retrieval for systematic reviews'. https://doi.org/10.2196/jmir.3369. *Journal of Medical Internet Research*, 16(10):223.

Dominian, H. 2014. *Basic types of pastoral care and counseling*. Nashville, TN: Abingdon Press.

Dowling, J.J. 1996. *Pastoral counseling*. Nashville, TN: Avindon.

Gichinga, E.M. 2008. *Marriage counselling: a counselling guide*. Nairobi: GEM Counselling Services.

Green, J.B. 2012. *Dictionary of scripture and ethic*. Grand Rapids, MI: Baker Academic.

Gyekye, K. 1997. *Tradition and modernity: philosophical reflections on the African experience*. New York: Oxford University Press.

Halpern, D.M. 1990. *Before sexuality: the construction of erotic experience in the ancient Greek world*. Princeton: Princeton University Press.

Kala, K. 2002. 'Cohabitation in Western Europe: trends, issues and implications'. In: A. Booth & A.C. Crouter. *Just living together: implications of cohabitation on families, children and social policy*. New Jersey: Routledge. 3-33.

Kathide, A. 2003. 'Teaching & talking about our sexuality: a means of combating HIV&AIDS'. In: M. Dube (ed), *HIV&AIDS and the curriculum*. Geneva: WCC.

Kessler, T. & McRae, R. 2014. *The Bible and sexuality*. Colorado Springs, CO: Nav Press Publishing Group.

Kiriswa, B. 2003. *Pastoral counselling in Africa: an integrated model*. Eldoret: AMECEA Gaba Publishers.

Levine, A. 1992. 'Ruth'. In: C.A. Newsom & S.H. Ringe (eds). *Women's Bible commentary*. Louisville, KY: Westminster John Knox Press. 80.

Longfellow, S.P. & Nelson, J.B. 2005. *Sexuality and the sacred: sources for theological reflection*. Louisville, KY: Westminster John Knox Press.

Madigele, T.J., Dube, M.W., Motswapong, E., Kebaneilwe, M.D., Gabaitse, R., Setume, S., Modie-Moroka, T. & Kgalemang, M. 2020. 'Premarital pastoral counselling/*go laya* on issues of gender and human sexuality: Naomi/Laban showers in Gaborone, Botswana'. *International Journal of African Catholicism*, 10(1):177-201.

Marsh, F.C. 2015. 'Integrating the psychological audit of interpersonal relationships into short-term pastoral marital counseling: help or hindrance?' Doctor of Ministry thesis, Faculty of Liberty University School of Divinity, Lynchburg, Virginia.

Marvasti, A.B. 2004. *Qualitative research in sociology: an introduction*. London: Sage. https://doi.org/10.4135/9781849209700

Masolo, D.A. 2004. 'Western and African communitarianism: a comparison'. In: K. Wiredu (ed). *A companion to African philosophy*. Malden, MA: Blackwell.

Mbiti, J. 1988. *African religions and philosophy*. Nairobi: General Printers Limited.

McLeod, J. 2001. *Qualitative research in counselling and psychotherapy*. London: Sage. https://doi.org/10.4135/9781849209663

Metz, T. & Gaie, J.B.R. 2010. 'The African ethic of *Ubuntu*/*Botho*: implications for research on morality'. *Journal of Moral Education*, 39: 273-290. https://doi.org/10.1080/03057240.2010.497609

Mullins, M. 2000. *Marriage-lite: the rise of cohabitation and its consequences*. London: Civitas: Institute for the Study of Civil Society.

Olutola, O.O. 2012. 'Wife-mother-in-law relationship and violence among Yoruba women of south-western Nigeria'. *American Journal of Sociological Research*. Department of Behavioural Studies, College of Management Sciences, Redeemer's University, Mowe, Ogun State, Nigeria.

Poiret, C.T. 1996. *Vision and time: the historical perspective of African centered paradigm*. Lanham, MD: University Press of America.

Sabalele, S.N. 2010. 'A traumatic experience faced by the second wife in a polygamous marriage: a challenge to pastoral care. A story of the proposed contribution of pastoral care and counselling model to the second wives, married in a polygamous marriage, with special reference to the people of Mogale Circuit and Mogale Methodist Church of Southern Africa in Gauteng Province'. University of Pretoria: Pretoria.

The Midweek Sun. 2011. 'Is marriage fading? The marital vow "till death do us part" is quickly losing its meaning considering the high prevalence of divorce rates'. 11 March.

Turner, W.D. 2010. 'Qualitative interview design: a practical guide for novice investigators'. *The Qualitative Report*, 15(3). Florida: Nova Southeastern University Press.

Venter, E. 2004. 'The notion of *ubuntu* and communalism in African educational discourse'. *Studies in Philosophy and Education*, 23(2/3):149-160. https://doi.org/10.1023/B:SPED.0000024428.29295.03

WHO (World Health Organization). 2006. 'Pregnant adolescents: delivering on global promises of hope'. Geneva: WHO.

Wiersma, W. & Jurs, S.G. 2005. *Research methods in education: an introduction.* New York: Pearson Education.

Yilmaz, T. 2010. 'Enrichment programme on relationship satisfaction'. Master's thesis, Ondokuz Mayis University, Turkey.

PART THREE

Botho/Ubuntu, Baby Showers and Mothering

10

'A LITTLE BABY IS ON THE WAY'

Botho/Ubuntu and community building in Gaborone baby showers

Abstract

The arrival of a baby has always played a significant role in many societies across the globe. Hence, there is a need to shower the mother-to-be and her forthcoming baby with gifts and advice, in preparation for welcoming, not only the baby, but also the additional member into the family. This chapter[1] is based on data that were collected from baby showers in greater Gaborone over a period of 12 months. The concept of *Botho/Ubuntu* drives these baby showers. The goal of this chapter is to establish what baby showers entail, how these initiatives started and how they are conducted. But most importantly, the chapter will argue that baby showers are a community-building initiative in the urban space. The chapter also seeks to establish the extent to which baby showers are gendered, using analytical insights from the theory of the 'good mother'.

Introduction

The chapter presents an analysis of data that were collected during baby showers celebrations over a period of a year in Gaborone, Botswana. The data came from 15 baby showers in which 183 attendants participated. The main aim of the chapter is to argue that baby showers are a community-building initiative in the urban space driven by the spirit of *Botho/Ubuntu.* In addition, the chapter discusses the objectives and aims of baby showers, how they started, and how they are conducted. Furthermore, the extent to which these baby showers are gendered, whether by design or by default. using a theory of motherhood, namely the 'good mother', will be employed. Though Western, the theory will be adopted, contextualised and introduced to Gaborone baby showers.

1 The article, '"A little baby is on the way": *Botho/Ubuntu* and community building in Gaborone baby showers' by Motswapong, E.P. et al., was first published in 2017 in *Gender Studies*, 16(1):50-70. It is republished in this volume by permission.

Background

The transitional stage from having no children to first-time motherhood is a universal phenomenon that includes social and cultural changes. Botswana is no exception, because motherhood is viewed as one of the most important stages in life. Therefore, welcoming and celebrating a newborn baby is nothing new. Batswana used to have the traditional baby celebrations called *mantsho a ngwana*, which literally means "taking the baby out" of the house. The celebration coincided with when the baby turned three months. After *botsetsi*, the 'confinement' period of a new mother, the relatives will come together to 'take the baby' out of the house and introduce them to the community. The activity was accompanied by feasting and gift giving. It was during this celebration that the whole village was invited to the indigenous shower. These events encompassed the principle of *Botho/Ubuntu*. According to Setiloane, a Sotho-Tswana baby is born into a social group whose pattern of behaviour has been formed by history and is constantly being modified by the interrelations of its individual members (1975:33).

From Setiloane's observation, the Sotho-Tswana group acknowledges each individual as unique when it comes to a particular social behaviour. However, the arrival of a newborn is closely connected to the interpersonal relationships within a community. Hence, the new individual is perceived as a continuation of life. In most African societies conception is received with great joy, excitement and blessings by the family and the whole community (Magesa, 1997). Amanze (2002) notes that pregnancy in Africa is the first phase, whereby a human being becomes a person. Consequently, when a woman becomes pregnant in the normal manner, there is a great deal of jubilation in the minds and hearts of those concerned, as well as the community at large (ibid.:133). According to Amanze, the safety and continuity of pregnancy are of paramount importance, hence the need for observation of specific taboos to ensure safety of both the expectant mother and the unborn baby. For instance, the expectant mother may use specific protective traditional herbs, and prayers may be offered to *badimo* (ancestors) requesting their protection. John Mbiti (1969) further observes that, "in many African societies the pregnant woman must observe certain taboos and regulations partly because pregnancy in effect makes her ritually 'impure' and chiefly in order to protect her child" (ibid.:111). Hence Mbiti argues that besides ensuring safety, certain taboos are for purity purposes.

Defining *Botho/Ubuntu*

Botho/Ubuntu is a deeply African philosophy that calls on human beings to mirror their humanity for each other. It can be seen and felt in the spirit of willing participation in community building, unquestioning cooperation, warmth, openness, and personal dignity demonstrated by the indigenous black population (see Mbiti, 1969; Biko, 1978). *Botho/Ubuntu* can also be seen as the African understanding of a being human and living in community. This can be summarised by a common African saying: "I am because we are, and we are because I am." According to Musa Dube et al. (2016:2), the saying with its recognition of the individual ("I am") emphasises that one's humanity is only realised in the context where "we are", that is, in a communal setting. The second part of the adage focuses on the community, that is, "we are". For Batswana, and most Bantu people, *Botho/Ubuntu* is a concept of acceptable relational living, which is measured by one's relationship to the family, community, the environment, and the divine powers (ancestors and God) (Dube, 2006:140, 2008). In Sotho-Tswana languages, this relational aspect is best captured by the adage "*motho ke motho ka batho*", or in Nguni languages "*umuntu ngu muntu nga bantu*". The saying holds that a human being is only human through other human beings, or that "a person in only human through living in the community" (Dube et al., 2016:1). Dumi Mmualefe adds "without others one cannot be" (2004:7). This adage articulates 'Bantu' as people, "*motho/umuntu*" as a human being, and *Botho/Ubuntu* as the quality of being human, and living according to the ethics of the community (Mmualefe, 2004). Lastly, *Vision 2016* has defined *Botho* "as a process of earning respect by first giving it and gaining empowerment by empowering other" (2016:5). Although the above definitions of *Botho/Ubuntu* are relevant to showers in general, that is, bridal, Naomi/Laban and the *Vision 2016* definition echoes the spirit of *Botho/Ubuntu* demonstrated during Gaborone baby showers. As a result, it will be adopted and applied to the general argument of the chapter.

Baby shower defined

The term 'baby shower' is often assumed to mean that the expectant mother is 'showered' with gifts. The custom can be defined in relation to a bridal shower, which may have derived its name from the custom in Victorian times. It was customary to put presents inside a parasol, which, when opened, would 'shower' the bride-to-be with gifts (Montemurro, 2006:3). The shower can be hosted by anyone from relatives, parents of the mother-to-be, her in-laws, her friends, office colleagues, and school friends. Baby showers can also be hosted by churches, but most people prefer a relaxed atmosphere, where people close to the mother-to-be participate, and have a great time. This becomes an opportunity to help the mother-to-be to feel completely relaxed, greeted and surrounded with support, so that she does not feel anxious with the new chapter that is about to begin in her life (Robinson, 2000:1).

Motherhood can be seen to be a transitional stage, and showers become testimony to that transition. Arnold van Gennep discovered that all rituals share or follow three stages: separation, transition, and incorporation (Dundes, 1999:101). Rites of passage are "ceremonies that mark important transitional periods in a person's life, such as birth, puberty, marriage, having children, and death. Rites of passage usually involve ritual activities and teachings designed to strip individuals of their original roles and prepare them for new roles".[2] Rites of passage, therefore, are rituals and or ceremonies that accompany major personal transitions by individuals as they move from birth to death (Fischer & Gainer, 1993:320). Van Gennep (1960) maintains that the mother-to-be is temporarily removed from the community. This is a form of separation. Although the mother-to-be was temporarily separated from the world of men, boys and girls during baby shower celebrations, once they are completed, she is reintegrated into the same community as a woman who is mature and responsible and ready to raise her child within her family.

As a result, baby showers somewhat create the narrative that connects the mother-to-be to her community, especially that of motherhood and womanhood. It is because of this self-exploration that the initiate (that is the mother-to-be) emerges with a stronger sense of personal responsibility to all aspects of her life. This stretches all the way to the larger world of which they are a part. In this way, both the community and the initiate or mother-to-be benefit from this rite of passage. During this rite of passage there is a space provided for the community to transfer its essential values and deliberate on the roles deemed appropriate to the initiate's (mother-to-be) stage of life. This will ultimately guarantee what could be termed as cultural continuity, where interweaving of generations is realised (Van Gennep, 1960).

'The good mother' as a theoretical framework

Despite decades of feminist critique of dominant presentation of mother and motherhood, images of 'the good mother' appear as prevalent as ever, especially in contemporary Gaborone baby showers. The critique of gender roles emblemised by Berry Friedan looks at the feminine mystique (1963), which articulated women's dissatisfaction with the conflicting roles of wife and mother. A feminist in the 1970s often represented this critique as anti-mother. According to *Encyclopaedia of Motherhood* (ibid.:748), representations of motherhood in 1980s to the 1990s, as portrayed by the media are as follows: The supermom: this is a working mother, who retains energy at the end of a long day for her children and husband. This was rejected when the *Bill Cosby Show* (1984–1992) was introduced and viewers started responding positively to portrayals of a mother who revealed the difficulty of child rearing, thus ironically rejecting the unruffled image of supermom. This

2 https://www.astrology.org.uk/wordpress/wp-content/uploads/MARCO-Presentation-website.pdf [Accessed 7 May 2023].

was followed by the working-class motherhood of *Roseanne* (1988–1997), and the defiant single motherhood of *Murphy Brown* (1988–1998).

During baby showers celebrations, it became apparent that contemporary mothers are expected to behave according to the prevailing ideology of 'intensive mothering'. It is as a result of the high expectations coming from the attendees of baby showers, that the theory of a "good mother or intensive mothering" by Sharon Hays was adopted for this chapter. The theory requires a mother to be a central caregiver to the child, to follow advice of experts, to always put the child's needs ahead of her own and be fully absorbed emotionally with the child. In addition, the 'good mother' discourse requires mothers to "act responsibly and present themselves in culturally recognizable and acceptable ways" (Miller, 2005:86). This became evident from the advice the participants shared with the mother-to-be. These included (among others), personal hygiene to the dos and don'ts of a mother in confinement, *botsetsi.* It is worth noting that the good mother "casts a long shadow over the women's lives, motherhood and continue to remain the subject close to social regulation" confirms Ruddick (2001:189). Even though Gaborone baby showers emphasise the 'good mother', it is worth noting that contemporary representations of a good mother are not uniform and stable. For instance, the 'good mother' appears differently in settings – she is nuanced and has multiple forms. Therefore, to take the 'good mother' literally means working on the ideological aspects of mother and motherhood and the notions of hegemonic motherhood.

It is in this regard that the 'good mother' becomes more of a social construct that puts pressure on women to conform to particular standards and ideals, against which they are judged and judge themselves. However, as noted by Porter and Kelso (2006:xii), "representations of motherhood and the accompanying expectation of mother are in a constant flux as they adapt to the changing socio-cultural context". As a result, these standards shape the identities of mother and noting how a woman should feel. For instance, "a good mother is a happy mother, and an unhappy mother is a failed mother. This myth attributes representation for the condition of mothering to individuals, not the system" concludes (Porter & Kelso, 2006:xii). Furthermore, she is expected to let everything go and protect her child. Sharon Hays (1996:150) adds: "A good mother would never simply put her child aside for her own convenience. And placing material wealth or power on a higher plane than the wellbeing of her children is strictly forbidden." As a result, a good mother discourse position women as intuitive nurturer naturally equipped and always readily available to care for their children, no matter what circumstances (see Krane & Davies, 2007).

Gaborone baby showers regulate women "through good and bad mother discourses and has a number of functions because it ensures that a woman takes on the child rearing, it ties women's identity to their roles as child raisers and nurturers of others" (Johnson & Swanson, 2003:23). This is very narrow considering that a woman in the urban space can do far better than nurturing and child raising. These are women who are not only single parents but are also in full-time employment and yet they never leave their jobs to raise the baby. In other words, these women are in full control of their day-to-day lives, because they continue as full-time workers, while simultaneously mothering. At the end of the day, they control their family and family lives are not regulated, resulting in freedom when it comes to reproduction. Being a working mother and in a full-time job has become possible as a result of 'group mothering'. This is where women from Gaborone showers have taken it upon themselves to take care of each other and assist in raising in the mothering because after all "it takes a village to raise a child" (as the popular African proverb confirms). The only difference is that they are in the urban space not in the village setting. Finally, the women in the Gaborone shower do not have problems of a set of norms, which are currently promoted by media as 'new monism'. These norms usually posit that increasing standard of perfection, making it difficult for mothers to either achieve the prescribed ideal or curve a space for individual identity. This can create anxiety, guilt and ambivalence for the experience of motherhood. It must be emphasised that these norms are not posing any problems to mothers at Gaborone baby showers. Simply because it is through baby showers that they have learnt to cope in the midst of all the hardships of 'intensive mothering' because they have a new support system in the urban space, that of friends, neighbours and acquaintances.

Botho project objectives and research questions

Before venturing into the methodology used in the study, research objectives and research questions will be presented. The title of the project was '*Botho/Ubuntu* and Community Building in the Urban Space: An Exploration of Naomi, Laban, Bridal and Baby Showers in Gaborone'. Although the study mapped out a number of objectives and research questions this chapter will only address baby showers as driven by *Botho* and community building in the urban space. The project's objectives and research questions as adopted from the original research proposal that was submitted when applying for the funding of the project have been introduced. This will assist and direct the reader from where this chapter is coming. The objectives of the *Botho/Ubuntu* project were as follows:

1. Explore the theological and spiritual base of the *Botho/Ubuntu* value/ethic.
2. Examine how the *Botho/Ubuntu* ethic was understood and manifested in traditional Botswana communities.

3. Analyse how *Botho/Ubuntu* ethic is expressed in the contemporary urban setting of Botswana.
4. Investigate how *Botho/Ubuntu* activities in the urban space construct and deconstruct gender.
5. Highlight how *Botho/Ubuntu* inform the building and maintenance of a justice-loving community.

Furthermore, the research questions of the study were:

1. How are *Botho/Ubuntu* ethics and spirituality founded and manifested in indigenous Botswana communities?
2. How does the *Botho/Ubuntu* ethic drive the Naomi/Laban, bridal and baby showers in the urban space?
3. What cultural traditions and roles are produced, reproduced, or deconstructed in the urban space through the Naomi/Laban, bridal and baby showers?
4. How do these *Botho/Ubuntu*-driven showers forge African spirituality?
5. How can *Botho/Ubuntu* spirituality foster a justice-loving community that rallies against the encroachment of poverty in urban spaces and empower women?

The chapter will address some of these objectives, while also attempting to answer some of the research questions.

Methodology

The study combined both quantitative and qualitative methods of inquiry. The study first carried out secondary desktop analysis, and second, conducted fieldwork-based research. The last two objectives were constituted by the analysis of the findings. Quantitative data were collected through a self-administered questionnaire from individuals who were attending the different showers. The qualitative approach allowed the researcher to explore in-depth descriptions, explanations, and narrations of the experiences of the respondents, as regards the *Botho/Ubuntu* ethic and other behaviours at showers. The collaborative nature of variables necessitated a blend of quantitative and qualitative methods of enquiry for interaction and to allow the strengths of one method to complement the other. Ethical approval for the study was obtained from the University of Botswana Internal Review Board (UB IRB). The UB IRB gave informed consent to take part in the study was obtained from each participant. The researchers read the consent form to the participants to inform them that their participation in the study was voluntary, therefore they could withdraw at any time during the research.

Gaborone was sampled as a site from which to carry out the study. The target population was people attending the baby showers. All attendees were suitable for participation. Purposive sampling was used to identify prospective recipients of the different showers. The researchers attended the showers; they recorded the events and the dealings that took place during the shower. The questionnaires were administered by the researchers during baby showers. The researchers personally joined the showers to observe, conduct the interviews using voice recorders, and, where permission was secured, used video cameras, to capture data from the participants. Notes were also taken by the researchers during showers and the interviews. Qualitative data were collected through participatory observations and in-depth interviews with key informants from each shower, such as organisers and the recipient of the shower.

The study used two instruments: the questionnaire and the in-depth interview guide, together with participatory observation, to collect quantitative and qualitative data, respectively. The instruments were prepared beforehand and piloted before the study was carried out. Data were gathered through in-depth interviews using a semi-structured interview guide. The events were recorded by the researchers on video and audio. The 'Shower Observation Instrument' included a description of the location of the shower, the location, how the organisers received and greeted the guests; 'off-camera' dialogue before and after the shower; evidence of who was invited, and the mode of invites; activities, games, refreshments, and gifts form part of the baby shower activities.

A 'Shower Observation Checklist' was designed, consisting of 14 items to which the researcher indicated with a 'Yes' or 'No', if they observed a particular behaviour during the shower. The items addressed 14 specific areas, such as the behaviour of shower organisers about guests, church membership, kin/relation, ethnicity, the guest behaviours and the types of gifts that were brought to the shower. A 'Baby Shower Participants Questionnaire' was developed to establish respondent's understanding of the baby shower: the purpose of the shower, whether it assists in community building and whether the shower furthers the cultural tradition of *Botho* or does it offer a new social gathering altogether. The survey instrument asked respondents to indicate their sex, marital status, educational status, their role in the shower and their relationship to the shower recipient.

As soon as the questionnaires were scanned for any discrepancies, data were coded and entered in SPSS version 2. The exercise was conducted on each question. The data collected through the observations and voice recorder, were first transcribed into text. The transcribed data and notes were then coded to make sense of them. Interviews were tape-recorded, transcribed and analysed through qualitative content analysis. Cross-reference was conducted in cases of overlaps. Lastly, the identification of themes was done. Respondents ranged in age from 20 to 50 years, which suggests a wide variability in the age of the sample. Gender of participants: male (1.8%); female (98.2%). Seventy per cent of the respondents were single (69.6%), and 30.4% were married women. All respondents had some form of formal education, therefore they were literate: junior certificate (10.7%), Form 5 (14.3%), certificate and diploma level (42.9%), bachelor's (25%) and master's (7.1%).

Emerging themes

There are themes that emerge during interviews that indicate that *Botho/Ubuntu* drives baby showers in the Gaborone showers. These recurring themes can be summed up as: baby showers as a Western concept, social networks, social support (material and emotional), empowerment, mutual trust, compassion and empathy. Although these themes are not exhaustive, they keep on recurring through the analysis.

Multiple origins and purposes for baby showers

The origins of baby showers were not clear, according to the respondents. When they were asked where the showers originated, the answers below were given:

> I have no idea.
>
> Clueless.
>
> I don't know *ke di fitlhelwa di dirwa* (I found them in practice).
>
> I am not sure how [the] baby shower originates, but I think it was an initiative to help women out.
>
> As a way to raise money to help the mother-to-be.
>
> I don't know but it is something that is not from our society. I think it's from the Bible.
>
> Baby showers I think are an extension of *mantsho a ngwana* (traditional showers).
>
> *Ke belaela moletlo wa bana o tswa mo go wa mantsho a ngwana.* (I suspect baby showers are a product of *mantsho a ngwana* [traditional showers]).
>
> It's an activity from the West, not from Botswana.
>
> *Mo seromamoweng* (from radio) and television.
>
> They were imported from outside therefore not our tradition [sic].

The respondents pointed out five possibilities for the origins of baby showers; firstly, the respondents said they did not know how the showers started, while the second group were of the view that it "was an initiative to raise money and a support structure for women to help the mother-to-be". The third group saw origins of showers coming from the Bible, however, there was no justification used to link baby showers or a relevant verse quoted from the Bible to support the claim. The fourth group saw the modern baby shower as nothing new but a mere extension of traditional showers, *mantsho a ngwana.* This was a traditional way of welcoming the baby after birth. Although there may be similarities between the two, both the Gaborone baby shower and traditional showers (*mantsho a ngwana*) are about the baby and gift giving, However, there are a number of characteristics that set them apart. This will be discussed in detail later in the chapter, when the two are compared. The fifth group of respondents, which was in the majority, the respondents maintained that modern baby showers were a result of a foreign influence. The media (television and media) is said to have had a great influence. Women heard about showers on some international radio stations or television and decided to introduce them to Botswana. *Ga se wa Batswana gotlhelele* (it has got nothing to do with Batswana in its entirety), therefore *e adimilwe mo bathong ba basweu* (it was borrowed from white people/Westerners).

How justified are the respondents' answers on the origins of baby showers in Gaborone? 'Baby shower' as a term is relatively new. However, the celebrations and rituals associated with pregnancy and child birth are both ancient and enduring and were celebrated in the form of *mantsho a ngwana* (see Moloi, 2006:1).

In Botswana, baby showers are common in urban and semi-urban areas, with the invitees mostly being "unmarried working or educated female adults" (Moloi 2006:1). As Moloi (2006) argues, the atmosphere during these rituals enables young women to learn from other women in a more relaxed manner. She is of the view that: a baby shower ritual, despite being borrowed from the Western cultures, is viewed by some young Batswana women as more or less a modern initiation school for literate women (ibid.:41). Her argument is that it is during such an occasion that the mother-to-be receives counselling on pertinent issues related to childbirth and motherhood. Furthermore, the baby shower is a platform where the mother-to-be is not only showered with gifts but is showered with necessary support, advice on what she ought to do and not do during and after her pregnancy, as well as good wishes.

Although Gaborone showers were seen as extensions of traditional showers (*mantsho a ngwana*), there are similarities and differences that can be drawn from these two showers respectively. They are similar, because women are still the chief organisers and at the centre of both the contemporary and traditional showers. One of the respondents said: *Ke bone tshoso e rweleng* (they are the brains behind the showers or the masterminds). Gifts also play a very important role in contemporary showers. During both showers there is gathering, feasting and exchange of gifts and counselling and giving of advice. In both showers, family members are participants. While in the traditional shower both men and women attend, cotemporary showers are mainly for women who are single. According to the data, there were 70% of women who attended were single, while only 30% were married. Furthermore, Gaborone showers are mostly organised by peers and friends, whereas in the traditional shower the family is involved extensively in the preparations.

Lastly, the baby shower is celebrated before the baby is born, while with *mantsho a ngwana* (traditional showers) the celebrations are done after the birth of the baby. Traditional showers did not have decorations like the modern showers, where a marquee was pitched and colour themes were chosen and used for decoration. Some of the places used as venues were ordinary houses or any space available outside the yard. For traditional showers there were no decorations, and music was not played during the celebrations. However, though men are not active participants in contemporary showers, they are still involved in a way because they give support by "contributing money towards the shower". They were restricted in the past, with men not being allowed to be part of raising the baby, especially during the confinement period (*botsetsi*). In contemporary baby showers, some men – especially the fathers-to-be – have been encouraged to become more active in the raising of the baby by attending. However, most men still shy away from the idea.

Networking, connection and socialisation platforms

Baby showers are seen as a platform where there is a chance of socialising, connecting with new people and building networks. Friends or relatives, co-workers, church mates and even total strangers build these networks. These platforms celebrate with the mother-to-be in welcoming the new baby. Through these showers, new relations are forged, which might either be short-term or for a lifetime. As one of the respondents put it, the main purpose of baby showers is *go kopanya batho le go dira botsala*, which translates to "unite people and to create friendships". Another one added to "liaise and meet well as make new friends to support each other especially women". Since new friendships were forged, the respondents were happy to invite the mother and other attendees to their celebration in the near future. Not only that, long-time friendships are forged, and these usually continue even after the baby is born; some respondents said they will "visit the family even after the baby has been born". There is no doubt that connection and socialisation becomes the pinnacle of baby showers in the urban space. And it is through these liaisons that the mother-to-be becomes socialised into a group of new acquaintances other than her family who are willing to share with her the joy of welcoming the new baby.

Support structure

Baby showers are also seen as a support structure. The support can be either material or emotional. As one respondent puts it: *Homme ba a tshegetsana ka meletlo ya bana* (women support each other through baby showers). Bringing a baby into this world can be a mammoth task, and it is highly unlikely that an individual will cope on her own. Therefore, it is important that other people support the mother-to-be *ka go fokotsa morwalo wa go reka dilwana tse dingwe ka o a bo a a setse a rekile dingwenyana* (baby showers assist the mother-to-be by buying some baby accessories that she might have left out). With the economic downturn, Botswana is currently facing, baby showers could not have come at an opportune time. The baby shower assists the expectant mother, as one respondent puts it: *Gore a seka a ba balelwa thata mo pateng fa a santse a baakanyetsa kgorogo ya lesea* (it relieves the mother from the financial burden associated with buying baby accessories). Although it is not compulsory for presents to be brought to the showers, it is an expectation from all attendees of the shower. Baby showers are seen as platforms, where gift giving becomes central to the celebration. As a result, it is expected that nobody comes empty-handed. The presents can be in the form of money or clothes and vouchers.

There is also an exchange of ideas where women advise how the mother-to-be should handle the baby. This advice, it should be noted, is not just for first-time mothers, but is also shared with second-time, even third-time mothers, for the simple reason that a lot might have happened since they last had a baby. The advice ranges from the personal hygiene of the mother and the baby's diet, as well as sexual matters. One participant advised the mother-to-be on her "delivery bag checklist": "Your bag should have cotton wool, surgical spirit, baby t-shirts, receiving blanket, sanitary pads (Dr Whites), toiletries for mom and baby, and mommy clothes."

The mother was cautioned on the type of medicine she gives her baby once the baby is born. She was encouraged to make sure that the baby receives all the vaccines as prescribed by the doctor, and to avoid over-the-counter medications. She was reminded to take her baby for routine check-ups every month, because this was the only way for her to know if her baby was growing well. Most of all, cleanliness of the environment where the baby is housed as well as the mother's personal hygiene were emphasised and considered paramount. A clean environment kept the baby safe from ailments, hence promoting their well-being. The mother-to-be was also advised not to neglect her partner once the baby has arrived. One participant said that most of the time after delivery, new mothers neglect the baby's daddy, and he becomes "the enemy in home". This has driven some men to be unfaithful. She encouraged the mother-to-be to make love to her partner as soon as she feels ready, but it should not take up to six months, because *ba tshwanetse go tiisa ngwana mokwatla* (they have to make the baby's back strong). This is a belief in Botswana culture that at some point after confinement time (*botsetsi*), a new mother is expected to make love to the father of her baby, because it is beneficial to the baby's overall health.

Prenatal counselling is among the important activities during this ritual. The counselling session, according to Moloi (2006), it is meant to educate the expectant mother on various issues relevant to "motherhood and womanhood in general" (ibid.:58). It is during this stage that attendees are expected to share their experiences with the expectant mother, in order to enlighten her of what to expect during delivery and motherhood. She is further advised on taboos regarding pregnancy, confinement and parenthood, specifically mothering. It is worth noting that these spaces are very 'sacred' spaces because women are free to exchange advice and ideas without fear of intimidation or being judged.

Women centred/gendered

Whether by design or by default, baby showers are indeed gendered and feminine. They become consumption avenues distinguished both by their 'feminine nature' and their seemingly role as a modern-day rite of passage (Fischer & Gainer, 1993). Since it is characterised by women, there is no doubt female solidarity is encompassed. The women further reinforce the personal relationships, which form the bonds of the community in which they live. In a number of showers, 98% of attendees were women, while only 1.8% were men. When the respondents were asked who should attend baby showers and why, the following answers were recorded:

> Everybody: women and those with or without children.
>
> Friends and family especially women to give her advice to share experience.
>
> Friends family and colleagues
>
> People who are close to the mother to be and the father because their experiences could be interesting to hear.
>
> Women because it is about a mother who is expecting.
>
> Women in order to support, encourage advice and give gifts to the mother-to-be.
>
> *O tsenelelwa ke bomme ba ba naleng maikarabelo e le go itumela le mme yoo itsholofetseng, re leboga Modimo ka lesea le le tlang* (it is attended by responsible women to celebrate with the mother–to-be and to thank God for the baby who is on the way).

From the answers given by the respondents, it is clear that baby showers are restricted to women. However, when further questioned on who should attend baby showers, opinions were split. Some respondents felt that everybody should attend, that is "men and women, with or without children". However, some of the respondents felt that baby showers should be reserved for friends and family over the age of 18, because they will be comfortable with each other; therefore, be open and sincere with their advice. Eighteen years was used as a yardstick, because it was felt that some of the topics discussed during these showers were not suitable for anyone under the age of 18. However, the majority of the respondents strongly felt that the restriction was unreasonable, because there were mothers under 18.

One respondent said: "Currently, baby showers are mostly restricted to women, but I feel even men should attend as they have a role to play in upbringing and nursing. Women are regarded as the pinnacle of the infant's upbringing, hence the restriction."

Emphasis seems to be not just on any other woman, but on *bomme ba bana leng maikarabelo* (women of integrity).

Botho/Ubuntu embedded in Gaborone showers

Although in the urban context an individual becomes entrenched in the reality of (Western) capitalism, it can still be argued that Gaborone baby showers are still motivated by the concept of *Botho/Ubuntu* (humanity). Baby showers are testimony to the fact that not all is lost during urbanisation. During these baby showers, *Botho* is expressed through *lorato, neelano le kutlwano* (love, giving and understanding). In addition, there is *tirisano mmogo* (spirit of togetherness), where there is respect and support. Furthermore, as one respondent puts it: "It is about team work and if there is no *Botho*, people won't be able to work together." All these are possible because people involved in the preparations are well mannered, tolerant and have mutual respect, which are the main ingredients of *Botho*.

In a way, baby showers can help to diffuse what Sparks (1990:249) sees "as the individual ego and make an African less prone to acts that do not contribute to community building". This comes across in a number of ways, for example, as respect for the person, the importance of community, personhood and morality. During baby showers, the community becomes the context for the manifestation of *motho* (human being) and *setho* (humanity). As demonstrated by baby showers, the value and dignity of persons is best realised in relationship with the other. As Mbiti (1969:108-109) rightly points out: "One cannot be a human being alone, only in a community." In the same way, the spirit encapsulated within baby showers show how a Motswana individual is a communal being, inseparable from and complete with other women coming together with a common goal to celebrate a life that is about to be born.

Furthermore, in baby showers we come across personal growth of individuals within the community of the attendees. Only through cooperation, influence and contribution of the other can one understand and bring to fulfilment one's personality. Through baby showers, a mother-to-be discovers a sense of identity in reference to the community with which she interacts, that of women who have been mothers themselves, or aspiring mothers. Since *Botho/Ubuntu* is based on the collective, baby showers become a collective endeavour, because it is driven by *Botho/Ubuntu.* Furthermore, the dignity displayed during the baby showers make a person divine, to be respected and valued, hence a woman or man is valuable in her- or himself: "not just as his[her] welfare, not his[her] material wellbeing but just man himself [humanself] and all his[her] ramifications" (Biko, 1978:46).

Within the context of *Botho/Ubuntu*, people are family, which is why women in the urban space come together in solidarity to support each other through baby showers even in the absence of immediate family. In that case, gift giving during baby showers is seen as supporting every member to live their full humanity in the urban-social space. The expectation for participants is to bring *sengwenyana* (something), as one respondent puts it. Sherry (1983:159) observes that "the giving of gifts is a way of conferring material benefit on a recipient". Sherry's contention confirms the role of gifts during baby showers in promoting *Botho* since "the act of giving takes precedence over the gift itself" (ibid.).

The central argument here is that in Botswana context giving and sharing are some of the most important values in the spirit of *Botho/Ubuntu* and community building. Besides having a well-rounded character and well mannered, a person with *Botho/Ubuntu* should realise their full potential and be fully involved in the activities of their community. Baby showers prove to be just one of those activities in the urban space. Arguably, those who were involved in the baby shower activities exhibited the spirit of *Botho/Ubuntu* by supporting the expectant mother. The code of conduct expected from them includes *setho le tshisibalo* (reverence and humility); they should be cooperative and show willingness to participate in all activities in the shower, as well as *ba supe maitseo, maitshwaro le maikarabelo* (display good behaviour and a sense of responsibility). Furthermore, maturity is taken for granted, because it is assumed that the participants are mature women who should be exemplary to the mother-to-be as well as to aspiring mothers within the group of attendees.

Community building and reciprocity

During Gaborone baby showers, there is no doubt that the spirit of community building and reciprocity prevails. By coming to the shower and participating, the baby shower attendee takes it for granted that the same favour will return when she has a shower or something similar in the future. The fact that the attendees leave everything they do to attend the showers show their selflessness and caring nature as they sacrifice their time to celebrate with the mother-to-be. There is a lot of collective efficacies from hatching the plan by organisers of the shower to the actual day of the shower when it is executed. As a result, baby showers become platforms where community building is realised in the urban space. This is put into perspective in Table 10.1, where 64% of the respondents saw showers as community building in the urban space.

Table 10.1 Showers create community building in urban space

Respondents	%
Strongly disagree	7.1
Disagree	14.3
Agree	64.3
Strongly agree	14.3
Total	100.0

While Gaborone baby showers are rooted in both Setswana and Western culture, they somehow challenge some Setswana cultural values. For instance, women who are not mothers counsel mothers-to-be, which is contrary to Setswana culture. Furthermore, mothers-to-be disclose information regarding the expected delivery of the baby. This transparency is a taboo in Setswana culture. In Setswana culture, *ga go segelwe ngwana thari mpeng*, meaning you cannot celebrate a baby before they are born. Data confirmed that there were norms of reciprocity expected amongst the attendees. Respondents believed that if they have attended a baby shower for X, they would expect X to attend their shower as well. Therefore, they made it clear that they would feel offended if they organised a baby shower for X and then X refuses to organise their baby shower. It is interesting to note that the attendees are expecting some form of reciprocity when it comes to organising showers, which take a lot of time, sacrifice, money and energy. Table 10.2 attests to the general feeling of the attendees regarding reciprocity.

Table 10.2 I will feel offended if I organise a shower for X and she refuses to organise mine

Respondents	%
Strongly disagree	17.9
Disagree	28.7
Agree	32.0
Strongly agree	21.4
Total	100.0

During baby showers, it was expected that one does not attend empty-handed to ensure that presents were given during the baby showers.

Women empowerment

With the economic downturn Botswana is facing since the 2007/8 global recession, Gaborone baby showers empower women by rallying against the encroachment of poverty in urban space. Besides empowering women economically, baby showers create both an opportunity and an environment for young women to share knowledge and skills. In this way, expectant mothers become independent, unlike their traditional counterparts who depended on their male partners. While the presence of attendees confirms care, support and love, gifts are another important aspect of the baby shower celebration. The economic empowerment becomes pivotal in the baby shower because the majority of these women are single mothers who are trying to make ends meet in the urban space. Table 10.3 gives an idea of the gifts given to the mother-to-be as an initiative to empower her materially and alleviate poverty.

Table 10.3 Gifts given materially empower the mother-to-be

Baby clothes	Baby accessories	Vouchers and cash
▪ Booties, gowns, hats	▪ Bed, feeding bottles	▪ Cash (P100-P5 000)
▪ Blankets, fleece bodysuits	▪ Pram/push car, car seats	▪ Vouchers (P500-P2 000)
▪ Baby bag	▪ Baby lotions, cotton wool	
▪ Socks, pull-on pants	▪ Potty, detergents	
▪ Jackets, sweaters	▪ Cot, washing powder	
▪ Vests	▪ Chest of drawers, diapers	

Table 10.3 demonstrates how women are empowered through gift giving in Gaborone showers. The gifts range from baby accessories to money. They give the mother peace of mind, because she has been empowered with the necessary items to assist her in raising her baby. This further explains why 51.8% of the respondents in Table 10.4 agree that the main purpose of a shower is to give presents to the mother-to-be.

Table 10.4 Main purpose is to give presents to the mother-to-be

Respondents	%
Strongly disagree	16.1
Disagree	21.4
Agree	51.8
Strongly agree	10.7
Total	**100.0**

The gift-giving ritual indicates that part of the social function that they serve to create and reinforce personal relationships (see Cheal, 1988; Fischer & Arnold, 1990). It is worth noting that the need for external support when one becomes a mother is not only moral, but also financial. This is exemplified through the giving of the necessary equipment for raising the child. Therefore, financial and material empowerment becomes a welcome development in the celebration of the unborn baby. Since gifts empower women materially, it does not come as a surprise when 35% of the respondents in Table 10.5 disagreed when they were asked if it was okay to attend showers without presents.

Table 10.5 It is okay to attend showers without bringing presents

Respondents	%
Strongly disagree	28.6
Disagree	35.7
Agree	32.1
Strongly agree	3.6
Total	100.0

Emotional empowerment

Women are also empowered emotionally through baby showers. It is in these showers where women create 'sacred spaces' for women to express themselves in a justice-loving community. In this setting, women are given an opportunity to counsel the mother-to-be regardless of whether they have children or not. In the village setting, this would be done by aunts and grandmothers or blood relatives who have children. This adds a new dimension to urban showers where we see freedom and equality as well as anti-oppression of women attendees. When the respondents in Table 10.6 were asked whether counselling should only be given by mothers, 62% of them disagreed.

Table 10.6 Counselling should only be given by mothers

Respondents	%
Strongly disagree	21.4
Disagree	62.5
Agree	12.5
Strongly agree	3.6
Total	100.0

It is worth noting that by letting everyone become involved in counselling, women at Gaborone showers are creating yet another new dimension that could be termed "group mothering". A group of women related or unrelated take it upon themselves to come together and help the mother-to-be. Through their actions, the famous African adage "it takes a village to raise a child" is fully demonstrated. Despite being in the urban space, by coming together, these women are creating a setup similar to what takes place in the traditional setting where blood relatives come together to raise the child.

The sharing of knowledge in the form of advice is very important in mothering. It is more rewarding when the exchange of knowledge was shared by not only the mother-to-be but also by all other mothers in attendance as a way of tapping into other aspects of motherhood, which were still kept secret. It is worth noting that baby showers are women "sacred spaces" where mothers are empowered. It is a space in the urban space where expertise in motherhood is nurtured. However, nurturing forms only a microscopic part of mothering and should be expanded further. For instance, viewing mothers "as vessels and birth giving as a task provokes reflection on the reduction of any woman to her reproductive capabilities, seeing it as a form of bio power exercised in patriarchal societies to control a large portion of their members" (Deszcz-Tryhubcazak & Marecki, 2015:192).

Conclusion and recommendations

In this chapter, we have demonstrated that a new baby has always been celebrated in Botswana. However, baby showers have taken the celebration to another level. Despite baby showers being partly foreign to Botswana, Batswana women in Gaborone have contextualised and indigenised the showers. These showers have become very significant in the lives of women in Botswana, because they empower them materially and emotionally in a number of ways. Most importantly, the chapter has demonstrated that the Gaborone baby showers are driven by the spirit of *Botho/Ubuntu*, which is embedded in Botswana culture. The women in the urban space become a support structure for another woman, regardless of class or whether they are related or not. It is through these baby showers that a justice loving community is supported – where there is equality and liberty. This is apparent in the way every women attendee, regardless of age, is given the platform to counsel the mother-to-be.

Despite the showers being largely urban, the spirit of *Botho/Ubuntu* continues to be deeply rooted in the celebrations. The mother-to-be becomes a mother within a community of those who share her ideals and aspirations but, most importantly, the net is cast wider to include even total strangers to further intensify character building. It is through our lived experience in an African setting that no person can be an island or live in isolation – "I am because you are". Little babies can tap into the spirit of *Botho/Ubuntu* even before they are born, when celebrating their coming into the community. We would like to recommend that similar studies be conducted in the rural areas and comparisons be drawn in the near future between urban and rural baby showers.

In conclusion, due to minimal and even non-participation of men in these showers, the chapter recommends that men should be fully engaged rather than passive witnesses. Their participation is necessary, because they form a very significant part of the baby's life, and whatever empowerment women are given will also be beneficial to them.

References

Amanze, J. 2002. *African traditional religions and cultures in Botswana: a comprehensive textbook*. Gaborone: Pula Press.

Biko, S. 1978. *Towards true humanity in South Africa: ecumenical review*. World Council of Churches. https://doi.org/10.1111/j.1758-6623.1978.tb03535.x

Cheal, D. 1988. *The gift economy*. London: Routledge.

Creswell, J.W. 2009. *Research design: qualitative, quantitative, and mixed methods approaches*. Los Angeles, CA: Sage.

Deszcz-Tryhubczak, J. & Marecki, M. 2015. 'Understanding motherhood as maturation: maternity scripts in Lois Lowry's *Son*'. *Children's Literature in Education*, 46:190-205. https://doi.org/10.1007/s10583-015-9249-z

Dube, M.W. 2006. 'On becoming healer-teachers of african indigenous religion/s in HIV&AIDS prevention'. In: I.A. Phiri & S. Nadar (eds). *African women, religion and health: essays in honor of Mercy Amba Ewudziwa Oduyoye*. Maryknoll, NY: Orbis. 131-156.

Dube, M.W. 2008. *A theology of compassion in the HIV&AIDS era*. Geneva: WCC. 1-153.

Dube, M.W., Kgalemang, M., Kebaneilwe M.D., Motswapong, E.P., Mmolai, S.K., Gabaitse, R., Kuswani-Ntloedibe, S., Setume, S.D., Sesiro, D. & Modie-Moroka, T. 2016. '*Botho/Ubuntu* and community building in the urban space: an exploration of Naomi, Laban, bridal and baby showers in Gaborone'. *Botho/Ubuntu* Project. Proposal submitted to Nagel Institute, USA.

Dundes, A. 1999. *International folkloristics: classic contributions by the founders of folklore*. Lanham, MD: Rowman & Littlefield.

Fischer, E. & Arnold, S.J. 1990. 'More than a labor of love: gender roles and Christmas gift shopping'. *Journal of Consumer Research*, 17:333-345. https://doi.org/10.1086/208561

Fischer, E. & Gainer, R.B. 1993. 'Baby showers: a rite of passage in transition'. In: L. McAllister & M.L. Rothschild (eds). *NA – advances in consumer research volume 20*. Provo, UT: Association for Consumer Research. 320-324.

Hays, S. 1996. *The cultural contradictions of motherhood*. New Haven, CT: Yale.

Johnston, D. & Swanson, D. 2003. 'Constructing the good mother: the experience of mothering ideologies by work status'. *Sex Roles*, 54(7-8):509-519. https://doi.org/10.1007/s11199-006-9021-3

Krane J. & Davies, L. 2007. 'Mothering under difficult and unusual circumstances: challenges to working with battered women'. *Affilia, Journal of Women and Social Work*, 22(1):23-38. https://doi.org/10.1177/0886109906295758

Magesa, L. 1997. *African religion: the moral traditions of abundant life*. New York: Orbis Books.

Mbiti, J.S. 1969. *African religions and philosophy*. London: Heinemann.

Mertens, D.M. 2010. *Research and evaluation in education and psychology: integrating diversity with quantitative, qualitative, and mixed methods*. 3rd Edition. Thousand Oaks, CA: Sage.

Miller, T. 2005. *From motherhood to mothering: the legacy of Adrienne Rich's of Woman Born*. New York: SUNY Press.

Mmualefe, D. 2000. '*Botho* and HIV &AIDS: a theological reflection'. In: J.B.R. Gaie & S.K. Mmolai (eds). *The concept of Botho and HIV/AIDS in Botswana*. Eldoret, Kenya: Zapf Chancery. 1-28. https://doi.org/10.2307/j.ctvgc61hd.4

Moloi, L. 2006. 'Celebrating womanhood through baby showers in Botswana: the case of Gaborone'. Unpublished dissertation, University of Botswana.

Montemurro, B. 2006. *Origins of bridal showers and bachelorette parties: something old, something bold.* New Brunswick, NJ: Rutgers University Press.

Motswapong, E.P., Kebaneilwe, M.D., Madigele, T.J., Dube, M.W., Setume, S.D. & Moroka-Modie, T. 2017. '"A little baby is on the way": *Botho/Ubuntu* and community building in Gaborone baby showers'. *Gender Studies*, 16(1):50-70. https://doi.org/10.2478/genst-2018-0006

Munyaka, M. & Motlhabi, M. 2009. 'Ubuntu and its social significance'. In: M.F. Murove (ed). *African ethics: an anthology of comparative and applied ethics*. Pietermaritzburg, South Africa: UKZN Press. 63-84.

Neyer, K. 2006. *What happens at a baby shower*? https://www.families.com/blog/what-happens-at-a-baby-shower

Porter, M. & Kelso, J. (eds). 2006. *Theorising and representing maternal realities*. Newcastle, UK: Cambridge Scholars Publishing.

Robinson, J. 2000. *Pride and joy: African American baby celebrations.* Collingdale, PA: Diane Publishing Co.

Ruddick, S. 2001. 'Making connections between parenting and peace'. *Journal of the Association for Research on Mothering*, 3(2):7-20.

Setiloane, G. 1975. *The image of God among the Sotho-Tswana*. Rotterdam: A.A. Balkema.

Sherry, J. 1983. 'Gift giving in anthropological perspective'. *Journal of Consumer Research*, 10(2):157-168. https://doi.org/10.1086/208956

Turner, V. 1968. *The ritual process: structure and anti structure*. Chicago, IL: Aldine.

Van Gennep, A. 1960. *The rites of passage.* (M.B. Vizedom & G.L. Caffee (Transl.), Chicago, IL: University of Chicago Press. https://doi.org/10.7208/chicago/9780226027180.001.0001

PART FOUR

Botho/Ubuntu, Love and Bedroom Talk

11

HOW I MET MY HUSBAND

Bridal narratives at bridal showers in Gaboreone

Abstract

The purpose of this chapter[1,2] is to explore how marital relations are established in Gaborone. This is done through analysing narratives at bridal showers. One of the most entertaining moments during any bridal shower is when the bride-to-be[3] is expected to narrate how she met her partner. The researchers carried out a qualitative study where in-depth interviews and participatory observations were the key data-collecting instruments. A total of 14 bridal showers[4] in Gaborone were attended and bridal shower narratives compiled. The following are important findings of the study: narratives can be used to understand the meaning that the brides create about the formation of their relationship; there is evidence of a shift from traditional Setswana perspectives of relation formation to modern ways of courtship – a paradox between modernity and the apparent conformity to the traditional perceptions that a man must always initiate the formation of a relationship. Bridal shower narratives in Gaborone further demonstrate the importance of love before marriage and personal choice in partner/spouse selection. The chapter further concludes, consistent with the findings of Oubuch, Veroff and Holmberg (1993), that each narrative presents a story making process, style and content of storytelling. The study recommends that future studies collect groom-to-be stag party narratives for comparison.

1 The article, 'How I met my husband: bridal narratives at bridal showers in Gaborone' by Setume, S.D. et al., was first published in 2021 in *Journal of the Interdenominational Theological Centre*, 50:82-113. It is republished in this volume by permission.

2 The phrase, 'How I Met My Husband' is adopted from the title of one of the short stories written by Alice Munro (1974). *Something I've Been Meaning to Tell You*. Canada: McGraw-Hill.

3 Hereinafter referred to as the 'bride'.

4 The data are extracted from a study, titled '*Botho/Ubuntu* and community building in the urban space: an exploration of Naomi/Laban, baby and bridal showers in Gaborone'. The study was generously sponsored by John Templeton Foundation and was done by women in the Theology and Religious Studies, Social Work and Centre for Continuing Education departments of the University of Botswana.

Introduction

> Cities are the height of human achievement. Cities are fraught with ambivalence. We adore city life, it stimulates, entertains and excites. Cities are open and tolerant, but perversely elitist and exclusionary. (Leary-Owhin, 2016:1)

City life has been an attraction for many young adults. Cities provide an opportunity for creativity as one journeys to find one's space within the busy city life. Women, especially the young and educated, have through bridal showers created spaces where they are able to empower each other and challenge some gender stereotypes. Hence, they enable themselves to cross social boundaries such as, for example, one that held that an unmarried woman cannot offer guidance to a bride (Setume et al., 2017). Bridal showers have further created spaces in which women can share personal information, such as how one met one's partner, for example. The sharing of such personal information is through narratives.

Over time, changes have taken place in relation to how men and women meet to form relationships. According to Hirsch and Wadlow (2006), research "around the world has suggested that the process of globalisation, transnational migration and modernisation have contributed to changing understanding of marriage and the role of love and intimacy in it". Hirsch (2003) further comments that there has been a significant shift from marriage of 'respect' to marriage of compassion, where marital relationships have become largely emotive and not just social obligations. As Botswana fast becomes part of the global village, changes regarding intimacy and personal choice have developed. Through bridal shower narratives, society can discuss the extent to which individuals have moved from the traditional kin-focused ways of establishing romantic relationships to an individual's autonomous choice. This plays out well in bridal showers in the urban space of Gaborone. Whereas in the past with marriages of 'respect' parents were responsible for the selection of spouses for their sons and daughters, in the contemporary Botswana women make their own choices of who to marry.

The purpose of this chapter is to explore the opportunities available to city dwellers to meet potential suitors/husbands through the analysis of narratives made by brides at their bridal showers. At any bridal shower, one important question that a bride needs to answer is 'how did you meet your partner?' The bride will be expected to narrate how she met her partner. In a way, the bride is trading the 'juicy' story for bridal advice and gifts. After this introduction, the chapter will explore what bridal showers are and what purpose they serve, then trace a development in the establishment of relationships over time. Then the chapter outlines a theoretical background that situates the understanding of how couples establish a relationship within the concept of personal narratives. After that, field data are presented and analysed.

Bridal showers

Bridal showers are ritual activities that prepare a woman for marriage. A bridal shower is "a ritual that dates back to 16th-century Western Europe as a gendered ritual organised by women for women" (Clark, 2000:7; Jenkins, 2000; Montemurro, 2005, Setume et al., 2017). The origins of bridal showers are traced to a legend in Holland. According to this legend, "a woman wanted to marry a poor man whom her father feared would not be able to support her, and thus her father refused to provide dowry. Sympathetic to the love between the two, the would-be-bride's friends gathered gifts so that she was able to wed" (Montemurro, 2005:13). This practice has since been adopted by women across the world in order to celebrate one another (Solway, 2016). Bridal showers offer women an opportunity to express how much they care about each other, because women are socialised to care (Gilligan, 1998).

Though bridal showers are neither exclusively urban centred nor for the elite, they are largely done by middle-class, educated and single women in urban spaces (Setume et al., 2017). While in America, the purpose of bridal showers is to shower the bride with gifts (Montemurro, 2002; 2005), in Botswana, the main purpose is to give advice to the bride (Setume et. al., 2017). Solway has observed that bridal showers in Botswana "have appeared as a new form of ritual combining both the consumerist driven allure of modern Botswana with aspects of didactic function of older instructional rituals and social connectedness" (2016:315). Solway notes that for Batswana women, bridal showers are not just about presenting the bride with gifts, but the bride is also presented with instructions such as, for example, how she needs to behave in relation to her in-laws. Women present at the shower would discuss, ask questions, and share views, experiences, and opinions with the bride to prepare her for married life. Solway further observes that bridal showers in Botswana offer women of all ages, including friends and kin to share instructions for the bride and indeed for themselves; she explains that "bridal showers offer a new way in which non-kin are incorporated into the marriage process, thus illustrating a 'social' expansion that contradicts the tendency of contraction" (Solway, 2016:315). Bridal showers are a very feminine social group and usually portray a carefree environment where very sensitive content can be trivialised and jokes made from it, for example, at one bridal shower, the bride was a widow. She narrated how she met her man, and at the point that she explained that her first husband had died, one attendant at the shower interjected and said "*lefu la gwe la mphidisa*"[5] ("through his death I am enabled to live on". This expression is drawn from a hymn, but has come to express how the death of spouse can also empower the widow, say, for example, with inheritance or insurance cover). In order to situate the current ways of how women

5 Intentionally misconstruing a line taken from a Christian song about how, through the death of Jesus Christ, humanity was saved.

in the urban space of Gaborone meet their spouses, it is of paramount importance that a brief history of relationship formation in the context of Botswana is offered.

Developments in the formation of intimate relationships

Culture in all its facets is dynamic. Equally, how women establish or meet the man that they are to marry has also changed over time. In this section we will describe three periods in how relationships are formed. The first period will cover the traditional Setswana ways of establishing a relationship; secondly, a discussion of formal education and urbanisation will follow, and thirdly, the formation of relationship in the era of modern technology will be discussed.

Setswana culture and relationship formation

Historical accounts about the formation of marital relationships centred on the kin (Kuper, 1940; Matthews, 1940; Schapera, 1939). In patriarchal societies, where marriage was seen as a vocation for all, parents could not leave such an enormous task of forming marital unions to the inexperienced youth. Marriages were arranged. In those days, becoming a wife or husband was such a mandatory role that it was impossible for one not to marry (Kuper, 1940; Matthews, 1940; Schapera, 1939). Failure to marry attracted derogatory terms, such as *lefetwa*[6] (one who has been 'passed by'), because marriage was arranged by parents and there was stigma attached to failure to marry and childbirth before marriage, especially for women. This was done with little or no consent from those getting married. Schapera (1939) poignantly captures that when he asserts that the issue was never who to marry, but when. With arranged marriages, romantic love was absent, implying that marriage came before love. However, over time, formal education and urbanisation had an impact on how sexual relationships were established.

Formal education, urbanisation and the formation of the relationship

With the arrival of formal education and migration to urban places, new social dynamics were shaped. These developments gave the younger generation more autonomy than the older generation. Gulbrandsen (1986) carried out a study in Botswana among the Bangwaketse in Kanye. He observed that parents have lost their grip on the younger generation and can no longer impose their wish as whether or not to marry, when to marry or who to marry. This was because due to formal education

6 A derogatory word used to refer to women that are perceived by the society to have passed a period/ age at which they should ideally been married, therefore they have been 'passed by marriage'.

and urbanisation the youth became independent in both thought and action when it came to matters of love. He notes that

> while a young man's ambitions were customarily directed towards acquiring rank in the hierarchically organised politico-jural forum of the *kgotla*,[7] where marriage was a basic condition for participation and where ownership of cattle was significant, the young men of today achieve esteem mainly through immediate and conspicuous consumption [...] in other words, there has been a dramatic transformation in idioms of rank, resulting in marriage not only becoming irrelevant but even 'just causing trouble' in the young man's achievements. Marriage means a young man might be hampered by a wife who 'makes noise' when he comes home, and who may bring a case against him of poor maintenance. (Gulbrandsen, 1986:15)

In contemporary Botswana as elsewhere (Sassler & Miller, 2015), young adults are increasingly "assuming what was historically the purview of parents and community: the right to manage their own relationship" (Sassler & Miller, 2015:142). Sassler and Miller further explain that courtship has increasingly moved away from the home into more anonymous, often public spaces where "parents and relatives continue to play important roles in romantic decision-making, though they are no longer the main gatekeepers. New technologies such as the Internet provide young adults with modern ways to meet prospective partners" (Sassler & Miller, 2015:142).

The bridal narratives poignantly point to the practice of self-selection of partners without much interference from their parents: a sole responsibility of the individuals who are to get married/get in a courtship hence has become a personal journey to explore. Analysing the bridal shower narratives allows for the exploration of how romantic relationships are formed in the modern cities.

Formal education and urbanisation created different social spaces within which a whole range of opportunities became available for the youth to meet. Schools, places of work and places of entertainment in cities are not gender sensitive as compared to a traditional Setswana set up. Therefore, these physical social spaces became vehicles for relationship formation. This was the case until the age of technology emerged.

Relationship formation and technology

It has been observed that social media has become an important vehicle in the formation of romantic relationships (Rainie & Wellman, 2013; Chambers, 2013; Kaya, 2009; Mesch & Talmud, 2007). Social media applications, such as WhatsApp, SMS, Facebook, etc. have rendered the need for a physical space to meet irrelevant and has greatly increased opportunities to meet online.

7 A *kgotla* refers to a local administrative system in Setswana villages.

Costa (2016) poignantly explains changes in ways of establishing intimate relationships. He does so by focusing on the role played by media in the expression of love when he describes how media has expanded:

> ...opportunities to satisfy pre-existing desires for pre-marital romantic love, which were traditionally limited to rare encounters in the few available and suitable offline space. New forms of romance first appeared with the arrival of the internet in the region: many people in their 30s and 40s note that internet chatting and MSN were used to meet, communicate and flirt with people of the opposite sex [...] diffusion of social media and the smart phone have made online pre-marital romance love and friendship among young people more frequent and thus more integrated into their daily lives. (Costa, 2016:103)

Therefore, through analysing bridal narratives at bridal showers, this study also explores the extent to which social media has become part of union formation and development. But what are narratives?

Narratives: stories about the self

The use of narratives in exploring marital and romantic relationships has been adopted in many qualitative research studies (Banks-Wallace, 1999; Maguire, 1998). The narrative approach to understanding relationships started in the late 1980s and early 1990s, with the postmodern and social constructivist approaches offered by Gergen (cf. Skerrett, 2010:504). A narrative or story is a report of connected events, real or imaginary, presented in a sequence of written or spoken words, or both. The word derives from the Latin verb *narrare* (to tell), which is derived from the adjective *gnarus*, 'knowing' or 'skilled'.

A personal narrative is a "form of auto-biographical storytelling that gives shape to life experiences" (Gaydos, 2005:255). Gaydos explains that people make sense of the world and themselves in it by creating self-stories, which have the qualities of narratives (2005:254). Such stories have a beginning, a middle, and an end. Narratives offer an understanding of how brides create meanings from self-defining memories (Gaydos, 2005). At bridal showers, the bride will create a beginning where she had no interest in the relationship, then she developed interest and love towards the groom and the end is reached when she accepts his advances and the marriage proposal. Most of the narratives will end with taglines such as '…and here we are' or '…and the rest is history'. Kotre (1996) cautions that the use of narratives should be done with the understanding that memory does not exactly conform to the facts of the actual events; the essential role of memory is the creation of meaning about the life of the self. It is therefore important to understand that the main purpose of analysing bridal shower narratives is to comprehend how brides make meaning of the formation of their romantic relationships, how they portray how they met their partners/husband instead of a very accurate factual presentation of what happened.

The use of personal narratives to explore romantic relationships is bountiful (Berger & Kellner, 1964; Oubuch, Veroff & Holmberg, 1993). Narratives therefore allow couples to construct their own realities. The research-adopting, narrative approach presents a researcher as "collecting and interpreting stories that people tell about themselves. Stories represent ways in which people organise views of themselves, of others and of the world in which they live" (Oubuch, Veroff & Holmberg, 1993:813, Bruner, 1990). It is further observed that narratives need to be understood as stories of self-representation. Therefore, narratives present the positive parts, an interplay of power dynamics and sensitivity to the spouse/partner and, above all, are biased self-representations (Oubuch, Veroff & Holmberg, 1993). Everyone makes stories out of their experiences. Therefore, each story that a bride shared during bridal showers in Gaborone, represents the choice of "which things to share in the story and how to say it" (Schneider, 2002:77). Skerrett (2010) carried out a qualitative study with long-term, middle-class heterosexual couples where the main objective was to explore the extent to which co-narratives relate to the development of the relationship over time. The study found out that the synthesis of each partner's life story into a couple's story promoted individual and relational development (Skerrett, 2010:504). Wamboldt (1999) carried out a study using a sample of premarital couples and adopted the narrative approach "to explore coherence, interaction and relations beliefs between the couples". The study concluded that the outcome of the couples' effort to construct an intimate consensual reality is the primary determinant of the psychosocial outcome for not only the individual, but also the relationship they form (1999:37-51).

Another study used a sample of 264 married couples, in which Oubuch, Veroff and Holmberg (1993) examined how these couples narrated the development of their relationship in the first year of their married life. The study found out that stories told by couples in the first year of their marriage helped to interpret the meanings that couples derive from becoming a couple. The study ably demonstrated the significance of the use of narratives. Most of the narratives used in literature were co-joint, that is, the husband and wife were asked to respond to the same research item with the aim of finding, for instance, consistency between couples; however, this study explores narrative consistency across brides.

Sassler and Miller (2015) carried out a study on the ecology of relationships. The purpose of the study was to explore the physical spaces where couples in contemporary society meet and the impact of these places on the quality of the relationships. The formation and development of a romantic relationship is largely "shaped by the type of network in which the initial" meeting took place (Sassler & Miller, 2015:143).

In their study, Sassler and Miller found out that some ways of meeting romantic partners, such as being introduced by friends or family members through shared interest or at work or school, may result in more homogenous relationships. They further concluded that such networks encourage partners to commit more to the relationship and develop more trusting bonds (Sassler & Miller, 2015; cf. Coleman, 1988), as couples might feel greater social support from the same networks.

The study found out that couples that met at less socially-approved places such as bars did not have strong family ties as compared to those couples that met at more accepted places such as church or place of work.

Methodology

Data were collected through a qualitative study in Gaborone, the capital city of Botswana. The target group were brides who were recipients of bridal showers. Purposive sampling was used to identify key participants. Participants were identified through a list from the District Commissioner's office in Broadhurst office, through churches and snowballing. This was largely a qualitative study that was complemented by quantitative data. The qualitative approach is ideal for the study since the study is interested in the experiences of the brides in their environment (Creswell, 2009; Chilisa & Preece, 2005; Wodak, 2001; Bogdan & Biklen, 2016). The principal data-collecting technique was in-depth interviews[8] with the brides. For this chapter, we focus on the narratives made by the bride and, in particular, how she answered the question "how did you meet your husband?". The bridal story was collected through voice recorders then transcribed verbatim, after which a thematic analysis was used to navigate data. Data are presented through narrative passages and verbatim quotes of the respondents. The next section presents the narratives and the findings of the study.

Narratives at bridal showers: how I met my husband

Love comes in many different forms and can present itself in the least expected environment. The narratives at bridal showers give a glimpse at how finding love can be a very exciting experience for the modern lady who has gradually shifted away from the traditional social context. She has shifted from how individuals traditionally became wives through the active involvement of their kin to a personal choice that is based on romantic love and companionship. Brides at bridal showers often have a quick response to the question "where/how did you meet your man?"

8 At the time of writing the chapter, a follow-up was made with brides KM and TE, since their narratives were not fully captured during the initial shower events.

Oubuch, Veroff and Holmberg (1993) reached a similar observation that "couples have a quick and easy response to inquiries of how they met, recounting how it all began and often tell a story of considerable interest" (1993:815).

Love can be found in the least expected areas as reflected in the narrative below.

> I was on a bus from Francistown to Maun. The bus stopped and we (passengers) went to the bathrooms. As I was going to the ladies' bathrooms, a gentleman tried to talk to me. I ignored him. As I came out of the ladies he was waiting by the entrance. He then says to me 'I think I have seen you in Gabs'. Well, I have never been to Gabs. Then he changes his story line to 'or it must have been in Francistown'. I looked at him and headed to the bus. He asked me for my cell number. I refused to give it to him. He followed me. As we approached the bus, he says to me 'If you don't give me your cell number, I am going to get inside of the bus with you and scream inside of the bus'. That scared me. I opted to give him my BBM (Black Berry Messenger) pin instead. He then explained to me that if I don't want to talk to him again, I can delete it and he won't be able to trace me. He sent the BBM. I did not respond to it the whole day before I accepted it. I accepted it the next day. We started chatting and everything fell into place.
> (Bride TE)

This narrative is an epitome of how social media has become an important part of formations of relationships.

As young couples move from rural to urban places, they create social networks that are based on friendship and church membership and less on blood ties (Setume et al., 2017). It is then not surprising that Mma MP is introduced to her potential lover through a friend as presented in her self-story:

> I met him through my friend. I was working at Barclays bank. One day a *sms* came through from him asking what time I was knocking off. I replied, '*Ka* 5'. (Then the bride pauses and says 'I am done'. The audience laughs and protests that the bride should continue). The next day he sends another message '*ke mo* parking'. Then we came this way ... (she describes the route they took as the audience screams with excitement of the detail). He then asked where I was going. I told him I am going to BBS mall. When we reached the mall, he went to a shop and bought some soft drinks. He dropped me off at home. He sent a few smses the next morning followed by more and more smses. That is how the relationship began. He explained to me that he was looking for a wife and did not want courtship. He suggested that I visit his home village to see what kind of people he comes from (murmurs among the audience). (Bride MT)

The above two samples demonstrate generally how the bridal personal narratives were generally conducted. Below, we proceed to make meaning of these narratives. A thematic approach is used to make meaning of the narratives shared by brides at bridal showers in the urban space of Gaborone. The themes were adopted from an

American study (Oubuch, Veroff & Holmberg, 1993:817). These themes are the story-making process, the style of storytelling and the content.

The story-making process across all bridal narratives

Storytelling in its broadest sense is anything that is told or recounted, normally in the form of a causally linked set of events or happenings, whether true or fictitious. Stories are a medium for sharing and a vehicle for assessing and interpreting events, experiences, and concepts to an audience. Through stories we explain how things are, why they are, and our role and purpose within them. They are the building blocks of knowledge and can be viewed as the foundation of memory and learning. Stories link past, present, and future and telling stories is an intrinsic and essential part of the human experience. Stories can be told in a wide variety of ways, which can be broadly categorised as oral, written and visual, and are so all-pervasive in our everyday lives that we are not always aware of their role as a tool of communication in all societies (Kelly, 2005:12).

As already stated above, all bridal shower recipients had to answer the question and therefore tell a story: How did you meet your spouse/husband? The bridal speech can be demanded by anyone in the audience. For instance, during RS's bridal shower, when it was time to give advice to the bride, one of the speakers instead of giving advice to the bride stood up and said: "*Nna ke batla go itse gore o kopane kae le monna wa gago*" (I want to know how you met your man). There was clapping and ululations in approval. Then the bride started her story:

> We met in 2004 when I was still a student at Gantsi brigade where I was doing a course in Accounting. We started the relationship then. In 2006, I left Gantsi to come to do my internship in Gaborone. *E be di phone di time go sena ope yoo o buwang le o mongwe.* Then we lost each other's contacts. After some years, God intervened and he also got transferred to Gaborone. I saw him in a cruiser, and he also saw me and stopped the car. That's how we got reunited. *Ebe re kopana mo Gaborone e be re tsweledisa ha re neng re eme teng, re itshokela dikgwetlho tsa botshelo ... ra utlwana. Ke fela last year a kopa gore 'mma jaanong ke batla go go nyala* (we met in Gaborone and continued from where we left. We were patient as we met challenges in life, and we committed to each other. It was last year that we decided that we want to get married to each other.
> (Bride RS)

The same lady had a follow-up question: "*A one a le romantic fa a proposa?*" (was he romantic when he made the proposal?).

The bride then explained:

> He invited me for dinner and suggested that we leave the children behind. We went to a restaurant at Airport Junction. We drank some coffee and he said to me: 'Lady, I mean it. I want to marry you.'

The style of storytelling

Different styles of storytelling were reflected at bridal showers. Mature brides were comfortable in answering the questions and therefore gave a detailed description of the events, while young brides were less comfortable and gave very scanty details and the audience would usually be sensitive to the nature of the bride and hesitant to probe. However, as demonstrated by Bride RS's narrative above, for more comfortable brides the probing was very evident. The more interesting narratives were given by brides, who were able to dramatise their storytelling. A comparison is given below from two narratives, namely Bride KM and Bride MPE.

> We met at a night prayer meeting in 2008. We became friends and the relationship started in 2014. (Bride MPF)

> We were colleagues (at work) and church mates. We worked closely together especially at church, him as an elder; myself as a youth leader. One day I was the preacher of the day as I usually did. This time it was a little different as I was giving testimony about my previous life. The message must have touched him because he said as I was preaching something told him 'that is your wife'. The following Sunday he calls me and informs me that he wants to see me. Apparently he summoned all fibre of his being to make the call. He came to my house and he told me that he had been looking and studying me, so he feels I would make him a good wife. I said, 'No ways, never, no interest in you at all, like zero interest and my body is not going to be touched by any man especially him.' He went back and devised other ways, apparently admiring my composure and moral standards. Later he tries another manoeuvre to coax me to share a house with him[9] as I was the only person who he could possibly share a house with. Still, I said no. He gave up. We continued to meet at work and at church. Later I started developing an interest in him, but he seemed to have moved on (murmuring and laughter from the attendants). I tried to flirt (more laughter and clapping). Apparently, he didn't pick it up, and regret set in, and I understood it was spilled milk. I got transferred to a different school. We barely communicated. Then one day, he says he woke up depressed and lonely and wondered who could pick his mood and bang, he thought of me! Me! Me! (Jeering clapping and laughter). He sends a message: 'I'm troubled and I think you are the answer to my troubles.' I then suggested he comes to town so that maybe I can help him (more laughter interjection and clapping). The day the schools closed he immediately ran to see me. We talked, he saying he still wants to marry, and I said I will think about it. But I had already made a decision. I waited for a week, still not being clear. Then finally I said 'let's give it a try'. We did and he said I want to marry you as soon as yesterday. I said there is no ring on my finger, be my guest. Then here we are... (Bride KM)

9 Sharing of houses by staff is a common practice as there is acute shortage of staff houses.

The social network that the couple had of working together and going to the same church provided a conducive environment for them to meet and establish a marital relationship.

Dramatising in storytelling is important because it captures the attention of the listener (Oubuch, Veroff & Holmberg, 1993). The listeners are engaged, entertained and interested in the story. Hence the laugher, interjection and ululations. In the case of more reserved brides, the most interesting part of 'how I met my partner' is left 'dry and disengaging'. However, what possible lessons came from all these narratives?

Cultural content of storytelling at bridal showers

Normative Setswana prescriptions played a very important underlying influence in the content of bridal narratives. Setswana culture is a patriarchal one. Therefore, the fact that in issues of love, it is the male partner that is expected to make the first move towards the formation of a romantic relationship is evident in the narratives. Males are therefore "perceived as the appropriate initiator of a relationship and proposal of marriage, more so than women" (Oubuch, Veroff & Holmberg, 1993:817). The findings are therefore consistent with our cultural expectations that only men can initiate the formation of both a courtship and marriage. In all cases, men initiated both the formation of the relationship and the proposal to marry. It seems women in the relationship were always responding to the man in question. For instance, in the case of Bride KM above, she initially rejected her partner's first intent to engage in a relationship with her. After she had developed some attraction towards him, she is not able to explain to him that she has developed interest and she would want them to give it a try. She flirts. From a cultural perspective, good women do not flirt. Thus, the fact that the bride describes her actions as flirting might suggest change of attitudes of women towards men. He doesn't read the signals. She gives up. She gets a transfer to another school, and it is only after the man sends Bride KM a message that: 'I'm troubled and I think you are the answer to my troubles' that Bride KM accepts, and the relationship is formed. Oubuch, Veroff and Holmberg (1993) in a study in America reach the same conclusion and further explain that "these cultural prescriptions are associated with greater psychological wellbeing".

Summary and conclusions

In all the cited narratives, romantic love and companionship are important elements in the formations of the relationships: women are getting married to men that they love. The narratives have a beginning as revealed in the process of storytelling; the middle is when the couple are dating and finally, the ending is when they get married.

All the narratives are consistent with the cultural expectations that a man should initiate relationships, all women in their narratives disclose that the man started the relationship. Bride KM's narratives depict how she almost gave up when the man could not read the signals. The desire for love and companionship among young couples is a worldwide trend (Twamsely, 2013). Twamsely carried out a study among the Guarani Indians in UK and India. The purpose of the study was to examine 'how ideologies of love are shaping marriage practices among middle class couples of 20–30 years' (2013:267). In this study, Twamsely found that in all cases cited, love came before marriage as all participants expressed a strong desire to marry someone they loved, making love the primary part of spouse selection (2013:273). While couples in her story preferred endogamy (marry within the Indian community) couples at bridal showers married across both the geographical and ethnic divide. Consistent with the narratives given by brides at bridal showers in Gaborone, love is the basis for getting into a relationship. Bridal shower narratives reflect how far women in the contemporary Botswana have moved away from the traditional parent centred physical space interaction to modern ways of finding romantic love in a very liberal and technology enhanced environment. The study suggests that future bridal shower narratives research should also involve the groom narratives as well for comparisons relating to gender.

This chapter, therefore, proposes that bridal shower narratives can be used as follows: to understand the meaning that brides create about their relationship formation; to explore the shift from traditional Setswana perspectives of relation formation to contemporary ways of courtship, and to solve the paradox between modernity and the apparent conformity to the traditional perceptions that a man must always initiate the formation of a relationship.

The contemporary relationship formation displays the extent to which the use of technology allows more social space for interaction in the development of romantic relationships. The absence of parental influence in the formation of such relationships reflects the extent to which the younger generation is gradually becoming independent of their parents or the older generation in matters of their love and the extent to which love and intimacy are of paramount importance, that is, 'marriage of respect' versus 'companionate marriage'.

References

Banks-Wallace, J. 1999. 'Storytelling as a tool for providing holistic care to women'. *Maternal Child Nursing*, 24:20-24. https://doi.org/10.1097/00005721-199901000-00005

Berger, L.P. & Kellner, H. 1964. 'Marriage and the construction of reality'. *Diogenes*, 46:1-23. https://doi.org/10.1177/039219216401204601

Bogdan, R.C. & Biklen, S.K. 2016. *Qualitative research for education: an introduction to theories and methods.* Bengaluru, India: Pearson India Educational Services.

Bruner, J. 1990. *Acts of meaning.* Cambridge, MA: Harvard University Press.

Chambers, D. 2013. *Social media and personal relationships: online intimacies and networked friendship.* Basingstoke, UK: Palgrave Macmillan.

Chilisa, B. & Preece, J. 2005. *Research methods for adult education in Africa.* Hamburg: Unesco Institute for Education. https://bit.ly/3BsmBh1 [Accessed 16 May 2023].

Clark, B. 2000. *Bridal showers.* Wiltshire, UK: Carpinteria.

Coleman, J.S. 1988. 'Social capital in the creation of human capital'. *American Journal of Sociology*, 94:S95-S120. https://doi.org/10.1086/228943

Costa, E. 2016. 'Hidden romance and love'. *Social media in southeast Turkey.* London: University College London. 102-127.

Creswell, J.W. 2009. *Research design: qualitative, quantitative and mixed methodology approaches.* 3rd Edition. London: Sage.

Gaydos, H.L. 2005. 'Understanding personal narratives: an approach to practice'. *Journal of Advanced Nursing*, 49(3):254-258. https://doi.org/10.1111/j.1365-2648.2004.03284.x

Gulbrandsen, O. 1986. 'To marry – or not to marry: marital strategies and sexual relations in a Tswana Society'. *Ethnos*, 51:7-28. https://doi.org/10.1080/00141844.1986.9981311

Hirsch, J.S. 2003. 'Un noviazgo después de ser casados' [Companionate marriage and modern Mexican family]. In: S. Szreter, H. Sholkamy & A. Dharmalingan (eds). *Categories and contexts: anthropological and historical studies in critical demography.* Oxford: Oxford University Press. 249-275. https://doi.org/10.1093/0199270570.003.0014

Hirsch J.S. & Wadlow, H. (eds). 2006. *Modern loves: anthropology of romantic courtship and companionate marriage.* Chicago, IL: University of Chicago Press. https://doi.org/10.3998/mpub.170440

Jenkins, J. 2000. *The everything wedding shower book.* Holbrook, MA: Adams Media.

Kaya, L.P. 2009. 'Dating in a sexually segregated society: embodied practices of online romance in Irbid, Jordan'. *Anthropological Quarterly*, 8(1):251-278. https://doi.org/10.1353/anq.0.0043

Kelly, G. 2005. *Storytelling Audit: An audit of personal story, narrative and testimony initiatives related to the conflict in and about Northern Ireland.* Healing through Remembering. https://bit.ly/3nZb3Pc

Kotre, J. 1996. *White gloves: how we create ourselves through memory.* New York: W.W. Norton.

Kuper, A. 1970. 'The Kgalagari and the jural consequences of marriage'. *Man New Series*, 5(3):466-482. https://doi.org/10.2307/2798953

Leary-Owhin, M.E. 2016. *Exploring the production of urban spaces: differential space in the post-industrial cities.*

Chicago, IL: The University of Chicago Press. https://doi.org/10.46692/9781447305750

Maguire, J. 1998. *The power of personal storytelling*. New York: Jeremy P. Tarcher.

Matthews, Z.K. 1940. 'Marriage Customs among the Barolong'. *Journal of International African Institute*, 13(1): 1-24. https://doi.org/10.2307/1156989

Mesch, G. & Talmud, I. 2007. 'Special issue on e-relationships – the blurring and reconfiguration of offline and online social boundaries'. *Information, Communication and Society*, 10(5):585-589. https://doi.org/10.1080/13691180701657899

Montemurro, B. 2002. 'You go 'cause you have to: the bridal shower as a ritual of obligation'. *Symbolic Interaction*, 25:67-92. https://doi.org/10.1525/si.2002.25.1.67

Montemurro, B. 2005. 'Add men, don't stir: reproducing traditional gender roles in modern wedding showers'. *Journal of Contemporary Ethnography*, 34(1):6-35. https://doi.org/10.1177/0891241604271332

Munro, A. 1974. *Something I've been meaning to tell you*. Canada: McGraw-Hill.

Oubuch, T.L., Veroff, J. & Holmberg, D. 1993. 'Becoming a married couple: the emergence of meaning in the first year of marriage'. *Journal of Marriage and Family Life*, 55(4):815-826. https://doi.org/10.2307/352764

Polkinghorne, D.E. 1988. *Narrative knowing and the human sciences*. New York: State University of New York Press.

Rainie, L. & Wellman. B. 2013. 'If Romeo and Juliet had mobile phones'. *Mobile Media & Communication*, 11:166-171. https://doi.org/10.1177/2050157912459505

Sassler, S. & Miller, A.J. 2015. 'The ecology of relationships: meeting locations and cohabitors' relationship perceptions'. *Journal of Social and Personal Relationships*, 32(2):141-160. https://doi.org/10.1177/0265407514525886

Schapera, I. 1939. *Married life in an African tribe*. London: Faber and Faber.

Schneider, W. 2002. *So they understand: cultural issues in oral history*. Logan, CO: Utah State University.

Setume, S.D. Gabaitse, R., Dube, M.W., Kgalemang, M., Modie-Moroka, T., Madigela, T., Kebaneilwe, M.D., Motswapong, E.P. & Matebekwane, A.K.M. 2017. 'Exploring the concept of *Botho/Ubuntu* through bridal showers in the urban space in Gaborone, Botswana'. *Managing Development in Africa*, 2(3):173-191.

Setume, S.D., Gabaitse, R.M. & Kebaneilwe, M.D. 2021. 'How I met my husband: bridal narratives at bridal showers in Gaborone'. *Journal of the Interdenominational Theological Centre*, 50(Spring/Fall):82-113. Republished with permission.

Skerrett, K. 2010. 'Good enough stories: helping couples invest in one another's growth'. *Family Process*, 49(4):503-516. https://doi.org/10.1111/j.1545-5300.2010.01336.x

Solway, J. 2017. 'Slow marriage, fast *bogadi*: change and continuity in marriage in Botswana'. *Anthropology Southern Africa*, 39(4):309-322. https://doi.org/10.1080/23323256.2016.1235980

Twamsely, K. 2013. 'The globalisation of love? Examining narratives of intimacy and marriage among middle-class Gujarati Indians in the UK and India'. *Families, Relationships and Societies*, 2(2):267-283. https://doi.org/10.1332/204674313X664923

Wamboldt, F.S. 1999. 'Co-constructing a marriage: analyses of young couples' relationship narratives'. *Monographs of the Society for Research in Child Development*, 37-51. https://doi.org/10.1111/1540-5834.00018

Wodak, R. 2001. 'The discourse historical approach'. In: R. Wodak & F. Meyer (eds). *Methods of Critical Discourse Analysis*. London: Sage. https://doi.org/10.4135/9780857028020

12

BOTHO/UBUNTU AND SEX IN THE SHOWER

Bridal showers and sexuality

Abstract

Candid conversation about sex and sexuality is difficult, challenging and taboo in many cultures, and the cultures of Botswana are no exception.[1] Botswana is an assertively heteronormative and patriarchal context guided by an indigenous value system called *Botho* or *ubuntu*.[2] The patriarchal culture conditions both men and women to suppress women's sexual pleasure while celebrating male sexual pleasure and libido. This makes conversations about sex by women attending bridal showers interesting as these exclusively female premarital ceremonies deconstruct patriarchal and cultural norms that deny women's sexuality. This chapter,[3] therefore, seeks to analyse the ways in which sex talk in bridal showers empowers women to deconstruct patriarchal heteronormative norms. It will further demonstrate how sex conversations embody life-giving values and ideals of *Botho* within marriage. This chapter draws on the data collected by a group of women researchers from the University of Botswana on *Botho* and bridal showers in Gaborone, the capital city of Botswana. The analysis of the

1 Botswana is a country with around two million people from different ethnic groups. While the official languages spoken in Botswana are Setswana and English, there are other languages such as Sesarwa and Sekgalagadi, which are spoken by ethnic groups that exist within the country, a fact that obviously creates differences among Batswana. Therefore, Botswana is heterogeneous, where some communities are more tradition bound than others. However, there are many cultural similarities between understandings of manhood and womanhood in Botswana because of shared beliefs, religion and language, hence performance of manhood and womanhood even within one city is influenced by a complex set of variables among them such as one's religion, level of education and upward mobility.

2 *Botho/Ubuntu/Uhunhu* are not just words, but are revered indigenous concepts as they communicate an African consciousness, philosophy, ethnic, spirituality, religion, moral compass, and culture that convey deep meanings translated into actions embodied in lived realities and ways of life, and performed daily through acts of mercy, love, justice, mutuality, interdependence, care and interconnectedness. In the specific context of Botswana, we say *motho ke motho ka batho*, meaning 'I in you and you in me', 'I am because we are', 'I exist because you exist' and 'your burdens are mine'. *Botho* is manifested in many ways. For instance, in a parent-child relationship blind obedience and respect from a child manifests *Botho*. However, in a husband-wife relationship, *Botho* is manifested when a wife cooks, cleans and submits to her husband.

3 The article, '*Botho/Ubuntu* and sex in the shower: Bridal showers and sexuality' by Gabaitse, R.M. et al., was first published in 2021 in *Journal of the Interdenominational Theological Centre*, 50:114-141. It is republished in this volume by permission.

data is guided by feminist theories of power, sexuality, culture, and masculinity. This chapter comprises of an introduction, methodology, a description of key features of bridal showers and conversations about sex. Having described the bridal showers, the chapter will proceed to discuss how bridal shower sex conversations have implications for sexual assertiveness among women, construction of positive masculinities and how these conversations affirm *Botho* in the Botswana context.

Introduction

Long before the arrival of Europeans and missionaries, African communities were organised in small groups separated by gender and age. In Botswana, young men and women of marriageable age would form a regiment and attend traditional schools called *bogwera* for young men and *bojale* for young women. The responsibilities of the schools were to train young people on issues of life as they transitioned from childhood to adulthood. This training included sex education, although the content of that education is not easily available because of the oral nature of the traditional cultures in Botswana (Schapera, 1970:112-124, 1971:229-233; Willoughby, 1909). The schools were guided by what is considered acceptable behaviours by invoking the Botswana indigenous value and ethical system of *Botho/Ubuntu*.

With the onset of Western education, the traditional schools were brought to an end. Perhaps this is partly the reason sex education was lost and the subject of human sexuality became taboo in most African communities.[4] Currently, most young people receive some information about sexuality informally from friends and acquaintances, and obviously this kind of education comes with all forms of risks and dangers. Botswana has witnessed an increase in teenage pregnancies in the past couple of decades, around the time when HIV and other sexually transmitted infections were on the rise (Heald, 2005). Communities within Botswana were forced to open up a little and talk to people about the basic facts of HIV prevention and reproductive health in general.[5] This period also saw a rise in civil organisations such as Botswana Family Welfare Association (BOFWA), which developed programmes that were aimed at disseminating information about sexual reproductive health within the constraints of a culture that is not fully open to sex education. While there is no formal subject on sex education in schools in Botswana, there are topics on reproductive health littered in numerous subjects in Botswana; hence more effective, comprehensive and properly organised curriculum on sex education is necessary (UNFPA, 2016).

4 There are other factors locally such as urbanisation and migration that led to the end of these schools. Though sex education was part of the curriculum of traditional schools, there is not much in existing literature that explicitly details the content of this education because Botswana is an oral culture. Whatever they were taught in traditional schools has largely been lost with the passing on of the older generation because it was not written down.

5 It is understandable that the information has to be relevant to the context.

At the moment, there are parents who are against schools offering comprehensive sex education to their children.[6] In addition to the meagreness of the vague sex education offered at schools, parents are not comfortable talking about sexuality with their children at home (Francoeur & Noonan, 2004; Mmegi Online, 2011). Moreover, honest and open conversations regarding sexual pleasure are difficult and uncomfortable even among grown-ups. Studies from within Botswana demonstrate that most mothers are comfortable discussing menstruation and hygiene with their daughters but nothing beyond that. This is because conversations between children and parents about sexuality in general and sexual pleasure in particular are deemed culturally unacceptable, inappropriate and therefore a societal taboo (Montgomery, 2017). Since "sexuality is socially constructed and historically located" (Preece, 2001:224-229), conversations about sex in Botswana are guided by, among other things, culture, religion and *Botho/Ubuntu.* Unfortunately, open conversations between parents and children about sexual pleasure go against the framework of both culture and *Botho/Ubuntu*, because the two require uncritical obedience and respect of parents by children.[7] The main religion practised in Botswana, Christianity, is not intentional about empowering parents to have these conversations even among themselves.

The absence of conversations regarding sexuality points to the fact that Botswana is not only patriarchal but is a high-context culture as well. According to Edward Hall and Mildred Hall, a high-context culture "is a culture where communication on everyday sensitive issues is mostly implicit and less direct" (Hall & Hall, 1990). High-context cultures specialise in, among other things, silence, secrecy little information and euphemisms for reproductive parts and topics of sex, gender and other related ones. Although there are words in the local languages for reproductive body parts, those words cannot be used freely as it is not culturally and socially acceptable to do so. In addition, there is a sense of shame attached to using those words as they are thought to be explicit.[8] Furthermore, high-context cultures are

6 Without assuming homogeneity and agreement on the existence of the sex education curriculum, sex education is part of the education system in some low context cultures such as Canada, where sex education is mandatory from age 5. The education goes beyond the metaphors and figurative language (see Montgomery, 2017). The same can happen in Botswana with age-appropriate illustrations and programmes.

7 This refers to the general culture of Botswana. There are obviously parents who engage with their children on issues of sexuality because of levels of education and upward mobility, among other things.

8 Not using names in the local language for body sexuality is socially constructed in Botswana, and how people speak and what they speak about must be framed within the *Botho* framework, which requires high levels of politeness. It is socially and culturally accepted that naming and calling out reproductive parts in Setswana (the language spoken by most Batswana) is impolite and disrespectful. A person who does that *wa rogana* (they are being obscene). Even when opportunities to use the local terms present themselves, for instance during HIV education and campaigns about HIV, most Batswana would use euphemisms such as *bonna* ('maleness' instead of 'penis'). Having attended numerous

slow in decisively and intentionally acting on issues regarding sexuality even when there is mounting evidence that lives are being lost. For example, there is evidence in Botswana that sex takes place among prisoners, but still there is resistance to avail condoms in prisons (Gabaitse, 2015; also see *Sunday Standard*, 2013). High-context cultures do not only undermine open conversations regarding sexuality, but rape cases go unreported, and the stigma associated with HIV grows, all in the name of secrecy and silence.

In addition, high-context cultures rob women of celebrating their sexuality freely, because sex talk is censored and when it happens, it is deeply coded or couched in language too difficult to understand. There are few spaces and opportunities for women to talk about sexual pleasure. For instance, some days before or after a wedding, before the bride is officially handed over to her in-laws, mostly senior married women from the bride's and the groom's family gather around the new bride to give her advice on married life; this is called *go laya* (to counsel, Gabaitse, 2017).[9] This process is taken seriously as part of culture[10] to help with the new bride's transition from singlehood to married life. The advice included what is culturally and socially acceptable behaviour within the *Botho/Ubuntu* framework. For example, the new bride is taught how to behave (to be gentle, kind and respectful) towards the husband and the in-laws and how to take care of children. It is during this time that patriarchy is ironically maintained, through teaching the bride that she should not ask about her husband's whereabouts and that she should tolerate her husband's extramarital affairs, because *monna poo ga a agelwe lesaka* (a man is a bull, one cannot build a kraal around him).[11]

campaigns on HIV and STIs, the author has observed that most people will be comfortable using the English word 'penis' than the equivalent local term.

9 *Go laya* is a Setswana word which means to give advice on good and acceptable social behaviour. However, its meaning is deeper; it is a lifelong process of giving sets of rules that govern good behaviour in order to avoid bad and unacceptable behaviour. It is also a rite, a counselling process, and a form of socialisation where expectations and attitudes are communicated. It usually happens during some form of transition such as children growing up, transitioning from childhood to teenagedom, from singledom to marriage, after the death of a loved one, when one enters university or when a child starts a new job, among others. In the contexts of bridal showers and weddings, it is a process, a ritual, a ceremony, where women intentionally come together in one place, gather around the bride and give her advice on what marriage is, what to expect, how to treat her in-laws, how to treat husband, how she should behave, handle money and, sometimes, on sex among others. *Go laya* helps in building and cultivating *Botho*. *Go laya* assumes different shapes depending on the contexts. It is never scripted but is spontaneous.

10 Although younger married women attend these ceremonies, they could never be as vocal as the senior ones because of the nature of hierarchical relations between younger women and older women within the *Botho* framework. Younger women are expected to give older women respect, and this includes being less vocal among elders.

11 There are many ways in which patriarchy is entrenched during this process. Not only is the new bride advised to accept infidelity, but she is advised to be submissive, demure and keep secrets about her marriage, no matter what happens because *matlo a na otlhe* (all house roofs leak). She is taught to be submissive and passive. It is during this process that gender roles and boundaries are drawn, a woman cooks, cleans the house, and takes care of children, but men are not expected to.

Sometimes the new bride is cautiously given advice on sex, but it is couched in parables and coded language.[12] It is common to hear elderly women saying, *monna wa alelwa*, which literally means, 'make the bed clean for your husband to sleep in', while in fact *monna wa alaelwa* means, 'have sex with your husband'. There are times when the language restriction is taken too far, whereupon young brides who are unfamiliar with the euphemism might leave the space not fully understanding what was meant. One of our bridal shower respondents who went through this process of *go laya* expressed her uneasiness with the language that was used. She said they (the older women) use deep and confusing terms such as '*go dirisa mogagolwane*' (to use a blanket). Whereas *go laya* takes place at bridal showers too, the conversations about sexual pleasure take place with some levels of ease in a flexible, relaxed environment among peers where questions and interjections are allowed for those who might not understand the language or some things during the ceremony.[13] In this regard, bridal showers are groundbreaking and deserve to be studied in relation to conversations about sex talk among women.

Methodology

A group of women scholars from the University of Botswana were sponsored by the John Templeton Foundation through the Nagel Insitute in America to research how *Botho/Ubuntu*, the African/Botswana value system and philosophy of care and mutuality was expressed and manifested in women-centreed events such as baby, bridal, Naomi/Laban showers in the urban space. While the core data for this project were the manifestation of *Botho/Ubuntu* in these showers, the research from the bridal showers yielded massive data on a range of topics, including human sexuality. Consequently, this chapter is based on the data collected from bridal showers only. The study, which took 15 months, was conducted in Gaborone, the capital city of

12 A member of the research team is a married woman who has gone through the process itself as a young bride and now frequently attends these ceremonies as it is culturally expected. In villages, women would hardly use explicit language for sex, let alone sexual pleasure, or teach a bride how to seduce her husband. There is some change in the cities because nowadays there are bedroom showers where the bride is given advice on sex by married women only. The showers can take place during the bridal showers or after the bridal shower. These showers are relatively very new. None took place during our research.

13 However, one should not imagine that bridal shower attendees were as free to discuss sex as they would discuss a soccer game or their favourite food. It was clear that the conversations about sex were laced with bits of unease and discomfort manifested through unspoken gestures such as giggling, laughter, face covering and shyness. This illustrates that these women are aware that sex conversations are not the norm in the patriarchal heterosexual space of Botswana. However, the shyness must not be confused with shame. The advantage of the bridal shower setting is that it is relaxed, in such a way that both single and married women can talk about sexual pleasure, and the bride is allowed to ask questions and engage with her peers. However, the traditional process of *go laya* is different; single women cannot be present, and the bride is expected to keep quiet during the entire process.

Botswana. The survey was largely qualitative using a triangulation of one-to-one in-depth interviews, open-ended questionnaires, and participant observation.

We attended 14 bridal showers; administered 110 close-ended questionnaires, and carried out 40 in-depth interviews. Most of the interviews were conducted at the venue of the bridal shower in some quieter space inside the house or at the corner of the yard. Some follow-up interviews were done at our offices or at restaurants days after the shower with willing participants. Any Motswana woman above the age of 18, who was attending the bridal shower, was eligible to participate in the research, as long as they were willing to talk to us.[14] Our respondents were Batswana women whose ages ranged from 20 to 45 and whose qualifications ranged from Form 5 certificates to master's degrees, with many women holding bachelor's degrees in different fields.

We identified the bridal showers through the marriage registry at the District Commissioner's office, church leaders, Facebook and others. We sent announcements through some radio stations requesting brides, families, and friends of brides to get in touch with us if they were comfortable participating in our research. We took care of the ethical issues regarding research with the University of Botswana Ehics Committee and sought permission from the relevant ministry within government to conduct the research. We met and established relationships with the main organisers and the brides before the day of the shower. It was then less challenging to introduce the research process and research objectives to the women attending the shower at the start of the shower.[15] We sought permission to observe, to audiotape the conversations, and to do interviews. We extensively addressed issues of confidentiality, voluntary participation and anonymity, among others. The languages that were used during the showers were Setswana and English as our respondents were comfortable with both or a mixture of both.

Several methods were used to obtain data, which included one-to-one interviews, open-ended questions and participant observation. Before the day of the event, the organisers of the bridal shower drew up a programme, which includes games, a gift-giving session and a session for *go laya*, among others. The programme for bridal showers differed from one shower to another. However, in all the showers we attended, the process of *go laya* was given a lot of time. One can conclude that *go laya* is the core curriculum of all bridal showers. During this session of *go laya*, the

14 In some showers, we had women from Zimbabwe, Zambia and Lesotho who were friends of the bride or were invited by one of the friends of the bride, but we excluded them.

15 Bridal showers bring together different women from the bride's workplace, sisters, friends and friends of friends. The bride produces a guest list, and the organisers send the invites. Those invitees sometimes bring along their friends or sisters. Some guests attend only because they know the bride-to-be. It is common to see women meet at the bridal showers and exchange phone numbers afterwards, because friendships are formed there.

director of ceremonies gives an open invitation for any woman to give advice or talk to the bride.[16] The topics covered are many; they include investments, taking care of the household, husband and children, personal hygiene and sex. This is the session that yielded a lot of data on sexuality.

We transcribed the data collected through tape recorders as accurately as possible, noting even when the respondents took pauses as well as leaving some sentences incomplete. We captured and noted the laughter, the giggles and the hesitancy in answering questions because these are also forms of communication, sometimes indicating discomfort or uneasiness. However, we were very much aware that transcription can never be adequate because it does not capture the non-verbal communications, which are also important for data analysis. We labelled data with numbers. For instance, data from shower 1 are labelled 1:1. Data field notes (FN), are also labelled using numbers, i.e., FN1 means data coming from shower 1. The data from *go laya* are indicated by the shower number and voice, for example, S3:26 means data come from shower 3, voice 26.

We use verbatim quotations from bridal showers, and those in Setswana are in italics followed by a translation and/or our own interpretation. If the quotations have a mix of both English and Setswana, and the Setswana bits are short, we interpret those parts within the quotations. If the quotations in Setswana are longer, we provide a full translation in English at the end of the quotation inside brackets. The respondents' verbatim quotations are interspersed throughout the chapter to give it credibility as well as to validate our findings and conclusions.

Describing the scene of the bridal showers

In order to prepare for the next section on women as sexual subjects and bridal showers sex conversation and the affirmation of *Botho/Ubuntu*, five crucial observations about bridal showers are critical. They are as follows:

First, the atmosphere during the showers was relaxed and calm as captured by one of the attendants:

> It is a free, flexible and calm environment. The setting allows the bride to be comfortable to express herself. Everything can be laid out on the table, provided people are willing to share. The language used in bridal showers makes it easier for everyone to relate. For example, in reference to sex, we use the term 'bedroom'.

16 We have already discussed how intense this process is when it is done by senior married women. In addition to the differences above, single women are able/allowed to advise the bride.

This means the shame attached to speaking about sex is minimised and mostly replaced by shyness, because sex is "celebrated as beautiful" (guest speaker, showers 3 and 4). The calmness was captured by women's acting out what they were advising the bride to do, for example, dramatic movements of hips when they advised the bride to seduce her husband. This was accompanied by lots of laughter and giggling (shower 1).

Second, bridal showers are hyper feminised gendered spaces where heterosexual romantic love and sex are celebrated within a patriarchal framework. It is not surprising that gender conformity sexist stereotypes were entrenched. Therefore, bridal showers entrench patriarchal attitudes in many ways, even as they deconstruct some of them. Bridal showers are not spaces where men are ridiculed; rather, they are to be respected and honoured through *cooking for them in the kitchen and bedroom.* Therefore, sex conversations are meant to stabilise heterosexual marriage in a patriarchal context.

Third, the bridal shower attendees do not talk about sex in crude and graphic ways. There was none where sex was spoken about in graphic terms and none of the shower attendees used the Setswana word for sex, hence the women still operate within the patriarchal and *Botho* framework. While they still maintain some levels of restraint on talking about sex, they have their own lingua to refer to sex. Throughout the research, in different places and different bridal shower groups, we heard about *the bedroom* over and over: "... cook for him both in the kitchen and in the bedroom ... There is one bowl that stays in the bedroom (shower 1:1).

Fourth, bridal showers had a different ambience and mood. We had showers that were low key and less interactive due to different dynamics, such as the bride who was not very cooperative or friendly towards people in general. When we had vivacious brides, the attendees were also vivacious and forthcoming with sexual conversations. In some showers we got more on sex and sexuality, while others were vague, with only sweeping statements from one or two attendees. Some surprised us since we got more than we anticipated on sexual pleasure. Shower 3, for example, was held at the bride-to-be's parent's home in the suburbs of Gaborone. The women participants were aged from 19 to 45, and most of the women belonged to the same church. Most women in this shower had university degrees. The bride-to-be was a lawyer and a dignified young woman herself. The group was highly charismatic, with lots of praying and reference to the Bible. There was no alcohol served, and only Christian music was played in the background the entire time. A lot of the young women stated that they were born again and were taught in the church that sex is private and exclusive to married couples. The guest speaker for the day was in her mid-40s and elegantly dressed, and had been married for 17 years. She was open about sex and romance, advising the young women to abstain from sex before marriage, while giving bride tips on how to seduce her husband, because that is her right as a Christian woman. She promoted sex as godly worship, the coming together of two bodies in a sacred institution ordained by God. The bride was further advised not to "use sex as a weapon … because it may lead to something else. So please, don't do that because God created you for a purpose".

After her speech, the director of ceremonies gave an open invitation for *go laya*, and the conversations were lively and active as the attendants spoke freely about sexuality. Although the conversation about sex was not unique to this group, we were surprised by the level of spirituality of this group, and yet they were the most comfortable ones to talk about sex, from abstinence to romance within marriage. Hence, different bridal showers have different moods and ambience.

Fifth, bridal showers offer practical information about sex, pleasure, romance, seduction and personal hygiene. The bride is advised on the art of seduction, which starts with personal hygiene.

> We believe that a woman is viewed as a beautiful flower ... her lips are not supposed to be dry and chapped ... use the gloss to bring out the beauty and the lips must be smooth. (3:24)
>
> I don't believe a woman should have dry hands. (3:62)

With smooth and glittery lips, moisturised hands, the bride is groomed and given practical information on the art of seduction. She is advised to create a romantic, conducive and calm environment in preparation for intimacy and sex with the husband:

> Get yourself a dining table just for you and your husband ... This will allow you to take time and relax with your husband ... Getting to the bedroom, I really like a white painted bedroom as this highlights the day. Keep on changing the bedding to make the bedroom lively and bright. (Guest speaker, Shower 3)
>
> *Monna hela ... a santse a diegile ko tirong ineye thothi...o sena go ya kwa, ga se dijo ... ebe o tshola o baya kwa ago fithele o apere mogo emang fa ... e bile o gwanta le ha ele sepe...ere ha gate ere swiii ... ago fitlhele o kwadile four mo setilong o sa apara le ha ele sepe ebile o eme hale ka kopi ya metsi a bothitho, hela ha a tsena o iteye lengole 'ao ntate, sweety, ao baby' le gaufi le monate.* (S5:1)[17]

Further, setting the mood for sex can happen anywhere, and the bride is told: "To take a bath with your husband is very good because you can continue the fun all

17 When your husband is still at work, bath, cook for him and wear a mini dress ... or do not wear anything ... when he opens the gate ... fold your legs while naked, hold a cup of warm water for him and call him by sweet names such as sweetie, babe or any other.

the way from the bathroom to the bedroom" (S4:3). She is further advised to dress seductively as well:

> *Rachel hare batle ere ha monna a chaisa o tlhola ka molenza mo tlhogong. Ha o itse gore Phemelo wa chaisa o ipaakanye. A go fitlhele o kwanyasela mo ntlong a ipotse gore o ya kae mme o sa ye gope. O tshwanetse gore o itlhokomele o seka wa tlhola ka melanza ntsalaka.*[18]

In one shower, the bride was advised to seduce her husband by wearing an apron only, while dusting or pretending to dust the lounge whenever the husband watches television. The woman who was giving this advice demonstrated it by moving her body seductively, while holding an imaginary feather duster. The plan is to have the husband take notice so that intimacy can take place (shower 3).[19]

Having painted a picture of the bridal showers and conversations about sex, I now proceed to analyse how the bridal shower sex conversations offer critical and positive contributions to studies on sexuality, locally and beyond the borders of Botswana. I will focus on how bridal shower sex talk has long term implications for affirming women as sexual subjects and for the construction of positive masculinities.

Women as sexual subjects

Bridal showers affirm women as sexual beings in two ways: first, they create a space for women to talk about sex, a privilege that all along has been monopolised by men. Sex talk is generally masculinised within assertively heteronormative cultures. The patriarchal performance of hegemonic masculinities allows men to engage in sex talk because, not only is sex talk normal among men within this framework, but it allows men to be sexual subjects. This means patriarchal attitudes permit men to act as subjects rather than objects in sexual encounters. They have confidence in sexual decision making, feeling, deserving of desire and seeking sexual satisfaction.

In addition, heterosexual sex talk becomes a way for men to achieve and demonstrate hegemonic masculinity, and also allows for the normalisation of their sexual desire and sexual activity (Montemurro et al., 2015:139 ff). While men can engage in sex talk, the same culture prevents women from doing the same. Because individual women's desire for sexual activity or sexual pleasure is rarely discussed within society,

18 "Rachel, my cousin, you should always be ready when your husband knocks off from work. Remove the *doek* (head scarf), beautify yourself and wear high-heeled shoes and make your husband wonder where you are going."

19 The women were aware that these tips might not work in some marriages. Some women expressed that this assertiveness might unsettle and bring insecurity to some husbands/men, who may feel threatened that their wives are not tamed, while some might wonder where they learned such moves. Women were cautioned to find out what works in their relationships, or to begin subtly when seducing their husbands (showers 1, 2 & 3).

women risk being labelled as "sluts" if they talk about this topic too frequently or openly … sex remains something women are afraid to talk about and thus feel conflicted about engaging in sex talk (ibid.).

In the specific context of Botswana, women are not expected to engage in sex talk, because doing so goes beyond the transcript of the hegemonic masculinity framework, which requires women and not men to be chaste, good, proper and well behaved (Schapera,1939:128, 1970:139). Because of the double standards of morality that Botswana as a patriarchal society holds about women and men, women who engage in sex talk express their desire for sex in public, perform a gender role reserved for men, and are judged harshly by both men and women.[20] Hence, a woman who intends to stay within the transcript of a 'good marriageable wife' does not explicitly express or act out her appetite for sex the same way men would. The women in our study were not aggressively detailing their sexual encounters. However, for the simple fact that these sex conversations took place, bridal showers are subversive spaces that challenge male entitlement to these sex conversations. Thus, they can be celebrated for defying patriarchal, heteronormative and high-context, cultural norms.

The second way bridal showers unambiguously affirm women is through empowering them to be more sexually assertive. While hegemonic masculinity constructs women as sexual objects, bridal showers on the other hand construct women as sexual subjects, who should take charge of their sexual pleasure within marriage. Brides are told that

> It's okay to ask for sex whenever you want it as much as your husband may ask for it. Also avoid going to bed with your clothes on. (Shower 3)

Conceiving of sexual pleasure as the right of the wife within marriage deconstructs the narrative of passive women and passive femininities – the narrative that subordinates women to men's sexual pleasure in the hegemonic masculinity framework.[21] Numerous studies indicate that women are generally powerless in negotiating terms for sex to take place. Within the Botswana context, married women have less power; they have lower self-esteem and confidence regarding issues of sexuality than single

20 The language used to refer to women who seem to be sexually untamed such as *bo mma dirabanyana* and *sefebe* communicates an unwritten and unspoken expectation about women and sexuality. These women are judged harshly within the *Botho* framework because they perform a role that could be performed by men. Some are judged harshly because they act outside of the *Botho* framework of a woman who is supposed to be chaste and contained. Recently, a young woman was stripped naked at the bus station by a group of men because 'she was not dressed properly' and so (in the men's minds) she was making herself available sexually. It is in these acts and moments that we see the harsh punishments that women who act and speak seductively and sexually can endure.

21 Sex is a private matter. Couples probably do discuss sex and sexual pleasure in the privacy of their bedrooms and home. However, sex talk is not a public narrative in Botswana. It is not common for women to gather and be explicit about issues of sex; bridal showers in the urban space are special because they present such a rare opportunity.

women (*Botswana Human Development Report 2000*). The report indicates that many times "sex is for man's pleasure and terms" and men assume a "directive role in sexual encounters initiating sex and thus forcing women to subordinate their desires to that of the man".

Godisang Mookodi confirms that there are defined "power relations within consensual relationships and … women occupy subordinate positions in relation to their consensual partners" (Mookodi, 2000:2). Prince Dibeela observes too that male entitlement to women's sexual subordination "often means that the man is in charge of the sexual life of the couple. … It is also the man who often decides when to have sex and how to have it" (Dibeela, 2007:13). Therefore, bridal showers deconstruct this subordination and powerlessness through offering practical information for women to act and be sexual subjects so that they can sexually assert themselves with confidence.

The young brides especially are told to take charge "in the bedroom" and to enjoy sex fully for pleasure's sake as it is their right to do so. They can ask for it and even initiate it. They can be as sexually expressive and seductive as they want through wearing nothing but high heeled shoes, moving hips seductively while cleaning and many more. As women engage in these conversations, their confidence is built and their ability to exercise basic bodily autonomy is strengthened. The bridal showers dismantle the construction of patriarchal hegemonic masculinity regarding female sexually passivity. From creating romantic moments, *parading naked in the house* and initiating sex, bridal showers speak against the powerlessness of women demanded by the patriarchal heterosexual narrative. The assertiveness and the confidence can encourage women to be decisive in other areas of their lives as well, such as politics and economics. This defies patriarchal hegemonic masculinity where these decisions are normally taken by men.

Bridal shower sex conversations do more than just affirm women as sexual subjects; they deconstruct the conservatives of culture which uphold the dominance of hegemonic masculinity over other versions of masculinities. This weakens the performance of hegemonic masculinity and instead a newer, softer masculinity emerges, where both men and women enjoy sex without being stigmatised. Since bridal showers encourage egalitarian pleasuring and acceptance of females as sexual subjects deserving sexual pleasure, men who accept this might be more open to egalitarian and inclusive existence and mutuality.[22] The existence of these qualities could help in reducing marital rape, which is not an offence according to the constitution of Botswana and the customary law, although married women can be raped by their

22 This is hoping that such assertiveness does not unsettle and bring insecurity to some husbands/men, who may feel threatened that their wives are 'taking over'.

husbands. Hegemonic masculinity supports marital rape because husbands have complete entitlement to women's bodies (Dube, 2012:323-354). The bridal showers are offering a new masculinity where husbands and wives should both joyfully participate in lovemaking. This egalitarian pleasuring has the potential to prevent marital rape. Therefore, narratives of sexual pleasuring are pointing to an emergence and maintenance of an egalitarian and inclusive masculinity that respects women sexual assertiveness and is not fearful of a woman's libido. Perhaps these women are not even aware that they are resisting hegemonic masculinity. However, they are constructing positive, softer masculinity even if this new masculinity operates within the dominant hegemonic masculinity framework.

Bridal shower sex talk: an affirmation of *Botho/Ubuntu*

Marriage in Botswana is guided by *Botho/Ubuntu.* Two strange families meet, engage each other out of respect and consideration with the aim of forming an alliance through marrying off their children. Bonds and relationship are formed during this process; hence, *Botho/Ubuntu* is at the heart of a marriage. When the two have been married off, the families continue to nourish the relationship through ongoing counselling and support. The good and positive that happen within marriage are supported by the ethics of *Botho/Ubuntu*, so that when the wife demands sex from her husband, she is in fact engaging in a positive thing that grows and nourishes the relationship. Whether it is done for pleasure or procreation, sex is an important component of marriage. Although sex does not guarantee a solid marriage, it, however, can strengthen a heterosexual marriage in keeping with the requirements of *Botho/Ubuntu.* Since *Botho/Ubuntu* is central to human existence among Botswana, it is the ideal value system that, if followed, allows for egalitarian existence, because it has kindness, generosity, good manners, solidarity, mutuality, shared humanity, mercy, love, justice, interdependence, and care as its central characteristics. What better place to demonstrate these qualities for both men and women than within the framework of *Botho/Ubuntu*!

Nonetheless, while *Botho/Ubuntu* has many positive qualities, it is also ambivalent because it seems to accommodate patriarchal attitudes where men have more privileges than women. Ezra Chitando elaborates on how *Botho/Ubuntu* is implicated in supporting the marginalisation of women:

> Whereas *Ubuntu* expresses the notion that, 'I am because we are, and we are because I am', in practice, the personhood in African cultures has been construed and constructed in a hierarchical manner, with men enjoying a full privileged status. The full membership of women in a community that places emphasis on the solidarity has not been taken as a given. (Chitando, 2015:276)

In the Botswana context, *Botho/Ubuntu* as a reference for morality and behaviour is sometimes used to encourage timidity and submission of women towards men in matters sexual and more. For instance, from a young age, women are socialised to be chaste, but the same level of morality is not expected from boys (Schapera, 1939). The girl child is raised in a way that she has to be more polite, more reserved than the boy child because she was scrutinised more before marriage than the boy child. These double standards are transferred to the behaviour expected from men and women. Men can engage in extra-marital affairs and women are punished harshly if that happens. These double standards result in the marginalisation of women and the elevation of men. Yet, they are often supported by using *Botho*.

While we completely agree with Chitando's observation that *Botho* exists in tensions and contradictions, it is difficult to reconcile how *Botho* as mutual existence, kindness, generosity, good manners, solidarity, shared humanity, mercy, love, justice and interdependence encourages the marginalisation of women. We hold that *Botho/Ubuntu* has been co-opted by patriarchal cultures to contain women who dare act and speak about sex in the same way that men do. They are denigrated as *ba ba ba sa bopegang, baba senang Botho* (as those whose manners are not guided by *Botho/Ubuntu*). *Botho/Ubuntu* has been co-opted in creating double standards of morality for men. On its own, *Botho/Ubuntu* should be liberating towards women, because it affirms the value of human beings regardless of their sex. A person who embodies *Botho/Ubuntu* does not thrive when others are diminished (Tutu, 1999:35). Therefore, when women talk about themselves as sexual beings, they are not defying the *Botho/Ubuntu* framework. Rather, they are defying the patriarchal capture of *Botho/Ubuntu*. In an ideal *Botho/Ubuntu* framework, men and women and husbands and wives should exist in mutuality and egalitarianism.

There should not be any reason a woman should not initiate sex with her husband, because the husband is *molekane wa mosadi* (the husband is an age-mate, friend, partner to the wife).[23] The concept of *bolekane* was emphasised using the Bible, especially Genesis 2:18, by guest speakers in showers 3 and 5. The two guest speakers submitted that in Genesis 2:18, the ideal of a companionate marriage involved partnership, egalitarian existence and mutual existence between couples, so that there is nothing *un-Botho/Ubuntu* if a woman asks for sex and seduces her husband. The woman's expression of sexual desire allows for egalitarian sexual existence and satisfaction that validates the sexuality of both men and women. Denying a woman to do this diminishes her and takes away her personhood (*setho*).

23 It is a term generally used in Botswana to refer to a spouse.

Conclusion

This chapter has sought to demonstrate the contribution that is made by bridal showers in the provision of liberative sex-education to brides in Botswana. It discussed the death of this critical form of education since the arrival of the missionaries and the abrogation of sex education in the Tswana culture, which left a vacuum for women. The men continued to be privileged in this regard since they could speak and learn freely about sex and human sexuality in a broader sense. The chapter then demonstrated that through the bridal showers there is a return of this education which is empowering women to take control of their sexual needs and satisfaction in their marriages by being sexually assertive.

I further demonstrated that bridal showers achieve much more than teaching women to be sexually assertive. The bridal showers are active in the construction of alternative masculinity which privileges mutual pleasuring and encourages affection and romance between spouses. The women's narratives, although still marginal, are a form of protest against the dominant hegemonic masculinity which disregards women's sexuality. The narratives are weaving a version of masculinity that has far more reaching implications such as encouraging emotional connection between spouses and dependence which may prevent marital rape. The children born in these unions are likely to resist sexist stereotypes and perform life giving masculinities and confident femininities. Bridal showers are already providing opportunities for women who have never had these sex conversations with their parents to learn that every human being has a right to sexual pleasure and, therefore, are transforming the sexuality conversations within Botswana.

References

Botswana Human Development Report 2000: Towards an AIDS-Free Generation. United Nations Development Programme. https://bit.ly/3Bvzreh

Chitando, E. 2015. 'Do not tell a person carrying you that s/he stinks: reflections on *ubuntu* and masculinities in the context of sexual and gender-based violence and HIV'. In: E. Mouton, G. Kapuma, L. Hansen & T. Togom (eds). *Living with dignity: African perspectives on gender equality*. Stellenbosch, South Africa: African Sun Media.

Dibeela, P. 2007. *A theology of life in the HIV&AIDS context*. Geneva: WCC.

Dube, M.W. 2012. 'Youth masculinities and violence in an HIV&AIDS context: sketches from Botswana cultures and Pentecostal churches'. In: E. Chitando. *Redemptive masculinities: men, HIV and religion*. Geneva: WCC. 323-354.

Francoeur, R.T. & Noonan, R.J. 2004. 'Botswana'. *International Encyclopaedia of Sexuality*. Kinsey Institute. https://doi.org/10.1093/acref/9780199754700.001.0001

Gabaitse, R. 2015. 'Partners in crime: Pentecostalism and Botswana HIV/AIDS policy on cross border migrants'. *Studia Historiae Ecclesiaticae*, 41(1). https://doi.org/10.17159/2412-4265/2015/v41n1a3

Gabaitse, R.M., Dube, M.W., Kgalemang, M. & Madigele, T. 2018. 'Reproducing or creating a new male: bridal showers in the urban space of Botswana'. *Journal of Gender and Religion in Africa*, 24(1):79-95.

Gabaitse, R.M., Setume, S.D. & Kebaneilwe, M.D. 2021. '*Botho/Ubuntu* and sex in the shower: bridal showers and sexuality'. *Journal of the Interdenominational Theological Centre*, 50(Spring/Fall):114-141. https://doi.org/10.14426/ajgr.v24i1.42

Hall, E.T. & Hall, M.R. 1990. *Understanding cultural differences: Germans, French and Americans*. Boston, MA: Intercultural Press.

Heald, S. 2005. *Abstain or die: the development of HIV/AIDS policy in Botswana*. Cambridge University Press (online publication). https://doi.org/10.1017/S0021932005000933

Mmegi Online. 2011. 'Minister withdraws moral education book from schools', 25 February. https://bit.ly/3WbCzWn

Montemurro, B., Bartasavich, J. & Wintermute, L. 2015. 'Let's (not) talk about sex: the gender of sexual discourse'. *Sexuality and Culture*, 19(1):139-156. https://doi.org/10.1007/s12119-014-9250-5

Montgomery, A. 2017. 'Quebec children to get sex ed starting in kindergarten. What will they learn?'. *CBC News*, 16 December. https://bit.ly/3Mud67d [Accessed 13 April 2018].

Mookodi, G. 2000. 'The complexities of female household headship'. *Pula: Botswana Journal of African Studies*, 14(2):2.

Preece, Julia. 2001. 'Gender power relations and the HIV/AIDS crisis in Botswana: some food for thought'. *Pula: Botswana Journal of African Studies*, 15(2):224-229.

Schapera, I. 1939. *Married life in an African tribe*. London: Faber and Faber.

Schapera, I. 1970. *A handbook of Tswana law and custom*. London: F. Cass.

Sunday Standard. 2013. 'Marked for death'. 18 February. http://www.sundaystandard.info/marked-for-death

Tutu, D. 1999. *No future without forgiveness*. New York: Double Day. 35. https://doi.org/10.1111/j.1540-5842.1999.tb00012.x

UNFPA (United Nations Fund for Population Activities). 2016. 'UNFPA calls for effective sex education', 21 October. https://bit.ly/3pQ3zyf [Accessed 12 May 2023].

Willoughby, W.C. 1909. 'Notes on the initiation ceremonies of the Bechuana'. *Journal of the Royal Anthropological Institute*, 39:228-245. https://doi.org/10.2307/2843294

CONTRIBUTING AUTHORS

Musa W. Dube (PhD) is the William Ragsdale Cannon distinguished professor of New Testament literature based at the Candler School Theology, Emery University (USA). She is the current continental coordinator of the Circle of Concerned African Women Theologians (2019-2024) and president of the Society of Biblical Literature (2022-2023). She studied the New Testament at the University of Durham (UK, 1990) and the University of Vanderbilt (USA, 1997). Her research interests include gender, postcolonialism, translation, earth, African literature, Ubuntu, and HIV and AIDS studies.

Rosinah M. Gabaitse (PhD) is a Biblical Studies lecturer at the University of Botswana. She writes, researches and publishes in the areas of Luke-Acts and women, Pentecostalism, feminist hermeneutics, and HIV and AIDS. Gabaitse is a Humboldt research fellow and a member of the Circle of Concerned African Women Theologians.

Mmapula D. Kebaneilwe (PhD) is a senior lecturer in Hebrew and Biblical Studies at the University of Botswana. She is currently a Humboldt research fellow with the Otto-Friedrich University of Bamberg, Germany. She studied the Old Testament at the University of Murdoch, Australia (2012), and at Stellenbosch University, South Africa (2003). She is co-editor (with S. Daniel and A. Savala) of *Mother Earth, Mother Africa and Mission* (Stellenbosch: African Sun Media, 2021). Her specialisation is the Hebrew Bible, gender-based violence, and ecology/environmental theology.

Malebogo Kgalemang is a New Testament scholar at the University of Botswana. Her research interests are postcolonialism, gender, African literature, Ngugi wa' Thiongo and Ubuntu studies. Kgalemang is the current national coordinator (Botswana) of the Circle of Concerned African Women Theologians.

Tshenolo J. Madigele (PhD) is a lecturer in the Department of Theology and Religious Studies at the University of Botswana. Her research and teaching are in the areas of pastoral care and counselling, systematic theology, human sexuality, LGBTIQ studies, health, spirituality and healing, and *Botho/Ubuntu* studies. Madigele is a member of the Circle of Concerned Women Theologians.

Tirelo Modie-Moroka (PhD) is an associate professor in the Department of Social Work at the University of Botswana. Her research interests are behavioural and social sciences, HIV and AIDS, public health, gender-based violence, Covid-19, Ubuntu and research methods. Modie-Moroka is on the Skillshare Advisory Board and has been a visiting instructor at the Institute of Health Sciences. She is a member of the Circle of Concerned African Women Theologians.

Pulane E. Motswapong (PhD) is a senior lecturer in the Department of Theology and Religious Studies at the University of Botswana, where she teaches in World Religions/ Comparative Religions, concentrating on Hindu Studies. She has published widely on gender studies, queer studies, and comparative religions. Motswapong's interest lies predominantly in comparative studies (especially in religion and spirituality) between Asian and Botswana religions (also called Indigenous Religions). She is currently working on religion and development. She is a member of the Circle of Concerned African Women Theologians.

Senzokuhle D. Setume (PhD) is the current head of the Department of Theology and Religious Studies at the University of Botswana, and a member of the Circle of Concerned African Women Theologians. Her area of speciality is African Indigenous Religions. Setume's research interests include anthropology, co-habitation, gender, research methodologies and Ubuntu.

www.ingramcontent.com/pod-product-compliance
Ingram Content Group UK Ltd.
Pitfield, Milton Keynes, MK11 3LW, UK
UKHW050146280726
14058UKWH00007B/856

9 781991 201980